starmaker

JIM HALSEY
starmaker

HOW TO MAKE IT IN THE MUSIC BUSINESS

WITH JOHN WOOLEY

Tate Publishing & Enterprises

Published by Tate Publishing & Enterprises, LLC
127 E. Trade Center Terrace | Mustang, Oklahoma 73064 USA
1.888.361.9473 | www.tatepublishing.com

Tate Publishing is committed to excellence in the publishing industry. The company reflects the philosophy established by the founders, based on Psalm 68:11,
"The Lord gave the word and great was the company of those who published it."

Book design copyright © 2009 by Tate Publishing, LLC. All rights reserved.
Cover & Interior design by Leah LeFlore

Published in the United States of America
ISBN: 978-1-60799-541-8

1. MUSIC / Recording and Reproduction
09.10.02

dedication

To my wife of 29 plus wonderful years, Minisa Crumbo—a
teacher, a spiritual guide, mentor, an inspiration, cheer
leader, a healer, a great artist, and my best friend.

★

To my family, my loved ones—

★

To my son Sherman, a creative, imaginative thinker
and visionary with great eyes, ears, ideas, a load of
talent, and a constant inspiration to me.

★

To my daughter Gina, the healer, physician,
and conscience for the world.

★

To my daughter Cris, the skier, the positive thinker, and mom.

★

To my son Woody, the airline pilot, musician, and family man.

★

To my mentors who have consulted, inspired, and taught:

Elon Robley	Simon Kalis
Leo Zabelin	Norman Weiser
Glenn Hybarger	Hank Thompson
Mack Sanders	Harry "Hap" Peebles
E.O. Stacy	Woody Herman
Lee Zhito	Larry Jones
Dr. Jerry Walker	Wayne Creasy
Marcellus Williams	

★

To my Cherokee and English Ancestors.

★

To Dick Howard and John Hitt.

★

To The Oak Ridge Boys: Duane, Joe, William Lee and Richard

★

Thanks to Mark Furnas for his tireless efforts
in helping me edit this book.

To the many people that were a part of The Jim Halsey
Company … and to our customers, artists, and clients.
It was always our goal to "make them satisfied."

table of contents

preface

In 1990, my company, The Jim Halsey Company, Inc., was the No. 1 country music agency in the world, representing 41 top country and pop acts. We had agents all over the globe. Every day, spotlights shone on our stars, as they entertained audiences from Birmingham to Bulgaria. After more than 40 years in the entertainment business, The Jim Halsey Company was at the very peak of its power and influence.

And that's when I decided to sell it.

A few months earlier, I'd begun holding music business classes in the agency's conference room in Nashville. Young people trying to get into the business would come in, and my agents and I, along with other industry professionals, would take turns teaching them what we knew.

We held classes twice weekly, and each session only lasted a month. But at the end of that month, those kids had found out that, most of the time, they were wasting their time doing what they'd been doing, and they'd rearranged their whole lives to reflect what they'd learned. They'd found out what to do and whom to call on, and they'd found out what was simply a waste of time.

As I saw the impact these classes were having, I began to realize that the time was right for me to sell The Jim Halsey Company. People, of course, thought I was nuts. "Why are you doing this?" they asked me. "Are you going to retire?"

I told them no. "I'm going to be doing something else," I said. "What I want to do now is tell young people about this business—

share my experiences, my formulas, my methods, so that maybe they can go out and become successful as well. "

I started writing this book in the last year that I had The Jim Halsey Company—which I ultimately sold to the giant William Morris Agency, making it the world's largest country music agency—and I've continued adding sections based on my experiences and observations ever since. After holding dozens of music business seminars all over the country in the first part of the '90s, I created the music and entertainment business program at Oklahoma City University, which became the first college in the world to offer a bachelor's degree in the business of entertainment, and I created, with Lee Zhito, the Billboard Song Contest, held annually under the auspices of the famed music-industry magazine, which offers aspiring songwriters a chance for their work to be heard by professionals. And I also continue to work with country music stars, managing the veteran supergroup The Oak Ridge Boys, who have been with me for more than 35 years. The Oaks join such stellar names as Roy Clark, Waylon Jennings, The Judds, Hank Thompson, Merle Haggard, Reba McEntire, Wanda Jackson, Freddy Fender, Roy Orbison, Tammy Wynette, Rick Nelson, Clint Black, Dwight Yoakam, Minnie Pearl, the Kentucky HeadHunters, Lee Greenwood, Ronnie Milsap and Mel Tillis, all of whom were guided—and in many cases discovered—by The Jim Halsey Company.

You've probably seen performances by several of these entertainers, either live or on television. And you've probably been impressed by their power of performance.

Have you ever stopped to consider that, onstage or off, we all have a performance to give? That you have your own unique Power of Performance? And that if you discover the ways to give the best performance possible, discover the ways of tapping the power within you, you can be a success in whatever you choose to pursue?

As you go through this book, you'll see a lot about the Power of Performance. In many ways, it's the whole key to what I'm writing about. Jim Halsey's (*Starmaker*) also gives you the behind-the-scenes facts about how the music industry works, covering all the varied components of the business and stripping away their mystery, showing you how they all work together—and guiding you in choosing the part you want to play.

This is a book about success, and how to achieve it. And this is a book about life, and how to live it. The plans, methods, and formulas you'll find in these pages all come from a life of trying and testing, of finding what works and what doesn't, of succeeding and failing, of embracing the hard-won positives and tossing away the misguided negatives. Here are the principles—and the secrets—that have guided me in my more than 50 years as an artist manager, agent, and impresario. They continue to work for me in my life. They will work for you in yours.

—Jim Halsey
Spirit Horse Ranch

an introduction

by Joseph S. Bonsall

GODFATHER–def. First appeared in the 12th century as, "One having a relation to someone or something analogous to that of a male sponsor to his godchild: and as one that founds, supports or inspires that child."

—from Compton's Dictionary

I am a firm believer in what I call the crossroads theory. In essence, I believe that there are many times in your life that you consciously or even unconsciously arrive at a meaningful crossroad where an event takes place that tends to mold, shape, and influence the rest of your life on earth. Sometimes it is merely a simple decision that we make in our hearts and minds to take the right road instead of the left. Or to choose the right thing to do instead of the wrong. Many of these decisions that we make are simple and very self-directed. Most, however, are divine interventions where God in His infinite wisdom has a definite plan in mind. But you must possess an open mind and an open heart to be aware of what it is that God is trying to tell you. So many missed opportunities exist because we just weren't listening.

I believe in my heart that at the most meaningful crossroads, God places a human being right there on the fork of the road at the appropriate time. A special human being whose influence changes our hearts and our very direction forever.

The Oak Ridge Boys, as a group and to a man, found ourselves at one such crossroad in July of 1975. We were a struggling and starving bunch of boys who were not really sure of our talent or worth, and we were just about to give it all up and go home. All of a sudden, there he was, standing right smack in the middle of the road, smiling and pointing out the right way to go. That man was Jim Halsey and for 33 years now we have respectfully referred to him as our Godfather.

On this night in July of 1975 Jim Halsey heard us sing for the first time. He told us that he believed that we were the most entertaining and energetic act that he had ever seen and that we were just "Three minutes away" from being the biggest act in Country Music. Of course, he meant that we needed a hit record. After all these years, Jim's famous "Three minutes away" speech has become a part of music business folklore.

Under his leadership and management, The Oak Ridge Boys did indeed become a household name, with a wall full of gold and platinum albums that are chock full of "three minute" miracles, for which we are all so very thankful.

We remain a hard working and popular act today because of the foundation that Jim helped us to build.

Jim Halsey has spent most of his life on the cutting edge of the music business. His booking agency, The Jim Halsey Company, Inc., out of Tulsa, Oklahoma once booked over half of the major acts in country music. I know that you are about to read a lot more about the Oaks and Jim in the pages that follow, but let me just provide for you, the reader, a slight recollection of milestones, a small collage of accomplishments that were simply unheard of B.H. (Before Halsey!):

1. Country music on "The Tonight Show" when Country wasn't as mainstream as today. The Oaks alone have been on the show twenty seven times.

2. Country music acts on variety shows from every major television network.

3. Country music acts under Jim's influence headlining all the major hotels on the Las Vegas Strip. (We still do it today!)

4. Roy Clark and The Oaks touring The Soviet Union.

5. Playing international festivals from Sweden to Switzerland and from Amsterdam to the Acropolis in Nice, France.

6. Headlining venues including Radio City Music Hall to Carnegie Hall and garnering major press for each performance.
7. Playing with big symphonies in major cities.
8. Shooting videos back when there was *no cable TV!*
9. Appearing at the famous Jim Halsey ranch parties in Tulsa where literally every fair buyer and concert hall booker in the world attended.
10. TV shows, concert halls, fairs, theaters. Jim could book us in all of them and make a huge, bigger-than-life event out of each and every one.
11. No idea too big. No problem that cannot be solved, no mountain that cannot be climbed.

This is Jim Halsey and, believe me, there is no one quite like him. But allow me just a few more words.

Jim Halsey is the most positive thinking man that I have ever known in my life. He is not only a man of knowledge and know how, but he is a man of God who puts his Family first.

He has always possessed in his soul certain ideals and values that come from years of studying the American Indian Way of Life, which teaches us to respect all of God's Creatures and to possess a child-like love for this great land in which we live.

So you see, Jim Halsey is so much more than our manager. He is a spiritual advisor, a healer, a peacemaker, a leader and a teacher.

I have seen him dance on top of a record company president's desk and I have seen him raise a family. I have seen him fight for what is fair and right and I have watched him light up and shine like an angel when he teaches his class.

Jim has never said, "Have a nice day." He always says, "This is a great day." It is always an "incredible week," and you had better believe, that "this year is going to be the best year yet!!," even "better than last year."

What a joy to have this man as a friend and what an opportunity for a young student of the music business to read this book and to learn from the very best.

I am honored to have been asked to write a few words here about our Godfather and Impresario, Jim Halsey.

Readers, look real hard at the road ahead. I guarantee there will be a crossroad around the next bend. Listen. Pay attention. Through the words of this book you will find Jim Halsey standing there ready to point the way down the right road. Listen to him. Learn from him. He is the best of us.

—Joseph S. Bonsall, The Oak Ridge Boys

May, 2009

Joseph S. Bonsall is a thirty-six year member of The Oak Ridge Boys and author of the Molly The Cat book series published by Ideals Children's Books, G.I. Joe and Lillie, An Inconvenient Christmas and An American Journey, published by New Leaf Press.

part one

SUCCESS AND THE POWER OF PERFORMANCE

chapter 1:

YOUR FOUNDATION FOR SUCCESS

What is success, and how do you achieve it?

First of all, you must determine what the word "success" means to you. It's easy to be confused or heavily influenced by other people's criteria for success, or to be misled by public opinion about what constitutes a successful life. For instance, far too many people believe that material wealth equals success, an equation reinforced by movies, television and the ads you read in newspapers and magazines. It's easy to be influenced by that image of success—but it doesn't necessarily have to be your image. Stop and think for yourself. Ask yourself what it would take to make you feel successful. Establish your own goals based on what you really want out of life, not what others want or think you should want.

As you'll read later, I formulated my early goals after absorbing the story of Sol Hurok, told in the book Impresario. But even before that, I was influenced heavily by those great old musicals featuring high-school kids, the kind MGM made with Mickey Rooney and Judy Garland. Although the stars were still in high school—at least for the purposes of the movie—they were doing musical plays, they had bands and producers, and it seemed as though the manager was always the person who called all the shots and the one who maybe got the most respect. So I started out wanting to become a manager.

Then, after I read the Sol Hurok book, I became entranced with the image of the impresario. He seemed to be the grandest—the one attending all the openings, carrying his ornate walking cane, his cape flung over his shoulder. That's when I decided that, instead of getting a real job, I'd promote shows.

After you have determined what you want out of life, ask for it. That's right, ask for it! You have the right. Whom do you ask? Start by asking the Creator, and you'll begin to get your answers.

Next, make a list for your life, just like you would make a shopping list. Write down your needs and your goals. Get them down on paper, in black and white, and then put them somewhere—on your desk, the refrigerator door, the bathroom mirror—where you'll often see them. That helps make them real to you.

When I am setting goals, I get a pad of legal paper and start writing down everything I can think of that will be needed for that particular project. I start at the top of the page, enumerating everything needed to make the project successful, including money, objects, people, talent, location, and time. Don't forget to add "luck."

You'll hear this from me time and again throughout this book: Write it down! This practice has been of great value to me, and it will be of great value to you. Write down your goals. Put the list where you can see it every day. This brings it into the present, into the real world, and that fact in itself helps you achieve what you've written down.

The list you come up with is really a recipe for achieving your goal, whether a specific, one-time project or a lifelong plan for your life. Once you've finished it, all you have to do is follow it to its conclusion.

That's not as easy as it sounds. Sometimes, we get thrown off the path because we get confused by what other people want from their own lists. Many times, for instance, we're guided by what our parents think we should become. That may not be compatible with what you want to become. True success must be fueled from within. The goals you strive toward must satisfy your own needs mentally, physically, emotionally, and spiritually. You must follow your own list, your own recipe for success.

Fortunately, I had parents who supported what I did, even if they didn't understand it and weren't even sure it was a real business. But they knew I was into it, and wanted to do it, and so they supported me. Of course, I always gave them free tickets to my shows.

If material gain is your measuring stick for success, that's fine. Recognize that it's not that way for everyone, though. If you write your list, set your goal, and follow the steps you've set for yourself, you will have your success. In certain professions, the monetary rewards are greater than others. Sometimes, when you achieve success in your projects, your reward will be both material gain and internal fulfillment. Believe me: the internal fulfillment is the most satisfying thing of all, and it should be what you seek above all else.

In building my career as an artist manager, booking agent, impresario, and businessman, I have measured my success in terms of the success of my projects and events. Some of them have benefited me materially, and some have not. My goal was always to maximize my creative process and to make a success of whatever project I took on. I didn't measure my success in material terms. Later on, you'll read about a couple of projects I did, The Oak Ridge Boys and The Judds at Radio City Music Hall and Roy Clark's Soviet tours, that were not financially rewarding but were richly successful on many other levels.

To be a success, you must focus on your goal. Surely, you've heard this phrase before, at a graduation speech or other motivational lectures. Somebody successful always seems to be standing at a podium saying, "Establish your goal and focus upon it."

There's no better piece of advice in the world than that. But let me add something important to it, and that is: have a purpose for your goal. When establishing the goals you hope to achieve, determine what their purpose is and what you hope to accomplish when you succeed.

A dog chases a car. Its goal is to catch the car. But what's the dog going to do when it catches the car? In other words, what's the purpose? So many of us are going through life chasing cars, putting a lot of work and energy into trying to catch something that's ultimately meaningless. If you know the purpose of your goals, if you can say why you pursue them, you'll dodge the empty pursuits that consume so many others.

The entertainment business is no different than any other kind of business. It may be a little more creatively stimulating than most, but the formulas for success are the same. It doesn't matter whether you're looking for financial, emotional, spiritual, or creative rewards, or a combination. You must have a goal and a purpose. When you determine your goal, identify the purpose. You can then plan how to achieve that goal.

From the beginning, I have always been interested in building projects and artists within this framework. I have always believed in making a project an event—in making life an event. Each one of my projects has had a specific goal, and each one has had a specific plan and a method of achieving success. And they all had a purpose!

★

I started my career as a promoter. It was through my early associations that I eventually became an artist manager and a booking agent. Learning to be a promoter, however, gave me an opportunity to understand all aspects of the music business: advertising, sales, marketing, promotion, artist relations, management, touring, agenting, the rodeo and fair business, television, and radio. I learned about record companies and music publishing companies and their importance to an artist's career. I learned, most importantly, about the power of teams and how their working together brought success. I learned about the Power of Performance each team member possessed.

I learned that by being a promoter of shows and music, I was also an important member of an essential structure, a player on the team. I learned to access my Power of Performance. I had the best of practical educations, with lots of planning and lots of trial and error combined with lots of failures. I worked with so many different artists that I was able to get a keen insight into how careers were being developed. I got to see a lot of the weaknesses of bad management and how disastrous it can be to an artist. I came to understand the differences between a good and a bad booking agent. As a working and learning observer, I could see when the synergy of the team members was missing—when the Power of Performance was lost, when all of its elements were not in working harmony. I found out in my early learning process that building a good team and harnessing every member's Power of Performance would bring success. Not doing so would bring failure.

While still a teenage promoter, I made up my mind that if I ever got the chance to manage an artist and exercise my Power of Performance, I would build a good team.

From the beginning of my show-business career, I actively sought knowledge about how to improve myself, including how to do a job better than somebody else was doing it. As a result, my on-the-job training had an early payoff.

I had been working as a promoter for Hank Thompson, an important recording artist, when he called me to be his manager. I'd been promoting Hank and his band, The Brazos Valley Boys, in various

towns throughout Kansas, Missouri, Oklahoma, and Arkansas. Sometimes, I would take a string of eight to ten dates and promote a small
tour. Hank told me his manager, John Hitt, was leaving for a position with Music Corporation of America (MCA), which was at that
time a very large booking agency. Hank had liked my "performances,"
my thoroughness in promoting his dates, and he wanted to know if I
would like to do it full time. In addition, he wanted me to be in charge
of everything else he did professionally—his bookings, all of his business arrangements, his record and television deals, corporate sponsorship, fairs and rodeos, the works. He asked me to be both his manager
and his agent.

At this time, manager-agent was not an unusual position, especially in the country field. Although Hank's western-swing style was a
mixture of country, R&B, and big-band, he was considered a country
act, and most of the big agencies knew very little about country music.
Managers of many country acts were also expected to book dates.

It was December of 1951. I had just turned 21 and was still in college, but it didn't take me long to recognize this was my opportunity to
put all of my dreams into action.

I had not really traveled outside of my four-state home area of
Kansas, Oklahoma, Missouri, and Arkansas. Now Hank Thompson
and his Brazos Valley Boys were asking me to book them nationally.

Before, Hank had been primarily a regional touring artist. His
records had sold nationally, but he had confined his personal appearances mainly to the southwest and West Coast, with an occasional
appearance in the East.

One of our first goals was to tour Hank in, at that time, all 48 states.
It was important to establish my relationship with Capitol Records,
Hank's recording company, and to work with them in trying to build
him into a national artist. Being a promoter, I was a constant reader
of the trade publications: Billboard, Cashbox, Variety, and Downbeat.
Using record-sale information gleaned from those magazines, I bought
a large map and systematically plotted the areas, states, and cities I
wanted to cover during my first year as Hank's manager and agent.

Take it from one who knows: timing is everything.

Just as Hank and I began our relationship, he released what turned
out to be one of the giant country records of all time, "The Wild Side
of Life." It sold well over a million copies and spawned many sequels
and parodies. I was in the right place at the right time!

Hank already had some good team members in place: the record company, Capitol Records; his record producer, Ken Nelson; a prominent music attorney, Harold Ornstein; and his music publisher, Hill and Range Songs. I was now an important member of the team, functioning both as manager and booking agent. It would be my job to coordinate the collective efforts of the team. For this, I had to access the very best of my own Power of Performance.

We came up with a five-year plan for Hank's career—a list of goals just like the list we talked about earlier. Our goals included expanding Hank's territory and his itinerary; getting more radio play nationwide; and creating a regional or national TV show with Hank at the center. He and I were firm believers in the power of television as a means of reaching masses of people. I went over the map, listened to the record company executives, took direction from Hank, booked the dates, went on the tour, met each promoter personally, and collected the money after every job. It was the important process of "learning the territory." It was on-the-job training!

We accomplished a lot the first year with Hank. I put all of my selling skills to work, designed a plan, established goals (with multiple purposes), and filled Hank's itinerary. Booking 225 dates in 40 states, I showed up at most of the venues with Hank. As a promoter, I had learned how an artist's personal appearances could be greatly enhanced if the team members' planning efforts were coordinated. The five-year plan was working, my methods were working, and they continued to work.

I have to confess that there were some dates included in Hank's itinerary that were more personal and meaningful to me than to anyone else. As I was getting my geography lesson firsthand, I booked some dates in areas I just wanted to see—places I had read about as a kid, but had never been able to visit. Now, I had an opportunity to see them as part of my job. Shows in places like Jackson Hole, Wyoming, the Grand Canyon, and the Cheyenne Frontier Days celebration in Cheyenne, Wyoming, were not only good dates for Hank, as we expanded his territory, but added to the color and flavor of what we were doing.

Hank Thompson is one of the most important people in my life. He is my mentor, business partner, teacher, and best of all, my friend. Because of my early relationship with Hank, I have been able to live my choice of lives. I recognized the opportunity. I accepted the challenge and used my Power of Performance. I asked, and I received, and I will always be grateful to God for answering my prayers and to Hank for a relationship that has lasted nearly half a century.

My long association with Hank Thompson illustrates two important things. One, you must be able to recognize opportunities. Two, you must be able to take action when the opportunities arise!

Much of my early training and most of my personal philosophy was developed while I was constantly traveling with Hank in those early years. When I took over management of this great artist, I formulated my first five-year plan, something I've done innumerable times since. I learned, early on, to follow my dreams. I agreed with the old truism, "If you don't follow your dreams, you are going to stop having them."

I had plenty of dreams and visions. I would write them down, along with my goals and their purpose. Once I had all of this down where I could see it and think about it, I'd discuss it all with Hank. I learned how to focus. All of this propelled me toward a performance that achieved the goals I'd set for myself.

So please, don't be afraid to follow your dreams!

Now is the time for you to begin. You have the right to ask for what you want. List your goals and their purpose, your dreams and visions, on a piece of paper. Put it in a conspicuous place, where you can't miss seeing it often. It is your plan for the future, your road map for your own personal journey. It's great to have more than one goal. Naturally, some are more important than others; you'll follow a lot of branches in the road to get to your ultimate destination.

Just as you have to pass through many cities and towns on a journey, you have to achieve some goals before going on to others. It helps to identify each goal and put it in order of importance to your overall plan. Once you've written them down, you'll be surprised how easy it is to focus on each one.

We talked about focus earlier. This is very important. You must be able to focus, and you must be able to stay focused—on your goals, and on your plan for achieving them.

Can you identify your goals, the ones you really want to achieve? Are they the product of your dreams? If they are, that's great! You are beginning to recognize the potential of your dreams. Now, you can begin turning those dreams into reality!

SOURCES OF REVENUE

Here are the ten main sources of revenue in the commercial music business:

1. Personal Appearances
2. Recordings (including CDs, DVDs, ringtones and downloads)
3. Songwriting
4. Music Publishing
5. Television, Movies, Video, and Internet (including websites)
6. Commercials
7. Product Endorsements
8. Corporate Sponsorship
9. Merchandise
10. Books and other Literature

Most of my life has been spent in the entertainment business, and what I've written in this book–including this list–comes from what I've seen and lived. I know that entertainment is about art and music, but I also know it's about product and the delivery of that product. Those of us who have a long-term love affair with the art and music know that our love can only be enabled and affirmed by dynamic sales and marketing.

Yes, the business changes. Twenty years ago, for example, the material listed beside the No. 2 revenue source would've been LPs and cassette tapes, rather than CDs, DVDs, ringtones and downloads. But change is creative. We learn by it. We grow by it. We even fail by it– and by failing, we grow and ultimately become more successful.

Success does not discriminate. On the other hand, it's not for everyone–just those who are prepared. Success, after all, isn't like Domino's Pizza. It's not delivered fresh and hot to your door. *You have to go for it!*

chapter 2

ACCEPTING THE CHALLENGE

In the music and entertainment business—as in all other businesses—the difference between excellence and mediocrity can be measured in degrees. Achieving excellence and not settling for mediocrity can be as simple as an extra boost of effort or a fraction more determination. The formula for consistent excellence is relatively simple, but that doesn't mean it's easy.

What must you do to seriously pursue excellence in a music and entertainment career?

You must commit yourself to attempting what most people will dismiss as impossible. You must be determined to stretch yourself to the limits of your ability. You must take on more than you believe is possible to achieve, and you must ask your spiritual and physical helpers for the strength and guidance to achieve it.

Go to the limit. Have a goal. Have a purpose. Access your Power of Performance, whether you're on stage or off.

Accepting the challenge to be consistently excellent is an important part of being successful. You must be able to recognize every challenge as an opportunity that triggers your Power of Performance.

In the music and entertainment business, challenges sometimes arrive unexpectedly or prematurely, at times when you seem to be least ready for them. Remember: every challenge is a test. Each challenge gives you a chance to excel, to pull past mediocrity and drive to the top.

When a new challenge comes along, ask yourself these questions:

- Am I ready for it?
- Is there a purpose for my taking it?
- Am I qualified to take it?
- Do I have the mental and physical stamina for it?
- Can I do it?
- Will it allow me to perform?

You'll notice that I repeat several principles and ideas throughout this book. Here's an important one: I never equate success with money, only with performance.

Material wealth can be a measure of success, but it's only one of many. Real success brings fulfillment and contentment. And performance, good or bad, determines everyone's level of success in the music and entertainment business.

Accessing your Power of Performance gives you the ability to excel, to achieve success and, ultimately, contentment. No matter what your field, it's all about performance.

And that's especially true in the fascinating, fabulous, frenetic, and occasionally frustrating business of music—my business.

chapter 3

THE POWER OF PERFORMANCE

Already, you've seen the term Power of Performance several times in this book. You're going to see it a lot more. That's because I firmly believe it is the single most important factor in anyone's success.

Learning about this power, and finding the best ways to unleash it, is really what this book is all about. So, before we go any further, let's define it.

Power of Performance is doing your job, performing your task, accepting your mission in life, all to the best of your ability. It is giving your best performance, whether you're on stage or off. It is going for excellence, with the understanding that you're capable of achieving it. It is, simply, accessing, perfecting, and projecting your abilities and talents to make yourself the best you can possibly be—mentally, physically, emotionally, and spiritually.

Every day, you give a performance. You may be on a stage, or you may be on a telephone. You may be behind a counter, across the table from a business acquaintance, in the home of someone close to you. By accessing your Power of Performance, you can shape your own life and influence others by expressing your abilities in an expressive and dynamic way. It is a sure path to success.

Whatever your skills are, perfect them beyond all insecurity or doubt of ability. Know everything about your job, your craft, your artistic talents. Go the extra mile, put in the overtime hours, push your talent and energy to the limit, and then go a little farther.

Every successful person has the Power of Performance. Artists and musicians have it, and the ones who have perfected their Power of Performance are usually big stars. I discovered the Power of Performance as a teenager, seeing how great artists connected with their audiences. I saw that these gifted people could conduct an audience through a range of emotions, from melancholia and sadness to exhilarating joy, just like a conductor changing mood and music with the wave of a baton.

I knew, however, I could never be one of these people. Playing saxophone in the school band and with a dance combo on weekends convinced me that my real talent lay elsewhere than the stage, despite the fact that I was in love with music.

Then, a high school book-report assignment changed my life.

The book I chose was a biography called Impresario: A Memoir of Sol Hurok (Random House, 1946). Once I began reading it, I couldn't put it down. During his many years in show business, Sol Hurok presented nearly every type of stage attraction, specializing in bringing talent from the Soviet Union and other parts of Eastern Europe to the United States. His life had been full of glamour, talented artists, events that required creative sales and marketing, and even a certain amount of risk. What could be better for me? All through school I had been selling something. So why not sell music and entertainment?

So, although my talent—and Sol Hurok's—didn't lie in performance on a stage, I made a decision to get into the music business and become, like my inspiration, an impresario. And once I made that decision, I began turning my energies in that direction, using my Power of Performance in a single-minded effort to become the impresario of southeastern Kansas!

★

It started when I booked the great western swing figure Leon McAuliffe and his band into my hometown of Independence, Kansas. It happened in October of 1949, the month I turned 19. Several months earlier, I'd begun thinking, "Well, maybe I'll get a band to put in the auditorium." I knew what to do: find a good night, put the posters out, put the handbills out, buy the ads in the paper, get on the radio stations. So finally, I decided to take the plunge, and access my mostly untried Power of Performance as a music promoter.

I was a big fan of western-swing pioneer Bob Wills, who had given Leon his start (as well as his trademark phrase, "Take it away, Leon"), and I'd followed Leon since his days as steel guitarist for Bob Wills' Texas Playboys. After World War II, Leon had put together his own popular Tulsa-based band, which was touring on a regional basis.

I wrote to Leon, and I got a letter back from C.M. Cooksey, his manager, saying they had a date in October that was available. They gave it to me on a straight percentage basis. While I was still at risk for the hall and everything that went along with it, as well as the advertising costs and the help, it was a minimal risk because Mr. Cooksey hadn't asked for a big guarantee.

The show night was a Thursday night, the night of the week that stores stayed open late in Independence. It was a beautiful evening, and before the show I walked the streets, wondering how everything was going to turn out. As I wandered, I noticed an unusual number of people in town, and cars with tags from Missouri, Oklahoma, and other states. I thought, "Something's going on, and maybe, just maybe, it's my dance."

It was. When I arrived at the auditorium to open the box office, there was already a line—an hour before Leon and his band were to begin. And when that dance kicked off with the words "Take it away, Leon," the place was full. It was jam-packed.

That was my entry into show business. I loved the music. I loved the excitement of seeing a promotion work. I loved the happiness on people's faces when they left, saying "Good dance, Jim," or "Good music, Jim," or "What a good time, Jim." That night, I knew I was in show business to stay. And even though I couldn't put it into words yet, I was learning the important idea of the Power of Performance.

After that, I branched out and started sending letters to other agencies and bands. I knew who to contact because I read Billboard and the other trade magazines that gave you performers' itineraries and told you who handled them. None of these people knew I was 19.

Neither did Mr. Cooksey, Leon McAuliffe's manager. When he came up to Independence, he was surprised to find a 19-year-old kid promoting the show. But I did a good job, and so we established a relationship that led to my playing Leon and his band about once a month in Independence and surrounding areas. By the time the mid-'50s rolled around, I was his agent, and we were busy expanding him beyond the Oklahoma, Kansas and Texas area, making him into the national figure that he and I both wanted him to be. He was a complement to Hank Thompson and Wanda Jackson, whom I was also handling, because I could call one promoter and make three sales. The efficiency and economy of having three national acts was better than having just one.

I took Leon all over the West Coast and through the Northwest. I represented him for four or five years. We remained friends forever.

★

There must have been something about Independence—as there is with my other hometown, Tulsa—that fostered and foreshadowed the development of my Power of Performance. Certainly, the town has been home to others who've accessed their own Power of Performance in lasting ways. They range from the brilliant American playwright William Inge, creator of such powerful works as Bus Stop, Picnic, The Dark at the Top of the Stairs, and Come Back, Little Sheba, to Harry Sinclair, the famed oil baron.

Supposedly, Harry Sinclair, in his early struggling days, shot off one of his toes to collect the insurance money, which he then used to drill his first well. True or not, that story went around Independence for many years. William Inge heard it, and he put a line in The Dark at the Top of the Stairs about how a man shot his toe off to get into the oil business.

Flash forward to the middle 1960s. I was promoting a touring stage production (known in the business as a bus and truck show) of The Dark at the Top of the Stairs, starring the veteran actress Joan Blondell. It came to Independence, and when the audience heard the line about shooting off a toe, it broke into uproarious laughter and cheers. Ms. Blondell and the rest of the cast were baffled. They'd been on tour for six weeks, and that was the first time the line had ever gotten a laugh. So as the play went on, they threw the line in three or four more times, just to see what response they'd get. It brought the house down every time.

When the play was over, Joan Blondell sought me out. "What is this deal about shooting your toe off and collecting insurance money?" she asked. I told them all the Harry Sinclair story.

If there's a moral to this story, maybe it's that, on rare occasions, your performance can take on a power that even leaves you baffled!

chapter 4

TEN KEYS TO POWER OF PERFORMANCE

O ver the years, I have developed a 10-key method for achieving success. It is simple and effective and it will always work, no matter what your profession. It is a formula for success in life. The better you understand and employ each of these keys, the more likely your Power of Performance will lead you to success. If your interest lies in becoming a manager, agent, or even a star, these 10 keys are essential. But they work in every profession, in every walk of life, and there is not a single one of them that you can't keep on developing every day of your life.

1. **Talent.** We all have talent. The lucky ones are born with it, but most of us have to develop it. I'm not talking just about artistic talent. I'm also talking about the talent that can help make you a successful artist manager, booking agent, record producer, executive and business person. Examine the talent you have, and see what you need to develop in order to advance toward your goal.

2. **Training and Education.** How do you develop your talent? Training and education is one good way. If you are a singer, songwriter, musician, or band member, for instance, you will always benefit from lessons, instructions, on-the-job training with other musicians and bands, working on the road, taking advice from other players, listening to tapes and CDs, watching television, reading, and attending concerts, confer-

ences, and workshops. You didn't know this was training and education? It's the best type of education, and it's available to everyone.

Always work toward refining your skills. If you're interested in the business aspects of the music industry, you can follow the same rules, but make a continuous study about how things are being done. Get as much education as possible, taking courses that will benefit you in your chosen profession.

Many people start in the booking or management business by taking jobs as apprentices or assistants with large agencies or management companies. These entry-level positions—file clerk, driver, etc.—may not seem important, but, believe me, they are. Everything you do for the company is part of your education, and the more education you have, the better your chances of getting off to a good start. So pay attention!

The same thing holds for careers in the record business, music publishing, and other music industry management positions. Watching how things are done, identifying the players, listening while negotiations are in progress, and finding out how to deal with artists, managers, booking agents, and record companies all adds to your overall knowledge. This is called apprenticeship, and it's the way a lot of people get started in the music and entertainment business.

You can increase your overall understanding of the music and entertainment business by reading the trade publications, called the "trades." These are magazines and newspapers dealing with various aspects of the business. They publish stories about what's happening in the music and entertainment business, review new products and artists, chart the popularity of records in current release, make forecasts, and give information on touring groups, among other things.

Some trades—Guitar Player, Bass Player, and Keyboard, for instance—are specialized, targeting a very specific music industry audience. Then there are general-interest trades, like Billboard magazine. The true bible of the industry, Billboard is a weekly that covers different aspects of music, television, video, personal appearances—and now, even computers.

Some colleges and universities also offer specialized training. A lot of schools have courses dealing with the performing arts, and some even offer songwriting courses. However, fewer than 50 schools deal with the practical aspects of the music business. This has always seemed strange to me, as a lot of graduates jump right in, thinking their business degree is all they need, and find out they know nothing about the basic elements of the music business—such as the functions of the manager, the agent, the unions and guilds, music publishers, copyrights, record companies, publicists, music and entertainment attorneys, and the sales and marketing of artists, records and events.

Not long ago, I completed my contract as the head of the music and entertainment business program at Oklahoma City University, and I thank OCU president Dr. Jerald Walker, who shared my vision about what that program should be. My main focus now is on the Halsey Institute in Tulsa, Oklahoma. The Halsey Institute provides accelerated learning for individuals interested in entering the music entertainment business.

If you don't have access to a program like this, a good part of your education will have to be learned by experience, often in the "school of hard knocks." You can find books and tapes that will help, and sometimes there are organizations in your area that offer seminars on the music business. Take advantage of these opportunities. Remember, it is a continual process of learning. The more knowledge you have, the better equipped you are to access your own personal Power of Performance.

3. **Personality.** Sometimes it seems as though personality is like talent; some people are simply born with it. This isn't so. There are people who have the ability to present themselves better than others, but they usually can do this only after training and lots of experience. And in making a good presentation of yourself, you develop your personality.

How do you develop your presentation? Well, if you don't have confidence in yourself, and if you tend to be unfocused and rambling when you speak before others, the best things you can do is write down exactly what you want to say, stand before a mirror, and say it over and over and over. Pretty soon you'll be able to go in and speak, and no distraction will bother you, because if you have to, you can go to your memory and say it just as you memorized it. When you're comfortable, you can ad-lib and free-flow. Becoming good at speaking gives you self-confidence, and that bolsters your personality.

I don't care if you are a singer, a band member, an agent, a manager, or filling one of the hundreds of other positions in the music business—you can develop a direct and positive approach to others. You can develop a good personality. It's an important part of your Power of Performance, your method for success.

There is a good course on how to present yourself, the famous Dale Carnegie course, available nationwide and usually offered in night sessions. I always encouraged the associates in my agency to improve their communication skills by taking the Carnegie course, and I still highly recommend it. The Carnegie course, and others like it, are immensely effective in sharpening your skills in dealing with people, whether on stage or off. In the music and entertainment business, you are constantly working with a dizzying number of people; to increase your Power of Performance to the maximum, your communication skills and your personality must be as effective as you can make them.

4. **Attitude.** This book is full of attitude; I bring it up again and again in these pages. That's because attitude is important for any accomplishment in life, and part of my method for success is developing a positive attitude and continuously maintaining it.

If your attitude is bad, nothing is going to work for you. If it's good, your attitude will enhance your dealings with others and make your performance better. If you're a performer, your good attitude will radiate out from the stage and engage the audience. If you're a musician in a band, a good attitude on the road will get you through many a trying time of bad schedules, long journeys, inadequate sound, and lousy hotel rooms. Keeping your attitude positive is only one of the important keys to making my method work, but without a good attitude, none of the others will be effective.

You have to understand that maintaining a positive attitude is, simply, an important aspect in the pursuit of a quality life. I am an eternal optimist. My attitude has always been positive. Having a good attitude doesn't mean I don't encounter problems or that difficulties don't arise. Life is a process of constant change, and with these changes often come problems, but these problems and changes bring growth. Sometimes, that's a hard fact to realize while working through one of life's difficulties, but maintaining a positive attitude always helps you get through.

When I think of attitude, I think of Leo Zabelin. Leo was, for more than 20 years, The Jim Halsey Company's in-house director of press and public relations; I had known him since the very early days of my career. Over the years, Leo had been involved with major publications and major motion picture studios. He was one of the great geniuses in the area of public relations, and Leo Zabelin knew everybody.

Because Leo was an early riser, he always arrived at our office before anyone else. While many of his colleagues were still in bed, Leo would be reading the trade magazines and the vast array of newspapers to which we subscribed. Normally, before I arrived, Leo would also go through all the telephone calls on the overnight telephone sheet, the overnight mail, and the numerous faxes or telexes that had arrived during the night. Every morning, I would enter the office full of ideas, new dreams, or just the excitement of starting a new day. And every morning, Leo would greet me with, "Hello. Well, we've got a problem today."

It was the same greeting each morning, and each morning there usually was a problem—often, more than one. Today, I cannot think of one which was not solvable. Some were more complex than others, but solving those is what makes us grow and learn. They are all just part of the territory.

I am a great believer in positive thoughts and positive energy and in doing everything I can to keep those energies free and flowing. This is what makes a positive performance. Since I try to be positive all the time, Leo's daily greeting didn't really bother me.

But finally, after several years, I sat down and tried to explain my approach to Leo. I told him that I saw problems as opportunities to learn. I stressed the fact that while "problem" situations were always going to be with us every day, we did not have to be negative. Maintaining a positive attitude, I said, was the key to solving all of these problems. Finally, I told him that I would prefer he not greet me every morning with "we've got a problem."

Leo understood my point and seemed to agree. He was a close friend; still, I wondered whether saying the kind of things I had to say to him had hurt his feelings and created some negative energy. I had so much respect for Leo and his knowledge that I felt he wouldn't be offended. I certainly hoped that was the case.

I was right. The morning after Leo and I had our talk, he met me at the door as usual—but for the first time, he had changed his salutation. "Good morning, Jim," he said. Then he hesitated. "This morning," he continued after a moment, "we've got a situation."

I complimented him on not starting the day with a problem. "It makes a positive change in our attitude when starting the day," I told him.

Then, I asked about the "situation."

"There's a fire," he said.

"Okay."

"A big fire!" Leo continued.

"All right, all right. Where's the big fire, Leo?"

"The MGM Hotel in Las Vegas," he replied. "It's burning down— and The Oak Ridge Boys open there Thursday."

"Now Leo," I said, "that is a problem!"

We spent the rest of the morning ascertaining the extent of the damage. It was a very serious fire. A number of people had lost their lives and the MGM Hotel would be closed for some time. Now was the time to show ourselves, and our clients, our Power of Performance. Our performance wasn't on stage; we performed for The Oak Ridge Boys behind the scenes, on telephones, making useful and productive time of the weeks we suddenly had open on The Oak Ridge Boys' performing schedule.

Because a few of our other stars had taken ill on the road—a not-uncommon occurrence with touring acts—we'd had to cancel some shows around the country. Now, we could use The Oak Ridge Boys to fill the dates those acts couldn't do. The rest of the time, The Oak Ridge Boys were able to do some press and public relations, guest-star in a couple of television shows, and prepare for their next album.

Taking care of "situations" is built into the day-to-day routine of simply doing business, and accepting the challenge of everyday life with a positive attitude is an important part of being successful. We have to recognize our challenges as opportunities and then act within our Power of Performance. Sometimes a challenge comes unexpectedly, such as the MGM Hotel fire. Sometimes, at least in our own minds, challenges come prematurely, before we're ready for them. But remember: You are being tested with every challenge. Are you ready for it? Are you qualified for it? Do you have the mental and physical stamina for it? Can you do it?

In the case of the MGM crisis and many other challenges that went along with the booking-agency business, we did it. And we did it by accepting the challenge.

Accept the challenge. Don't be afraid to fail. If you're always afraid to fail, then you'll never accept the first assignment. And so what if you do fail? Isn't that the best way of learning how not to fail with the next challenge that comes your way?

Sure, it takes a little courage to set off into the unknown. But remember: You have established your goals, and you have written them down. Now is the time to get started.

Challenges come in many forms, and they don't always look like opportunities. Often, they do not even seem to fit in your scheme of things. Having the proper attitude when faced with these things helps you achieve success.

Examine each challenge and opportunity to determine if it will be a learning experience. Will it help make you better as a person? Will it open up new opportunities down the road? Will it bring you satisfaction and happiness? Will you grow through the challenge? Does it fit into the overall plan for achieving your goals? Can you salvage the misfortune that happens, as The Jim Halsey Company did in the MGM crisis? Have you learned to access your power?

- If it fits, go for it!
- Get excited about it!
- Get enthused about it!
- Give it all you can!

5. **Enthusiasm.** Get enthused! Get excited about your life, your talent, your job, your career, and the selling of yourself or your product.

Another important part of my method, an essential key, is to deal always with every aspect of the business with enthusiasm. After all, more sales are made because of a salesperson's enthusiasm than for any other reason.

Our life is comprised of selling. If you are a player, you sell from the stage, but no matter what part of the music business you're in, genuine enthusiasm will produce results and sales beyond your expectations. Sometimes things won't go as planned. The breaks may not come. But if you have prepared yourself, you'll know you have what it takes to persevere and to triumph.

Stay focused and stay enthused! Enthusiasm is one of your best sources of energy. Always greet the day with it, realizing it is an important key to your success.

By the way, I'm enthused about passing this knowledge on to you, so you can put your Power of Performance to work!

6. **Desire.** You have to have desire. It fuels your enthusiasm and helps

you overcome a lot of disappointment and rejection. If you have the desire to make it, in spite of all adversities, you will make it.

When I think about the power of desire, I often think of Lee Greenwood, whose "God Bless the USA" is the best known of his many country music chart-toppers. For years, Lee dealt blackjack in the Las Vegas casinos by day and worked the lounges at night, determined to get out of there and get his songs heard and become a recognized international performer. He did, and I'm happy to say that The Jim Halsey Company helped him achieve his goals.

Lee Greenwood and his subsequent stardom is an impressive example of how much desire is involved in accessing your personal Power of Performance.

7. Persistence. My method stresses persistence: not wavering from your path, not losing focus on your goal. Stick your foot in the door of success and do not take it out until you have wedged the door open far enough for you to get through it. Do not get discouraged and give up.

Persistence keeps you on the road to success—persistence in the quality of your performance, persistence in the dedication to the work you've chosen. Realize, please, that persistence is all-important. Without it, my method won't work.

8. Self-Confidence. Self-confidence is something you develop for yourself. It comes with learning your craft. The more you do any task, the more comfortable you are with it. It is this repetition in perfecting your skills, your own Power of Performance, that develops self-confidence. The more you train, study, and work with your music-business skills, the more you will develop self-confidence. The more you work, the more you perform, the more comfortable you will be with the knowledge that you can do it. This is self-confidence, and it is attainable by anyone!

9. Recognize Opportunities. If you are going to be successful, you not only have to be able to recognize opportunities, you have to act when an opportunity comes your way. So many times, people pass over an opportunity because they're afraid to take action. Acting might mean changes in their lives—they could face risk and uncertainties, and they lack the self-confidence to face all of that.

If you're really going for success, you have to be able to make decisions and take risks. Examine every opportunity that comes your way.

Does it offer an advancement in the areas you're interested in? What are the risks? What are the rewards? What are the sacrifices you will need to make? Write all of the risks and rewards, listing potentially positive things on one side, potentially negative things on the other. When you are through, look at it objectively. It will help you decide how to act. And remember: Even inaction is an action.

10. **Commitment.** This one tells the story. Commitment is different from desire. It is your promise to yourself to focus on your goal and do what is necessary to achieve it. Can you be a success at anything if you do not have a commitment to your family, your job, your friends, your ideas, your country; to God, life, and yourself? If you are committed to yourself, then you'll know what you have to do to make your life a success. The challenges you face will come more easily because you will understand how to make the necessary commitment.

Make a goal, develop a plan, and follow it through. Have a purpose. Be committed. As you become more and more involved with people, as you continue to develop your Power of Performance, a personal commitment will be indispensable for making your relationships grow and prosper. Do not be afraid to make a commitment and stick to it. When you do, it brings forth commitment from others.

Here's a simple equation: Power of Performance is a commitment, and commitment is Power of Performance.

In my business as artist manager and agent for a number of stars, I was constantly renewing my commitment to myself, my company, and the people we represented. We established game plans for our artists' careers—and for our own careers as well. Each year, usually, we would put down in writing what we hoped to achieve, where we wanted to go, and then we would make a commitment, or a recommitment, to the artist and the plan.

Do not be afraid to speak about your commitment or to put it in writing. People like to know where you stand. This is part of your Power of Performance. Even if others are sure of your ability and loyalty, when you say—as we did—"I am committing myself and the resources of my company to your career," it seems to assure success.

It is positive. It is commitment. It is Power of Performance.

If you are not willing to commit, how can you expect others to commit to you? How can you access your Power of Performance if you are not committed? After all, aren't you going for success? Aren't you willing to give all that you can?

It all goes back to that commitment to yourself. That's your first commitment and your most important one. Access your power and get your performance going for you through commitment. Do not waste your time or anyone else's if you are not ready to make a commitment.

Once you understand the importance of commitment, your life will change. It will become more interesting, because what you do with it will be solid and meaningful. Commit and be glad you did; it will reshape your life more and sooner than you can imagine.

★

Each one of these keys is important to your Power of Performance; taken together, they will be of immense help in establishing your own personal discipline, learning, and work habits. Include all ten of these keys in your life. Read them and reread them. Understand them and put them into action.

And then, be ready for the trickster that can throw a wrench into even the best-laid plans: *rejection!*

The lesson of rejection, as painful as it is, must be learned by all of us. If you're lucky it will come early in your career, and you'll be able to deal with it and learn from it. Unfortunately, you probably won't see it coming.

I sure didn't, when Roy Clark and I got schooled in rejection by one of Hollywood's real heavyweights, Jack Webb.

It happened in the early 1960s, when Roy and I were getting started together. Even then, I knew that Roy Clark was, quite simply, the single most talented person I had ever met. I knew it. He knew it. Our job was getting the rest of the world to know it.

Roy was recording then for Capitol Records. He hadn't yet scored a big hit, but that didn't bother Capitol or Roy's producer, Ken Nelson, who saw the same potential in him that I did.

The movie No Time For Sergeants, starring Andy Griffith, had been a boxoffice blockbuster, and Warner Bros. was planning a television series based on the picture. Because of the efforts of some Capitol Records executives, Roy's name had been pitched as a possible star of the series, and he was subsequently invited to audition for the role originated by Griffith. We were told that if his reading went well, he'd have a screen test and then, if all went right, the lead in the series.

What a break for us! It was the kind of break that launches a career, and to say we were excited about the opportunity is an incredible understatement. We were ecstatic about the possibility of Roy becoming an instant television star.

I was confident, of course, that he would get the role. Things were starting to happen for us. We were on a roll, and this just felt right.

Spurred by excitement and optimism, Roy and I climbed into my car and headed across the country to California, scarcely stopping for anything. I drove. He studied his script and went over his lines as I listened and made suggestions. After three days of this, we were in Southern California and Roy, I felt, was a shoo-in for the part.

Our meeting was at Warner Bros. Studios with the series producer, Jack Webb. For years, both of us had been fans of Webb, who'd soared to fame as the laconic, no-nonsense Joe Friday on the famed TV series Dragnet. I have to admit that we were a little intimidated by the to-the-point character we'd seen on TV. But we weren't really worried. Roy had been over and over the script, and he was ready for his reading.

Then, we saw Webb's office. I have seen a lot of executive offices in my time, but never one as huge as this was.

We were early for our appointment, and a rather stiff and unfriendly secretary ushered us into Webb's cavernous quarters. It was really more of a palace. Dark walls rose up to impossibly high ceilings and down to marble floors full of massive oak furniture. Even all these years later, I can still see the place. It was immense—so big that every little sound echoed like thunder.

Left alone, Roy and I glanced around at the intimidating opulence and awaited the arrival of the powerful Jack Webb, this palace's king. Finally, an assistant arrived to do what pages have been doing for kings for hundreds of years: he announced to all within earshot that Mr. Webb would arrive shortly. Then we heard the echoes of leather heels snapping on the shiny marble floor. The King had arrived.

One look at Jack Webb and I knew what getting the role could do for Roy's career. I can't speak for Roy's feelings at the time, but my heart was in my throat.

By now, Webb and another associate were standing in front of us. We rose out of our chairs, ready to shake hands. Webb's assistant—the page—said, "This is Mr. Halsey, and this is Roy Clark."

And there, floating motionless in the great expanse of the king's throne room, our extended hands remained. They were not accepted by either Jack Webb or his associate.

The King looked at both of us.

I waited for him to speak.

Jack Webb didn't say "Hello."

Jack Webb didn't say "How do you do?"

In fact, he only said two words: "Too fat."

And with that he did a military about-face and left the room, his leather heels clicking on the shiny marble floor.

He might as well have said, "Off with their heads." In that instant, our dreams of Roy becoming that instant television star vanished. We were speechless. We looked at each other, open-mouthed, the weeks of anticipation and preparation, the days of driving, the dreams of TV stardom, all flashing through our minds, all dashed to pieces.

We could've reacted in several different ways to the sentence of the King. We could've given up, become angry, lost faith. For us, though, there was only one thing to do. Maybe we remembered the old adage about how you might as well laugh as cry, or perhaps it was simply spontaneous. Whatever the reason, we both broke out laughing. Our laughter filled the cavernous space of Jack Webb's office, and the echoes must have been heard throughout the whole castle.

And so, we put a humorous spin on our rejection, overshadowing our disappointment at our treatment by the King. Jack Webb had certainly exercised his Power of Performance; in fact, he'd done it with just two words. And we'd reacted with laughter instead of tears or anger.

There is a lesson here on rejection. Ours was direct, to-the-point, brutal, and personal. We had to accept it and make it a part of learning, a part of growing. At some point in your own career, perhaps at many points, you will have to accept it, too. Accepting and working with rejection is one of the most important elements of your growth, and you must learn to use it. If you can turn it around and make it a positive part of your process, you'll be well on your way to success.

★

Everyone in the music business has an ego. Artists are usually thought to have the biggest egos, but ego is one of the things that make you a success, no matter what part of the business you're in. Ego is your drive, your desire for acceptance and recognition. It must be acknowledged, and a certain amount of it is beneficial.

All of us, I guess, have been put in our places many times, and our egos have been bruised and bent. If you can accept reality, if you can understand what the real truth is in your life, then you can be at peace with yourself.

Part of accepting reality is striving to understand why people make the decisions they do. As I said earlier, I'm grateful to have two hometowns that I feel comfortable in and love, Independence, Kansas, and Tulsa, Oklahoma. I grew up in Independence, and sometimes, by Independence standards, my ideas may have been a little too extreme for the town, or not as important to others as they were to me. And, of course, having your ideas go unaccepted or unappreciated is a form of rejection.

In my early days with Hank Thompson, booking a lot of package tours, I became involved with two more great country stars, Tex Ritter and Merle Travis. They not only became good friends, but I bought and promoted a lot of dates with them. The three of them—Hank, Tex, and Merle—went out together on a number of package shows, and we'd all travel in the same car.

During one of these trips in the early '60s, I was telling them about Tom Mix, whom I admired a great deal, and how he'd been a city marshal in Independence before making the jump to silent-movie stardom. And Merle Travis said, " Well, you know, a friend of mine has got all of Tom Mix's memorabilia stored in a garage, out in the San Fernando Valley or someplace. You think you'd be interested in that?"

Sure, I told him. With that material, maybe we could start a Tom Mix museum in Independence.

"If you wanted it to start a museum, I think he'd give it to you," Merle said.

So I went to the Independence city fathers, and I said, "There's a possibility that we could get all the Tom Mix memorabilia—his medicine chest, his silver saddles, his pictures, his ropes, his trophies, everything. It's in storage, and some friends of mine think there's a possibility we could get it for no cost at all."

So they mulled it over, and they came back to me in a couple of weeks and said, "No, we don't think we're interested. We already have one museum in Independence."

It was only a couple of years after that, Dewey, Oklahoma, purchased the same collection for $50,000, and started what I think is a really interesting and wonderful museum. Now, of course, one of those silver saddles is worth what the town paid for the collection.

I thought that Independence should pay attention to Tom Mix, because he's a part of town history. But I guess the city fathers at the time just didn't think the idea was very good.

Many years later, in 1994, I came up with the idea of celebrating an event that happened in 1926. It was the first coast-to-coast network radio broadcast, and Independence was a big part of it. General Sarnoff, the head of NBC, rounded up all the big stars of the day, people like John Philip Sousa and Paul Whiteman, to participate in the broadcast, and he knew he had to have Will Rogers on the roster. But Rogers was appearing live in Independence that night, and he told General Sarnoff, "If you want me, you're going to have to come to Independence, Kansas."

You can imagine the kind of electronic equipment it took in those days to make a remote broadcast. But General Sarnoff got NBC hooked up to Independence and broadcast 15 or 20 minutes of Rogers' show coast to coast.

I thought it would be a good idea to commemorate the anniversary of that broadcast in Independence each year with a banquet and the presentation of a Will Rogers Commemorative Award to a celebrity. We could even broadcast it nationally. A lot of the townspeople also thought the notion had merit, and we got underway, selling tickets to the banquet.

It was a big success. Some 250 people saw Roy Clark and Hank Thompson receive the award, and the Great Empire Broadcasting chain picked it up for broadcast on their stations. Johnny Western, the singer and air personality on Great Empire's KFDI in Wichita, told me we reached an audience of five million that evening—more people, probably, than General Sarnoff reached with his broadcast 75 years earlier.

But after that first success—the banquet, the celebrities, the national broadcast, stories and press all over America—the event was never repeated.

Sometimes, you get excited and enthused about something, and then you find that no one picks up on your excitement and enthusiasm. Although a little bit more subtle, this is a form of rejection that you may well find yourself dealing with, as I did.

★

Accepting reality is the most important factor in a harmonious life. Accepting rejection and even giving thanks for it is a good learning experience, because rejection teaches you something. It teaches you

that everybody does not think the same as you do. It gives you toler-
ance for other thoughts, opinions, and ideas. It's easy to get so caught
up in your own ideas and opinions that you begin to think you're the
only person who's important, the only one who matters.

You have to listen to other people. You have to hear their ideas and
take them into consideration. When you are representing an artist, for
instance, you have to listen to that artist. There will be times when you
do not agree, but if you have the privilege of expressing your thoughts,
you can get your own point across.

Sometimes, for instance, you'll disagree on the way something's
going to be promoted, or an artist will have a certain idea about the
way he or she is presented in a show. In most cases, you try to make
your compromises.

A good example of this is album titles. An artist may come up with
a title for their disc that they think suits their image perfectly, but their
suggestion may sound anachronistic and dated. They may like what
the title says to them, but to the record-buying public, it might sound
totally out of date. So, delicately, you have to tell them, "You know, I
think it'd be more contemporary sounding if we did this." You can't
just say, "This won't work." You have to say why and make another
suggestion. And in most cases, they can still tell you "no."

As I've said before, the music business is a sales business, and in
the sales business, you're going to be told "no" many times. It is your
averages that will take care of you. If you present one show and it is
a dismal failure, it does not necessarily mean that you are a failure. It
only means that this one particular show was not right. But if you go
out and do ten shows, the law of averages will level things out. You
will learn from the mistakes and grow with each show. Most likely,
the majority of those shows will be successes. Learn from the failures,
make adjustments and corrections, and remain flexible in your resolve
to work for success.

Are you ready for some hard work? Nobody said it would be easy.
But it will be rewarding.

Are you willing to sacrifice? Are you willing to apply yourself to
achieving? Do you believe you have the talent? Will you train and educate yourself? Can you develop your personality? Will you maintain
your positive attitude? Can you get enthused? Do you have a burning desire? Will you be persistent in achieving your goal? Will you

continue building your self-confidence? Are you learning to recognize opportunities when they appear?

If you can honestly answer "yes" to these questions, then all that's left is commitment. Establish your goal with a purpose. Strive to activate your Power of Performance, and you'll be on your way to success.

What's next? When I began my own career, I quickly learned that the music business was many related businesses working together as a team—many teams, working as one, to support the artist. As I promoted shows, I met managers, booking agents, publicists, entertainment attorneys, record company executives, record producers, music publishers, and members of sound, lighting, and production crews. As a promoter, I was becoming a part of the team.

In Part Two of this book, I'll identify the team members and their duties. Use it to find and focus on the music-business position that you want!

chapter 5

TWENTY HELPFUL SUGGESTIONS

Here are 20 good suggestions for cultivating habits that will help you develop your Power of Performance. Remember: Success is your ultimate goal, and success comes with accessing your Power of Performance. These suggestions will help.

1. Follow the Boy Scout motto: Be Prepared*
2. Establish goals with a purpose.
3. Always maintain a positive attitude.
4. Be sincere.
5. Look professional.
6. Hand out business cards.
7. Shake hands firmly.
8. Look people in the eye.
9. Believe in yourself.
10. Believe in your employer.
11. Work as part of the team.
12. Know your product.
13. Know your customer.
14. Treat your customers with respect.
15. Give your customers what they need.
16. Have answers to objections.
17. Ask for the sale (or the job).

18. Develop your memory.
19. Follow the rules.
20. Enjoy what you do!

Make these 20 guidelines a part of your life, your day-to-day routine. When you follow them, you are building your self-confidence—and self-confidence is what Power of Performance is all about.

*When Roy Clark and I were just taking our first steps on the path to stardom, we'd try to play any place where music-industry members could discover the talents that Roy possessed. A singer and comedian, Roy was also one of the world's greatest musicians, and part of my job was to expose all his talents to as many people as I could.

At this time, Capitol Records wasn't quite sure what to do with Roy as a recording act. Ken Nelson, his producer, was having Roy record a variety of music, including instrumental versions of great standards that showed off Roy's prowess on guitar. Two of those instrumentals, "Under the Double Eagle" and "Black Sapphire," were released as the A and B-side of a Capitol single. Although there weren't a lot of instrumentals on country and pop radio at the time, the record got some radio-station airplay. Its biggest success, however, came from jukeboxes. I think it was on every jukebox in America.

Its success in that arena was so great that Roy received an award from the Music Operators of America (MOA), the jukebox operators' organization, for Most Played Instrumental of the Year on America's jukeboxes. As a result, he was invited to perform at the annual MOA convention in Chicago, appearing with other jukebox favorites like Tony Bennett and Ella Fitzgerald. The event would be covered by the news media and various trade publications, and the audience would be full of record buyers. At this time in Roy's career, the appearance would be what I refer to in this book as a Power Booster.

The gala affair was held in the Grand Ballroom of Chicago's Conrad Hilton Hotel. Roy was scheduled for a featured spot during the main event that evening, with a rehearsal scheduled for the afternoon. We came in with Roy, his Fender Stratocasters, and his amplifiers. The MOA was providing a 22-piece orchestra.

As I passed out Roy's arrangements to the 22 musicians, the show's producer asked me about Roy's conductor.

Conductor? Roy didn't carry a conductor.

Everyone else had one, though. So I didn't have much choice. As a musician myself, I could read music, and I knew the two songs Roy had picked to play—"Under the Double Eagle" and "Kansas City." So I stepped forward and took the baton. Tapping it on the podium, I watched as the orchestra members came to attention with their instruments, ready for my downbeat.

I have to tell you, this is still one of the greatest moments in my life. I was in charge of these fantastic Chicago musicians, none of whom had a clue that I wasn't really a conductor at all. Even Roy was amazed. I led that orchestra with zest and gusto, and this Music Operators of America event helped move us along on our quest for further success.

And why was I able to step onto that podium? Because ... like the Boy Scouts, I was prepared–even if I wasn't expecting it.

chapter 6

EARLY ETHICS LESSONS

I t's time now to talk about honesty and ethics, how important they are, and how fundamental they are to your Power of Performance. They are, in fact, essential to your success.

Where do you learn about honesty and ethics? Ideally in your home, as you grow up. You can also acquire a good sense of ethics from your early associations with adults in your community and from businesses, churches, temples, mosques, clubs, organizations, and schools. I acquired my own basics from my family. They were merchants in Independence, Kansas, owning and operating the Halsey Brothers Department Store, and they included my grandfather H.E., my great uncle Will, my aunt Helen, and my father Ed.

From the time I was 6 or 7 years old, I was hanging around the store. Everything about it fascinated me, from the elevator to the zippy way that cash and sales slips shot from the clerk's station to the mezzanine cashier's office.

These were still the days of the traveling salesman. And when one came to town to pitch his wares to the Halsey Brothers Department Store, I was always an interested audience. The salesmen would bring in new dresses, the latest in women's coats, woolen and cotton goods, cosmetics, notions. Especially enjoyable was the theatrical flair with which a skilled salesman would unfurl a bolt of English worsted or Scottish glen plaid. Many of these men were from New York, Chicago, or St. Louis; Grandfather would often bring them home to have dinner with us, and their tales of traveling, of seeing other merchants in other, faraway cities were spellbinding.

But even at this early age, I was most interested in listening to the negotiations, keeping in mind my grandfather's dictum: "It's only a good deal when it's a good deal for all parties." As I watched and listened, I was learning by osmosis the art of sales and negotiation, as well as getting a good lesson in business ethics—just by being there. I also learned about how the store staged events: a fall opening, a spring opening, a special sales promotion. I learned the language of the retail business: 50% off, 10% down, layaway, two of the same item for a better price than if the same items were bought individually. There were always sales, always promotions. And every so often, there were special events. I was fascinated with how things were marketed.

It was during this time that I learned the concept of the "satisfied customer." In our home, that was the key phrase that described our family's success. My grandfather and father both drilled into me that a satisfied customer is the main element in any sales transaction. The Halsey Brothers Department Store was built upon that principle, and I would later build my own entertainment business around it.

When I was 10 years old, I started selling on my own. After answering an ad on the back of a comic book, I set out to sell flower seeds door to door, first covering the immediate neighborhood and then branching out over town. By instinct, I made a presentation and politely asked for the sale, and I was very successful. My success wouldn't be measured in money, but in the prize I could claim based on the number of seed packets I sold.

I remember to this day the excitement that welled up in me as I finally achieved enough sales to get the item I wanted most…a telescope! It looked fantastic in the beautiful catalog the company had sent with the seeds. For the first time in my young life, I joyfully anticipated a big reward for doing something fun—selling. It sure beat all of the sweat and toil of mowing lawns. Intensely, I anticipated the arrival of the telescope, my big payoff for selling umpteen packages of flower seeds.

The package finally arrived. It was so small. How could it contain a telescope that looked from the catalog picture as though it might take up my whole backyard?

To this day, I have never been as disappointed as when I opened that package and saw the two cardboard tubes, one inside the other, with window glass at either end. This was not a telescope! The boy pictured in the catalog could hardly hold it, it was so big. I had been taken. It was a fraud! I was mad! Having worked every day after school and on Saturdays for a month to sell enough seeds for my prize, I didn't know what to do.

Actually, there was nothing I could do. My dad explained to me how certain unscrupulous people in business take advantage of their customers by cheating them, not giving them what they think they've bought and charging an unfair price for what they do get. It was not the way the Halsey Brothers Department Store operated. There, everyone worked hard to please customers, finding good merchandise and giving value at a fair price. By doing this, the Halsey Brothers assured that their clientele would continue to be not only customers, but satisfied customers! That sense of honesty and ethics is what kept the store open and fed our family for three generations.

My father taught me to accept my disappointment about the telescope, and to use it as a lesson. With a positive attitude, I accepted it, learned from it, and grew from it. It had taught me that I not only could sell, but that I enjoyed it. It also taught my 10-year-old self to go for cash next time, not prizes.

So, I found the perfect item and set out again. This time, I was selling a metal pot scrubber called Dolly Dozit, a small tool full of metal strips coiled tighter than Little Orphan Annie's hair. After some experimentation in the Halsey kitchen, I knew they worked, so I ventured out confidently, offering them to prospective customers for 10 cents each—and knowing that I would make a penny on each sale. If I sold a hundred, I told myself, I would make a dollar, and that was better than mowing lawns. After all, a dollar would buy 20 movie admissions at the local theater, or 20 nickel ice cream sodas at the Garden, a combination soda shop and beer joint. And I knew I could make a lot more than a dollar!

The term "marketing" had yet to be invented, so I didn't know anything about that, but I did know about selling and satisfying customers. My dad's sales events had taught me that it was better to offer a more attractive price if the customer bought two of something rather than just one. I applied that to my Dolly Dozits campaign. After taking part of a Saturday to mark off streets and blocks within the streets, and then to check the list I had kept of all my flower-seed customers,

I was off. Filled with enthusiasm and eager to sell door-to-door in my hometown, I offered my potential customers a deal: one Dolly Dozit, the best pot-scrubber ever made and unavailable in any local store, for 10 cents—or, as a special incentive, two for a quarter.

I couldn't sell them fast enough. Everybody bought two. I don't remember exactly how many I sold that day, but it was at least two or three hundred. I sold out and made it home before dark, flushed with success.

Now comes the big lesson in ethics.

You've probably already figured it out. The price shouldn't have been two for a quarter, because that made the individual price 12 1/2 cents, not 10 cents. I had been more interested in finding a catchy sales price than doing my math, and I had failed to add things up properly.

It hit me that I had charged nearly every customer extra for buying two of something instead of one. With each transaction, I had unintentionally cheated each customer out of five cents. I felt terrible. I felt like an idiot. I was embarrassed.

Worrying all night, I realized some folks might think I had cheated them intentionally. That was hardly something that made for satisfied customers. If I were to continue selling Dolly Dozits—or anything else—I was going to have to rely on the same customers for repeat business. What was to be done? Somehow I had to rectify my mistake.

Deciding to retrace my steps, I explained to each customer that I had inadvertently made a mistake in my arithmetic, and that I would refund five cents for every two Dolly Dozits he or she had purchased. But an interesting thing happened. Because of my mistake, I inadvertently learned the concept of "up sale." Up sale is a term used a lot by the makers of today's infomercials, who try to get their call-in customers to buy another, higher-priced item than the one being advertised. What happened was that I hit upon the idea of offering a third Dolly Dozit to those customers who had already bought two.

First I apologized, telling them of my mistake and advising them they were entitled to a five-cent refund. Then I told them they could add another five cents instead, and receive another Dolly Dozit. Believe it or not, everyone brought out another nickel. They increased the number of Dolly Dozits in their house by one; I increased my gross revenues by 20%.

This lesson in honesty and ethics was a good one. It encompassed lessons about offering good products for good value and the then-unknown idea of up sale.

Years later, when I got into the business of promoting shows and managing and booking artists, the principle of the satisfied customer kept my company in business for a long time.

Remember, then, that ethics are the cornerstone of any sale. As a 10-year-old, I didn't understand that principle—at least in those terms—but I put it into practice as I began to develop my own Power of Performance.

part two

FINDING YOUR PLACE ON THE TEAM

chapter 7

THE POWER OF TEAMS

As I told you in Chapter 4, I learned very early that the music business is in fact many businesses, all working together. And, like any other good team, a music-business team working harmoniously provides a power far greater than any of its individual parts. Here are five important things that a team can provide:

1. A group of specialists working together as one.
2. A collective exchange of ideas.
3. Enhanced and expanded performance.
4. Extended support and multiple skills.
5. Collective problem-solving.

Building any kind of business always requires planning; it involves many other elements besides yourself. The success of my career as a talent manager, booking agent, and impresario has not been my success alone. It has been the result of careful planning and the assembling of other specialists into a team.

The "team method," with related specialists and businesses working together, is a major part of my formula for success. Even within our own company, The Jim Halsey Company, we had internal teams. You must understand this team-method principle and know that it's important for the team members to function to the best of their ability, each utilizing his or her own Power of Performance.

Now, let's talk about the basic members of any music-business team. There are nine essential team elements necessary to begin building an artist's career. We'll call these nine the Star Team. No matter what style of music you're doing, the Star Team will determine the level of your success.

Envision an old-time wagon wheel, with the spokes extending from the center out to the rim. The center of the wheel, the hub that supports all the spokes—or team members—is talent. Talent is the primary member of the team, the No. 1 component. All the spokes extend from the center, because without talent we wouldn't have a music business.

Here, then, are the nine essential members of the Star Team:

1. *Talent*
2. Artist manager
3. Record company
4. Record producer
5. Booking agent
6. Music / entertainment attorney
7. Music publisher
8. Press and public relations person
9. Promoter

These are the essential members of any music-business team. As an artist's career grows, other important components get plugged into the extended team, such as radio, television, video, performing-rights organizations, touring companies, road managers, crew, set designers, arrangers, musicians, and sound and light technicians. These are extended team members that come along later.

Miraculous performance can be expected and unbelievable energy can be harnessed when every team member is performing together in sync. Understand the Star Team method, and you are on your way to success. Now all that remains is for you to decide which part of the team you want to be!

chapter 8

THE TALENT

How do you become a star in the music business? It's simple. Since this business starts with a song, all you have to do is write a hit song, sing a hit song, and get discovered!

The Jim Halsey Company represented many great talents, including The Oak Ridge Boys, Roy Clark, Tammy Wynette, Hank Thompson, Clint Black, The Judds, James Brown, Leon Russell, Ronnie Milsap, Woody Herman, Roy Orbison, Pam and Mel Tillis, Reba McEntire, Dwight Yoakam, the Kentucky Headhunters, Waylon Jennings, and Merle Haggard. All of these star acts had one thing in common: They were exceptional songwriters. In today's music business, most of the artists who break out of the pack are the ones who can create their own material.

That's what the record companies are looking for, even if much of a star's recorded material ends up being written by someone else. Check out any of the Billboard magazine charts and look who's on top. It's people like Radiohead, Garth Brooks, Steve Wariner, Michael W. Smith, Bruce Springsteen, Mariah Carey, Phil Collins, and Dwight Yoakam, Shooter Jennings, U2, Alicia Keys—acts and bands who are great songwriters as well as great performers.

A hit song is one that becomes popular with great masses of people. Maybe it's the melody, the lyric, the subject matter, or a combination of all three, but somehow it strikes a chord within the public that resonates for a good long time, translating into sales and stardom for its creator.

What makes a hit song? One thing is for sure: Every hit has a hook, a memorable phrase, word, or melodic line that immediately identifies the song. Good songwriters—and good singers—know about the hook and how to use it.

Let's take the late Tammy Wynette, one of my favorite clients. There is no doubt that her songs were written and delivered so you would remember both the hook and her. Who doesn't know the hook of her signature song, "Stand By Your Man," which she and her producer Billy Sherrill wrote in a few minutes to finish out a recording session? Think of that phrase, that hook, and you'll hear Tammy's soaring vocal in your mind, a perfect blend of words and melody.

And talk about a hook! How about The Oak Ridge Boys multi-platinum seller "Elvira," with Richard Sterban's resonant "oom papa, oom papa, oom papa mau mau" bass line? After managing The Oak Ridge Boys for more than 35 years, watching hundreds of their shows, and listening to hour after hour of their albums, I still enjoy hearing them do that song—as well as their other great hits.

Another of my clients was James Brown, "The Godfather of Soul," who crossed all barriers with "It's a Man's World," "Please, Please, Please," "Papa's Got a Brand New Bag" and many more huge hits. His unique material, distinctive style, unusual arrangements, and great performances have earned him another well-deserved nickname, "The Hardest-Working Man in Show Business." I have never worked with anybody who had more focus than James Brown. He knew exactly where he wanted to go, and he had a plan for getting there. I learned a lot from him; he is an inspiration to me still.

Leon Russell's distinctive style, both vocally and instrumentally, has made him one of the great singer-songwriters of all time. He's had several hits with his own material and hundreds of other artists around the world have also recorded his compositions. A unique pianist, composer, singer, song craftsman, and showman, Leon combined his skills to create such evergreens as "Masquerade," a song that will be around forever. We were pleased to represent him.

It was my great honor to be the agent for a man I consider truly the master of singing writing and performing: Roy Orbison. Roy's great genius was in his ability to put an enchanting melody with a haunting and beautiful lyric, as he did in "Only the Lonely," "Blue Bayou," "Crying," and many others. Because he presented his masterpieces in such a unique vocal style, his records were instantly recognizable. To me, Orbison was the perfect example of a songwriter-singer whose talents work together to make both a hit song and a star.

One of the greatest artists of all time was Woody Herman. Best known as a bandleader, he also was a composer—his best-known composition, "Woodchopper's Ball," is still around today. Instrumentally, this piece has a great hook—no words, but a memorable rhythmic melody that people found easy to hum or whistle.

Another of Woody's trademark hooks was a driving, crescendo-building arrangement, bringing a musical piece to a climax that would leave the audience exhausted, only to be lifted to even greater heights by the next number. His sound was unique, with five trumpets, arrangements built around three tenor saxophones, a baritone sax and, of course, the famous Herman rhythm. A lot of Woody's style wasn't based so much on his own clarinet or alto sax solos, or his singing, but his personification of the teamwork and discipline within the whole band, working like a well-oiled machine. Woody Herman inspired respect from his players, but he also forged a discipline that pushed them to play beyond the limits of any band I've ever heard. As a leader, he produced results greater than anyone else could have. That whole band was fed by Woody's driving energy.

There's a lesson here. Like Woody Herman, always strive to be better. Always push beyond your limits.

Another of our clients, and a favorite one, was Merle Haggard. He is a good one for budding songwriters to study—and you'll notice I say "study," not "copy." Study the best, but be your own person, your own talent, even as you learn from the masters. Merle Haggard is one of these masters. He knows about hooks, and he also knows about song structure and composition. His songs about the working man are brilliant, to the point, and every hook is in place. Think of lyrical hooks like "Now I've got swingin' doors/A jukebox/And a barstool," "I turned 21 in prison/Doin' life without parole," or even "I'm proud to be an Okie from Muskogee/A place where even squares can have a ball." Add to that a distinctive vocal style that can always be recognized in the first few bars of anything he sings, and you'll see that Merle Haggard is one of the world's great song stylists.

All of these artists are not only good songwriters, but great performers as well. Each used his or her personal Power of Performance as a key to achieving success.

What can we learn from them?

For one thing, to succeed as a singer-songwriter, you need to come up with great hooks, both lyrically and musically. As a beginning songwriter, make your own examination of different styles, different stylists and songwriters. Use analysis, listen to the words, the music, the structure, and the vocal interpretation. Find the hooks. Don't copy. By listening to others, you can learn how to improve your own style.

Also, learn to use your own gifts. Many songwriters are inspired and creatively blessed. It's important to learn your craft so you can most effectively use what gifts you have. A great songwriter must be inspired, but anyone can learn to be a good songwriter. In fact, I have a theory that everybody is a songwriter, because all people have a song in their hearts.

There is a difference, however, between being simply a songwriter and being a good, professional songwriter. Just as someone who dashes off a poem one day isn't a professional poet, someone who writes a song or two isn't really a songwriter. As is the case with any other craft, becoming a professional takes commitment and work.

How can you become a good songwriter? First of all, find out all you can about the craft of songwriting. Some colleges and universities offer songwriting courses as part of their community-outreach or continuing education programs. Almost every large city has a songwriters' group that meets regularly, with members offering information, critiques, and support to one another. Nashville, for instance, has the Nashville Songwriters Association International, which you can check out on the Internet at www.songs.org/nsai. These groups, as well as the college classes, are also excellent places to find collaborators, people who bring in fresh perspective and synergistic energy to your efforts.

If neither of these options are available in your area, investigate some of the many books available on the subject. Billboard magazine, the leading weekly music publication, has a big book division, with many songwriting titles available. Check your local bookstore for Billboard book titles like 'This Business of Songwriting,' Blume; 'The Billboard Book of Number One Hits,' Bronson; 'This Business of Music' and Mollyanne Lincoln's 'How to Make a Good Song a Hit Song.' The Cincinnati-based Writers Digest Books offer several good, informative books on songwriting, too, with their Songwriters Market leading the way. Updated annually, Songwriters Market gives you a complete how-to and where-to market your songs. Writers Digest also publishes what I think is one of the best: The Craft and Business of Songwriting by John Braheney. Be sure to seek out and read "Everything you Always Wanted to Know About Songwriting" (Showdown Enterprises), written by the late country music star and songwriter, Cliffie Stone.

A big part of becoming a songwriter is self-taught, so it's essential to absorb all the information you can. If you happen to live in or near a city that has a lot of music activities, it will be a lot easier. You'll have activities available for songwriters, as well as regular meetings where your own songs can be played and critiqued. Some cities have clubs that feature an open-mike night for singer-songwriters. You may get the opportunity to attend seminars and workshops on writing sponsored by local organizations. Music stores and churches are also good places to find songwriting colleagues.

The more you study, the more you observe, and the more you write, the better you will become. Get all the information and help you can. If contemporary music is your interest, know what's being played on the radio in your musical genre. Keep up with music by reading Billboard magazine; it covers all areas of music on a weekly basis, from rock to classical. The more you understand the music business, the better equipped you'll be to proceed with your business of songwriting. Take advantage of whatever is available. When it comes to writing and performing your songs, there's no such thing as too much information.

Then, once you get your songs written and you're confident about them, what do you do? After you get past the local options of peer critique and public performance, where can you go next? Who will listen? How will you be discovered?

First, you must get someone to listen who can do something for you. And the way to begin this process is to put your songs on a demonstration CD, commonly referred to as a "demo." Your demo will be your calling card, the first way the music business will know of you and your work. It is the first and best way to be discovered.

Unfortunately, badly produced or poorly presented demos can drastically reduce your chances. While music-industry executives don't have time to listen to every demo that comes across their desks, they don't want to miss out on finding someone with real talent. One of the ways they can simplify the demo-listening process is by giving only cursory attention—or no attention at all—to unprofessional demos.

How, then, can you create a demo that appeals to the eyes and ears of someone who can help you?

HERE ARE NINE IMPORTANT TIPS:

1. Your demo must be on a quality CD. You would not believe the number of demos I've received over the years that were poorly produced. Let's get real! If you're trying to sell an automobile, would you show it to a prospective buyer when it was covered with dirt, or had a flat tire? Of course not! You would make the best possible presentation.

2. Do not put more than three songs on a CD. Because of limited time, a music publisher or other industry figure will be more likely to listen to three songs than a whole string of them. If your songs show promise, believe me, your listener will ask for more.

3. Have lyrics typed out for easy reading. This is very important. I have received CDs that have no lyric sheets included; if your lyrics can't be understood, the person you're trying to impress can become rapidly disinterested. I have also had lyric sheets sent to me that were totally unreadable because they were marked on and through. Make them neat and professional looking!

4. Put your best song in the first position on the CD. I've had people disagree with me about this. Some have said that putting your best song last builds more interest. The problem is that you can't be sure your listener will hear all three songs! I speak from experience. If you do not put your best song first, the listening party may not even get to the second or third song. You must command interest right away.

5. Put your hook in the first thirty seconds of your song. Use that hook, that memorable part of the lyric or melody, to put your song in the listener's mind forever.

6. Have someone competent sing your song. If you are not a good singer, find someone who is. A poorly performed song will turn a listener off and take attention away from lyrics and melody. This is simply human nature.

7. Type your name, address, email and telephone number on both CD and CD package. This way, your demo will not get lost in the shuffle. Many times, producers and publishers have desks covered

with CDs. They are not always careful about putting each CD back into its package. You do not want them to discover you and then not be able to find out who you are.

8. Always get permission to send your CD. Make the necessary phone calls, write a letter, send an email or go to the offices in person to ask for that permission. Do not send the CD until you get the green light.

9. Be prepared for rejection. As a songwriter, you must prepare to be the recipient of much rejection in your professional life. People, for one reason or another, may not like your masterpiece. Maybe it's just not for them, their companies, or the artists they represent. Do not despair. A lot of songs have gone around, getting turned down by everybody—and then suddenly, someone has heard something in it, and a song that was a big loser has been recorded and become a giant hit. Remember not to take rejection personally. People are rejecting the content of a song—they are not rejecting you. It is part of the growing process in the business to get rejection and then move on.

Over the years, I have heard thousands of demos. There was a time when I tried to listen to them all, but it finally became impossible. There was just too much material and too little time. I always felt badly about sending these songs back to the writer unopened, knowing I was driving a coffin nail into their dreams and hopes. There had to be a solution.

That solution came during lunch a few years ago with my close friend, the late Lee Zhito of Billboard magazine. Our conversation that day laid the groundwork for the Billboard Song Contest, a way for any amateur songwriter to be heard by music-industry professionals. The Billboard Song Contest now accepts original songs in twelve categories of music—pop, rock, country, gospel, Latin, jazz, world, rap/hi-/hop, dance, Americana/folk, soundtrack/electronica and R&B/Blues—and uses music figures as judges at every level of competition, offering substantial prizes to those songs deemed the best in their categories.

It is getting tougher and tougher to get publishers, artists, and record companies to listen to new material. It can be done, however, and those who stick with it and do not get discouraged will eventually get through to the right people. If you are really serious about your songs, and you're not getting any response to your written requests, take your vacation time and travel to the leading recording centers: Nashville, New York, Austin, Seattle, Toronto, Vancouver, and Los Angeles. Try making personal appeals at the various offices of the music publishers, record companies, and artists. Try to get your foot in the door long enough to get a meeting. Find out what's happening in the music business community in those cities. Become involved. Search out the songwriting organizations and the open-mike nights. Check with the offices of the performing-rights organizations—BMI, ASCAP, SESAC—about their artist-development programs. Maybe two weeks of vacation is not long enough to do all of this, but it's enough for you to begin to find out for yourself how the system works. Learn all you can in the time you have.

Song contests are a viable way to get noticed and to build credibility for your songwriting. Our Billboard Song Contest has helped numerous winning songwriters gain notoriety for their talent and contributed to their success by exposing their music to industry contacts. Other contests such as the John Lennon Song Contest, and the International Songwriting Competition (ISC) are helpful to a songwriters resume.'

Billboard Song Contest partners like Taxi (www.taxi.com), Sonicbids (www.sonicbids.com), GoGirlsMusic.com (www.gogirlsmusic.com) also provide important support services to songwriters to help them get noticed.

When you become an established songwriter, it doesn't matter where you live. But when you're getting started, it's tough to do it long-distance, which is why many dedicated songwriters move to Nashville, New York, L.A., or another music city. They need to be in the middle of it all, meeting people and networking.

Incidentally, the more songs you write, the better songwriter you will become. When aspiring songwriters tell me they've written two or three songs, I know the likelihood of any of these tunes being good is pretty slim. But if they tell me they have written 25 or 30 songs, I figure they probably have one or two good ones in the bunch.

Songwriting is a craft that can be developed with work, discipline, and time. If you are serious about being a songwriter, you need to write something every day. It doesn't have to be a complete song. Daily, you can develop ideas, work on melody and lyrics. If you make the commitment and apply the discipline to work a certain amount of time every day on your music, you will be surprised at how much you'll get done and how much easier inspiration will come.

I'm sure you've heard the stories about Willie Nelson writing a hit song on the back of an envelope, sitting in a taxi on his way to the airport. Those moments of inspiration happen to all gifted songwriters. They have done their homework. They have already learned their craft, the basics of songwriting. They have achieved a certain discipline, so that when that lightning bolt of inspiration hits them, they are well-equipped to turn it into a hit song. This is where the art and the craft of songwriting meet. It's another example of the Power of Performance.

As a songwriter, you must accept the fact that selling is part of your business too. The more songs you offer and the more people you offer them to, the better your chances of getting them accepted. Just be prepared for the rejection we talked about and overcome it by making more calls. We've said before that self-confidence is an important part of your Power of Performance, and no other professional in the world has a bigger need for self-confidence than a songwriter. You must believe in your own work before anyone else will. You gain self-confidence by doing what you do best, over and over, and becoming completely at ease with your skills. Even when you do get a "no," a rejection, you can get past it by knowing it has nothing to do with your ability.

This, of course, doesn't just apply to songwriters. It applies to any talented person who strives for stardom. Being a star is an art. Recognize that it is also a business. The more you understand the business aspects, such as knowing who the players are and how everything functions together, the more you know how to deal with rejection and the more successful you'll be.

I'm not suggesting that an artist should handle his or her own business affairs—that would be counterproductive. The artist's energy should be focused totally on the stage and the studio, with managers, agents, and attorneys handling the business. What I am saying is that artists must know enough about the business to recognize whether their associates are doing the right kind of job.

An artist, like any other businessperson, must be honest and honorable. It is the artist who signs the contract with the promoter, the booking agency, the record company, the music publisher, and the artist manager. Some artists do not honor their work or their commitments. Their signature on a contract means nothing. These people may be few and far between, but they are often the ones you read about. Just as the Power of Performance lasts a long time after the artist has left the stage, so will an honorable reputation last a lifetime, long after the stardom and hit records are over.

Talent is not enough to make a star. You must go farther. In classroom discussions, many of my students have said that an artist's honesty and sincerity are more important than talent. Credibility ranks high. Charisma and stage presence are essential. To be viable artists, performers must be able to project their music and themselves. They must be able to connect and to have rapport with the audience.

For the performer/songwriter in today's market, individual style is important. Each must master his or her own technique and strive for quality of performance. This takes confidence, which comes with practice and dedication. An artist must have a willingness to learn, a love of music and entertainment, and an ability to handle rejection. An artist must recognize the importance of being a team member. There are many more things involved than talent.

An artist must be able to deliver. An artist must be unique, with that something special that sets him or her apart from all the others and makes him or her unforgettable. There is already a Reba McEntire, a Clint Black, a Shania Twain, an Oak Ridge Boys. Do not try to sound or look like one of them, or any other popular performer. Develop your own style, your own brand of uniqueness, because that's what will work for you.

All of the good players are not from Los Angeles, New York, or Nashville. They don't all live in big cities. Stars can come from anywhere, but they must be discovered.

Here are two stories, both offering important lessons about talent, discovery, and stardom.

★

All of us in the entertainment business have, at one time or another, claimed to "discover" a talent. In reality, however, the discovery is almost always a team effort, the combined result of people working together.

Here's an example. In the early '70s, The Jim Halsey Company packaged and promoted shows for the Howard Hughes-owned hotels in Las Vegas. Our big hit at one of those hotels, the Landmark, was a continuously running revue called "Country Music USA." This revue usually played to full houses, changing headliners every two or three weeks. Since we used our own talent in the show, we were able to rotate new acts in as we added them to the Halsey Company roster.

The contract with Hughes was an important one. It brought cash flow to our company and to the artists who played the hotels. It allowed us to keep our stars steadily employed for long periods in one place, which saved them travel time, road expenses, and wear and tear on their touring vehicles. It also gave them more time for rehearsal.

There were other pluses. Because our acts were playing hotels, rooms and food were included in the contract, which cut their costs. And because they were in high-visibility Las Vegas venues, we could get higher prices for their other appearances. And because Vegas was so close to Los Angeles, we were able to bring big-time entertainment buyers in to see our artists perform under very favorable circumstances.

During one of our successful Vegas runs, I got a call from my close friend, Jim Foglesong, the president of Dot Records. Jim had just "discovered" and signed a new artist, who had first been "discovered" by a record producer in Houston named Huey P. Meaux. Meaux's own label, in fact, had released a regional hit by the artist.

"I think you'll like this artist," Jim told me. "We've just released his record on Dot, and I'm sure it's going to go to No. 1 in two or three weeks."

I told him he had contacted me at just the right time. I had an opening in "Country Music USA" for a headliner. "But," I asked him, "who's ever heard of this guy, Freddy Fender, and this song of his, 'Before the Next Teardrop Falls'?"

"They'll hear of him," Jim returned. "Believe me, they will. This record is on radio stations all over the country as we're talking. Next week, it will be in heavy rotation on every radio station in America."

I told him that I'd never put anybody into a show that I hadn't seen, and I'd never signed an act for my agency who had not turned me on with his talent and a knockout performance.

"Well," Jim said, "time is of the essence."

So I took a chance. I told Jim okay. I would put Freddy Fender into an already-running hit show, and I would do it as soon as he arrived. I explained to Walter Kane, Howard Hughes' entertainment director and my friend, that I had not seen Freddy Fender, but that he came with the strongest of recommendations from Mr. Foglesong. Walter, being the impresario that he was, agreed to take a chance.

The next day during rehearsals, I asked Leo Zabelin to go to the airport and pick up our new "headliner." Not long afterwards, I had a call. It was Leo, phoning from the airport.

"You won't believe this," he said, "but all this guy has is his guitar and the shirt on his back! You're going to headline him tonight?"

I said, "Look, Leo. Take him into town and get him whatever he needs. Tonight, we're going to make Mr. Fender a star!"

While Leo and Freddy were in town, we changed the Landmark's marquee, spelling out F-R-E-D-D-Y F-E-N-D-E-R in letters 12 feet high. That night, with very little rehearsal, Freddy went on and displayed amazing charisma, establishing immediate rapport with the audience. He captivated them. He was a natural talent who knew how to access his Power of Performance.

Freddy Fender came off that stage a star. By the time his Landmark engagement closed, there were lines around the block to see him. We represented Freddy for the next dozen years, and he grew to be one of country music's biggest acts, cutting lots of hit records and playing major venues all over the world. Freddy Fender had been "discovered" by Jim Halsey... and Jim Foglesong... and Walter Kane... and Huey Meaux... and the audiences who came to see "Country Music USA" at the Landmark. His discovery had been a collective one, shared by many.

★

As Freddy's story shows, timing is important in this business. When Jim Foglesong called about Freddy, I just happened to have a show going with a spot that Jim's new artist could fill.

Equally as important as timing is desire. In fact, desire has to outweigh all other interests for someone to succeed. It's easy to lose your Power of Performance to other priorities and obligations.

I have a friend in my hometown named Jerry Webb. The Webb family has had a funeral home in Independence for several generations, and Jerry is a dedicated mortician. However, he's always had a flair for show business. A natural comedian, he's in constant demand in southeast Kansas, with all kinds of groups and organizations after him to be master of ceremonies for their events. Jerry has both the talent and the timing it takes to do comedy right—even with borrowed material, he's as funny as any big-name comedian.

Thirty years ago, the Buena Vista Club in Safford, Arizona, ran two shows a night, six nights a week. All of my artists played there at one time or another, and Earl Perrin, the owner, paid well. Plus, anytime I got stuck for a date for Roy Clark, Wanda Jackson, Mary Taylor, or Hank Thompson, Earl could always be counted on for a short-notice booking.

Then one day Earl called me. He'd booked a standup comedian for a two-week run, and the guy had suddenly canceled. Who did I have who could come in and take the date?

I told him about my friend, the undertaker, and Earl agreed to try him. He made Jerry his first real show-business offer to play for two weeks in Safford—good pay, accommodations and food, as well as billing on the club's marquee. Webb thought about it for a long time. Finally, though, he declined.

Three decades later, during a telephone conversation, I asked him why he hadn't seized that opportunity.

"It's funny," he said with a laugh. "I was just telling them at the coffee shop this morning that I should've taken that job. But I'd never heard of the place, and I would've had to leave my ambulance business for two weeks, so I decided I'd better stick around."

Who knows? Maybe Jerry would have been discovered in Safford, Arizona, by some big network television producer or an important talent scout. If he'd taken the job, he might be hosting a late-night television show or headlining in Las Vegas today.

(Although Jerry remained in Independence and didn't pursue a national career as a performer, he was instrumental in getting a couple of excellent celebrity golf tournaments into the town. Held in 1980 and 1981 and patterned after the Roy Clark Celebrity Golf Tournaments we were doing in Tulsa, the Independence tournaments attracted such high-caliber stars as Ernest Borgnine, David Huddleston, Fred Mac-Murray, and Roy—who, like me, remains friends with Jerry Webb.)

★

I tell these two stories to illustrate an important point: you have to be able to recognize opportunity when it knocks. Maybe it will knock while you're playing a club. Maybe it will knock when someone in the industry hears your demo tape. Maybe, if you can finagle an audition before someone who can help your career, it will knock then. Several years ago, I was in my office in Nashville when two young ladies came in. They told our office staff that they were singer-songwriters, they wanted to get into the music business, and they were looking for an agent. Our staff advised them to submit a demo for consideration.

"What's a demo?" one of them asked.

Someone in our office explained that "demo" was music-biz lingo for a demonstration tape, adding, "You put your songs on a demonstration tape, and we'll listen to them."

Well, they didn't need that, they said. They had their guitars in the car. And before we knew it, they'd retrieved their instruments and were giving us an impromptu concert right there in the office.

It didn't take us long to realize that both their songs and their singing were very good. And once we found out they were mother and daughter, we felt that they had something unique to offer the country music market.

They were, of course, Naomi and Wynonna, The Judds, and they had been making the Music City rounds, knocking on the doors of managers, booking agents, record companies, music publishers—anyone who might help them break into the business.

They found their managers, Ken Stilts and Woody Bowles, the same way they found us, via a live audition. The managers got them their record company deal. After their audition for the Halsey Company, we began booking them all over the country. It was, like all music-business success stories, a team effort.

Remember Chapter 4, and the ten keys to the Power of Performance? The Judds walked into our office holding all those keys. Their attitude was geared for success. They had the enthusiasm and the desire. Through their persistence, they had made themselves known within the music community in Nashville. Certainly, they had self-confidence; it radiated from them. They also had the dedication to their music. They had talent—loads of it! They had personality for sure, along with enough training to get them started in the big time.

★

Another of our soon-to-be big stars started in a different way. He was a Las Vegas lounge performer, brought to my attention by Larry McFaden.

Larry was a musician in Mel Tillis' band, the Statesiders. I had Mel headlining at the Frontier Hotel in Las Vegas, and Larry kept telling me about an entertainer who was appearing in the lounge at the Tropicana Hotel. Sure I would be interested, Larry persisted in trying to get me to see this act. Frankly, I was lukewarm, feeling that anyone who had been working in a Vegas lounge for a long time had already had his opportunities and, for whatever reason, stardom had passed him by.

Was I ever wrong. As it turned out, this lounge artist had all of the attributes necessary to make it. He was a great singer and entertainer just waiting to happen nationally. We became his agent, Larry McFaden became his manager, and that's how Lee Greenwood became a star.

Lee's success story reinforces that big secret to success: you have to be seen and heard by someone who can help you. As a Vegas lounge act, Lee had been seen and heard by thousands. Finally, one person—Larry McFaden—saw him and believed in him as much as Lee believed in himself. Larry brought Lee to the attention of The Jim Halsey Company, and the team that would launch Lee's stellar career began to come together.

★

There's another way to try to get the attention of the music industry. It's called showcasing, and it's one very practical way of introducing your talent to a large number of potential team members.

How do you showcase? It's simple. You rent a venue and invite prospective managers, booking agents, record-company representatives, music publishers, and press people. Once you get them there, you try to impress them all with a dynamite show, so that at least some will express an interest in helping you get your career off the ground by offering you management, booking, or a potential record deal.

There are a number of music conferences across the country that also offer opportunities to be discovered. These events offer lectures, seminars, and workshops along with showcases designed to present bands and performers to conference attendees. Because the showcasing acts perform before an audience of industry professionals, a lot of deals get made at these conferences.

I have been a guest speaker at many, including South by Southwest in Austin, Texas; Atlantis Music Conference in Atlanta, GA; Dfest in Tulsa, OK; Canadian Music Week in Toronto, Canada; Popkomm in Berlin, Germany; North by Northeast in Toronto, Canada; and North by Northwest in Portland, Oregon; and MIDEM in Cannes, France.

Training and education, you'll remember, make up one of my keys to the Power of Performance, and attending conferences is one vital way of achieving this key. At least part of your success in the music and entertainment business will come from the people you know within the business. So you should always make it a point to meet as many people as you can, not just those on the business side, but other songwriters and musicians as well. If you're attending a conference or other industry function, be prepared! Have a good-quality demo tape, some professional pictures of yourself, a biographical sheet, etc. Certainly have an adequate supply of business cards.

Remember that getting a manager or a record deal is only the beginning. You still must have a team to get to the top.

Managers and their philosophies are as individual and unique as the artist's talents. Finding a good manager can be as difficult as finding a good artist. Irving Azoff, Front Line Management (Eagles, Fleetwood Mac, Christina Aquilera), one of the most important and inventive managers in the business in 2008 sold controlling interest in Frontline Management to Ticketmaster. Front Line also owned interest in 80 other management companies that collectively has more artists and stars than any other management company. Azoff became CEO of the new company called Ticketmaster Entertainment. Azoff was president of MCA Records during the time of my renegotiation of the Oak Ridge Boys' MCA contract. I liked him and have great respect for him. He's one of the best.

Jim Mazza and associate Bob Burwell (Kenny Rogers), Doc McGhee (Kiss, Bon Jovi), are some of the best.

When The Kentucky Headhunters made their first record deal, with Harold Shedd at Polygram, they already had their manager, Mitchell Fox, on board. Before their first record hit the shelves, The HeadHunters did a showcase at a Nashville club, sponsored by Polygram, in an effort to find a booking agency and other team members for the band. One of my associates, Terry Cline, had already seen the band and was singing its praises to the rest of our company. When the Polygram showcase happened, our agency turned out en masse, as did the other agencies in Nashville. I was knocked out by The HeadHunters' music, but as much as anything else I liked their aura, their collective personality. I liked each one of them individually as well. Making a deal to represent them as their booking agency, we became another member of the team.

We've talked about cutting demos, playing places where people can see you, attending music conferences, and showcasing your talents. What are some other ways a beginning act can be seen or heard?

In the past several years, a lot of corporate entities—from beer and cigarette companies to hardware stores and sausage manufacturers—have begun sponsoring national talent searches, usually co-sponsored by local radio stations. Audition for these shows. Try to get into the contests. These have led to the discovery of several artists and lots of record deals.

Try in every way to build your act locally or regionally and try to enlist the help of the local media. Many times, a hometown radio personality or newspaper writer can bring you to the attention of record companies, managers, or agents.

Above all, be persistent. Getting discovered is not easy, but it is done every day. Remember, too, that when you hear about some new "overnight sensation" being discovered, it's likely to be an act that's been trying for years to break out of a limited scene into national prominence.

CHAPTER 9

THE MIGHTY OAKS

The Oak Ridge Boys and I discovered each other back in 1974 at a Nashville showcase put on by CBS Records. I forget what act I had gone to see. All I remember was that my attention was captured, and I was thoroughly entertained that night by a terrific gospel group, The Oak Ridge Boys. What a show! They had energy, excitement, beautiful harmonizing, good looks, lots of movement on stage—everything they needed for superstardom.

The Oak Ridge Boys were in gospel music, which was, at that time, enjoyed by a limited and very specific audience. And even though I love gospel music, I saw their potential to go past that niche audience into country, country-pop, or pop, where they could reach many, many more people.

Going backstage after the performance, I introduced myself to the four Oaks—Duane Allen, Joe Bonsall, Richard Sterban, and William Lee Golden—explained my excitement for their broader potential, and gave them my card. I came away not only deeply impressed with the excitement they created on stage, but by their enthusiasm for the business and their desire for success. They had dedication and commitment. They knew about the Power of Performance. They had everything but a manager and a good team working for them. I wanted to be that manager and to help them put together their own star team.

It took them awhile to make their decision. Trying to expand their audience base would mean jeopardizing their position as the No. 1 gospel group in America. They liked country music but were not exactly sure if country fans would accept them.

We decided to work together on a trial basis, and I hired them to open shows with Mel Tillis and Roy Clark, two of my biggest stars. The first date was in Buster Bonif's Theater in Warwick, Rhode Island, opening for Mel. Opening night, I made the date, anxious to see the audiences' reaction and wanting to make sure that Mel, a very important client to us, was satisfied.

I wasn't the only one blown away by The Oak Ridge Boys' opening set. That night, they received standing ovations for their show!

I remember so vividly talking with the four guys after the show that night. Standing out in the theater's parking lot, I reassured them they could entertain any audience, anywhere. I wanted to be their manager. I wanted to start building their team. I gave them an old music-biz axiom: they were only three minutes away from being superstars. That three minutes, of course, represents the playing time of a hit record.

The Oak Ridge Boys saw an opportunity. They recognized it. They went for it. They got it. Our collective Power of Performance would create one of the biggest country music success stories ever—and we haven't yet written its final chapter.

First, I had to let the world outside of gospel music know how great The Oak Ridge Boys were. I worked to get them in front of buyers for fairs, rodeos and special events. And I wanted the buyers for the Las Vegas showrooms to see them, too. I thought The Oak Ridge Boys could be very successful playing Vegas.

At the time, my company's three big headliners were Roy Clark, Mel Tillis, and Hank Thompson. All three agreed to use The Oak Ridge Boys to open their shows, and our relationships with other stars enabled us to put The Oak Ridge Boys in front of many other acts as well. In the risky transition from gospel to country, I needed to cover a lot of territory in the shortest amount of time possible. I had to make sure that people, including the loyal gospel fans, understood the group's new focus and where we were going with it. We needed to be on sure footing without much down time.

The Jim Halsey Company made the commitment to The Oak Ridge Boys, and that meant we would make it work! We were sure we could. But, truth to tell, we were just a little nervous, too.

Imaging–look and attitude–has always been important to the Oak

Ridge boys. From the very beginning, it was their contemporary look and sense of style that set them apart. It's also what got them in trouble with the gospel-music industry, as well as some fans, in the early '70s.

I was convinced there was no better act in America at the time. Yet, they were relegated to a genre of music that tried to put limits on their performance and sense of style on stage. The Oaks resisted that. When I saw them, they were ahead of any act in country music, let alone gospel. I fell immediately for their mesmerizing four-part harmonies, their up-to-the-minute *GQ* look, and their focus and desire to make it to the very top of the entertainment business—as well as their devout faith in God and their belief that they were on the right path.

A few months after the showcase, we began working together. I had a plan, and they had the talent and desire. We met, we stood in a circle, held hands, and prayed for guidance, the first of many, many times we'd do so.

With the help of my associates Dick Howard and John Hitt, along with lots of conferences with Duane, Joe, William Lee, and Richard, we set into motion the first five-year plan.

We all knew it would be a big departure and a courageous step to expand beyond gospel music, where they had already achieved as much success as that genre, with its limited opportunities, would allow. They were leaping forward into a field where they were relatively unknown by fans and industry people alike.

Our *first plan* was simplicity itself, with five basic points as our immediate goals:

1. Eat
2. Pay bills, salaries, rent
3. Get exposure to the secular world of fans, press & promoters
4. A new record deal
5. Las Vegas for career exposure and food, shelter, and salaries

Before the Oak Ridge Boys and the Jim Halsey Company joined forces, the Oaks' entire itinerary consisted of gospel shows in auditoriums, theaters, and schoolhouses, where they sometimes shared the bill with as many as a half-dozen other gospel acts. The revenue was meager, with sales of merchandise supplementing their performance income.

When we entered the music-business mainstream, the Oaks made a great leap of faith. I recognized the responsibility I had to them and their chances of succeeding, and I readily accepted the challenge. I knew we could make it happen.

As all of this was happening, I was producing the "Country Music USA" shows for Howard Hughes' Landmark Hotel, which you'll remember from the Freddy Fender story. At this time, I was constantly in Las Vegas, and Walter Kane—Hughes' entertainment director—and I had become very close friends. You'll recall that we changed the "Country Music USA" headliners every two or three weeks. Walter wasn't always familiar with the headliner names I suggested, but he had learned to trust my judgment.

With that in mind, I made my pitch for The Oak Ridge Boys.

I told Walter I knew they would be great. As an opening act, they had been wowing the country audiences who had come to see Roy Clark and Mel Tillis. And because I always leveled with Walter, I told him The Oak Ridge Boys were a gospel act, making the transition into country, with a repertoire that was 70 percent country and 30 percent gospel. Then I asked Walter if he felt there would be any objections to their doing religious music in a Las Vegas showroom.

His answer to me was very positive. "Our showrooms have Christians in them, too," he said.

I knew that the "Country Music USA" production would be a great place to showcase the talents of The Oak Ridge Boys. Although they were relatively unknown outside the gospel music world, I was able to give them 100% headline billing, good sound and lights, a good audience, and their name 12 feet high on the marquee. I brought in talent buyers, concert promoters, and a lot of television producers and talent coordinators to see this new group of ours. I wanted John Hitt, head of the Halsey Company's fair department, to see them. I also wanted my colleague Dick Howard in the audience. Dick's main responsibility was securing television bookings for our company's artists, but he also was one of my main sources for creative thinking. I knew he would have some good marketing ideas. He did, and both John and Dick became an important part of the team that built The Oak Ridge Boys.

There was another reason I pushed for The Oak Ridge Boys to headline "Country Music USA." I can laugh about it now, but then it was deadly serious. Very simply, I needed that three-week date to meet the payroll—and the hotel rooms and food that came in the package were very important parts of the contract. Believe it or not, things were running that close in the beginning.

Over the next year or so, we were able to make The Oak Ridge Boys into one of the most popular acts in Las Vegas. We finally graduated to the Frontier Hotel, and later made deals for them to appear on a regular basis at Caesar's Palace and The MGM Grand. Over more than a quarter-century, they have continued to be a popular attraction in Las Vegas, working several weeks each year at Bally's (formerly the MGM Grand). I know of no other act in show business that understands the Power of Performance better than The Oak Ridge Boys.

★

You see that being discovered takes many different forms. Once you're discovered, you have to examine, every now and then, your quest for your goals. You must keep asking yourself about your dedication and commitment to those goals. In other words, you must do what The Oak Ridge Boys continually do: keep affirming that you are fully dedicated and fully committed.

You must say to yourself, "I am determined to be a success. I have goals. I have purpose. I know I have access to my own Power of Performance. And I know how to deal with rejection and turn it into a positive force." The artists I've represented over the years can say this. I can say this as well.

I always stress how important it is not to give up, because the ones who give up won't make it. It takes a special dedication and unwillingness to throw in the towel to make it big in the music business. A lot of people say they want it, but when it comes down to the hardships, long hours, hard work, and personal and professional rejection, a lot of people fall by the wayside. Eventually you get to a very important crossroads, and it's there that you answer the question, "Do I really want this?"

What I am constantly looking for is the next superstar. And when I ask him or her that question, I want to hear this answer: "Yes, I really want it. No matter what. I have to have it!" That's when I'll know that I really have something to work with.

Talent is not enough. You have to get the commitment! You have to make the commitment!

IN THE BEGINNING

In the beginning, I remember... Duane Allen, Joe Bonsall, William Lee Golden, Richard Sterban, and me, standing in a circle, holding hands and asking the Creator, God, to bless this union and to let the songs be felt by all in attendance. We gave thanks for so many blessings bestowed, and asked that we could recognize our opportunities to help heal and bring people together in a spirit of harmony and friendship through our work. We asked God to help us never forget that we did it all in His name.

I remember the first time we did this, more than 30 years ago, when the five of us first came together. It was a powerful action then, and, although we've repeated it hundreds or maybe thousands of times since that first night, it's *still* powerful. Sometimes it's just the four Oaks and me, but at other times the circle expands, taking in everyone backstage at a concert, or a television taping, or an important meeting. We do it because it recognizes and reaffirms how we operate: under His guidance and asking for His blessing on our work and lives.

More than three decades ago, the Oak Ridge Boys made a move into the mainstream of the music and entertainment business. It was considered a controversial decision in some circles, but it wasn't about getting out of gospel music, where they'd been very successful. Instead, it was about broadening their scope. As a mainstream act, the Oaks could attract bigger audiences and perform songs that crossed all sorts of borders.

And with shows and material that stressed the positive, bring the kind of healing to people that was sorely needed then and is still needed today.

It's been proven that music can reduce stress and create harmony in people's lives. "Harmony" has a double meaning here, as anyone knows who's heard the unique four-part harmonies of Duane, Joe, William Lee, and Richard. Those harmonies, coupled with their lyrics and stage presence, leave audiences worldwide with a great feeling of satisfaction and joy. That's the business of the Oak Ridge Boys–to make lives better and more expectant, to bring harmony through their performances.

I've always thought that a spark of the Divine brought us together back in the '70s, beginning a 30-plus-year run of ideas, sounds, hard work, vision, and goals that continues today, even as we move forward into tomorrow. A major reason for the Oaks' long history of success is the fact that their existence is one of planned, constant change and reinvention. They continue moving ahead with new songs, hit songs, television imaging, important and meaningful personal appearances, and always a great, entertaining, show. While they may have a different look and some different songs in their current concerts than they did 20, 10 or even five years ago, that four-part harmony remains the foundation on which everything is built.

In 2005, when we reflected upon our 30 years together, we understood that it had been a collective effort. As you know, my blueprint for success has always involved assembling a great team, one that can move mountains, work great magic, build a great star attraction, and maintain an important career. Almost from the beginning, the Oaks have been one of those star attractions. But it took a lot of combined effort on behalf of the whole team to get them on top and then to keep them there.

Of course, it started with the Oak Ridge Boys themselves. Duane, Joe, William Lee and Richard were already together when I discovered them, back in 1974.Once we started working together, our first goal was to keep working so that we could all keep eating. Everything else fell into line after that. In getting work for the Oaks, our company relied on many of the team members—promoters, theater managers, and tour packagers—that had successfully utilized our other headline artists like Roy Clark, Mel Tillis, Donna Fargo, Jimmy Dean, and Hank Thompson. At the time, the Jim Halsey Company represented a big group of country-music acts, and we had a great team. A part of my philosophy as a manager and agent: use common sense, honestly and intelligently integrate a plan–a master plan. Build a great team. As the act becomes more successful, the team will grow along with it if the plan is followed.

One of the most important considerations in building a team is making sure everyone understands the overall goals. If a powerful team gets focused on an integrated plan, most of those goals can be achieved. Of course, the artist is always the focal point, with all elements working in harmony with the artist. It's the artist manager, along with the artist, who chooses and plugs in the rest of the team members.

When it came to the Oak Ridge Boys, everything worked well because they were very goal-oriented. They had a collective goal. We were all on the same page, so all we had to do was implement the plan, working with major players like the record company and press and PR people. Of course, there were many other members of the team that helped catapult the Oak Ridge Boys into the kind of stardom few acts will ever achieve.

THE RECORD COMPANY—1975
OAK RIDGE BOYS PLAN

When the Oaks and I joined forces, they were still with Columbia Records. You'll recall that I first saw them at a showcase of Columbia artists, all with new albums for release in the fall of the year.

Columbia was a big, major, important record label, but the executives there didn't have a clue about what they had on their hands with the Oaks. Maybe nobody else saw the potential I saw, a potential the Oak Ridge Boys themselves believed in.

Again, my whole marketing philosophy is one of team effort, with all members working in harmony toward a common goal. The people at the record label are important components of the team. But I felt that Columbia, as storied a label as it was, didn't share in the vision, the goal, and the dream.

In fact, it wasn't just Columbia. Executives at other labels, many of whom worked with Halsey Company artists, told me again and again how hard it was to take an act from gospel music into the mainstream.

I knew we could do it. We had the strength within our agency to move them via personal appearances and television. But we needed the records, too.

During this time, the mid-'70s, many of my main stars were successfully recording for a small but powerful independent label, Dot Records. Roy Clark had recorded his million-selling signature song, "Yesterday, When I Was Young," for Dot, and Hank Thompson's huge hits "Six Pack to Go" and "Oklahoma Hills" had been released on the label. Dot's roster included the likes of country stars Mary Taylor, Donna Fargo, Tommy Overstreet, Rex Allen Sr. and Curtis Potter. All Halsey acts.

Jim Foglesong, president of Dot Records, was already an important part of our star team. With Larry Baunach as the head of its marketing arm and a small but solid lineup of recording artists, Dot had produced an amazing array of successful discs.

As close a friend as he was, however, Jim Foglesong expressed the same reluctance as the other label execs when it came to the Oak Ridge

Boys. It would be a tough project, he believed, to make mainstream recording stars out of a Southern gospel quartet.

A legendary event called the Halsey Ranch Party changed his mind.

Our company had a great working relationship with Jim Foglesong and Dot Records. He understood the value of collective team effort. But while he'd said "yes" to many of my artists, he kept saying "no" to the Oak Ridge Boys.

I wanted Jim and his team for the Oaks. So I kept pitching. Finally, the big breakthrough came. It was in August 1976, during something we dubbed the Halsey Ranch Party. Nobody has ever copied it. It was the ultimate in a "controlled" setting and marketing promotion.

It was at the 1976 edition of our Halsey Ranch Party that Jim Foglesong was finally convinced to get on board with the Oak Ridge Boys. Standing in front of the stage, watching the Oaks entertain our crowd of industry VIPs, Jim looked at me and said, "I'm sold. I believe. Let's do it!"

That in itself made the whole Halsey Ranch Party that year worthwhile. I was elated. Because of the recording deal Jim Foglesong offered that day, a new and very important team member was now in place. A missing ingredient had been added. Soon, another key man would be added to the team–producer Ron Chancey. His run with the Oaks would be long and productive, beginning with the hit 1977 single "Y'All Come Back Saloon,' the first in a long line of chartbusters that would help the Oaks become country, pop and rock stars with, eventually, an amazing 27 No. 1 records to their credit.

chapter 10

THE RANCH PARTY

ere's how it came about. I had been inspired by the early Oklahoma Wild West shows, especially those emanating from the famous 101 Ranch and Pawnee Bill's Wild West Show. These popular internationally touring shows featuring cowboys, Indians and Rough Riders would launch their season each year with a spectacular rodeo and Wild West show. Invitations were extended to celebrities, political dignitaries and, of course, lots and lots of press. The Philips Petroleum brothers in Bartlesville would also feature parties with invited guests from around the world. Their famous "Outlaws and Oilmen" party would gather much notoriety.

Roy Clark, Hank Thompson and I, along with our business associates Wayne Creasy and Stan Synar bought a 2,500-acre cattle ranch. Located twenty-five minutes south of Tulsa, it became our company's headquarters. We later leased another 2,500 acres, and the 5,000 acres included over 1,000 head of cattle. Following the colorful Oklahoma tradition, we designed our own "Halsey Ranch Party" that would become as well known worldwide as any of our predecessors.

Our acreage also boasted a beautiful 8,000 square foot ranch house, along with a large swimming pool and picnic area, all situated atop one of Northeast Oklahoma's tallest hills, overlooking verdant valleys and peacefully grazing cattle. We only used the ranch house for entertaining.

With another partner, Mack Sanders, we owned two Tulsa radio stations, an AM and an FM, Both were country stations, of course.

Once a year, all of us partners would host a private, invitation-only, event, usually on a weekend in September. These were dubbed the Halsey Ranch Parties. The guest list included our preferred buyers and promoters, major casino operators, fair and rodeo executives, important radio-station program directors and general managers, TV talent coordinators and producers, entertainment-industry executives, and newspaper feature writers and members of other media. Just about everyone who was anyone in the business showed up, and the Associated Press, *New York Times, Los Angeles Times,* and *Billboard* and *Variety* and other national entertainment publications generously covered each year's party.

We provided our guests with transportation, lodging, and meals for the weekend. Amenities included limo and helicopter rides back and forth from Tulsa to the Ranch, where most of the events occurred.

In conjunction with the weekend, we always taped an hour-long TV special for Buick, which would air later in the fall, when the company unveiled its new models. The weekend also included the Roy Clark Celebrity Golf Tournament, a star-studded event that raised money for Tulsa's Children's Medical Center. On the Saturday evening after the tournament, we presented Roy Clark's Star Night at the 11,000-seat Mabee Center on the Oral Roberts University campus. This was also a charity event benefiting Children's Medical Center. It featured performances by many stars both within and outside the Halsey roster. Bob Hope came in to host the event numerous times.

The big function at the ranch was an all-day barbecue feast on Sunday. All of our artists attended, from stars on our exclusive roster—Roy Clark, Tammy Wynette, Freddy Fender, Jimmy Dean, Mel Tillis, Hank Thompson, Jody Miller—to new acts we were just getting started. Our stage was located atop the hill in a natural amphitheater, and as the event unfolded on Sunday, the wildly enticing aroma from our big barbecue pit–where Stan Synar presided over the cooking of whole sides of beef and other Oklahoma delicacies–mingled with the sights of flying banners, tents and Indian teepees, Indian dancers and an art show and the sounds of our acts performing against the beautiful early autumn backdrop of the Oklahoma hills. It was an event that only the power of the collective partners could produce, and it served a couple of purposes.

First, it was a big personal thank-you to our many friends and purchasers of Halsey Company talent over the preceding year.

Second, it was a very subtle sales event. As our artists performed, Halsey Company agents stood watching and listening beside their preferred buyers—who, as likely as not, would have a big barbecue sandwich in hand. Our agents didn't have to ask for an order. In this sales-conducive atmosphere, people like the aforementioned Vegas heavyweight Walter Kane, Holmes Hendrickson from Harrah's in Lake Tahoe and Reno, producer Freddy DeCordova from "The Tonight Show with Johnny Carson," and representatives of the Cheyenne, Wyoming, Frontier Days Committee, would make the first comment, asking if they could have Tammy, Freddy, Roy, or Hank–or someone else—for a specific date.

While the Ranch Party may not have been an overt sales promotion, it was one of the best ones ever assembled. We specifically planned it for a couple of months before the big IAFE (International Association of Fair Buyers) fair buyers' meeting in Las Vegas. This annual gathering includes all of the major fair, rodeo, and exhibition buyers. Elaborate displays, promotions and artists showcases highlight this five day event. The future year's talent contracts were discussed, promoted and dates arranged. When we showed up for that event, most of the buyers had already been to the Ranch Party and made their talent selections for the next year.

The Halsey Ranch Parties were major, major events, drawing international celebrities and important entertainment-industry executives into Tulsa for a weekend. It took almost a full year to plan and thousands of hours to put together, with every Halsey Company employee assigned specific duties. Then, our company associates worked almost 24 hours a day over the weekend, in order to maximize the benefits for everyone involved. The cost of each Ranch Party was more than a quarter of a million dollars, but it was well worth it. The Halsey Company secured millions of dollars of future business for our artists, and the positive press went on for the next several months. People still talk about this innovative and imaginative sales, marketing, and press event.

The Ranch Party and its surrounding activities were a great example of layered events and marketing. They showed that when you put one event on top on another, with celebrities, cross-promotion, and press, everything increases in importance.

In addition to Jim Foglesong, many other people saw the Oaks perform for the first time at the 1976 Ranch Party. They included talent buyers who'd become believers after seeing the group on stage. And while the event would've been a success for the Oaks if the recording deal was the only thing we'd gotten out of it, they reaped other benefits as well, including TV shows and fair and rodeo dates. Harrah's Holmes Henderson bought them for his showrooms. And, because Walter Kane was in attendance and impressed by what he saw and heard, we were able to move the Oaks from their "Country Music USA" slot at the Landmark over to the main showroom at the Frontier Hotel. In addition, the press was all over the Oaks, and many stories came out of their Ranch Party appearances and interviews.

This and subsequent Halsey Ranch Parties were extremely important to our first five-year plan for the Oak Ridge Boys. You hear a lot about Hollywood parties, but in terms of productivity and success, I'll put the Halsey Company's Ranch Parties up against any of them.

Chapter 11

MORE MAGIC: NEW YORK CITY

Y ou can play all over the United States and Canada, but one city
will always be set apart from the rest. It is, of course, New York
City.

I've always considered it important to play a big engagement every so
often in the Big Apple. In fact, playing New York City has been a big
component of all my five-year plans for my acts. If you can make some
noise in New York, it will reverberate across the country. There's an
American mindset that says, "You must be good, or you wouldn't be
playing in New York City."

The first five-year plan I ever crafted for the Oaks was in 1975,
when we charged into the mainstream and pulled out all the stops on
our creativity, striving to play important venues and trying to share
bills with top acts, so we could become recognized as more than just
a gospel act. We were making headway, too, playing top casino-hotels
in Las Vegas and lots of state fairs, and, in 1976, going to the Soviet
Union with Roy Clark, making Roy and the Oaks the very first big-
name country-music show to tour the USSR. (Once again, I stress how
important it is to be the first to do something.)

Back then, we were able to leave Columbia Records, whose executives only wanted the group to record gospel music, and switch to
the ABC-Dot label. ABC-Dot's Jim Foglesong saw the Oaks' potential early, when they performed at the Jim Halsey Company's annual

ranch party in Tulsa. Jim teamed–once again, the "team" concept arises–Duane, Joe, William Lee and Richard with creative producer Ron Chancey, and their first single out of the box was an irreverent, instantly memorable country hit called

"Y'All Come Back Saloon." We hadn't planned on a big single that quickly, but it certainly helped bring us into the mainstream.

The first five-year plan for the Oaks also included television exposure. You have the potential to reach millions and millions of people via TV, making those all-important repetitious impressions. Radio is great, but usually your audience is limited to people who like the kind of music a particular station plays. With television, you reach people who aren't just tuning in to get country or pop music, but a whole variety of entertainment.

In the beginning, my associates Dick Howard and John Hitt agreed with me about the potential of the Oaks, and Dick, as the head of the Halsey Company's West Coast office, was in the best position to get the group television bookings. The first time he saw them perform he got the picture, and it was his dedication to getting them on television that really helped move the Oak Ridge Boys into the mainstream. He started at the very beginning of our association with the Oaks, in 1975, when there were a lot of variety shows on morning, afternoon and evening TV hosted by personalities like Dinah Shore, Dean Martin, Flip Wilson, Johnny Carson, Merv Griffin, Mike Douglas and Joey Bishop. Dick made it his business to get the Oaks on as many of those programs as he could. No matter how inconvenient it might be, we'd always rearrange our schedule if we could get the Oak Ridge Boys a television spot.

The thing is, no matter how big a record you have, television puts both you and your music in front of millions. If you're constantly on TV, you receive the multiple benefits of repetitious impressions. This, coupled with your records and important venues and dates, gives you what I call a multiple-layered building block. And, again, New York City is one of those important–probably *the* most important–place you can play. If you're a major act, you play there. New York is full of industry leaders–not just in music, but also in media and finance–and you want them to know you, or at least to know *about* you. So our plans for our artists always included New York City.

In 1977, the first reinventing of the Oaks was going full speed ahead. ABC, which owned the ABC-Dot label, was excited about the group and its new music. We had momentum. It was time to play New York City.

Ask anyone what the most prestigious concert hall in the world is, and chances are that they'll answer "Carnegie Hall." It's not a country-music venue, of course, but it's a deeply respected stage that hosts the world's finest performers. We decided that would be it. An Oaks show at Carnegie Hall would be the biggest country-music event of the year!

We needed to have every seat filled for the show, so I called my old friend Ed Salamon, the general manager at radio station WHN, which was the country-music voice of the city. From the beginning of my career, I'd worked with him and his station.

Ed asked why we didn't go to Madison Square Garden, where we'd paired with WHN to put on a successful show with Roy Clark and Diana Trask three years earlier. Madison Square Garden was considered friendlier to country-music audiences.

"Nobody would expect us at Carnegie Hall," I told him. I figured that, by performing at Carnegie Hall and playing up the "bringing country to the city" angle, we'd draw some serious press attention. To me, that outweighed all other considerations.

Ed came on board, knowing it would be great to have WHN connected with a Carnegie Hall event. And I set about building a package of acts to appear on the bill with the Oaks, a package that would help attract reviewers and sell out the show. These performers had to believe the same way we believed—that there were great advantages to appearing at Carnegie Hall—and agree to do the event for expenses. All Halsey company acts, Mel Tillis and Donna Fargo, both of whom had Top Ten country records at the time, came aboard, and the Texas-based western-swing act Alvin Crow also signed on. We had our show, and it was a strong one.

Here's a secret about playing Carnegie Hall: You don't make any money. Even with a sellout crowd, there isn't any profit because of the high expenses of playing the venue. You play your artist in Carnegie Hall for two reasons, which I call the two "P's:" *press and prestige.* This event would bring press and prestige to all of us—the performers, WHN, and the Jim Halsey Company, Inc., co-producer of the concert.

From the beginning of my career, many of my contemporaries in country-music management thought I was crazy because I emphasized getting my artists on television, where they were only paid union scale most of the time.

It was the same with the Carnegie Hall concert. Some country-music managers thought that Dick Howard, John Hitt and I had gone off the deep end. "Carnegie Hall?" they'd ask in disbelief, "Where you can't break even with a sellout?"

But we knew. With the Oaks, we had a supergroup in the making, and no sacrifice was too great in pursuing our collective dreams. The point of playing Carnegie Hall was, again, *press and prestige*. The industry people knew we were in town, playing the most respected venue in the world. Our reviews noted that country music had finally come into its own. After all, country acts were playing Carnegie Hall. Prior to the show, all four acts gave interview upon interview, and when the night finally came, the powers that be saw a great show–and it was all country music.

One night of magic in New York City gave us lots of new business, with follow-up calls to make and contracts to be negotiated. The press and prestige generated by the sold-out event helped move the Oak Ridge Boys to a new plateau. Some of the TV programs that had passed on them before the Carnegie Hall show now became eager to sign them up. Top Las Vegas casinos began talking deals. The record company (thanks, Jim Foglesong) saw a new pop and rock potential in the group.

All of that came along with the very first five-year plan for the Oaks, which ran from 1975 to 1980.

INVENTORY

At this point, I'd like to explain one of the most important philosophies behind the Jim Halsey Company. It applies to all the artists I've represented over the years and it's a business strategy I've used with the Oaks ever since the mid'70s, when they crossed over from Southern gospel to the mainstream.

First, let me introduce a new term. It's a word you've heard before, but probably not in conjunction with show business. It's "inventory." For our purposes, it means the number of dates that an artist wants to work, or *will* work. In the country-music business, most acts work a certain inventory of dates each month, with some months busier than others. Most artists in rock music–and these days, country artists like Tim McGraw, Alan Jackson, George Strait, Toby Keith, and Kenny

Chesney—work an inventory that only runs a month or two, the length of one tour, and then devote the rest of the year to other endeavors.

From the beginning, the Oak Ridge Boys gave us a large inventory. They worked 160 to 170 days each year, sometimes doing as many as 30 consecutive days in the summer concert season and around Christmastime. That's a lot of potential dates—and this is where my philosophy comes in. The strategy from the beginning was to divide the Oaks' inventory into several different categories. (We first did this when the Jim Halsey Company was doing their booking, and we continued to do it when the William Morris Agency became their booking agent.) These days, those categories include (1) fairs and celebrations, (2) performing arts centers and theaters, (3) casinos, (4) private and corporate dates, (5) television appearances, (6) recording dates, (7) Branson, Mo. (usually for 30 days), (8) the annual Christmas Show tour. In addition, we always create several special events per year.

When you distribute the inventory this way, it does three things. First of all, it lessens your risk in any one category, so if one segment of the business sags, you won't lose a lot of dates. Second, it diversifies both the Oaks' income and the audiences they reach. And finally, it keeps things interesting, because it's not the same place and same thing all of the time.

1995 MASTER PLAN

In 1995, I presented my fifth five-year plan for the continued reinvention of the Oaks. As a part of that plan, I stated what I believed should be our priorities, goals and purpose. Here's what I wrote:

Nothing is impossible!
Put dreams and visions on the table.
Make decisions—focus
Follow directions of the manager
Purpose: *Reshape the image and inspire renewed confidence among buyers, fans, employees, and the industry.*
Priorities:
1. Maintain itinerary and plan
2. Secure meaningful dates
3. Insure cash flow
4. Build career and prestigious dates
5. Television, television, television … 'nuff said.

My five-year plan included 50 points. The first point–have William Lee Golden return to the group (thought of simultaneously by Duane, Joe and Richard). I felt it was essential that the Oaks return to the William Morris Agency. When they did, after two years with another agency, we all had a reunion party. The Oaks, William Morris and I. We started implementing the 50-point plan I'd worked out for them, as we set about rebuilding our team.

One of the first things we wanted to do was get the Oak Ridge Boys on television–and fast! I had an idea that the best way to do that would be to record a direct-response album, a CD sold through television spots. A forceful and effective 60-second commercial could achieve a couple of things. Not only would it sell new Oaks product, but it would also tell the world that the Oak Ridge Boys were back together and singing better than ever.

It had to be a special record, though, for maximum effectiveness. And when my son Sherman–by now a well-known music-video and television director–suggested a double-length gospel CD featuring 25 all-time standards, produced by music legend Leon Russell, I knew he'd hit on the perfect package to accompany the Oaks' reinvention. We engaged our friend Richard Sutter, one of the most clever and successful direct-response marketers in the business, to handle our marketing.

The spot went on the air, and both the campaign and the CD package itself *Reunion I* and *Reunion II* became a big success. You couldn't turn on the TV without seeing the Oak Ridge Boys, and even the most casual fan had to notice that the very distinctive-looking William Lee Golden was back in the group. It was one of the fastest reinventing campaigns ever, and it included many other components, including the work of Paul Moore, head of the William Morris Agency's Nashville operation and an old friend. With the TV ads saturating the market and making people aware of the Oaks—with William Lee once again aboard—Paul and the agency were able to go about booking the "new" Oak Ridge Boys with a renewed zeal. The new album and new TV exposure, coupled with the group's old magic, attracted the attention of talent buyers. The date book started to fill. The industry was talking, and there was a new excitement surrounding the Oak Ridge Boys.

Now, while they were hot, was the time to implement some of the other important parts of our five-year plan. Let's now look at a few of them in detail.

THE RECORD COMPANY–1995 PLAN

We needed a label to release our product to mainstream audiences. Problem was, hit-country radio had changed so much since the Oaks run of hits in the '70s, '80s and early '90s. Record companies were more interested in new artists than established acts. By the mid-'90s, commercial radio had become locked into formulaic music, with "consultants" replacing local programmers, and stations paring down their playlists. Neither of these developments was good, especially when it came to artists and new music. A consultant, hired by a corporation, might program all the songs for dozens of radio stations across the country from a headquarters in one particular city, not taking into account regional tastes and other local factors, homogenizing the music with a one-size-fits-all mentality. And the major radio stations (known in the business as "reporting stations") that gave weekly reports on what they were playing to *Billboard* magazine and other entities with record charts were now only playing 20–25 different songs a week. As a result, listeners were not only hearing fewer different songs each time they turned on their radios—the chance of getting a new record on the charts became harder and harder also. There were just as many, or more, singles coming out than before, but there were fewer slots on playlists. In one sense, the repetition helped sell records for those lucky enough to have a song in rotation on enough reporting stations. But the tightness of those playlists took a lot of the creativity out of the business by limiting the selection that a deejay could play.

We finally found a label, Platinum, that had seen some reasonable success, especially with veteran hitmakers like the Bellamy Brothers. Platinum had a full sales and promotion staff, and their staff was excited about signing the Oak Ridge Boys.

One of the longtime members of the Oaks team was Nashville-based producer Ron Chancey, who'd been responsible for most of their major hits. He was a great producer who could be a valuable member of the team, someone who could help in the reinventing of the Oak Ridge Boys. Was there a chance we could get him on board?

There was, and we did. And, with both a record label and a hit-record producer, we were plugging back in!

GOT A MINUTE

It's like the story of new Coke. "It didn't work as planned but achieved a goal of revitalizing the brand and re-attracted the public to Coke," says Sergio Zyman in his book, "The End of Marketing as We Know It."

This is what the Oak Ridge Boys first single release in seven years did for them...a sixty second version of their regular three minute record. A sixty second record? YES! Never in the history of the recording industry had a commercially released record been 60 seconds or less. (Another first, by the way).

The idea of course was to make the Oak Ridge Boys attractive to radio–who was not playing the Oaks, or any others from this era.

Only sixty seconds, one minute long, catch phrase, "Got a Minute."

The song was good, but resistance at radio was still strong. The ingenuity of a one-minute record however caught on like wildfire with the media.

Was this one minute record a publicity gimmick, or as I defended, a unique and useful mini marketing event.

It did get a lot of airplay however, not consistent and not enough on the monitored stations to get charted–but for the first time in several years we were getting airplay.

Just as rewarding, lengthy interviews on radio and TV, and stories galore in major newspapers, magazines and press in all of the syndicates. USA Today ran a major story with the four guys' picture!

The "Got a Minute" campaign re-introduced the Oak Ridge Boys to a new and younger radio audience. On Donny and Marie's network show the Oaks were featured, singing the song standing next to a giant stopwatch, with the second hand timing them as they performed. Yes, it was just exactly one minute long.

This campaign did what it was supposed to do. Reawakened an audience to the Oak Ridge Boys. Part of re-inventing the "original Coke," or in this case "the original Oak Ridge Boys." In a short period of eight weeks, *300 million impressions* were accumulated.

Sometimes the campaign's original purpose takes a turn and heads another direction.

In the case of the one minute record release, we didn't get a hit record, but we got more press and PR than if we'd had a number one radio hit.

Being creative and inventive like this makes it sound like "genius at work." It's not that complicated. This just happened to be one idea that worked. A lot of others haven't, but you haven't heard them.

In keeping a band, or shall we say, a "Brand" alive and well there has to be a steady flow of campaign ideas, projects, and as with the Oak Ridge Boys, they are their own best subject.

They stay current with their music, sound, look and attitude. That's why they are "The Oak Ridge Boys" and 30-plus years in the mainstream (since 1975) is just a beginning for them.

OAK RIDGE BOYS PRESS AND PUBLIC RELATIONS

Not all of our 50-point program was done one point at a time. Sometimes, we were able to do more than one at the same time—as happened when we both achieved a goal and got simultaneous publicity about it.

Understand that, in the team philosophy, success is a direct result of all efforts working together. And, as we put the various elements into place and began implementing them, the press and PR people were always essential because they got the word out about what we were doing and what was happening with the Oaks. With each newspaper story, magazine article, or press release, they reminded the world that the Oak Ridge Boys were a major act.

Press and PR are very important because public perception is very important to success. We can be successful doing our projects, but if the world doesn't know about them, we've lost a big "enhancer."

As the reinvention of the Oaks geared up, their longtime press agent, Kathy Gangwisch, pitched in to implement the 50-point program by scheduling rounds of radio, television, and print interviews. She made sure that the media knew there was a lot of fresh stuff to talk about with the Oaks—the reunion with Golden, their signing with William Morris, my return as their manager, the direct-response TV album, a new tour. In the middle of the 1990s, when the reinvention began, we had to let the world know about the exciting "new" Oak Ridge Boys and where they were going. We had to let the public know that the "new" Oaks were the "old" Oaks, together again, and to do that, we had to aggressively seek new and different avenues to get our story out. So, the team—Halsey, Gangwisch, and the Oaks—focused on both old and new opportunities for press coverage. We went after international press. We explored cable television and interactive media. Carefully, we coordinated our press plan.

A few years after the reinvention of the Oaks began, Kathy Gang-wisch retired. We were fortunate to get Sandy Brokaw, an excellent press and PR person, to take her place on our team. Sandy and his brother David operate the Los Angeles-based Brokaw Company, one of the most successful and capable PR firms in the business. And they continue to do a great job as the Press and PR team of the Oak Ridge Boys. We also use Nashville based Webster PR in joint efforts between Kirt Webster and Sandy Brokaw to produce magic.

AWARDS

When we began the reinvention of the Oaks, they'd gone through a period during which they hadn't received any special recognition or a single award. I planned to change all that. After all, they'd achieved much since 1975, when they'd moved from the niche market of South-ern gospel into the musical mainstream. They'd sold millions of records since then, and while they hadn't seen anything in the way of awards since the early '90s, they'd received many before that time.

Unfortunately, when we began our five-year plan in '95, we couldn't capitalize on the fact that it was the 20th anniversary of the Oaks cross-ing over into the country, pop, and rock markets. It takes a few years to gear up for a meaningful promotion, so we couldn't take advantage of that ready-made opportunity for accolades and awards.

As a board member of the National Music Council, though, I was aware of that prestigious organization's American Eagle Award, which recognized outstanding performers and their achievements each year. The nominations came from the council's various member organiza-tions and were voted on by the board of directors. At the time, the likes of Benny Goodman, Ella Fitzgerald, and Dizzy Gillespie had been honored with the award. There hadn't been one recipient from the field of country music.

On June 11, 1997, that changed, as the Oak Ridge Boys were given the American Eagle Award "for their unique contributions to the gospel and country genres of American music" at a banquet and gala in New York City, where they also performed for the crowd of music-industry professionals. Larry Jones, president of the Oklahoma City-based international relief organization Feed The Children, presented Duane, Joe, William Lee and Richard with the crystal tro-phy, and National Music Council president David Sanders told the crowd of their pioneering work before international audiences and their great philanthropic and humanitarian activities.

Interestingly enough, the other American Eagle recipient that year was the legendary rock producer Phil Ramone, who produced Paul Simon's hit 1977 single "Slip Slidin' Away'–which featured backing vocals from the Oak Ridge Boys!

The American Eagle Award put the Oaks in the national spotlight, providing plenty of newsworthy material for our press person, Kathy Gangwisch, to use with the media. It also further broadened their visibility beyond country and gospel audiences. While they were in New York City, the Oaks also had the opportunity to help Larry Jones and Feed the Children do a feeding in Harlem. That area of New York was a regular stop for Larry's organization, but, while the Oaks had assisted Feed The Children with many feedings over the past decade and a half, this was the first time they were able to help with the efforts in Harlem.

On that day, five semi-trailers, full of much-needed, nourishing, food, rolled into Harlem's Joe Louis Park, where representatives of more than 30 local agencies waited to distribute it to the needy and hungry. It was an important day, long to be remembered, and the Oaks did their part by not only helping to hand out the food, but also to raise awareness of the event by making an early-morning appearance on Geraldo Rivera's network TV show and, throughout the day, doing interviews with newspapers, trade magazines, and radio. They were also videotaped for a future Feed The Children television program.

It was another example of networking, something that goes on through the business, and throughout our lives.

As pointed out earlier, part of this five-year plan was getting the group an important award or recognition, which happened in 1997 with the National Music Council's American Eagle Award–given in New York City, of course.

As we prepared to head for New York to receive the award, I wondered, "What would be the coolest way to hype the Oaks' latest Big Apple appearance?" We'd done Carnegie Hall in 1977 and then Radio City Music Hall in 1986. We'd made lots of visits to the city for TV and radio appearances and interviews. But this time, we decided we'd announce our presence in the town by playing B.B. King's hot club on 52nd and Broadway. It was a small venue, but everyone knew the blues king and his famous nightspot. We got the booking there and spent two days in town, doing interviews, the "Imus in the Morning" radio show, an appearance on the MSNBC network, another Feed the Children feeding with Larry Jones, and an impromptu performance with the Boys & Girls Choir of Harlem.

Throughout this book, I emphasize the importance of networking, and how important it is to retain friendships. Remember Ed Salamon, the general manager of radio station WHN, who co-sponsored the Oaks' Carnegie Hall event in 1977? Twenty years later, he was president of Westwood One Broadcasting, with 1,800 radio stations under its umbrella. His assistant in '77, Pam Green, was still with him, and in 1997 she scheduled the Oak Ridge Boys for a whole day at Westwood One and Lee Arnold, America's number one on-air personality at New York's WHN, was host and emcee at our Carnegie Hall event. Today, he is still one of America's most important radio personalities on Sirius/XM satellite radio. Ed Salamon today is president of CRS (Country Radio Seminar) who's annual gathering in Nashville are an important networking event.

Once again, the power of the two P's—press and prestige—worked for the Oaks. These NYC appearances also enabled Duane, Joe, William Lee, and Richard to meet many of the people from the William Morris Agency who were working on their behalf. Making the most of the opportunity, the Oaks shook hands with and thanked the agents, one on one.

These sorts of things have long-lasting benefits and continue to build relationships on a personal basis.

Every item in my 50-point plan reflected the accumulation of other items and events. No one point stands alone or is all-important. It's the layering of the points that makes the sum more important than the parts. The same can be said for the assemblage of the team. Every team member is important, but all team members working together produces pure magic.

SURVIVING WITHOUT MONITORED RADIO

There is a lot of difference when we talk about radio play. Every artist will have a certain period of time when there's just no end of hit records. Or so it seems.

Some artists only have one record that ever reaches the hallowed halls of monitored radio. *Most artists never have any* so called hit records. Everybody tries. Effort and money. Just nothing happens.

We talk about timing. This business is all about time. Good timing is like good luck. It comes every so often to all of us. If we recognize it, *grab it, work it, use it.*

Because timing and luck are fleeting and intangible, some will have it last longer; others will be able to maximize it to stick around for a while and get the most of it.

Unfortunately, there are too many of those that just flat don't recognize good timing and good luck, even if it hits them squarely between the eyes.

Radio, monitored radio, is what drives the "Hit record" category.

With the Oak Ridge Boys, we had a long run of "good timing and good luck." Through the coordination of marketing and promotion plans we were able to extend the virtue of great performance use with product into 30 top charted records, 30 million sales.

The Oaks have a charted record life longer than most other artists.

The charted record play lists that make up the top charts are selected from less than a couple of hundred radio stations in country music out of 3,500 stations all over the country that play country music.

These 100 or so stations making charting decisions are referred to as the "monitoring stations" or "reporting stations." The other 3300 or so country music stations are called secondary stations. The same percentage of reporting stations to the number of overall stations is about the same in all genres of music. Pop, Rock, Latin, Jazz and so forth.

The major record companies are only concerned about airplay on the monitored stations. Times change, everything changes. That's part of life. Most CD buyers, music buyers (so far) have younger demographics than a few years ago. Most young buyers are not buying CDs at all and many don't even own a CD player. They're purchasing their music by download. Country music is still a CD marketplace, but more and more downloads are sold each year. Our Oak Ridge Boys demographics are still buying CDs, but our download sales are continually increasing.

As manager of the Oak Ridge Boys, this presents a challenge to still get our music out there, in service, so to speak.

Most of the 100 plus stations (monitored) are programmed by station consultants, usually not in the same town as the radio stations. Some consultants program for multiple stations.

We know people still like the Oak Ridge Boys music. The Oaks have stayed musically current and always, *always* present a great show.

So, how is success maintained when not being in the charts (songs selected from play lists on the 100 or so monitored stations)? *We're on TV!*

We have to be inventive in order to overcome this obstacle. This book reflects on the Oak Ridge Boys being in the main stream for over 30 years.

We found a *Good* independent record company, well staffed and motivated, that caught our vision of successful reality... good songs, good product, good marketing and promotion.

Spring Hill Records. They became an integral part of the team. They are the ones that successfully marketed and promoted the CDs mentioned in the previous paragraphs.

Look at all of the things we discussed here, plus, an important element about distribution. Spring Hill sells and distributes the Oak Ridge Boys record product to the stores... Wal-Mart, Target, Best Buy, etc... through the distribution giant EMI.

So, as far as the Oak Ridge Boys are concerned, it's better than being with one of the four major record companies! (read the chapter on record companies to learn more about the difference between majors and independents).

We have a close working relationship—on a day-to-day basis. Spring Hill is creative in their marketing and sales. And they work hard on supporting all of our personal appearances.

A big plus for us, is the nature of Spring Hill's business. They are an important Christian and Gospel record company, too. Because of the Oak Ridge Boys background and personal beliefs; the Christian/Gospel audience is still an important part of the focus.

Have we gone past our "record charted prime?" I don't think so. But as the charts move on with new criteria, we, the Oak Ridge Boys move on too. We're still recording new songs and new material and have several big CDs in the last few years, a patriotic CD "Colors," a gospel CD "From the Heart," a bluegrass CD "The Journey," two spectacular Christmas albums "An Inconvenient Christmas" and "Christmas Cookies," and an excellent contemporary country CD "The Boys Are Back," produced by Shooter Jennings producer David Cobb. Singles from all of these have charted on various playlists.

We have produced television shows with all of these albums as the featured music. These have been part of regular broadcast features of Larry Jones' Feed The Children television shows. The multiple airings on large cable networks producing over one hundred million impressions yearly have been as beneficial to selling our inventory of dates and keeping our venues sold out as having a top five record constantly in the charts. *Wow!* The power of television!

Just to give you an idea, in 2008, the Oak Ridge Boys worked 170 plus concert dates, including major fairs and celebrations, Performing Art Centers and important venues, casinos, 37-day Christmas tour and 30 dates in Branson, MO. We sold out almost every single date, even adding extra performances on many.

How? How in the world do the Oak Ridge Boys keep doing this?

We're still getting lots of radio play (though not on the 100 monitored stations). And TV, TV, TV. Plus many, many press interviews.

Being in the main stream as we call the last 30 plus years, means their exposure of repertoire to include pop, country and rock music has also expanded the Oaks audience.

PODCASTING

Podcasting your music puts you in reach of millions around the world that can either listen or download. Normally this alternative distribution method is thought only to be for the very youthful demographic.

Downloading of music in recent years has become so popular that many are not buying CD's, but downloading directly into their iPod or computer. A lot of big music buyers do not even have a CD player. The same downloading with video and TV with iPod type of receivers is expanding on a daily basis.

As a means of marketing your original music with your band, certainly look into podcasting. There are phenomenal success stories coming from podcasting—and it's for everybody.

We podcast with the Oak Ridge Boys, too. We started a few years with a podcast of our Public Domain (PD) Christmas recordings. Our record company and The Oaks waived their royalty. The podcast program included Oaks music and some reading of the Christmas book by Oaks' member Joe Bonsall. The guys did a lot of interviews about what was probably the first such "podcast" of a traditional, big name country music group.

Why would a group like The Oak Ridge Boys, with a commercially distributed CD in the marketplace do such a cutting edge presentation? I think "Cutting Edge" says it. They were interested in reaching an audience less traditional than might be expected. By podcasting, this put them in an "around the world" arena that extended their audience, new focus, new territory and in the long run, new buyers. This Podcasting by the Oak Ridge Boys was one of the first by a big name, popular music group into areas of alternative marketing.

It doesn't seem so new and cutting edge now. We still have to rely on the tried and tested methods—-retail, direct response and on the merchandise tables of artists in concert. We are seeing more and more sales coming from downloading and less and less from the retail bins in stores.

Building your own internet radio station is becoming easier and less expensive everyday. This adds to another creative way to get your music, your product, your ideas into the hands of consumers with little expense, using your computer. And best of all, you are in control.

You'll need the appropriate licensing from BMI, ASCAP or SESAC if you're playing copyrighted music. Rights have to be acquired and composers rightfully compensated. All regular broadcast stations (radio and television) are licensed.

Your own radio station would need the appropriate computer software and special phone lines, maybe an upgrade of your computer. Basically, you can get into internet broadcasting with your own station and programming selections for a few thousand dollars. And, this is your ability to reach thousand, maybe millions.

Many books are available that give you good information on both Podcasting and internet radio. It's all changing—everyday and it's exciting.

Want to know something real important? We are in the black with our record company. In the chapter on Record Companies, you can see the pit fall of getting into debt with the record company. You never get out. We *are* out!

BRANSON

As I write this, there are 52 show-presenting theaters in Branson, Mo, and more hotel rooms than in Kansas City and St. Louis combined. But when we began our five-year plan with the Oaks in 1975, Branson was barely a dot on the entertainment map, presenting only a couple of local shows.

The Oak Ridge Boys were eager to work then, and they still are today, more than 30 years later. In fact, they did 160 dates in 2008. They realize that to stay active and current in this business, any artist or group has to be seen and heard on stage.

And within the past several years, Branson has been a great place to get that done.

When the Oaks began their transition from gospel to country music, Branson was a sleepy southwestern Missouri town whose main attractions consisted of a cave and a couple of highly entertaining live shows featuring country and hillbilly music and comedy from the Presley Family and the Baldknobbers. They remain popular mainstays in a much larger Branson of today, but it was, in many ways, the direct opposite of Vegas–a small town with a wholesome, family-friendly image that offered down-home entertainment *sans* booze, gambling, and half-naked women.

In 1984, Roy Clark became the first celebrity to lend his name to a Branson theater. The Roy Clark Theater caught on from the beginning, and a rush of other stars flocked to Branson–Mel Tillis, Box Car Willie, Jim Stafford, Ray Stevens, Mickey Gilley, Moe Bandy, and many more. While most were country-oriented acts in the beginning, major performers from other genres also came to town, including pop superstar Andy Williams, who's beautiful Moon River Theater also hosts many other big-name attractions. The Russian comedian, Yakoff Smirnoff, has a successful theatre there, as does violin virtuoso Shoji Tabuchi; Dick Clark's American Bandstand, Dolly Parton's Dixie Stampede. Other varied attractions such as Chinese Acrobats at the Shanghai Theatre, Ripley's Believe It or Not Museum, The Titanic Museum and the internationally renowned theme park Silver Dollar City add to Branson's appeal. Add to that a progressive downtown plan that combines restored historic charm with a state-of-the-art shopping experience dubbed the Branson Landing located on the shore of beautiful Lake Taneycomo. All of these features are situated within reach of major Ozark lakes Table Rock and Bull Shoals, making Branson a mega tourist mecca unparalleled in America.

For a number of years, the Oak Ridge Boys performed regularly at the Grand Palace Theatre. We'd do 30-plus days every year at the Grand Palace, and we've also taped several Feed the Children TV specials with Larry Jones there.

2008 marked the beginning in a new chapter in the Oaks' Branson history…our own Oak Ridge Boys Theatre. Mr. Gene Bicknell, producer, theatre owner (Mansion Entertainment and Media Center) constructed a deal to license our brand, The Oak Ridge Boys for one of his theatres. The Theatre has state of the art lights and sound, 2,200 seats, and is now the Branson home for Oak Ridge Boys. It's a head-quarters for us, where we can entertain visiting friends and VIPs, do interviews for national media, perform, and sell some merchandise. It also serves as a base for their heavy 160 date touring schedule where they can create a place where their fans can feel "at home." They play nine 3-day stays each visit to Branson. Each stint is timed so that it can be made into an event. Wedding weekend, Patriotic Tribute, Harmony Convention, Harvest Festival, Christmas Show debut, etc. The advantage to having a regular base is to create special event type promotions to expand our press and PR and our audience base.

We know, also, that bus tours are an important part of Branson's entertainment scene, and certainly of our own Branson appearances. Vacationers throughout the country flock to buses bound for Branson, knowing they'll see several great shows, eat well and often, and have the opportunity for lots of discount shopping before returning home. The bus companies offer shows as part of their packages, and the Oaks are always an important act for their passengers to see. Each bus holds about 50 people, and we'll have anywhere from 10 to 30 busloads of folks come in to see us each day we play Branson.

It's always important to have a regular performance situation that can be tied to events promotion and PR. The Branson community has developed into this type of situation. In developing Branson for other Halsey company artists, it supplied the same type of opportunity as Vegas where we could bring in other press and buyers. It also provided a state of the art location from which to do TV shows. Over the years the Oak Ridge Boys have been built into one of the major Branson attractions and appear there 27–30 days a year annually.

THE NATIONAL ANTHEM PROJECT

By now, you must realize that my whole life has been about events and projects. Every year has brought opportunities that could be shaped into projects, which in turn could become important in the growth of my artists and our company. All have benefited.

Some projects, of course, are more important than others. But all of them are fueled by an underlying philosophy: Devise plans that can be expanded, so that the original goal can be given room to grow.

In some cases, this just naturally unfolds, with everyone contributing ideas and thoughts that add to the excitement.

That description fits the National Anthem Project. It all started, like a lot of my projects, with networking. In this case, it was my position as a member of the board of directors of the National Music Council that allowed me to network with other board members.

(The National Music Council is a quasi-governmental board composed of representatives from all the organizations that deal with music and performance rights. Those groups include Broadcast Music Inc. (BMI), the American Society of Composers (ASCAP), and the American Federation of Musicians (AFM), along with the National Symphony League and some 30 other organizations. Formed in 1945, it's an important lobbying group that functions much like a chamber of commerce for the music industry. Because of my role as president and President of Honor of FIDOF, the International Federation of Music Festivals, I've been a member of the National Music Council's board of directors since 1990.)

A couple of years ago at a board meeting, Dr. John Mahlman, president of MENC (Music Education National Conference, the organization representing American music teachers), explained an important project his group was discussing. One of his associates, Earl Hurrey, had devised a patriotic program. It was to be called the National Anthem Project and its purpose would be to stimulate Americans' interest in "The Star Spangled Banner." Research had shown that many could not recite the words, let alone sing them. Even when the National Anthem opened sporting events, it was usually sung by a guest performer, with spectators simply standing with their hands over their hearts. MENC wanted to restore the importance of knowing the words to, and singing, our National Anthem.

Joe Lamond, president of the National Association of Music Merchants (NAMM), was another National Music Council board member, and his group became a sponsor of the project. More sponsorships would be forthcoming. And then, Dr. Mahlman announced that the National Anthem Project needed a National Musical Ambassador.

There's that WOW factor again! It would be a perfect fit for the Oak Ridge Boys, whose patriotic dedication was, and is, well known. And while more than 500 worthy celebrities were considered for the position, the project's committee ultimately picked the Oaks.

The announcement of the new National Music Ambassadors took

place, with much pomp and circumstance, on the lawn of the U.S. Capitol in Washington, D.C. It featured dignitaries, celebrities, the United States Marine Corps Band, school choirs, Dr. Mahlman, and Dr. Dieter Zetsche (president of Daimler Chrysler–another national sponsor). It was featured on that morning's broadcast of ABC-TV's *Good Morning, America.*

We were now the official spokespeople for an important, patriotic project in which we all deeply believed. As such, the Oaks became part of a dizzying variety of events. They sang "The Star Spangled Banner" at numerous sporting events, including a high-profile major-league baseball game between the Yankees and Mets. They also were a part of the MENC-sponsored World's Largest Concert. Televised over both the PBS and PAX networks, it featured the Oaks with several high school choirs, choruses and an orchestra, all led by MENC instructors. The broadcast reached out to music classrooms, where students from all across America joined in. It was estimated that more than six million students participated in the World's Largest Event.

The Oaks also appeared at the MENC conference in Salt Lake City, where they were joined by the Mormon Tabernacle Choir for a concert given before a crowd of more than 21,000. This event was so important that it also became a television program, the basis of one of our featured specials for Larry Jones and Feed the Children. The project also fit well with our Feed the Children patriotic show, "Let Freedom Ring."

Because of their work in the National Anthem Project, the Oak Ridge Boys received the FAME Award, MENC's highest honor.

All of this certainly illustrates our philosophy of Layered Marketing and Repetitious Impressions. You make Layered Marketing work by tying all elements into almost everything you're doing. Layered Marketing opens up new interview opportunities–you don't just have a new CD or tour, but something beyond that, something of great general interest. That was the case with the Oaks' participation in the National Anthem Project.

A big plus of the National Anthem Project was many unique opportunities arising for the Oak Ridge Boys. On January 1, 2007, for instance, one and a half *billion* TV viewers saw them during the Rose Bowl Parade, center stage on the parade's second-largest float, accompanied by a 100-person choir, Joe Lamond's drum circle and the Oaks' singing a one-minute version of their hit "It's Hard to be Cool in a Mini Van." They were invited there by representatives of NAMM, which sponsored the massive float.

The National Anthem Project, which has been going for nearly three years at this writing, has been one of our most worthwhile endeavors. I know that each of the Oaks–Duane Allen, Joe Bonsall, William Lee Golden, and Richard Sterban–feel gratified that they were the ones chosen to help rebuild the visibility and popularity of our National Anthem.

OAK RIDGE BOYS AND BRANDING

The Oak Ridge Boys are a great singing group, and have been for years. Over the years of concert performances, hit records, television appearances and constant press, they have also become and important "brand name."

A Brand Name is what every marketer is hoping to build. Name Recognition. An identifying logo. Coca-Cola, Tide, Dial, Kelloggs, Ford, Hershey, Tabasco, BluBlocker Sunglasses (had to get these two in). These product names and logos should bring instant recognition and conjure up a vision of the product itself. Marketers work to build a positive image.

That's what we collectively decided to build 30-plus years ago, as we worked to build the Oak Ridge Boys into a "mainstream" act.

First, their unique four part vocal harmony is a style or "brand" itself. No one sounds like Duane Allen, Joe Bonsall, William Lee Golden and Richard Sterban.

The look has changed over the years, but the energy and harmonies haven't.

Entertain the audience and stay positive. Treat everyone fairly. Don't burn bridges. Constantly continue building. That's our philosophy.

Our company, the Jim Halsey Company, Inc. represented many big stars, and for each one a policy and plan was formulated to make his or her name a "Brand Name," Roy Clark, The Judds, Clint Black, Dwight Yoakam, Hank Thompson, Freddy Fender, Minnie Pearl, and others. Identifying music, pictures, press and PR into name recognition. This branding helps sell tickets, records and merchandise.

The Oak Ridge Boys became one of the best, prime examples of "Brand" building. They understood the value of "layered" marketing and the value of combined press and PR with all of the other elements working together.

This is where the real "power of performance" became evident.

The Oak Ridge Boys are a dream to work with. They recognize the importance of how records, books, BluBlocker sunglasses, promoters and venues, concentrated promotions, plus press and PR working together spells success. Their work as Musical Ambassadors for the National Anthem Project and the numerous Larry Jones' Feed The Children television specials push the combined "brand" value higher.

Once again, the coordination and cooperation of the team partners need to be carefully orchestrated to maximize the benefits.

The Oak Ridge Boys. Every time you hear that "Brand Name," you get the picture. Four guys stylishly dressed, you can almost hear the four-part harmony, envision William Lee Golden's 23–1/2 inch beard or Joe Bonsall's tireless energy, hear Richard Sterbans' window rattling bass or Duane Allen's smooth lead. All of this brings to mind a vision of their powerful logo, The Oak Ridge Boys.

For over 30 years, this is the designed plan. The powerful Oak Ridge Boys logo was created early in our "building the artist" period by Nick Fasciano. He is the same artist that designed the distinctive *Chicago* logo.

The logo has been with the Oaks all of these years in the main stream and has helped to solidify a positive and wholesome image.

Realize, this group of four guys, Duane, Joe, William Lee and Richard have been together making their mark in the mainstream music business for over 40 years.

Their momentum of success is part of careful planning and coordination of their team.

We stress emphatically how important it is to build a solid team.

The Oak Ridge Boys have one of the best organizations. It's not by chance. Each member has been carefully chosen.

I have been blessed to have been a part of this team for 30-plus years as their personal manager. Our Jim Halsey Company, Inc. acted as their booking agents from 1975 to 1990, when our booking company was sold to the William Morris Agency. The management team within the Oak Ridge Boys Office, Kathy Harris, Jon Mir, Karin Warf, Darrick Kinslow, Erma Smith, and their long-time attorney Gary Spicer are the core basis of what goes on within the company.

As manager these 35 plus years, part of my responsibility has been to help build a visible team: A booking agency, record company, Press & PR representation, promoters, music publishers, music & entertainment attorneys, book publishers, corporate sponsors and the list expands from there.

The big success factor, in this situation, is the fact that the Oak Ridge Boys understand the music and entertainment business.

Their ideas, wants and desires can best be achieved with the coordination of working with common sense.

I stress throughout this book, it's really about viewing and approaching this business with common sense. Sure, there are some prescribed methods and formulas that can reach the achievement of goals. Apply these to your own time schedule and way of working.

I don't know of anybody that has ever achieved success alone! They may claim it, but it's always a combination of talented team members working together to make this magic happen.

For some, the success seems to come easier and faster. Maybe so, but you can hasten this achievement by making your plans, coordinating the efforts of your teams.

I must add, if a team member is not working for the best interests of the artist, get rid of them.

There are enough stress factors in business when everything is going just fine, there is no need to accumulate stress from team members with negative attitudes and lack of ability.

The artist's salvation, many times, through stressful times or seemingly unproductive time periods, is the strength that comes from building the "Brand Name." This Brand will keep the group booked and audiences coming.

The Oak Ridge Boys have continually reinvented themselves over the years, keeping themselves and their music fresh. This just doesn't happen. It takes work, thought and execution.

Developing the consistency of your "Brand." Your "Brand," our brand the Oak Ridge Boys means the quality and integrity it has represented over the years. These years have added meaning and a solid base that just doesn't come with overnight success. You have to work for it. You have to earn it. Beginning artists and "brands" need to realize from their very first appearance before an audience, it starts to build— it's called *reputation*. Good or bad you'll earn a piece of it with every performance or encounter with the public. Pay attention. Be careful. It all will be accounted.

For the ticket buyer, record buyer or someone buying our books, our "brand" represents quality, integrity and value. If you don't get this in a brand, you're disappointed.

Brands like Wal-mart, Walgreens, Best Buy, Target, Home Depot, Dunkin' Donuts, Quik Trip are all retail stores, but they are "brand names" too. Same with web e-tailers Amazon, iTunes, ebay. Shopping at one of these "brand" stores will mean the same consistent quality wherever in the US you're shopping.

You know the quality, integrity and value. It's the same in all of the "brand" stores or websites. All of the big retail stores have websites, too. Consistency of value gives confidence to the customers.

It's the same with the Oak Ridge Boys. You are going to get your value—consistently—concerts, television, records, and books. This has been a goal for the past 30-plus years.

You can see the Oak Ridge Boys are much more than a singing group.

This is what you should strive for in building your career.

The value of this "Brand" makes The Oak Ridge Boys an asset, an in-demand brand for corporate sponsors and television shows.

And branding is more than just advertising and repetitious impressions. With us it's the magnificent buses and rolling stock, it's posters and trade ads, it's on our BluBlocker Oak Ridge Boys official sunglasses, coffee mugs, coaster, T-shirts, ball caps - posters, letterhead, CD's, DVD's, books, broadcast television shows. It's always projected in our featured interviews and news stories. Our purpose is to create the image—-both in print, and on stage.

Take it home with you. The look, the sound—the positive image! The goal is for everybody to recognize and remember.

Thirty years later the "Oak Ridge Boys" only gets bigger and better. Today, after years of image "Brand" building they are one of the most recognizable groups in the business.

This is a goal for you as a beginning artist and band. Even if you're established, it's never too late to turn your image around. Start reinventing yourself now.

Remember, in the earlier chapters we talk about our goals … with a purpose.

Building our Oak Ridge Boys Brand name has had a purpose. To make the best, most harmonious music is just part of the goal. I know, from my part, and can say with assurance: the one goal of the Oak

Ridge Boys has been to help make people's lives better through their music.

I think this overview, while simplified, speaks to our vast audience.

chapter 12

A DENT IN THE IRON CURTAIN: THE FIRST SOVIET TOUR

I n May 1974, an event took shape that would change my life.

Roy Clark was headlining in Las Vegas, doing one of his two-week engagements at the Frontier Hotel. Late one afternoon, he and I were sitting around in his hotel suite, watching the evening news, when a segment appeared about a group of Soviet dignitaries at the Seattle World's Fair. They were on an official visit to America, and the TV interviewer asked them if there was any place in the US not on their official itinerary that they'd really like to see.

"Yes," immediately answered Alexi Stepunin, the delegates' leader. "We had hoped to visit Las Vegas, but it was not included in our trip."

I think Roy and I both got the idea simultaneously.

"Roy" I said, "let's invite them to Vegas to see your show, as your guests."

Roy was all for it. Both of us, however, figured it would be impossible. The main thing was that it would have to be done on very short notice and there obviously would be a lot of—if you'll excuse the expression—red tape.

Nevertheless, I made the call the next day to our State Department. I'd already talked to the Frontier Hotel, and, seeing the possibilities of some great press, hotel management had agreed to fly the Russians from Seattle to Las Vegas and return them to Los Angeles via Hughes Air West. (This was a regional airline owned by Howard Hughes, who also owned the Frontier Hotel.) Further, the delegation would be housed at the Frontier and would be guests at Roy's dinner show.

To our surprise, the State Department approved. It turned out that the Soviets had an open date in their itinerary, and it was okay with the US officials as long as it didn't cost the government anything extra. I don't think any deal between the US and USSR had ever been struck so fast. Two days later, 18 Soviets—doctors, scientists, economists, farm specialists, and other dignitaries—arrived in Las Vegas, the guests of Roy Clark and the Howard Hughes organization. When we met them at the Vegas airport, a string of Hughes-provided limousines was waiting. Upon the delegation's arrival at the Frontier Hotel, each member was given a bag of $25 worth of quarters to play the slot machines—and they dispersed through the casino like mercury hitting a slick surface.

That's when I began to doubt the wisdom of our invitation. Would we see our Russian friends again? Would they show up for Roy's dinner performance? Would they defect? Our brainstorm and the swiftness with which we carried it out hadn't left much time to consider any possible negative outcomes.

Thankfully, any fears or doubts were alleviated at the opening of Roy's dinner show, when all 18 showed up right on time. We seated them front and center, waiting to see how they'd react to his performance.

Roy always does a great show. I don't know if this show was greater than usual, but his Power of Performance on stage that night could have been felt all the way to Moscow! After he concluded the show with a rousing performance of "Malaguaña" on his Ovation twelve-string guitar, the Soviets, along with everyone else in the sold-out showroom, gave him a standing ovation.

After the show, Roy received all 18 Soviets in his dressing room. The delegation, under the leadership of Mr. Stepunin, presented Roy with many gifts—the best of which was an official invitation for him to present his concert in the Soviet Union!

Although Roy's journey to the Soviet Union was a long way from starting at this point, the story of his initial invitation to the Soviet

Union, their attending his show, and their subsequent return invitation for him to perform in the USSR garnered enormous amounts of international press in those Cold War times. Once again, our Power of Performance was enhanced by plugging in a Star Team member—publicist Kathy Gangwisch. We all worked together to get as much press and PR as this unusual set of circumstances warranted.

Then, after that initial flurry of publicity, the real work began.

Our first step was to deliver our official proposal to State Department officials, who were delighted with the idea. Through the US government's cultural-exchange program, they'd had presented many American shows to Soviet audiences. But even with all of the artists involved in the State Department's program, they'd had few stars the magnitude of Roy Clark to work with—and they'd never presented an American country-music artist in the Soviet Union.

But the whole thing was going to take months of negotiations, beginning with financial ones. The State Department's cultural-exchange program wasn't heavily funded, and the Soviets had only rubles, which couldn't be exchanged for American dollars. Roy agreed to go for no fee, but he insisted that all his musicians and crew be paid. The Oak Ridge Boys were invited to go as well, becoming important impact enhancers for the event.

In addition to working out the financial details, we had to jump a lot of other hurdles to make the tour happen. At one point, the Soviets sent three different delegates to view Roy's show, and then asked that he delete one number from his show before presenting it in Russia. The offending song? It was the main theme to the hit movie Doctor Zhivago, which had been a staple of Roy's concert for years. It offended the Soviets because its Russian emigre author, Boris Pasternak, was persona non grata in the USSR, and Soviet officials wanted no reference to him or his works.

Much of the time between the actual invitation, which came in May 1974, and the tour, which began in January 1976, was spent in negotiating details to the minutest degree. It was also spent in utilizing the upcoming tour as a wonderful vehicle for press and public relations.

From the time it was conceived, the Roy Clark Soviet Union tour represented a milestone—not just for country music, but in the realm of human relations. I have never seen the personification of our Power of Performance philosophy more dramatically demonstrated than during Roy's first performance in the USSR.

In 1976, the Oak Ridge Boys accompanied Roy Clark on his groundbreaking tour of the Soviet Union–18 sold-out shows in 21 days. It was a major breakthrough for us, establishing the Oaks as an internationally known music group, but it also had far wider implications. During those Cold War days, the tension was very high between the USA and the USSR. But Roy and the Oaks made friends for America at every stop–on stage, off stage, at diplomatic events, private parties, and on the streets of cities like Moscow, Leningrad, and Raga.

At that time, the Soviet Union had only one television network, and we were on it. There was no changing channels. If you were watching television and we came on, you saw us. By the time the Oak Ridge Boys and Roy Clark left Moscow, 750 million people knew who they were. That's right, 750 million! That single network beamed us into all 18 Eastern European countries of the Soviet Union Bloc.

It began on January 18, 1976, when we arrived in Moscow. Many hours earlier, we'd had a sendoff from Tulsa International Airport with press and television in attendance, and evangelist Oral Roberts asking God for a blessing of safety, harmony, success, and friendship. Now, we were suddenly facing a Moscow temperature of 25°F below zero and heavy snow. Our path from the plane to the airport was lined on both sides with Soviet soldiers carrying wicked-looking Kalashnikov machine guns, each soldier holding his finger on the trigger! After an 18-hour flight, that was quite a reception.

MIDNIGHT TRAIN TO RIGA

Then we found out there'd been a change in schedule. We weren't starting the tour in Moscow at all, but in Riga, Latvia, 14 hours north of Moscow by train. After an 18-hour flight, we were greeted with the prospect of a 14-hour train ride.

(I should mention here that, at this time, the political relationship between our two countries was at a low ebb. Later, we found out that the Soviets were afraid the US was going to bomb them at any time—which would make anyone a little nervous, I guess.)

Taken to the Moscow train station directly from our flight, we boarded the midnight train to Riga. None of us had ever been this far from home, and in the kind of environment where Americans didn't appear to be particularly welcome. Wearily, Roy and I looked at each other. Had we made a mistake? Although we didn't say it, I'm sure we both thought it: Will we ever see home again?

As we all boarded the train, however, we began to experience a revelation of the human spirit.

There had been enormous publicity in the Soviet press and on Russian television about Roy and his upcoming shows. And the passengers in the crowded train knew who we were. Not long after the train pulled away from the station, one of the Russians broke out a guitar and started playing Hank Williams' old classic, "I'm So Lonesome I Could Cry." Other passengers joined in. Members of our entourage started taking out their instruments. The Oak Ridge Boys began singing some harmonies.

Power of Performance? You bet! Our troupe and the Russians on the train couldn't communicate—except through performance. And it was powerful! For that entire 14 hours, as the train pulled us slowly through the Russian night, music rang out from singing hillbillies—both American and Russian. By the time our train arrived in Riga, I may have been a lot sleepier than I wanted to be, but I was also feeling much better about our reception in the USSR.

THE FIRST CONCERT

Our premier Russian concert, the first of 18 sold-out shows, was set to begin promptly at 8 p.m. the night after our arrival in Riga. Despite a busy day of setting up, rehearsal, and time with the Soviet press, everybody was up for this debut—and, truth to tell, a little apprehensive as well.

The concert began with a cold audience, and the well-below-zero temperature outside had little to do with it. You could feel the attitude rising off the entire opening-night crowd. Okay, Americans, they seemed to be saying, prove to us how good you are. Make us enjoy it.

This was going to be the test. Our first night. Our first concert. And before they even heard the first note, the audience was hostile. Those old misgivings about this whole trip began creeping back in.

What happened next is impossible to describe adequately. As I stood backstage, watching, Roy came out and began the show. Within 30 seconds, he'd changed the entire audience's mood from cold, impassive hostility to warm, loving friendship. A few more minutes into the show, and he was getting the kind of reception and acceptance these

Soviet citizens would've given their country's biggest hero. He was not only entertaining them; he had won them over!

That audience loved Roy Clark, calling him out again and again for encores when his regular concert concluded. He introduced The Oak Ridge Boys in the middle of his show, and they got the same kind of response. It was a magical night for everyone.

In all my years in show business, I have never seen any performance move an audience more than those performances did. And their reception was a portent of things to come, because the same kind of thing happened every night, at every performance, on our Russian tour.

It was, simply, the pure essence of the Power of Performance.

Do you see how it works? Sure, we all understand how a gifted artist can give a powerful performance on stage. But this goes beyond the simple musical or entertainment aspects of a show into an even vaster territory, and it has to do with the obligation of everyone involved to evoke all the individual power that comes with performance.

In this case, it was our mission not just to entertain, but to show people through music and art that we all have a common heritage. All of us can live in peace and harmony together; the first step is to meet on the common ground of performance. Roy and The Oak Ridge Boys had a responsibility not only to themselves to give the best performance they could give, but to our country, the United States of America, to be the best representatives and goodwill ambassadors they possibly could be. Through these kinds of efforts, we all make a contribution toward a better world.

★

During those 21 days, I saw attitudes toward Americans changing. The Oak Ridge Boys and Roy Clark had come to entertain, and they did, but they also made millions of friends for themselves and our fellow Americans back home. Upon our return, the State Department issued us an official thank-you, calling our cultural-exchange program one of the most successful ever. And in the USSR, a front-page review on the cover of the official Soviet newspaper *Pravda*, said in part: "The American guys and girls sang here of their striving for peace, happiness and love. And this is the best confirmation, that people of good will always understand one another."

Пролетарии всех стран, соединяйтесь!

Коммунистическая партия Советского Союза

ПРАВДА

Газета основана
5 мая 1912 года
В. И. ЛЕНИНЫМ   № 34 [21003]   ●   Вторник, 3 февраля 1976 г.   ●   Цена 3 коп.

Орган Центрального Комитета КПСС

О ЧЕМ ПОЕТ БАНДЖО

Лассо, кольты, мустанг под седлом — вот тот «джентльменский» набор, без которого обычно не представляет себе ковбой. И между тем в Америке называют отнюдь не искателей приключений, а сельских жителей, которые занимаются нелегким и не очень романтичным трудом — разведением скота. И многие ковбои, если выберется свободная минутка, предпочитают «укрощать» не непослушных животных, а банджо или гитару.

В этом легко можно убедиться, побывав на музыкальном представлении артистов из США «Рой Кларк кантри шоу». Гастроли этого коллектива проводятся у нас в стране в соответствии с программой культурных обменов между СССР и США. Участники «Кантри шоу» — популярнейший певец и музыкант американской эстрады Рой Кларк, его партнер Бак Трент, вокально-инструментальный ансамбль «Оук Ридж бойз» и ансамбль «Шуга» — исполняют песни американских фермеров и ковбоев.

Сочинения этого жанра, получившего название «кантри» (на русский язык это можно перевести как сельская, деревенская музыка), сейчас пользуются большим успехом в США. Нет ничего удивительного в том, что в наше время — время политических и экономических кризисов в странах капитала, рождающих общественное беспокойство, неуверенность в завтрашнем дне, — американцы с удовольствием слушают песни о любви, о радости труда, мирной жизни: ведь эти вечные понятия близки и дороги всем.

«Посади зернышко, — поется в одном из таких произведений, — ухаживай за ним, и у тебя вырастет прекрасный цветок. Если бы каждый посадил зернышко любви, освещаемое солнцем, — мир в человечестве стали бы еще более прекрасным». Вот так неприхотливо, но искренне выражается в пес-

не стремление к миру, честному труду многих и многих рядовых американцев.

Артисты «Рой Кларк кантри шоу» выгодно отличаются от «звезд» вульгарной коммерческой западной эстрады и репертуаром, и манерой исполнения. Они представляют особое, независимое направление общедоступной, популярной музыки — «кантри мьюзик», — опирающееся на национальные традиции вековой давности. Не случайно некоторые из них не имеют специального музыкального образования, пришли на эстра-

ду исключительно из любви к пению, музицированию на гитаре, рояле, банджо. Аудитория «кантри» — не избранная публика фешенебельных концертных залов Нью-Йорка и Бостона, а сельские труженики, рабочие южной «глубинки» Америки, иногда даже просто уличные прохожие. Из этого направления, кстати, возникли в 60-е годы знаменитые песни протеста, осуждавшие насилие, войны в США, социальную несправедливость.

Собственно, «кантри мьюзик» проповедует общегуманистиче-

ские идеалы — о добре и зле, о том, что нужно сделать, чтобы это было во имя жизни на мирной земле.

Один из своих номеров ансамбль «Оук Ридж бойз» исполняет так: первая часть песни была распространена 20 лет тому назад, вторая — в современном ритме. Изменился стиль исполнения, пришла новая мода на одежду и длину волос, но прежними остались слова, которые поют влюбленные, но не прошло восхищение человека перед красотой природы и полнотой жизни. Кровная связь с музыкальным творчеством народа — тружеников юга Америки, богатые традиции вокально-инструментального типа музицирования, существующие в этой стране, обусловливают непринужденность, несомненно высокую культуру исполнения артистов «Кантри шоу».

«Гвоздь» программы — выступление Роя Кларка. В звуках его банджо присутствует, кажется, самый дух талантливого и трудолюбивого американского народа с его динамизмом, любовью к озорной шутке, которая помогает переносить все жизненные невзгоды, схрашивает самый изнурительный труд. Недаром Кларк, начав свою карьеру с выступлений в маленьких клубах, сегодня является ведущим в США исполнителем и комментатором «кантри мьюзик», дающим около 300 концертов в год, участником и ведущим самых популярных телевизионных передач.

Рой Кларк — блестящий инструменталист. Его игру на банджо, гитаре и скрипке отличают великолепная техника, художественный вкус, чувство формы. Не принужденно, артистично ведет он номер с Баком Трентом «Дуэль банджо», а пьеса для гитары действительно звучит в его исполнении как соната-произведение, написанное для оркестра.

Завершает программу «Рой Кларк кантри шоу» пламенный «Малягенья», виртуозно исполняемая Кларком на гитаре. Эта народная мелодия как бы еще раз напоминает: если с эстрады звучат, хотя и в современной обработке, песни и танцы тех, кто живет трудом и мечтает о счастье, они обязательно найдут отклик в сердцах слушателей.

Сами участники «Кантри шоу», как они сказали корреспонденту «Правды», в восторге от того приема, который оказывают им советские зрители. Да, еще десятилетие назад это трудно было бы представить: сельские, почти самодеятельные артисты из тех районов США, которые у нас принято называть «медвежьей глубинкой», выступают в советской столице, легко налаживая непринужденный контакт с публикой. Зал принимает шутки гостей. Как говорится, «на лету — этому не мешают даже особенности южного диалекта, на котором говорят и поют артисты-из-за океана.

В одном из песен, исполняемой ансамблем, рассказывается о поезде, который везет из Флориды на север фрукты, падающие и еще всякую всячину, какой богата щедрая земля этого штата. Образно выражаясь, можно сказать, что сегодня этот поезд делает остановки в Москве, Ленинграде, Риге. Американские парни и девушки поют здесь о мире, счастье и любви, и это — лучшее подтверждение тому, что люди доброй воли всегда поймут друг друга.

Н. АГИШЕВА

◇

На снимке: руководитель ансамбля, певец и музыкант Рой К---рк.

Фото А. Ляпина.

Pravda review translation on following page

Pravda Reviews Mr. Clark

The members of the "Country Show" include the most popular singer and musician of the American show business, Roy Clark, his partner Buck Trent, the vocal-instrumental ensemble "Oak Ridge Boys" and the ensemble "Shugah." They perform songs of the American farmers and cowboys.

The compositions of this genre, which has been named "country" (in Russian it could be translated as rural or village music), are now enjoying great success in the United States. There is nothing surprising in the fact that in our time—a time of political and economic crisis in the capitalist countries, giving birth to public uneasiness, lack of confidence in the future—the Americans listen with pleasure to songs about love, about the joy of work, a peaceful life; these are the eternal concepts that are near and dear to everyone.

"Plant a seed," goes one of such compositions, "look after it, and you'll have a beautiful flower grown. If everyone would plant a seed of love, lit by the sun—then the world and mankind would become even more beautiful." Thus unpretentiously but sincerely the song expresses a striving for peace and honest work by lots and lots of ordinary Americans.

The artists of the Roy Clark Country Show advantageously differ from the "idols" of vulgar commercial western entertainment, both in repertoire and manner of performance. They represent a special independent trend of easily accessible, popular music—"country music"—which relies on the centuries-old national traditions. It is not accidental that some of them don't have special musical education and come to the stage exclusively out of love for singing and making music on the guitar, piano and banjo. The "country audience" is not a select public of fashionable concert halls of New York and Boston, but rural toilers and workers of the southern "depths" of America and sometimes even simply passersby. From this trend, by the way, there arose in the 60's the famous songs of protest which denounced violence, wars and social injustice. Actually, "country music" preaches broad humanistic ideals—about good and evil, and what should be done so that all people on earth would live under a peaceful sky.

One of the numbers of the Oak Ridge Boys group goes as follows: the first part of the song is sung in the manner which was widespread 20 years ago, and the second in contemporary rhythm. The style of the performance has changed, a new fashion for the clothing and length of hair has arrived, but the words remained as previously, which they say to a sweetheart, and the admiration of a man for the beauty of nature and fullness of life has not passed. The close connection with the musical creations of the people of the American south, the rich traditions of the vocal-instrumental type of music-making which exist in that country, precondition a natural easiness and an indisputable culture of performance of the artists of the country show.

The highlight of the program is the performance of Roy Clark. In the sounds of his banjo is present, it seems, the very spirit of the talented and industrious American people with their dynamism and love for a mischevous joke, which helps to bear all the troubles of life and softens the most exhausting labor. It is not for nothing that Clark, having started his career with performing at small clubs, is today the United States' leading performer and comedian of "country music," giving nearly 300 concerts a year, a participant and leading figure of the most popular television broadcasts.

The program of the Roy Clark Country Show winds up with the fiery "Malaguena" which Clark performs on the guitar like a virtuoso. This folk melody seems to remind once more: if from the stage their sound, even in a contemporary style, the songs and dances of those who live by their labor and dream of happiness, they will inevitably find a response in the hearts of the listeners.

The participants themselves of the Country Show, as they told the Pravda correspondent, are delighted by the reception which is shown them by the Soviet spectators. Yes, even a decade ago, it would have been difficult to imagine: rural, almost amateur artists from those areas of the United States which we habitually call "bear's corners" are performing in the Soviet capital, easily establishing natural contact with the public. The hall accepts the jokes of the guests, as they say, "in mid-air," and this is not inhibited even by the peculiarities of the southern dialect in which the artists from across the ocean speak and sing.

In one of the songs, sung by the ensemble, they tell about a train, which carries from Florida to the north fruit, turkeys and various things, in which the fertile land of this state is rich. Figuratively speaking, one could say that today this train makes stops at Moscow, Leningrad and Riga. The American guys and girls sings here of their striving for peace, happiness and love. And this is the best confirmation that people of good will always understand one another.

N. AGISHEVA

The New York Times

© 1976 The New York Times Company

— NEW YORK, TUESDAY, FEBRUARY 3, 1976 —

25 cents beyond 50-mile zone from New York City, except Long Island. Higher in air delivery cities.

U. S. Country Music Wins Following in Soviet Cities

By CHRISTOPHER S. WREN
Special to The New York Times

MOSCOW, Feb. 2.—On the advice of a Soviet official, the country music star Roy Clark dropped the "Doctor Zhivago" film theme from his guitar medley. And to avoid pricking Moscow's official atheism, the Oak Ridge Boys put aside their customary opener, "Nobody Wants to Play, Rhythm Guitar Behind Jesus."

The omissions were never noticed in the dazzling profusion of five-string banjo licks that the Roy Clark Country Music Show brought to three Soviet cities in the first American cultural exchange to visit the Soviet Union this year.

American country music, with its simple celebrations of love, work and hard times, bears a distinct resemblance to some aspects of Russian folk music. But because of the heavy reliance on lyrics, it faces a formidable language

and cultural obstacle in a country like the Soviet Union.

Barrier Surmounted

It says something for Mr. Clark's versatility that during this tour, which wound up its final show in Moscow today, he surmounted the barrier by emphasizing his mastery of the music instruments of country music — banjo, guitar and fiddle. He was complemented in his brisk picking also by an accomplished sideman Buck Trent, banjoist.

The Oak Ridge Boys, a Nashville gospel group that has emerged into the broader realm of country-non-plused by the country music approach, but became caught up in tunes like the now classic "Dueling Banjos," played with formidable speed by Mr. Clark and Mr. Trent. Mr. Clark changed one show last week, with a flamenco rendition of "Malaguena" on his 12-string guitar.

The Oak Ridge Boys, a

of the 6,000-seat Sports Palace.

An affable performer likes to banter with his listeners between songs, Mr. Clark found himself at first facing a stone-faced audience in Riga who could not understand his quips. The problem was remedied by adding a quick-witted Leningrad graduate student, Aleksandr Puchkin, who not only put across the humor in his onstage translations but also sharpened some of the punch lines for the Russian-language listeners.

The audiences, used to more formality in their own performers, seemed initially non-plused by the casual country music approach, but became caught up in tunes like the now classic "Dueling Banjos," played with formidable speed by Mr. Clark and profusion. After the end of Mr. Clark changed one show last week, with a flamenco rendition of "Malaguena" on his 12-string guitar.

The Oak Ridge Boys, a

and musicians, steered away from what the group's leader, Duane Allen, called the "heavy Jesus" numbers, but still glided over the boundaries of gospel and rock. After at least one show, they all but rattled the mirrors of one Leningrad restaurant with impromptu revival songs like "Gonna Have a Little Talk With Jesus."

The reception the show got indicated that there is an audience for more country musicians, if they are as adaptable as Mr. Clark and have an interpreter like Mr. Puchkin on tap. The sheer Americana of country performers appears to fascinate Russians more than have some classical musicians or ballet dancers, which the Soviet Union already has in abundance.

After the end of one show last week, a young Leningrad man in Leningrad ran up to the departing bus and asked anxiously, "And when can we expect the next American stage built directly on the ice personable octet of singers group'".

Monday, February 2, 1976   THE CHRISTIAN SCIENCE MONITOR

Country music in U.S.S.R.

Soviet listeners cheer Roy Clark group

By Elizabeth Pond
Staff correspondent of
The Christian Science Monitor

Moscow

The first-night protocol audience was not exactly stomping in the aisles. But by the end of the Roy Clark country music show the listeners were applauding rhymthically and shouting bravo. And if the ticketless youths outside the theater offering 40 rubles (almost $60) a seat had been able to get in, there might have been a real hootenanny.

As it was, the rambunctious Roy Clark and the Oak Ridge Boys wowed Moscow, as they had wowed Riga and Leningrad earlier. They were on a two-week tour of the Soviet Union on the cultural exchange program.

The Oak Ridge Boys pranced onto the Moscow stage: the tenor in an Afro and embroidered orange bell bottoms, the lead singer with a beard and a green bell-bottom suit, the baritone in blow-dried hair and beige, the bass in a five-o'clock shadow and red. "Plant a Seed and Watch It Grow" came first, followed by a medley including "Love Will Keep Us Together."

The cherub-faced, piano player in cowboy hat and sequined black duds put on a virtuoso show, now pounding the keyboard with his fists, now jumping to his feet without missing a beat, now resembling a hunt-and-peck typist.

As if all this exotica were not enough, there was the long-haired sound man in jeans roaming about the auditorium to check decibels and blends. He cajoled his way past suspicious ushers by displaying a hand-lettered card saying in Russian, "Let him go everywhere: sound operator." And there was cornball humor: "This is a violin. I would like to do a piece that was originally for the piano, but it's difficult to get a piano under my chin."

Any Soviet combo that affected this styl would be expelled from the Komsomol, th Communist youth league, forthwith. But th Roy Clark group was acceptable because i was here too short a time to set off . dangerous fad — and because, as the bouffant coiffed Russian announcer in black evenin gown soberly explained, this is "a democrati popular genre."

By the time they did "Rockey Top, Ten nessee," the audience was beginning to shou its approval.

The group did not alter its program much t make the Soviet tour. Out of deference t Soviet atheistic sensibilities, it omitte straight gospel singing after a Soviet preview of the lyrics. But the Russians did not ask tha any rock, loud guitar, or other musical style be changed.

Besides giving sold-out performances in th three Soviet cities, the Roy Clark group me topflight Soviet musicians in friendship club in each place. There were no joint jan sessions, but each side played and sang for th other, and Roy Clark himself will return to th United States with a gift of a balalaika, and balalaika instruction book in Russian — fron the top Soviet player.

The Americans have found a surprising number of country music fans in the Sovie Union. Presumably most of them develo their taste from Voice of America broadcasts.

Not realizing the strong barriers put up by theater ushers, the American musicians were surprised at first at how few people cam backstage after a concert. But they were touched a number of times by the eagerness and appreciation of the listeners who did ge to them, often after recognizing them outside their hotel.

It made us feel good to present our culture, our American songs and music, to millions of Russians who'd never been exposed to this kind of down-home, family-oriented performance. It was funny. The Russian censors had restrictions on anything religious–among other things, they asked The Oak Ridge Boys to change "Canaanland" to "Disneyland" in the song "Where the Soul Never Dies." But the Oaks and Roy closed every concert with the rousing spiritual "Have A Little Talk With Jesus," and no official ever said a word.

At the time of the Soviet tour, we'd been working for a year and a half, presenting new, mainstream-oriented songs designed to help the Oaks break down the barriers to other markets. They opened for Roy Clark, Mel Tillis, Jimmy Dean and many others. They successfully played Las Vegas and other major events, But were still struggling to break through.

Before leaving for the Russian tour with Roy, the Oaks had completed two weeks at the Frontier Hotel in Vegas as his opening act. Well, they weren't exactly billed as an opening act, although they did open the shows. You see, one of my policies was that the main artists I represented would always receive 100 percent billing. That meant that their names on a marquee would not be any smaller than the names of the other act or acts. Regardless of which performer was opening, the lettering of their names would be the same size. This made everyone look equal in status. Roy, Jimmy, Mel, and the other acts the Oaks opened for didn't have a problem with this, and we were thankful to them. As a result, when selling the Oaks to other buyers, we could say that the Oaks were co-headlining with Roy or Mel or Jimmy. That 100 percent billing we got for those jobs was even more important than the money we earned.

This is the way an act is built–one step at a time, one date at a time, one tour at a time. After the 1976 Soviet tour, things seemed to magically happen for the Oak Ridge Boys. The Frontier show they'd done with Roy had been taped for a national television special, and it began playing nationally after our return, which generated more press for us. The cumulative impact of media exposure grew with each interview and appearance. Although the Oaks were still in a fragile financial position, they had reached an obvious turning point. They were now international stars. The momentum had begun, and it was up to the team to keep it rolling.

There are a lot of these breakthrough turning points in any artist's career. Usually, you can count them on your fingers. I felt that the Soviet tour in January of '76 was a big one for the Oaks. The sacrifices we made and the solidarity we showed during those 21 days bonded us together in a unique brotherhood, gave us a deep spiritual connection. We became one, spiritually and emotionally, and our goals have been common ones since then.

These are feelings that can't be put on paper. But they exist. They are felt not only by the five of us, but by everyone connected to our lives for the past 35-plus years.

POSITIVE REVIEWS

By the time the tour concluded three weeks later, at the Rossiya Theatre in Moscow, it was a tremendous success by any standards. Journalist A. Agisheva, writing in the national paper *Pravda*, gave the concert a glowing report. He concluded his front-page review with this statement: "In one of the songs ["Orange Blossom Special"] sung by the ensemble, they tell about a train, which carries from Florida to the North fruit, turkeys and various things, in which the fertile land of this state is rich. Figuratively speaking, one could say that today this train makes stops in Moscow, Leningrad and Riga. The American guys and girls sang here of their striving for peace, happiness and love. And this is the best confirmation, that people of good will always understand one another."

This Roy Clark-Oak Ridge Boys tour opened lots of doors, culturally as well as diplomatically. And it doesn't just make a good story; it also provides an example of how, when all elements are working together, you can achieve success in anything.

The elements involved in this Soviet tour were legion. Roy Clark and The Oak Ridge Boys, of course, were the talent. Then there was The Jim Halsey Company as booking agent and management, and Kathy Gangwisch for press and public relations. (Kathy came up with the idea of having all the performers' bios and other press material translated into the Soviet language before we left America, which made everyone's job easier.)

In addition, the team included our music-business attorneys Bill Coben and Dan Sklar to review the contracts; ABC-Dot Records head Jim Foglesong, for whose label Roy Clark and The Oak Ridge Boys recorded; and the musicians, road crew, and sound and lights people. That was the Star Team, and it worked with lots of other elements:

the US State Department—which could be seen as the promoter—the American Embassy, the Voice of America radio network, the Howard Hughes organizations (including the Frontier Hotel and Hughes Air West), the Soviet Embassy, the Soviet Ministry of Culture, Gostel Radio, Gosconcert, Intourist, Alexi Stepunin, and the thousands of newspapers, radio and television stations, and magazines that carried stories about this tour before, during, and after the trip. In addition, the makers of Clark candy bars (no relation to Roy) gave us plenty of their product to pass out along the way, as did the Wrigley company, providing packets of Juicy Fruit gum. Everyone worked in harmony, using his or her individual talents and skills to enable the Soviet tour to become a history-making event—not just for country music, but for American music!

See how the Power of Performance philosophy works? We didn't just go to Moscow for a concert; we created an event that the whole world knew about. When everyone's performance works together, it produces a spectrum of power. When all team members work together, the power takes on a life of its own. It's a power that should be used only in the most wholesome and positive of ways. And when it is, it produces results greater than anything imagined or planned.

It worked for the Soviet Tour event. From conception to implementation, it took 18 months to get it done, but it was worth all the effort and planning. Its success lifted the Iron Curtain, helping other American artists to enter eastern Europe and make their own contributions to harmony and peace in the world.

chapter 13

THE ARTIST MANAGER

T alent—whether singer, singer-songwriter, or band—is the essential component, the hub of the music-business wheel. But, you remember, that hub must have spokes radiating from it, spokes that work together to support the center and form the wheel that moves everything forward.

Each of these spokes is a member of the Star Team. And the first spoke, the first team member to join up with the talent, is usually responsible for putting the rest of the group together—for making sure all the spokes are in the wheel, and in the right places. Like a well-built wagon wheel, a good Star Team can be counted on to hold up in any situation. Assembled and functioning correctly, a team shows that there is strength in cooperation and power in unity. Every member of a Star Team has an opportunity—and a responsibility—to tap into his or her individual Power of Performance.

Sometimes, the artist signs a recording contract very early in his career, making the record company his first team member. Other times, a booking agent is the first to "discover" an act. More often than not, however, it's the artist manager who becomes the first member of a budding performer's Star Team, the first spoke in the wheel.

The manager is the one who catches the artist's dreams. It is his business to e-x-p-a-n-d on the artist's vision and help discover, access, and perfect the artist's Power of Performance. Perhaps most important, the artist manager develops a plan! It's true that everything starts with a dream—but nothing will happen without a plan.

Why then, is a manager important?
- The manager gets the team in motion.
- The manager plans the career.
- The manager chooses the projects.
- The manager helps build the organization.
- The manager provides motivation.

During my first few years as a promoter of concerts and shows, I gradually became more interested in becoming an artist manager. There were a couple of reasons for this. First, I wanted to be able to focus my creative talents on one artist. Second, I wanted to help develop and build a career for that artist and reap the long-term rewards that would come with managing a successful performer.

Artist management is one of the most delicate areas of the entertainment business. By nature, musical artists are sensitive people—it's this sensitivity that helps them create their art. One of the reasons they're great artists is that they feel things deeply. Working as an artist manager, you have to be sensitive to their emotional sides. I think it all boils down to respect, which I talk about throughout this book. If you can respect someone's art and respect the artist as a person, then you can deal with him or her on sensitive issues in a comfortable and friendly manner.

When you look at the big stars appearing on television, hear their records on the radio, read of their gold and platinum record sales and big-figure incomes, you probably wonder how they got where they are. It's really no secret. Most of them started the same way, with talent and desire. Then they found someone who would help them formulate a plan to reach their goals, someone who believed in them, someone who helped them develop their Power of Performance. They found, in other words, a good manager.

What do you need to be an artist manager? You need good ears. You need good eyes. You need intuition, and you need the instinct it takes to discover artists with the special quality that puts them above the pack. You need to be able to set goals and develop a plan to achieve them. You need to be a salesperson, marketing expert, business planner, dreamer, psychiatrist, and good friend all wrapped into one. And you need even more. You need to learn the true meaning of two important words: respect and heart.

Respect is essential in dealing with any creative person. If you don't have real respect for artists and their art, you're not going to be effective in dealing with them. If you don't give respect, you won't get it. If you want respect from both artists and the music industry, you must respect them and it.

You also need to have heart, something that's very important when dealing with sensitive, creative people. Artists, after all, are about heart, and you must understand that if you want to be a good manager. A lot of people can make decisions based on cold, hard facts, but when you are dealing with talent and creativity, you must deal with the aspect of heart. While the best interests of your artist's career are always essential elements in effective management, being sensitive to the needs of the artist's heart should come first. Plus, on a personal level, having heart is going to make your life a lot better, more interesting, more fulfilling, and much more worthwhile

Talent is only one element—albeit an essential one—in creating a star. It must be complemented by many other elements, many of which are the responsibility of the manager. The manager, working with the artist, must set goals with a purpose and determine how those goals can be achieved. The manager must put together the rest of the spokes in the wheel to create the Star Team that will work toward those goals together.

Of course, it helps to be in the right place at the right time and to have a little bit of luck and timing. But knowing how to orchestrate plans and goals will help create the timing and the luck.

Let's get down to nuts and bolts. As an artist manager, just what can you do to create a star?

Again, we start with the essential element: the artist, the hub of the wheel, around whom all the team members revolve. Where can the artist manager find an artist, and where can an artist find the artist manager?

Everywhere!

There are fine singers, songwriters, musicians, and bands all over the world. The key is finding someone special, using good eyes and good ears to discover an act with something different, something unique. Then, the real work begins.

How do you find this special performer, the one you want to spend time and energy with? As a manager myself, as well as an agent, I've found acts by listening to demos and going to showcases, among other things. I've even had artists I'm already managing help me discover another act. That's what happened with my first-ever management client, the great Hank Thompson.

We were doing a live television show with Hank every Saturday afternoon on Oklahoma City's WKY-TV. From time to time, Hank would feature a young singer from the area, a high school senior named Wanda Jackson. Wanda couldn't wait to get into the music business full-time and, after she graduated, Hank helped to get her first recording contract with Decca Records. It wasn't long before her first hit single, "You Can't Have My Love," a duet with Billy Gray, was burning up the charts.

At that time, I was finishing up a two-year hitch in the Army. Luckily, I'd been able to maintain my management agreement and booking arrangement with Hank, and following my discharge, I met with Wanda and made a deal to become her representative. Now I had two important artists under exclusive representation: Hank Thompson and Wanda Jackson.

Because of her Decca Records action, Wanda was able to get a deal with Capitol Records—Hank's label—and their becoming labelmates was an important step for both of them, as well as for me.

Wanda had all of the requirements for stardom. She had an original vocal style—one that you only had to hear once to remember. She developed a good show. She was an excellent performer with a good show and a wonderful rapport with the audience. Plus, she was a good songwriter, contributing to many of her hit records. She had the desire. She had the dedication. She was unique.

She had the Power of Performance.

Wanda went on to score many country and rockabilly hits, becoming a successful star in a very short time. Because of pop-crossover songs like "Right or Wrong" and "In the Middle of a Heartache," she was able to play many venues not normally available to country artists. In demand as co-headliner for many artists of the day, she also opened several shows for Elvis! Dick Clark used her many times on his American Bandstand, the long-lived music-and-dance TV show that influenced teenagers and pop music for decades.

I tell Wanda's story to illustrate how, from the very beginning of my career, I understood the magic of the Power of Performance. I found out quickly how connecting and networking make things happen, and how being in the right place at the right time can give a career a needed boost.

The lessons here for you? When you plan with a purpose, set your goals, and follow your dreams, success will come.

Hank Thompson introduced Wanda to the world, and after Wanda made it, she helped usher in another new star, one who would become one of my biggest stars and dearest friends.

I had just completed a contract for Wanda to appear at the Golden Nugget in Las Vegas. It was a long-term arrangement calling for her to play through the year of 1960. Before that string of dates started, Wanda informed me she was hiring a guitar player she'd found working in a Washington, D.C., nightclub. Envisioning him as the front man for her band, Wanda described him as a multi-talented musician, singer, and showman.

When I saw him play his first concert with her, I saw that she'd been conservative in her description. He turned out to be all she'd said he was—and a whole lot more. To this day, I have not seen a greater talent.

His name? Roy Clark.

Even in 1959, fronting someone else's band, Roy had "superstardom" written all over his performance. He connected with an audience like nobody I had ever seen. I immediately recognized in Roy his magical ability to entertain anybody, anywhere, and after that show we began a relationship that has lasted for 50 years. There was no doubt then, and there is no doubt now, that Roy Clark has that "something special," a uniqueness that sets him apart from every other performer. Wherever he appears, from the finest Las Vegas casino showrooms to huge international music festivals, Roy Clark is a talent the world recognizes and enjoys as a superstar.

In the beginning, we recognized each other as having the two main ingredients of the Star Team. He had the unique talent, and I had the skills to be his manager, as well as his agent—his impresario. We soon established a friendship and rapport.

Early in an artist's career, it's important to get them onto a stage where they can be seen and heard by people who can do them some good. In the first year of my association with Roy, Wanda Jackson provided that stage. I would bring in various concert promoters and buyers to see her perform, and of course they would also have the chance to see her front man, Roy Clark.

Wanda's popularity opened a lot of doors for Roy. Her producer at Capitol Records, Ken Nelson, was the first major record-company executive to see Roy perform, and Roy piqued his interest. Eventually, Nelson and Capitol Records decided to give Roy a shot at his own recordings. We were now beginning to get the key players in place. First, as always, it was the artist. Then the manager-agent. And now a very important player, the record company.

As Wanda and her band traveled the country, Roy Clark's performances were connecting with the various critics, reviewers, and promoters for whom we were playing. They liked him! We made sure they would notice Roy, writing personal letters to everyone we could think of at each tour stop about this fantastic singer, comedian, and guitar player with Wanda's band, advising them to take notice. Roy was becoming known within the industry, and the public was enjoying him, too. He was not just hot with one segment, but with both!

It's a great situation to be hot within the industry and hot with the public at the same time, because that's something that usually doesn't happen. Most of the time, an artist gets hot within the industry before he or she becomes popular with the fans. If you read the trades, you'll see articles predicting that an artist is "going to happen." An artist manager should keep an eye on those acts. Many times they don't have management, or the relationship with their current management is almost over. Find the opportunity; use your *Power of Performance* to make it happen.

And once you find them, remember the two most important things you can do for new acts: get them exposure, and be in the right place at the right time. Help your artist connect with both the fans and the industry. As a manager, I realized I must get exposure for my artists in many ways, including television, radio, personal appearances, press and promotion, and of course, records. Hopefully, hit records!

Some artists and managers come together with a rare chemistry that makes success inevitable. Roy and I had that chemistry, but we had a lot of work to do, too. With a common purpose, we established our goals early in our relationship. We determined our plan and we set to work exercising our *Power of Performance*—his on stage, mine in developing his career. Part of our plan was building a good team, which was my job as manager. We did, and the rest is history!

Roy and I would spend the next 32 years together blazing new trails, setting new records, and achieving what might have seemed impossible to a lot of people. We made 1+1=100! That's the kind of payoff you can get when you fully access your *Power of Performance.*

DISCOVERY

An artist like Roy Clark doesn't come along every day, of course. A manager is lucky to get one superstar like that in a lifetime. But all successful acts are, to a greater or lesser extent, unique, and finding this uniqueness in an unknown performer is an important part of the artist manager's job. Listen for a particular tonal quality, an unusual style or phrasing, a curious glitch in the voice. You want someone so distinctive and unique that people will be able to recognize the voice after only a few records come out. You want people to turn on the radio, hear a few bars of a song, and know it's your artist.

Being a good, unique singer is a fine start. In today's marketplace, however, you also need someone who creates his or her own material. Look for this whole package of talent by listening to demo tapes, watching acts perform before an audience, and imagining how an artist will look on television. In a live situation, observe the audience's reactions and listen for comments.

Suppose you, as artist manager, find the artist you believe in. What comes next?

First of all, you should find out where the artist really wants to go, his or her dreams, his or her desires. Then, you should set your goals together. Is it television, records, personal appearances, performing at top venues? A combination of all of these things? Whatever the objective, plan how to get there. As manager, it's your job to get the artist seen and heard by the other members of the industry, including music publishers, record company executives, talent buyers, and other leaders. As manager, you can start putting the Star Team together by providing showcases and inviting industry representatives, some of whom will have influence with established artists. If these representatives like your act, they can help get him or her on the front half of shows, exposing your performer to a wider audience. (This usually happens after you've gotten a record deal.)

Artist manager: do you understand the job description?

A manager is a person who manages and guides the careers of artists by generating creative suggestions and discussions aimed toward proper career-building. Don't get this confused with the job of the booking agent. A booking agent books dates and events, arranges tours, television shows, and generally creates cash flow. We'll talk about the booking agent in Chapter 17; he's not quite ready to be plugged into our scenario.

I bring up the booking agent because there's a lot of confusion regarding the jobs of manager and agent. Maybe it's because the same person sometimes has to do both jobs, as I did with Hank Thompson early in my career. After starting in the business as a promoter, I became a combined manager-agent because someone had to do the whole job; in country music at that time, the big agencies were not equipped to handle booking for country music artists. They didn't know about country music, and they weren't really all that interested in it.

As a manager, remember that many times artists aren't really sure what they want. They know that they want to have hit records, or that they want to be stars. You must design and set in motion the plans to achieve their goals, and to make their dreams more focused. It is up to you to develop their careers.

How do you start? First, put in writing where you and the artist want to go. Lay out your plan in increments of 12, 24, and 36 months. Develop the plan and write it down in detail. I have written a plan for every artist with whom I have ever been involved. Even if the act has already achieved superstardom, you can still develop him or her in a multitude of other areas and expand the career to be bigger, better, and even more rewarding.

Another of the manager's jobs is to make certain that the artist's creative needs are fulfilled. Creativity is an important part of any artist's being; sometimes it's more important than financial needs.

For example, there's the show that Merle Haggard and the Strangers put on at the Cain's Ballroom in 1984. Larry Shaeffer, the Tulsa entrepreneur and impresario, had Hank Williams Jr. on a nationwide tour at the time, and Merle was on that tour. According to Larry, they were having coffee after one of the shows, and he happened to mention that he owned Tulsa's Cain's Ballroom, the venue that launched Bob Wills and the Texas Playboys. Merle Haggard just got all beside himself with admiration for Bob Wills, and he ended up telling Larry, "I want to go back there and play one of those noontime shows like Bob used to play every day, live over KVOO radio. I want to come in and do the whole thing."

We were Merle's agents at the time, and we arranged things with Larry at the Cain's. I even called Mr. O.W. Mayo, who'd been Bob's financial manager and announcer, and asked him to come down and do the announcing. He did, KVOO radio broadcast it, and Merle and his band did an entire program of Bob Wills songs, playing to a packed house.

It was exciting for me, because it took me back to my roots. Growing up in Independence, I listened religiously to Bob Wills over KVOO every day, with Leon McAuliffe playing steel guitar. And it was exciting for Merle Haggard. I'm sure Larry had expenses and Merle had expenses, but that was a free deal. They didn't charge any admission. To compensate financially, we had Merle booked somewhere else that night. But this show was a labor of love for him. He wanted to do it. For that period of time, he was Bob Wills. And that was more important to him than drawing a big check.

★

A good manager must be able to tie the Star Team together and then creatively work with each member. For example, let's assume that you are down the line a bit, and you've already gotten your artist a record deal. The next thing you're talking about is touring, so you hook up with the booking agent. The booking agent creates the cash flow, the revenue, but the career direction is given by the manager, working in conjunction with the artist. Usually, in a situation like this, the manager, the booking agent, a record-company executive, and the artist all meet to coordinate plans and determine direction.

If you have a major artist, it's pointless to tour if there isn't any record product in the marketplace, since touring helps sell records. Sometimes, of course, you have to tour an act just to keep the cash coming in. Once an artist is big enough, you can usually maintain cash flow with a once-a-year tour—timed to coincide with the release of a new disc. That's when the record company wants your act out in the marketplace.

As the manager of a recording act, you must determine three things:

Why to tour.

When to tour.

Where to tour.

First of all, why? Is it for cash flow, record promotion, or just to maintain your presence in the marketplace? Answering that question will help provide the when and where.

For example, let's say that you as manager, along with the record company and the booking agent, decide to put an artist on tour. The company has just put out new product by that artist. So working together, you find a specific territory where the record is hot. Concentrate on booking your act there, excite the interest of prospective buyers with things like well-timed new media promotions, promotional flyers, and telephone calls, and a successful series of dates is all but assured.

Although a tour is really the booking agent's responsibility, it's your job as manager to feed information to the agent so he'll know what to do and when to do it.

WEBSITE

You, with creative planning, must develop the advertising campaign, email and direct-mail promotion, e-marketing, a good website and other new media marketing plans for your artist. It's important to develop an attractive and professional website for your artist. This can be linked to other associates such as record company, corporate sponsor, booking agent, press and PR firm, and other interested parties. Many times, however, this marketing campaign will be worked in conjunction with the booking agent who's planning to take the artist on tour and the record company that's planning a release. All of these entities should work hand in hand, guided by an overall plan, enhancing the artist's Power of Performance. In fact, when they perform in tandem with one another, I call them power enhancers, individual components that make the whole effort more meaningful and important than it would be if they didn't contribute.

Are you getting the point? It's a simple one. Combined energies create Power of Performance, and an artist manager must be able to coordinate efforts among many entities, including the record company, the press, public relations, and the booking agency. It is all about marketing.

Basically, a really good manager designs a plan, makes the connections, and markets an act. The energy put into marketing ties into an artist's whole career, not just one specific area. It's far more complex and important than just getting your act booked. Working with the rest of the Star Team, a manager can choreograph the Power of Performance as beautifully as a fine ballet.

★

Opportunities come every day. One of the keys to success is learning to recognize opportunities when you see them—even when they come in the form of people. Every achievement in life relies on your ability to learn from people, and putting a Star Team together is partially about learning to deal with others. As you become more sophisticated through learning to recognize opportunities and achieving your goals, you'll expand your relationships and your team.

Start today to develop the ability to recognize opportunities as they are presented to you. They come no matter what walk of life you're in. If you're an artist manger, you'll have many business-related opportunities, as well as opportunities with your artists and others.

Everyone has dreams and visions. Maybe as a child you even lived in a dream world part of the time. You know that there is nothing you cannot achieve in your dreams and visions. Don't question those dreams and visions. Test them. I know that if you stop believing in and following your dreams, they'll stop coming. Dreams are especially important in a creative business like ours; in fact, dreams are what show business is all about. So pay attention to them.

It is the artist manager who helps bring dreams into reality, using the elements of sales and marketing. Success comes when you put everything together, utilizing not only your own Power of Performance, but that of the other Star Team members. Are you beginning to see how it works?

We're talking about being an artist manager, but this teamwork principle also applies to the artist and all the other members of the Star Team. And it applies throughout an act's career. Even when he's got a big-name artist, the manager has to continue to stay on top of the career, making plans and projections and setting new goals. This is all part of it. One of the most important things in dealing with an artist is the need to constantly make things happen. If an artist has been around for a long time and is still successful, his or her career surely has been nurtured well, and there's usually been a good artist manager there in the background, still exercising a collective Power of Performance.

Keep this in mind: The artist manager has to make an artist happen. And to do that takes total dedication.

Whether an artist is just getting started in the business, or whether he or she has been around a long time, the manager's total commitment is required. A total focus on the artist and the art he or she produces is indispensable. The first time a manager stops thinking or working with dedication, someone else will pull out in front.

As a manager, you must be dedicated. You must give attention to detail. And you must be willing to follow dreams. When dealing with an artist's career, expand your thoughts even beyond your hopes for that career. Don't be afraid to dream. If an idea seems ridiculous at the time, you can always bring it back into focus and find ways to make it practical. To understand your ideas better, always write them down. Remember how writing things down is important to our formula for success!

When you are thinking about doing one thing with your artist— one concert or one tour, for example—explore every avenue imaginable. Work on publicity through the press and radio stations, through fan organizations, through websites, through advertising. Try to get corporate sponsorship, and go to the most powerful and influential corporations first. Work from the national to the local; local sponsorship is important as well, whether in the form of actual money or in services—a rental-car company providing transportation for the artist, a hotel giving rooms in exchange for a sponsorship mention. Expand your thoughts, and you can expand your plan. Concentrate on details. You cannot just put an artist out there and hope things will happen. As a manager, you are responsible for making things happen! And you can't make things happen without a plan!

When you sit down to make a plan, ask yourself questions like these:

- Where am I starting from?
- Where am I going?
- Where do I want to be at the end of my plan?
- What is my goal?
- What is the purpose?
- What will be the final results?

Once you have outlined your plan, start building a staff to help you implement the plan. These people may include Star Team members like booking agents, publicists, and promoters as well as specialists in production, lighting, and sound. You need them all to help build a show around your artist, who cannot be thrown out there on stage without some kind of presentation. It is up to you, as the artist manager, to make sure you have the best people to help make that happen. If you aren't qualified to stage the show yourself, find someone who is. A concert must be designed, paced, and most importantly, delivered in a way that connects with the audience. There's a lot of competition in the world today. If you do not have good, well-planned shows, you are going to be passed by.

As you progress, there may be literally hundreds of people involved in helping a show or tour work. Like you and your artist, they all have a performance to give. It takes a lot of people to make any project happen, whether it's a show, a tour, an album, or a personal appearance. And if everyone from artist to stagehand utilizes his or her Power of Performance to the utmost, the result will be those two key words dear to the heart of every agent, artist, publicist, and booking agent: repeat business.

If there's one thing above all else that's important in selling and marketing, it's making sure the customer is satisfied. And in the music business, it's an artist's performance that's being marketed to customers. It's marketed to a record company, to a promoter, and finally, to ticket buyers. Remember those ticket-buying customers. They've paid good money to see the show, and maybe they've hired a baby sitter, driven a good distance, eaten dinner out, and paid for other things along the way. Your performer has an obligation to give them the best show possible.

Make sure your artist knows that his or her Power of Performance should be perfected before he or she ever sets foot on stage. Feeling good or bad has nothing to do with it. Performers are obligated to give their customers, the ticket buyers, the very best they have to offer. If they do, your customers becomes satisfied customers! Satisfied customers will buy a ticket to see your act again, buy your artist's CDs, tapes, videos and other merchandise. Best of all, they will tell other potential customers about your act, helping to build a fan base.

The worst thing that can happen is for your performer to acquire unhappy customers. Not only will they not spend another dime on your act for the rest of his or her career, they will tell everybody else about what they considered a bad performance. This trickle-up effect will touch everybody and impact everything from record sales to future bookings.

It takes a long time to build an act. A moment or two of some stupid performance, either on stage or off, can seriously damage or even destroy a career.

The manager and artist cannot always expect new places, new buildings, new promoters. If you are going to build your success, you have to establish good venues and good promoters and continue to work with them. With proper planning and promotion, you must work to make each date successful, so your artist can go back to a venue next season, and the season after that. In a perfect world, the talent always takes care of the buyer, and the buyer always takes care of the talent. But our world isn't perfect. As long as an artist has hot records, things are great! But as a manager, you must plan for the 90% of the time when your act will not be hot. There is only a certain period of time, a window, in which to take full advantage, and that's when your act is at the top of the charts. You may think hit records and hot acts last forever. They never do.

I am sure you have seen cases when artists who've been very hot become very cold. A few lucky and talented ones are cool for years and then surge back with another hot record, and their careers start all over again. As artist manager, it's up to you to establish your act's name, and the time to do that is when the artist gets his or her first hot records. Get the name recognition, the image, and the stage show established during this time, because the hot period will sooner or later come to an end. If the manager and the artist have done their jobs, they are going to be established forever.

★

All that's necessary to accomplish all of this is to deliver, to perform! Get it? It's not just the artist's Power of Performance; it's the manager's as well!

Remember, satisfied customers create repeat business. And it's not just the ticket buyers. You also want satisfied promoters, which leads to repeat business. Take care of the promoters who've helped establish your artist. See that they make money on your act. Help them if they don't. There are times when, because of one circumstance or another, the show doesn't turn out financially the way you want it to. In that case, remember two adages you'll find again and again in this book: It's only a good deal if it's a good deal for everyone involved, and the only good customer is a satisfied customer.

The great Woody Herman, one of my earliest clients, had a philosophy that revolved around always keeping the promoter in business.

And I know of literally hundreds of times that The Oak Ridge Boys gave money back to a promoter when something happened—a flood, disastrous weather—that wasn't the fault of either the promoter or The Oak Ridge Boys.

A few years ago, Roy Clark played the Colorado State Fair, and his contract had a very big guarantee. Once he got out there, he found out they'd been experiencing a serious drought in the area, and a lot of the farmers hadn't been able to make it on their crops that year or the year before. During his show, Roy made the announcement that he just couldn't come out there and take their money, so he was donating his performance to the Colorado State Fair.

★

It doesn't hurt to repeat successful plans and promotions. Usually, all you have to do is change an aspect or two of the plan or promotion, and it'll work successfully over and over again, just like the movie themes that come back every year in new pictures. Later, you'll read about the promotions The Jim Halsey Company did during the annual fair buyers' convention in Las Vegas, where we reworked our sales and marketing approaches each time, building on an established base.

As we've noted before, artists are very creative people, and creative people are sensitive by nature. A lot of artists also have delicate egos. Their ideas are creative and imaginative, and their thought processes are not always as logical as those of the business person who directs and guides their careers. As a person with a business background, I have also tried to be sensitive to my artist's needs, both personal and creative. When they receive this kind of respect, they will flourish.

There are a lot of words that describe my own philosophy of living. As I told you earlier, respect is one of these words. I deal with people with respect. I offer respect, and I expect to get respect in return. If I cannot respect an artist with whom I am involved, it is impossible for me to do a good job. Not only do I have to respect artists as people; I also have to respect their art and their creative ability. I have been brought up to appreciate and respect anything that is done creatively and well. I'm in the country music business, but that doesn't mean I only like country music. I like jazz and classical. In fact, I like every type of music, and have albums of all kinds in my own library. I am certainly in agreement with Duke Ellington's famous statement about how there are only two kinds of music: good and bad. Good music broadens the scope of my being.

If an artist, no matter what his musical style, feels respect from you and feels that you understand what he is doing creatively, your relationship is going to be richer. You will be able to accomplish more together, because you are both working on the same plan.

Finally, then, as an artist manager, it's of paramount importance to be sensitive to your artists and their needs—it is the foundation of a successful relationship! Do not forget, perfecting your own Power of Performance is in your best interest, as well as in the best interest of your artists and the other members of the Star Team.

FEES AND CONTRACTS

Most managers work on a commission basis. A commission on everything that happens during the term of the agreement between the artist and the artist manager. Generally, the artist manager's commission will range from 15% to 25% of everything happening within the artist's career. i.e. personal appearances, recordings, merchandise, endorsements, corporate sponsorships, books, licensing agreements, almost everything. In some cases, a common exclusion is the artist's songwriting and music publishing. If the artist manager is active in these areas, that will be included in these commission fees as well. In other words, 360, everything. Additionally, most artists are required to pay for the artist manager's travel and entertainment costs as a part of doing business.

Length of contract: for a beginning artist it takes about 3–5 years to bring this artist into a reasonable expectation of gross. Most artist contracts will be 3–5 years in length. Sometimes these contracts, based on shorter time periods, will have a performance clause. This means if the artist achieves certain goals during the initial time period of the contract, it automatically extends the length of the contract by a certain time period.

Expectations of both the artist and the artist manager should be discussed and, if reasonable, can be included in the contract. Remember my constantly stating "if there is a contract or legal document to be signed always have your experienced, specialized music industry attorney review!"

Remember, the reason the artist manager is included in all areas of the artist' business is because it is generally the artist manager's obligation to put the star team together. 360, if you will.

chapter 14

THE RECORD COMPANY

We've talked about talent, the hub of the Star Team wheel. We've talked about artist management, usually the first important spoke in that wheel. Now it's time to add another essential spoke: the record company.

Once a record company has been plugged into the Star Team, a whole new set of circumstances comes into play. Discs are important to a career for a number of reasons. They preserve an artists' work for all eternity. They give an artist new status with family and friends. Most important, if radio plays songs from a disc and a demand is created, they reward the performer financially. If the discs yield hits, and enough of them, a star is born. Now, it's more than discs. It's recording music digitally and downloading from specific sites. It's for sale by download as well. Bands not acceptable to record labels are now successful without the help from a record company.

When Thomas A. Edison invented the cylinder disc in 1877, I'm sure he never anticipated what worldwide commerce his invention would spawn. Viewed largely as a novelty, Edison's phonograph was seen as a possible way of preserving historic talks, special events, and music for posterity.

Now, recordings are a multi-billion dollar business, and one of America's principal exports. And a record company—whose Power of

Performance lies in producing, promoting, marketing, and distribution—plays a definite and integral part in any artist's development.

Most record labels have great resources at their disposal, along with a worldwide network of people power. The creative workforce at most record companies is a great resource for the artist and artist manager, with individual departments that deal with production, artists and repertoire, press and public relations, new media, sales and marketing, distribution, and video promotion. The heads of these departments should all be a part of your extended planning team.

A label's promotional facilities are extensive, with the ability to get your records to radio stations worldwide, as well as in retail stores. They also can get your product to most popular internet download sites. They will finance and place your videos on music-video programs and in clubs, and they can help you get proper reviews and press. A lot of times, the artist-development department can even help in booking dates or arranging guest appearances on radio and television. A record company can help set tours and finance any shortfall (tour support)—the difference between what a performer actually needs in order to do a performance properly and the amount of money he or she gets paid to do it—on an important tour, or book one of its acts into an opening slot on some major artist's tour. Many times, usually in conjunction with a manager, they'll bring other professionals onto the tour to help with staging and costuming.

The record company is a major part of the Star Team. An artist and artist manager's good working relationship with a record company not only helps shake loose advertising and promotion dollars, but also helps assure that the label's network of sales and marketing people, press-relations department, and systems of distribution are all engaged in helping build and sustain a career.

It sounds great and so easy, doesn't it? But how do you find a record company willing to be a part of your Star Team? Frankly, a lot of times even a good artist with a good manager finds it hard to get a record deal—and if the music isn't there, forget about it.

Whether artist or artist manager, you can increase your chances of landing a label by starting with good demos and a professional-looking presentation packet that includes good photos. Remember, your photo will be the very first thing anybody sees upon opening your package.

Spend a little money. Have some professional photos taken. Get a good photographer. I have had people send me presentations with pictures of themselves taken in front of Christmas trees, or in a group with a circle drawn around their face with a "this is me" scrawled across the picture. It'd be funny if it weren't so sad. Crummy amateur photos like these not only turn me off, they also influence the rest of my thinking about the artists who sent them. It may not be fair, but it's true, and it's not just true for me, but for any music-industry professional.

A good demo is an act's best sales tool. Put it with a good photo, a brief resume, any press clippings you might have, and you've got a presentation. Put it in a nice cardboard folder, one that you can buy at any department or office-supply store, and you have a professional presentation to submit to a record company. Now it's popular to have your demo music and other band information online (EPK). Flash sticks, flashbands, or other digital transfer devices that insure a professional presentation are also viable.

See how simple it is? When it comes across somebody's desk, it won't be thrown out because it looks too sloppy or unprofessional. Putting together a good presentation package is generally the job of a manager; the artist can make it easier by giving the manager something to work with.

Again, it's important to emphasize that if the music isn't there, the greatest demo and the best presentation in the world won't make any difference.

Once you've got your package together, it's time to start knocking on doors. As either artist or manager, you may know someone at a record company. If you do, get permission to send your package. If you don't, it's time for some creative thinking and planning. Somehow, you must figure out a way to make contact with someone in a record company. Maybe you can get a label's attention in ways I've mentioned earlier—by showcasing your talent or attending a music industry conference. If you are properly prepared—and make sure you are—for one of these conferences, it can give you a shortcut to the music business profession. A first-class conference will cost you some money in admission fees, but it will be well worth it.

THE TEST MARKET

No, it's not your family, or close friends. That's a start, but to find out if your song, your band, your project really has legs, it needs to be tested on an objective audience, or non-relative customers.

Your music, your song, your band should get as many opinions as possible in several different locations as you preview your music.

If it's a CD, send it to some qualified professionals for opinion. Try radio program directors, DJs for their opinion. Get involved with contests (i.e. Billboard Song Contest, John Lennon Song Contest, USA Song Contest, etc.) to get feedback. Maybe you'll win something. Even an "honorable mention" gives you a positive opinion and an idea you're on the right track. Most song contests give a critique of your entry.

If you are producing, manufacturing and releasing on your own label, get some opinions (a test market) before you run off 10,000 copies. Most people don't have that many friends and relatives.

If you have product, i.e. CDs, T-Shirts, sunglasses, whatever is going to be offered to the public for sale, test it in several markets.

If you're selling CDs or DVDs by direct response selling on radio or TV, test the product. The music as well as the packaging will have varying results depending on your presentation. That could be as simple as getting the proper sequencing on the CD, or getting the right colors or photos on the packaging.

If you're testing in 3 or more cities, the campaign could circulate public performance reviews and stories, ads in local newspapers and magazines, promotion on radio and TV and direct mail and email to qualified, targeted names (database) in the markets being tested.

Put the new product on your website. You do have a website, don't you? Maybe run some contests, give away some samples. Work these test markets, usually a minimum of three, which would include a small, medium and large market.

Thirty days will usually give you enough results to analyze and determine your further course of action.

Ask for feedback—maybe to your email or download. Listen to it and make your decision accordingly. Other product, use the same procedure.

A lot of record companies are now testing 2 or 3 songs on the websites before determining to release on CD. Maybe it will become only downloading or podcasting.

★

It may surprise you to know that over 3,000 record labels are licensed in the United States. Many thousands more are active in other countries. So how do you know which and what kind of label you want to pitch your material to?

Here are five classifications to help you sort things out:

1. **The Major Labels (Full Service).** These have all of the components necessary for full-scale business. Of these—UMG(Universal), is the largest, representing over 20% of the marketplace. UMG, Sony/BMG, Warner Brothers, EMI/Capitol—are multinational corporations with their own manufacturing and distribution companies. They also distribute labels other than their own. Besides these four multinationals, there are many successful labels with full staffing and big stars. Some, like Arista, RCA, Columbia and Epic are subsidiaries of the multinational Sony/BMG. MCA and Mercury are subsidiaries of Universal.

2. **Independent Labels.** These are labels operating with independent distribution, sometimes distributed through the multinationals or other direct sources. Some of the bigger independents—like Curb Records, for instance—have fully staffed departments for promotion, marketing, development, etc. Most indies make deals for foreign sales through other record companies, on a country by country basis.

3. **Telemarketing Labels.** Over the past couple of decades, labels specializing in telemarketing have become very successful. Usually these companies license previously released tracks from an artist and repackage them, offering their collection for sale in television spots. They do not put artists under contract, nor do they usually make new recordings themselves. Their success comes from marketing already proven hits or artists. Generally, records released by these companies are only available through their TV ads rather than in stores. (This is called "direct response" marketing.) Big telemarketing labels include Heartland Records, Razor and Tie, Suffolk, Time-Life, and Reader's Digest.

4. **Speciality Labels.** Specialty labels release product for a limited, specialized audience; you'll find specialty companies that concentrate only on jazz (like Pablo or Concorde/Blue Note), or bluegrass (Skaggs Family), or classical (Angel). Ethnic and folk music also have their own specialty labels. Even a genre as far-reaching as comedy has specialty companies releasing discs and videos.

Some specialty labels will also package and produce "special project" tapes and CDs. These are much like telemarketed albums—usually they're a compilation of hits by various artists, released via special marketing plans. You'll see stacks of these kinds of discs and tapes in places like service stations, convenience stores, and truck stops; a lot of Christmas albums fall into this category. And even major labels will sometimes get involved in this kind of special marketing.

5. **Private Labels.** Certain artists, commercial companies, and organizations make discs intended for their own use. Often, these are done as promotional albums to celebrate, publicize, or tie into some special event. Certain societies have their own private label; an organization like the Knights of Columbus, for instance, might put out a special as a fundraiser.

For most—but not all—artists, the big multinational labels are the most alluring, and not just for the obvious reasons.

Most multinationals have a policy now, 360. This includes revenue from every artist source beyond what the record company produces, including but not limited to:

Merchandise
Personal Appearances
Corporate Sponsorship and Endorsements.
Television
And more

In some cases, having all of these connected companies works to an artist's advantage. If a label has the clout to get an artist' CD into more and larger stores it can boost the artist' recognition and sales considerably. If they can buy and manufacture t-shirts cheaper and get them into more retailers than you can by yourself, there's potential for more profit. If the label has connections that can land you better and more prestigious appearances, it can advance your career faster than you can on your own. Some labels have relationships with potential sponsors that might take you years to cultivate. It is these relationships the label has that create value for the artist. Unless an artist has all of these connections themselves, letting the record company share in the financial rewards of these revenue streams must be considered. If an artist and manager are aware of what's potentially available from a record company, they'll be ready for the opportunities that lie beyond simply recording. Here again it's important for the artist manager and specialized music attorney to be involved.

Our company, The Jim Halsey Co., Inc., worked closely with all of the record companies in designing and promoting our artists' careers. It was important to us, and for the artists we represented, to maintain a daily working relationship with the different record companies. Many labels became partners on promotions and projects. Sometimes, new artists they discovered and signed also hooked up with us. After several decades in the music business, I have yet to work with a more important record-company person than Jim Foglesong. Jim was president of Dot Records when I met him, and after an uncertain start, we became good friends. He was one of the reasons The Jim Halsey Company became such a successful agency. His vision and creative ideas, coupled with his understanding of the artists' needs and the importance of cooperation between the team members, were all important. But even more than that, he was and is a man of great integrity and a gentleman.

In 1967, I made an independent production deal with Dot Records, giving the opportunity to deliver a certain number of artists to Dot over a period of years. Our main act at the time was Hank Thompson, and the label required Hank to be one of the artists. Hank was also my partner in the deal, he and I having recently formed the production company Swingin' "T" Productions. Because of Hank, I was able to get Roy Clark, Rex Allen, Mary Taylor, and other of my acts onto the label.

At this particular time, Roy was a puzzle to record companies. They all respected his ability as a great musician, but instrumentals were not selling, and his previous vocal hits on Capitol Records, "The Tips of My Fingers" and "When the Wind Blows in Chicago," had not been fully promoted and were looked at, in the jargon of the record industry, as "possibly not consistent." Roy could do too many different things. He could sing several different styles of music—pop, country, and blues—and he could play great instrumentals. One of the things record companies do is put a label on an artist, fitting him or her into an identifiable niche, and that was impossible to do with Roy, because he was so multi-talented.

Because of our production deal at Dot, we had a free hand to experiment with Roy's sound. Joe Allison, both a longtime believer in Roy's talents and a good friend, became his producer. (He would ultimately be responsible for Roy's great hit "Yesterday, When I Was Young").

Working at Dot Records, however, was a bumpy ride. Presidents were fired and hired, and our creative energies were simply not being appreciated. With each new president came a new staffing of the sales, marketing, and promotion departments. Chaos seemed to be the order of the day. What was going on here? We needed the cohesiveness of a well-balanced company, but Dot Records was floundering.

Finally, Dot was sold to Gulf & Western. At the time, I was in Las Vegas with Roy Clark, who was performing at the Hughes Landmark Hotel, and I was pretty discouraged with Dot Records. Then I got a call from Jim Foglesong. He introduced himself as "the new president of Dot Records."

I had not met him previously, but he sounded nice enough. He explained how he was going to change a lot of the policies at Dot and bring in a great promotion person, Larry Baunach, to head up marketing and sales. A new distribution system was to be put in place along with a total restructuring of the company. As the conversation came to a close, he once again assured me that things would now be different at Dot.

Then it was my turn.

"Mr. Foglesong," I said, "this all sounds great to me and it's something we've been hoping for. But I must tell you this: within the last two years we have gone through five new presidents at Dot Records, and as many new sales, marketing, and promotion heads. How will we know you'll be around long enough to implement our plans?"

There was a long silence on the other end. But Jim Foglesong recovered enough to give me the assurance he had the mandate. I then pledged my cooperation, and we agreed to work together on what would become one of the most rewarding and personally satisfying relationships in my entire career.

Jim Foglesong believed in our multi-focused projects for our artists. Much of our company's success, and the success of our artists on Dot Records, came because of Jim's cooperation in the marketing and promotion departments. Dot (Gulf & Western owned) later merged with ABC, and eventually was purchased by MCA. Foglesong and his staff members remained in place through all of the changes, and our friendship and working relationship deepened.

Part of my method in establishing an artist has always been to come up with projects or programs that draw attention, build careers, and sell records. We call these projects events! Being the first in a new venue or territory, or with a festival or television show, has long been important to me. I believe that being first establishes the importance of the project. Being the best is important, too, but being first is going to get you more recognition, and it only happens once.

Jim Foglesong helped with the events for many of our artists on his label. We devised unusual, unique events and then worked together to achieve press, record sales, and success. We combined our ideas and sales plans and by teaming up the artists, our company, and the record label, we multiplied our Power of Performance. I'll give you some good illustrations in the third part of this book, "Secrets of The Jim Halsey Company."

Before we leave Jim Foglesong and Dot Records, however, I want to acknowledge a woman named Dottie Vance. During all of the change and upheaval before Jim took the helm, there was one believer who managed to remain through each change of command. This was Dottie, a legendary record promoter, who helped make hits out of a lot of early Hank Thompson and Roy Clark songs. She had a great reputation at the radio stations. If Dottie called, she always reached the right people.

Legends like Dottie and Jim remind us that this is still a people business. Even though each company has a certain prescribed structure, its success depends on its people. If the departments are staffed by ineffective personnel and the proper leadership is not involved, all of the other elements will fail. This is why most people picked to head a company bring in many of their own team members. They know that in the pressure cooker of the big-time music business they'd better have people around them they can count on to do the job right, to fit into the team, and to access their Power of Performance for the good of everyone involved.

chapter 15

THE RECORD PRODUCER

The record producer is the next spoke in the wheel of our Star Team. Usually added to the team at the same time as the record company, the producer works hand in hand with the company, creating recordings calculated to grab the public's interest and make things profitable for both artist and label.

When a record company becomes interested in signing an artist, the big question is: who'll be the producer? The producer goes into the studio with the artist and helps select the material, the musicians, the studio, the engineers, the arrangements, the background singers, and the sound.

You thought the singer did all of that? Sometimes that's true. More often, though, hit records have been more the producer's creation than the artist's. Most of the time it's a collaboration between the two, a meeting of minds and songs and the ways things should be done. Most producers actually work for the record companies, but others have their own studios or produce master sessions that they sell or lease to the labels.

Producing your music is more than just going into a studio, turning on the microphones and machines, and running through the material to be recorded. A lot of thought goes into the production of a record. You have to make sure to get the best songs possible. You must strive to get the best musicians, and the best sound, mixing and balancing correctly, and getting the best performance possible from the singer, singers or band. It's not uncommon for a producer to ask for several takes of the same song, even as many as 20 or 30. Through this kind of repetition, the producer is assured of a perfect track, but can sometimes get the artist to stretch into new and unexpected levels of performance. This repetition and deliberation is why the process of recording a new 10-song disc can take weeks or even months.

When the musicians and artists are through in the studio, the producer's job continues, as he masters and mixes the recording, often with the help of the artist. That means he takes every track and every take recorded, picks the best, gets the sound he wants, equalizes the selection and flow of material, discovers any hidden mistakes or blemishes, and finishes with a perfect or near-perfect product. With the new electronic, digital equipment much of the editing can be accomplished with new programs such as ProTools that can tune the instruments and voices. Even individual notes can be eliminated or moved around in the recording process.

It's a big job. It takes lots of skill and talent. Like the artist recorded, the producer is looking for a hit!

As I said earlier, some record companies employ their own in-house producers. The part of the company they work for is called the A&R (artists and repertoire) department. Early in the recording careers of Hank Thompson, Wanda Jackson, and Roy Clark, a man named Ken Nelson was an important member of their Star Team. Ken was a producer in the A&R department of Capitol Records. It was his job to discover and record artists exclusively for Capitol.

Remember that the Star Team doesn't always come together in perfect order, with talent followed by manager, then record company, record producer, booking agent, etc. When our company signed as agents for Dwight Yoakam, for instance, he already had a manager—my son Sherman, who served as vice-chairman of The Jim Halsey Company. Although he had no record deal, he did have an important team member, Pete Anderson, in place as his record producer.

It was Sherman's undying belief in Dwight that convinced the rest of the Halsey Company to take notice. Sherman became Dwight's manager, and our company became the booking agent. This also was a little out of sequence, since the record company should have been the next element in place after Sherman signed on as manager. Sherman, however, was so convinced he could get Dwight a record deal that we all got aboard, even if things were a bit out of order.

Dwight is not only a uniquely individual artist, he's a great songwriter. But every time Sherman went to one of the Nashville labels trying to land a record deal for Dwight, he'd get the same kind of negative response.

"Sounds too country," they'd tell Sherman. "Sounds hillbilly."

"If he could just get rid of that glitch in his voice," someone else would say.

"Maybe if he would come into Nashville and record with Nashville musicians instead of his own band," still another would suggest.

This, along with a dozen other turndowns only fueled Sherman's belief that Dwight was an unusual performer, outside the mainstream and different from the norm, who could nonetheless capture the public's attention. Finally he found a Nashville ally, Paige Levy at Warner Bros. Records, who really believed in Dwight and worked hard to get him on the label. He did sign with Warner Bros., but it was Warner Bros. in Los Angeles where Sherman found two more people who believed in his vision: Mo Austin and Jeff Ayeroff. Finally convinced of Dwight's potential—in large part because of Sherman's persistence and dedication, as well as Nashville Warner president, Jim Ed Norman and Paige Levy's belief in the project—they gave Dwight a contract.

Sherman's plan also included introducing Dwight to the public in an unorthodox manner. Instead of taking the usual route of putting a new country artist on tour as an opening act for a big-name country star, he booked Dwight as an opener for alternative-rock groups and went after the alternative press. It was unorthodox and extreme! But Warner Bros. liked it, and even more important, it worked.

Additionally, Sherman's vision called for Dwight to do a very stylized, state-of-the-art music video for his first Warner Bros. single, "Honky Tonk Man," a revved-up version of the old Johnny Horton hit. The song was great, Dwight's vocals were superb, and the video—produced and directed by Sherman on 35mm film—set a new standard for visual promotions through videos.

"Honky Tonk Man" launched Dwight's career. The record company had a new hit artist, and the video won countless awards worldwide, including a prestigious New York International Film Festival gold medal for Sherman's directing. Sherman also was named Manager of the Year by Cash Box magazine for his innovative approach to launching and managing Dwight's career.

I certainly want to give Pete Anderson, Dwight's creative record producer, a lot of credit for Dwight's success as well, recognizing again that the record producer is one of the nine key members of the Star Team. Pete, from the beginning, saw something unique in Dwight—in his voice, in his songs, and in his style. By using his skills, his Power of Performance as a gifted producer, Pete Anderson was able to capture Dwight's own Power of Performance in the studio.

The launching of Dwight Yoakam's national career is a good illustration of the power of a team. Although not all the spokes were in place, there were enough to get the wheel rolling: Dwight, the talent; Sherman, the artist manager; Warner Bros., the record company; Pete Anderson, the record producer; Bill Coben, music business specialized attorney; and The Jim Halsey Company, the booking agent. With these, we had the fundamentals of a solid Star Team. As we all worked together, our collective energy produced a collective Power of Performance, driving us to success.

Pete Anderson became a part of the Dwight Yoakam Star Team early. This happened because he was an independent producer who recorded material with Dwight "on spec" before the Warner Bros. contract. Sometimes, as in Pete's case, the producer is the first member of a potential Star Team, by virtue of his doing the artist's early demos, as well as the master recordings that make up the finished product.

An independent record producer is a good way for an artist to get his or her material to a record company. If the producer has a good track record of discovering new artists or producing hits, the record companies can make a deal on the producer's reputation alone. It's just another way this essential team member can be important to success in the music business.

When we made our deal with Dot Records in the late '60s, Roy Clark and I wanted an independent producer to do our product. A good friend, Joe Allison, had come to us with material and had been instrumental in some of our previous recordings, so he became our producer at Dot. Joe was creative and a good songwriter himself. He was also ahead of his time, as far as country music was concerned.

While we were looking for material for Roy, a friend named Scotty Turner, who was also a successful record producer, brought us a song left over from another recording session. It just hadn't been right for the artist doing the session. Scotty thought it might be right for Roy.

It was. When Roy encountered the tune for the first time, he said, simply, "This is me." Joe liked it, too, and he produced it as a pop, rather than a country record. When it was released, it became an instant hit on both the pop and country charts, and remains Roy's biggest record to date, having sold more than a million copies.

The song was "Yesterday, When I Was Young" by the great French composer, Charles Aznavour.

Interestingly enough, it was not a No. 1 hit. It had plenty of sustaining power on radio, and because of that it stayed on the charts for a long time, but it never jumped up to the top spot. Instead, it made a slow and steady climb to No. 2 on Billboard magazine's country chart, No. 11 on the pop chart. But it was in rotation on radio playlists and in the nation's consciousness a lot longer than many No. 1 records, and because of that it established Roy Clark as a major recording artist.

Joe Allison continued to produce Roy, Hank Thompson, and several other Halsey Company artists for quite a while, scoring other hits and helping to create some great records. Eventually, as often happens, it came time for a change, but before I leave Joe here, I'd like to say to him, "Thanks, Joe, for some good action!"

We were looking for another producer and another hit for Roy. We had considered a number of producers but couldn't seem to find the right combination. By this time, Jim Foglesong had become the head of Dot Records, and when he offered his services as a producer, it sounded like a good idea.

And it was. Jim started a string of records with Roy that would all be successful. In fact, the only No. 1 records Roy has had to date were produced by Jim Foglesong. Those top hits began with "Come Live With Me" by famed songwriters Boudleaux and Felice Bryant, and included such singles as "Honeymoon Feeling" and "Thank God and Greyhound." When you consider the contributions of producers like Jim Foglesong, Joe Allison, Pete Anderson, and Ron Chancey— who's produced 11 No. 1 hits with The Oak Ridge Boys—you can understand why I consider a record producer an essential part of the Star Team.

If you're not in the business of making records, it looks a lot easier than it is. One time, when Roy Clark was in Nashville taping the long-running Hee Haw TV series, we also had a recording session scheduled. Roy, as many of his fans know, got his start in the music business playing in a band composed of his dad Hester, uncles Paul and Dudley, and several other cousins and family members. The Clarks had continued to play together on weekends over the years, and they were great. As it turned out, Roy's family was in Nashville to do an episode of Hee Haw, and we prevailed on Jim Foglesong to cut a family album at the upcoming session.

I remember it well. The session was set for a Sunday evening. All of the members, along with Roy, gathered in the recording studio to run through the songs for producer Foglesong. Roy and his family members did about 45 minutes of run-through with tape rolling, and then Roy went into the control room with Jim, where the two of them listened to the rough tapes, made notes about where to put solos, and what to emphasize in certain places.

Finally Jim said, "I think we have it, Roy. Let's start recording."

Agreeing, Roy left the control room and went back out into the studio—which was now empty! After a short search, Roy found his father and uncles waiting outside in the car, their instruments packed up and put away.

"Come on," Roy said. "We're going to record now."

His father looked at him incredulously. "I thought that's what we just did," he replied.

Indeed, recording an album is more difficult than most people—even some musicians—realize.

★

How do producers get paid? Those who work within the record-company structure are usually paid by the label. Good producers will always receive a royalty from the company, separate from the artist's royalties.

Independent producers, those who don't work for the label, many times become part-owner of the masters they produce. All kinds of other deals are made with indie producers—sole ownerships, partnerships, joint ventures, royalty sharing, etc.

Most producers are paid an advance sum for their services, based on each side, or song, that they produce. Additionally, they'll receive a royalty payment for each record sold. Normally this royalty is between three and five percent of gross retail sales. Sometimes it's more. Sometimes, in the case of big-name producers, it's a lot more. In many cases a creditable producer will receive a guaranteed cash amount for each song produced.

Finally, whether a producer is an independent or a cog in the wheel of a giant record company, they all share one thing: the evidence of their Power of Performance that lies in their finished product, polished and preserved for all to hear.

10 TIPS ON GETTING THE MOST OUT OF YOUR RECORDING SESSION

1. Know your music, the words to the songs, vocal and instrumental parts, arrangements before going into the studio. Studio time is expensive. Not a place to rehearse.
2. Arrive at your session rested and with good energy. This is one of the most important moments in your life. Respect it. Prepare for it.
3. Be on time. It's your money that's being spent. Even if the record company is advancing your session costs, it's still money that will be recouped from your royalties.
4. Bring enough equipment, instruments, supplies. Extra strings, reeds (woodwind players), cords, maybe batteries.
5. Keep distractions and interruptions out of the studio. It's your time and money. Not a place to chat and visit with friends.
6. Play in tune.
7. Take a break, deep breaths, drink some water. A few down minutes can cure a "creative block."
8. Back up everything. Make sure before leaving the studio.
9. Have additional songs ready if you have some time left at the end of your session. Some of the biggest hits have been "extras" recorded in the last 20 minutes of a session.
10. Stay focused on your music.

chapter 16

THE MUSIC VIDEO

There used to be a saying in the music business: "It has to be in the grooves."

Now, of course, with recorded music being delivered digitally and on CDs, there *aren't* any grooves to deal with any more. But the wisdom conveyed by that old truism still applies–the song, the music, has to be there.

Today, video is an important part of a performer's career. Still, if the music isn't good, there's not much point in doing a music video. If the music's there, however, video can be an exciting and important complement.

In the beginning, music videos were thought of as simply promotional tools. If you could get the artist's image and an exciting visual presentation of the song on video, coupled with radio airplay, then people would be more likely to remember and purchase the record. It worked, too. The Power of Performance on a CD, added to the Power of Performance on a music video, stimulated record sales. Interestingly enough, this synergy also produced a new product that people wanted to buy. The music video became a consumer product, too!

The video-production company constitutes still another team. It includes producers, directors, camera technicians, makeup people, production assistants and many more crewmembers—sometimes numbering as many as 50 or 75 for a single shoot.

In the short period of time it takes to produce the video–beginning with concept and storyboard, then shooting, then a final edit–the video company is exercising its own Power of Performance, the members doing their own brand of magic to deliver a piece of video art. Hopefully, it will be equal to the recording artist's art and will stimulate sales and help build a pertinent image of the artist.

If the video is good, all that will happen. In some instances, a video has come out before the artist's song was released to radio, and the video has forced radio stations to add the song to their playlists. The video created the virtual demand, and it translated to radio play.

Are you beginning to understand how important it is to have a plan–a set of goals with a purpose? An artist behind a microphone, doing his or her performance, is only one element of success in the music business. Orchestrating the Power of Performance among all of the essential and extended team members is the key to success. It's not a one-person show. It's a show that depends on the Power of Performance of all the elements. The essential Ten Keys to Success are a place to start.

When an artist becomes a star, all of the elements and various teams expand like crazy. Then, it becomes more than just the "Ten Keys," the essential team members on the wheel. It extends to show producers, production, sound and light, travel agencies, choreographers, arrangers, researchers, costumers, tour managers, road crews, bus drivers, transportation specialists–on and on.

You thought it was just a one-person show? Just a hit record and the star did it all? You know differently now. It's a big business. It *is* big business, taking many people to make it work successfully–hundreds, maybe thousands, maybe, in the whole picture, millions.

Somewhere in the wonderful, crazy, creative world of music, there's a place for you. A lot of people set their sights on stardom. That's not always possible, of course. So, if you have the drive and desire to be involved in music, you should prepare yourself not only for stardom, but also for one of the other creatively satisfying positions in this business.

Who pays for the video? Usually, the record company advances the money. In most cases, at least 50% of the advance will be recouped from the artists' royalties. A lot of bands are now making their own videos with new high quality and inexpensive cameras and computer editing programs. It's possible to create some quite interesting videos from within your own resources. If you don't have a record company or you *are* the record company and you're putting your band video on You-Tube, your website, or other programming entities, you can still get your desired "impressions" and promotional benefits.

chapter 17

THE BOOKING AGENT

It's all about selling!

You've probably noticed that this chapter is the longest chapter in the book. That's not only because a booking agent is one of the most important members of the Star Team. It's also because my company, The Jim Halsey Company, was the biggest country music booking agency in the world, and I want to share some of my greatest learning experiences. You'll also note that many of the ideas and theories here touch on several other spokes in the Star Team wheel and can be used by managers, artists, and others.

As a booking agency, our company was in the business of marketing and selling artists. We were famous for our marketing campaigns, individually tailored for each artist. Designed and implemented in a way that maintained respect and appreciation for the art of our clients, our campaigns were still innovative and effective enough to get that "call to action."

When you're selling entertainment, you must condition your buyer—whether a talent buyer for a club or some other venue, or a concert promoter—to make the offer, the call to action. To help do that, we made progressive promotions via email, new media, phone, press and PR, and radio, all reinforcing a concept called "repetitious impressions," which I'll discuss in greater detail later. All of these promotions were part of a marketing plan to build up our artists and to educate the buyer, a plan coordinated with the overall master career plan established in cooperation with each artist, manager, and record company, and usually put into play around the release of a new record.

As a vital Star Team member, the booking agency contributes important ideas and input. Some people think an agent simply waits for the phone to ring, and then discusses an act's open dates and issues a contract.

To quote the title of our client Waylon Jennings' hit: *wrong!*

Unless you're an agent with a superstar act, you have to stimulate a buyer's interest enough to make him or her call, and then you must negotiate the sale. Most acts don't sell themselves. They have to be sold, and they're sold more effectively with proper marketing. As sales agent for an artist, a booking agent should know all of the important venues, promoters, clubs, television buyers, and the representatives of any other establishments or events that might be able to use the performer's talents. An agent must be a specialized salesperson, knowing all there is to know about both artist and buyer.

SELLING BY PHONE

No matter whether you use time-tested tools like direct mail and trade journal ads or high-tech, up-to-the-minute approaches like spectacular websites and sophisticated email, it all boils down to the same two things when it comes to selling your act–*getting* the deal, and *closing* the deal. Both of these are often best accomplished when you're face to face, one on one, where you can give a sales presentation with visual aids and answer any questions immediately and directly. If you can't have a personal meeting, some presentations can be successfully adapted to the Internet.

In the business of music booking and management, however, one of the most effective selling tools remains the telephone. These days, most of us are on the phone more than ever, and the always-expanding cell-phone technology allows us not only mobility in our communication, but the ability to transmit photos and other data as well as our voices across the country and the world.

Here are a few tips on how to be more effective, manage your time better, and *get and close more deals* on the telephone.

First of all, remember that everybody's time is important. Begin your call by (1) identifying yourself, (2) asking for the person you want to talk with, and (3) stating briefly the nature of your call. Once you're in touch with the party you're seeking, remember these 12 tips.

12 TIPS

1. Keep your **solicitation brief** and to the point.
2. Present your facts and **sales points concisely**. If you get interest from the other end, you can go into more detail.
3. Be polite.
4. Smile as you talk. Believe it or not, this comes through even though the other party can't see your face.
5. Have **notes in front** of you with important facts about the person you're talking to and other things relevant to the conversation.
6. IMPORTANT! If you are not comfortable talking on the phone, you may tense up, forget important points, and lose your focus—and probably your sale. It happens to a lot of people. If you think you could be one of them, let me suggest that you *write a script outlining* what you want to say. Have it in front of you for easy reference, in case you tense up. At the least, you'll get your message across. After you've made a number of calls, you'll become more relaxed and eventually eliminate your need for a script.
7. Keep the information on your artists **updated**. Know when they're in the recording studio, where they are in their tour, where their records are on the charts, etc.
8. Use a **call sheet**. Before starting your calls, make a list of everyone you'd like to contact during your calling time. Have each phone number in front of you, along with some refresher notes on what you're calling about. If you're contacting people regarding a specific act, make sure to have the relevant information handy. You don't want to forget an important point or fact.
9. *Listening* is important, too. You're not the only one on the line with information to share.
10. Sometimes, it's worthwhile to **record your conversation**, just to monitor the effectiveness of your presentation. Listening to yourself will give you good ideas about how to improve your telephone skills.
11. A good way to begin every phone call is to take a deep **breath** and fully **exhale**, as you clear your mind of any thoughts other than the purpose of the call.
12. *Think positive!*

And finally, five things to *avoid* when making a sales call:

1. **Don't talk politics or religion.** At worst, these two topics can be horribly divisive and anger-inducing. At best–when the person on the other end thinks like you do–they can take you off track and make you lost sight of the sale, which was the reason for the call in the first place.
2. **Don't talk sports.** If you don't know what you're talking about, you'll sound like an idiot.
3. **Don't talk fishing.** It wastes too much time.
4. **Don't rely on your memory.** Keep notes of the conversations, and make sure to have your own facts and figures on hand for the call.
5. **Don't lose focus.** Always keep the purpose of the call uppermost in your mind and your words.

If the agent's plans are not carefully orchestrated with the other Star Team members, it can spell disaster. For an artist with a national release, everything must be laid out in a logical order for maximum effectiveness, taking into consideration such things as the artist' product release date; sales campaigns in retail outlets; proper cities, venues, and presenters for live shows; a well-devised press and public relations campaign; television and video coverage; radio promotion; and whatever else is needed to make the tour a success.

It may sound to you like the artist manager and the booking agent have similar responsibilities. It's true that their job descriptions often overlap, but they each have a distinct function in the career of an artist.

The manager usually concentrates on a small roster of acts, making sure none of the planning, contracts, and details are overlooked. Remember, it's the manager's job to plan a career and develop the other team members, and for the most part a manager is more long-range in thinking about an artist's career. The booking agent, on the other hand, is responsible for creating a steady cash flow through the artist's touring and personal appearances.

What are some keys to a booking agent's Power of Performance? Unique and inventive marketing programs, for one. Also, you can measure performance by the revenue that comes from dates the agent books. Other criteria include the signing of new acts and the servicing of artists and dates. But remember: the main job of the agent is to sell—to book dates for his artists. Most of the creative and esoteric areas of the artist's career are handled by the manager.

If you're an artist, it's very important for you to find a good agent, one who wants you, will work for you, and won't just add your name to a long list of clients. A good booking agency sometimes represents hundreds of artists. If you sign with one of the big agencies, how can you be sure you'll get the kind of personal attention you and your career need?

This is a question answered by one word: teamwork. The artist, manager, and booking agent must develop a team relationship—a smaller team, within the Star Team. The manager, because of his job description, will usually have more day-to-day contact with the agent than the artist will, and it's the working together of manager and agent in developing itineraries, accurate fees, and the right venues that will help the agent's own Power of Performance. If the artist is a recording act, they'll coordinate touring plans with the release of the latest disc, with tour stops planned to stimulate record play on radio and video play on television, which in turn should help ticket sales for the tour.

See how cooperation between all the Star Team members becomes essential? On the artist's behalf, the manager, booking agent, and record company, along with publicist and promoter, work together on this one touring project. And on a worldwide basis, the big booking agencies will have organizational ties to the top venues, top promoters, and most importantly, the prestigious dates that can be worked by the artist.

The booking agent and the manager should study their artist's potential. What are the act's most marketable attributes? The agent and manager must do research, just as though they were selling automobiles, insurance, or refrigerators instead of talent.

CONTROLLED BUSINESS

We developed a philosophy in the most ethical of understandings we called "controlled business."

By mid-1975, the year my relationship with the Oaks began, our Jim Halsey Company was the largest country-music booking agency in the business. We were the experts. We had the superstars, a virtual "who's who" in the business, with a talent roster that included Roy Clark, Mel Tillis, Donna Fargo, Jimmy Dean, Freddy Fender, Minnie

Pearl, Tammy Wynette, Jody Miller, Hank Thompson and more than 30 other top country-music names.

Our approach to our artists, buyers and customers, as well as to our artists' fans and public, was unique. We were booking agents who operated with the heart and philosophy of managers. (In fact, at that time I managed as well as booked two acts, Roy Clark and Hank Thompson.) We dealt with every matter that came up with the utmost integrity and honesty, and our reputation helped us acquire more business—and stay in business.

The Halsey Company developed a growing business of supplying stars for major fairs and events. John Hitt, my key man in the booking agency, established a rapport with buyers for fairs and rodeos across the country, and our company became the major talent supplier for more than 400 fairs annually.

Meanwhile, Dick Howard, my other key person, ran the West Coast branch of the office, becoming the single most successful booker of country music for television.

One of my own areas of concentration was Las Vegas casinos. They were important for four reasons:

1. The two P's: press and prestige. Headlining or appearing at a major casino gave notice that the act was worthy of attention.
2. Playing a casino for two, four, six, or even 10 weeks during the year assured a positive cash flow and a savings on expenses. Hotel rooms and food were furnished, so the tour bus and traveling stock didn't have to stay out on the road, going from one date to another and accumulating expenses.
3. Remember "inventory"? Because most artists work a designated number of dates each year–their inventory—dedicating a number of weeks to casino appearances left fewer dates to be filled. Because there were fewer dates, we could be more selective in what we chose to complete the performer's inventory for the year.
4. In addition to being desirable bookings for our acts, the casino shows were important to the business of the agency. We could bring in prospective talent buyers and give them great hotel rooms and VIP seating in the showroom, where they would see our stars perform under the most favorable of circumstances.

In the mid-1970s, as we developed our plans for our newly

acquired Oak Ridge Boys to make the leap from gospel to an extended a greater market, we had to draw heavily from what I term "controlled business."

The phrase "controlled business" refers to situations in which we were able to influence buying and selling, and I tell you about it with the utmost candor, emphasizing that we never misused the trust with our buyers or our artists. An example of controlled business is our use, in the early 1960s, of Roy Clark as an opening act for Wanda Jackson. We booked Wanda Jackson, who then had Roy in her band. But we knew that Roy had superstar potential, so we began featuring Roy as an opening act on the Wanda Jackson shows we put together. The plan worked, and Roy became one of the biggest country stars of all time.

In 1975, our first year of representing the Oaks, we utilized the same kinds of opportunities. We had to keep the transition going. We had to expose their dynamic show and unique way with harmonies to the country-music audience, as well as to buyers and promoters. And we had to achieve the first two goals of our first five-point year plan, which meant we had to make enough to pay salaries, bills, and rent— and keep eating!

Luckily, many of the packages—that is, touring shows that feature more than one performer—headlined by our big stars Roy Clark and Mel Tillis needed an opening act. Since our company "controlled" the sales of these packages, we were able, with the utmost integrity, to present the Oaks as openers on these shows. It was revenue as well as a chance to expose our new Oak Ridge Boys to thousands of prospective fans. That was what we needed it at that particular time, and it worked.

As I noted earlier, the Jim Halsey Company was an important player in the Las Vegas entertainment scene. At the time the Oaks started with us, we were booking our stars into the Howard Hughes hotel chain, which included the Frontier, the Desert Inn, the Sands, the Silver Slipper and the Landmark. We were also supplying talent to the Sahara, the Stardust, Caesars Palace, the Hacienda, the MGM Grand and the Showboat. We were, in fact, the only suppliers of country music to Las Vegas!

In 1975, our company had a continuously running show called "Country Music USA" at the Landmark, a big production with state-of-the-art lights and sound. It ran for more than two years, changing headline performers every three weeks.

'Landmark Hotel Las Vegas, circa 1976, the beginning
of the Oak Ridge Boys crossover to country.'
Photo courtesy of Jim Halsey Co. archives

You can see where I'm going here. A "sit down" date for the Oak Ridge Boys, like the one "Country Music USA" offered our other stars, would genereate much-needed revenue. Also, we needed the credibility that a 100-percent top headline billing would bring us. We knew that influential Vegas reviewers like JoeDelaney, Bill Willard, Forrest Duke and Sig Sagowitz would write about us, (if their reviews were positive. As it turned out, they were), they would be some of the first bridges we could use in our crossover to the mainstream. Getting the Oaks as headliners for several weeks of "Country Music USA" was a perfect example of making "controlled business" work.

By being in a passive but controlling situation in both concert packaging and our Las Vegas bookings, we were able to move things along for the Oak Ridge Boys at a more "controlled" pace. Earlier, they'd appeared with Johnny Cash at the Las Vegas Hilton, and that gave them the confidence they needed to make the "Country Music USA" commitment.

I'll never forget that opening night at the Landmark. Once again, we gathered backstage before the show, forming a circle and holding hands, asking the Mighty Creator to bless our work and endeavors, to guide us in our music, to enable us to make people's lives better through our performance. And it was that very first "Country Music USA' show that grew the Oaks into one of the most successful and in-demand of the Las Vegas stars.

All of the attending critics wrote glowing reviews, and because it was a sit-down date and we were in one place for three weeks, Dick Howard, John Hitt and I were able to maximize our opportunities by bringing in TV buyers from Los Angeles, fair and rodeo buyers from the Midwest, and prospective sponsors from all over. Our "controlled business" had propelled us into the mainstream. Our master plan, the beginning of the first five-year plan, was underway.

God had heard our prayers.

The maximizing use of our controlled business philosophy helped to establish our Jim Halsey Company as the leading purveyor of country music artists in fairs, on television and in the casinos for 20 years.

★

You know I recommend making lists of goals. I also recommend that an agent make a list of reasons why talent buyers would want to buy an act. First, of course, is that the artist will make money for a buyer. A good show is capable of building an audience for repeat dates, and this is important to agents and buyers alike. It's simply not practical always to always be finding new venues and new buyers. An agent needs to establish a following of good, substantial buyers and satisfied customers, and you do that by building a buyer's faith and confidence. As you go along in this business, who you know and who knows you is going to be important.

From the beginning, you must keep it straight and honest. A booking agent's good reputation is worth more than money in the bank, and it stays forever and ever. It is important for an agent not to sell a buyer something not right for him or his venue. Once the sale is made, the buyer has put his faith and trust in the agent and the agent's belief that the act will make money. Happy customers enhance an agent's standing and reputation, which translates into repeat business.

You'll read about promoters in a later chapter, but I want to note now that being a promoter, a talent buyer, a presenter of artists, has many rewards. It's a money-making business that satisfies certain creative needs in a person. But promoting is a very risky business as well. Circumstances and elements that change on a daily basis can mean the difference between success or failure, between making or losing money. It's the booking agent's responsibility to the promoter to provide as many elements as possible to ensure a successful date. That means an agency—in coordination with management and press and publicity—should supply buyers with the essentials, including discs, videos, and photos, to help the buyer get the message to their buying public. An agency should also have the artist available for interviews, if possible.

The booking agent has a responsibility to the buyer, but he also has a responsibility to the artist. For that reason, he should be sure that he's always dealing with reliable promoters, people who'll treat the artists with respect, present them properly, advertise the date correctly, and compensate them for the work.

Most major agencies require at least half of the money in advance once a contract is issued for a specific date. To protect his artist, an agent dealing with a buyer for the first time should get all of the money in advance unless he can gather enough information to convince himself that the buyer is honest and reliable.

If you're an artist or manager, investigate before you sign with a booking agency. Is the agency good at keeping its artists booked? Does it have access to special events, conventions, trade shows, and private parties? Can it fill your particular needs for cash flow and revenue?

Does it deal with important promotional venues—halls like the House of Blues in L.A. or the Beacon Theater in New York—that are prestigious for the artist to play and have record-selling cachet?

What are the agency's international connections? How many of the artists on the agency's roster have been there for a long time? What is the agency's reputation for honesty and ethics? Do you like the people?

Having a good individual agent is necessary, but it's not the only reason to sign with an agency. If the agency represents some big acts, that fact can help the once-great, near-great, or the just-getting-started artists, because they'll get sales and opportunities that wouldn't be available if the big acts and their sales strength weren't with the agency. Often a lesser-known act can be sent on tour with a big performer from the same agency, or packages can be put together with several acts supporting the star attraction. For these reasons, it's a distinct advantage to be with an agency that has a number of top, in-demand artists. They give what is known as "accumulated clout."

When working with a new artist, an agent and/or manager can be very effective with a marketing plan that includes an effective website, direct mail, a barrage of emails, trade and consumer advertising, videos, television guest appearances, and extensive promotions targeted for radio, record stores, distributors, and consumers. The idea of repetitious impressions works when one impression after another is made within a short period. This is called "impact enhancing" and creates a measurable increase in the name recognition and identification of the artist or product.

I've seen this work so many times. As you repeat the impressions via your marketing plan, planting the name of the artist over and over, your act becomes hot in the minds of the talent buyers—hotter, in fact, than he or she actually is with the general public. If all of the marketing elements come together at the same time, the promoter will be stimulated to call the agent, ready to buy that artist he's heard so much about—answering the call to action.

In a way, the booking agent is a telemarketer. But instead of selling juicers, skin care products, real estate, or auto wax, he is selling talent, and 90 percent of his sales are achieved over the phone. It sounds impersonal, but if you are giving your artists the proper respect. It's not. It is marketing, however, and you can be successful at it by always keeping these six things in mind:

1. Offer a good product.
2. Create the image.
3. Fill the need.
4. Identify the buyer.
5. Make the call.
6. Close the sale.

Our company, representing 40 great artists, never failed to appreciate the fact that we were selling our artists' creative efforts, and that our product—their art—was good. We had respect for our artists, and we demanded that the buyers respect them as well. Our company revolved around the performer.

The Jim Halsey Company was a sales organization; booking acts was our business. Each different sales and marketing plan we devised for our artists exhibited our Power of Performance as an agency. It was important to get buyers to call us. If a buyer calls an agent, there is a decided advantage for the agent in making the sale. When the agent has to call the buyer, the advantage switches to the buyer's side. We developed our call to action advertising pieces, mailers, emails, electronic messages, trade magazine ads, and other inventive methods for one reason: to stimulate the buyer to call us. Are you getting the idea?

CLINT BLACK FORMULA

We became the agents for Clint Black long before Clint Black became a household name. His team, preparing him for stardom, included Bill Ham, his manager; RCA, his record company; and The Jim Halsey Company, Inc., his booking agency. All of us had been working together for nearly a year before RCA released Clint's first single, "A Better Man." When it hit the streets in March 1989, our agency kicked in with the plan that all Clint's Star Team members had agreed on. The goal? To get Clint Black in front of audiences, no matter what the cost, and thereby lend support to his newly released record.

The Jim Halsey Company, RCA, and Bill Ham all worked together toward this goal. We needed every bit of exposure we could get. We needed it within the time frame of the record's release and promotion campaign. Getting an unknown artist to perform in important venues, on important shows, and to open for important established stars is no easy task. But it was the Halsey Company's job.

With that specific goal in mind (along with a very tight time schedule), our company developed a selling and marketing plan, coordinating it with the concurrently running plans of manager Ham and RCA. The action really heated up when "A Better Man" came out. That was the time to call in favors. Every day counted. We had to get as much exposure as possible in a very short amount of time.

Fortunately, Clint is a great artist with appealing looks and a unique sound. Just as important, he's a gentleman, easy to get along with, the kind of man everyone likes. Because Clint had all those attributes, people willingly helped promote him—which made our job a lot easier. Within The Jim Halsey Company, we harnessed our own creative resources and developed a three-part plan, putting our own Power of Performance to work for Clint Black.

The plan's three parts involved (1) power boosters, (2) repetitious impressions, and (3) impact enhancers. Here's how it worked:

1.Power boosters. The goal was to book Clint on as many important dates in important markets as we could in a very short period of time, putting him in front of the biggest audiences possible. After many conversations and calling in lots of favors, we had Clint opening 50 major shows—with guaranteed large audiences—in 50 cities, appearing on the same bill with such major stars as The Judds, Reba McEntire, The Oak Ridge Boys, and Alabama.

Soon, we knew we'd need more money to support Clint's tour. Everyone agreed we needed to present Clint with his own band, duplicating the sound he had on record. The problem was that his opening-slot payment for these fifty shows would be $1,000 to $1,500 a night, and providing hotels, meals, and travel for his band members would cost an additional $250,000. Because everyone thought it was imperative for Clint to work these dates with his band, RCA agreed to provide the shortfall—the difference between what he needed and what he was getting paid—even though the company already had big money invested in Clint.

Once the record was out and Clint and his band were on the road, we were in a very critical time period. Every move we now made was very important.

Our collective goal was to make Clint Black a mega-star. The record company was doing its part. Bill Ham, the manager, was doing his. It was up to us, as Clint's agents, to make the final part of the puzzle fit. By mid-summer—three months after the release of the album—we were in the midst of our concentrated promotion. The Country Music

Association was sending out ballots for its prestigious awards, with winners announced October 1 on the organization's annual CBS-TV awards show.

We had to work fast, as did the other members of the team. First, we worked to get Clint nominated for a CMA award. If we were able to get his name on the ballot, then we'd have to try to get him elected. Winning an award would solidify what we had built so far and would give him the much-needed Power of Performance within the industry.

Even though we had boosted Clint's power by getting him on a lot of big concerts in a short time period, his winning a CMA award was by no means a sure thing. So, to complement the blitz by his record company and management, The Jim Halsey Company developed its own special promotion, putting our particular formula of repetitious impressions into action. As I noted earlier, this is one of the most effective methods of establishing name identification and stimulating sales.

2.Repetitious impressions. Our special Clint Black promotion encompassed three ways of securing massive print and direct-mail exposure, all within a 14- to 21-day time period.

First, we developed an artistically designed brochure highlighting Clint, his hit record, and his being destined for mega-stardom. This was mailed to our massive list of over 25,000 industry professionals that included press, TV, and movie people; buyers for fairs, rodeos, performing art centers, casinos, theaters, exhibitions, and festivals; industry executives; and the top promoters and entertainment packagers. Additionally, the brochure was sent to every country music radio station in America—all 3,000 of them.

Then, this same brochure, enhanced with artwork, was paid for and placed strategically by our company in various trade magazines, including Billboard, Variety, Amusement Business and The Hollywood Reporter. (Amusement Business is read by promoters, theater managers, and buyers for fairs, festivals, and rodeos. The Hollywood Reporter and Daily Variety are respected daily papers for the motion picture and television industry.)

Finally, as a follow-up to our repetitious impressions campaign, I sent a personal letter to more than 10,000 industry buyers and executives. Yes, I signed them all personally—and then added postscripts to more than a quarter of them!

And that wasn't all I did. Before sending them out, I stacked up all 10,000 letters in the back room of my office building and took a blow-torch to the right edge of the stack! The text of the letters explained that Clint Black was so hot, even the mention of his name would sear paper. Those letters received attention … a lot of attention!

The personal letters were the final step in repeating the impressions. Designed to arrive after the ads and the printed brochure, the mailings were timed within a 21-day period, coinciding with the time that "A Better Man" was getting its heaviest airplay. It was important not only to identify the record, but also to solidify the name, Clint Black, in the minds of listeners. Too many times a hit record will be so powerful it will overshadow its artist. While it is important to establish both act and song at the same time, you must make sure the artist lives long after the hit record has passed. This is part of the overall building process.

3. Impact enhancers. The impact enhancement method allows you to add to a promotion that's already working, making it even more important—enhancing its impact. With the repetitious impressions part of our campaign working powerfully for Clint, we began booking him on as many television shows as we could, making sure his appearances fell within the time frame of the other elements of our promotion. This impact enhancing part of the promotion kicked off when Ralph Emery introduced him to the vast audience of TNN's Nashville Now—Clint's first appearance on a network TV show.

I called Fred deCordova and Peter Lasally, producers of The Tonight Show with Johnny Carson. I needed a favor. We needed this show. And we got it! Clint ended up appearing on Good Morning, America, too, and other major programs. And because all of these guest appearances appeared within the time frame of our direct mail and print advertising campaign, they enhanced the impact of the repetitious impressions.

By this time, Clint was touring, appearing on stage in 50 major cities, and doing local press and TV along the way. It would be hard to calculate the number of impressions that Clint made during this short period of time, but when it was over, he was a star.

You'll remember that all of this activity from us, management, and record company was timed to give Clint the best chance possible of getting a CMA nomination. We felt that if Clint showed up on the CMA's nominee list for at least one award, it would show that our promotion had been both well-timed and effective. As it turned out, the CMA nominated Clint for three awards.

What a break for us! The nominees' names were announced by all the major news services and TV networks, and USA Today carried his picture on the cover of its "Life" section.

Our timing with this campaign, coupled with the efforts from RCA and Bill Ham, proved once again the power of collective energies working together as the Star Team, as well as the importance of power boosters, repetitive impressions, and impact enhancers in stimulating the call to action. Buyers, TV producers, members of the press, and radio station programmers began picking up phones all over the country, calling to inquire about Clint Black. So as booking agents, we were helping build another important star for our roster.

You'll remember that in March, when "A Better Man" came out and our campaign began, Clint was getting $1,000 or $1,500 an engagement. Six months later, in September, we booked his first $25,000 gig; and by the first of the year, we were booking him for $125,000 per night. Twenty years later Clint Black is still a major star enjoying a productive career.

You may be dealing with personal feelings and artistic temperaments when you're selling a performer, but remember: selling is the same, no matter what you're selling.

What a booking agent sells is, simply, people and their art.

REBA

An agent's work is never done. Along with the required booking of dates, creating and being involved with events is an important, ongoing part of your daily life.

Reba McEntire was destined to be the mega-star she is today. Sure, she's one of the most talented performers ever to sing a song, or step on a stage, but she also willed her stardom years ago. She has every qualification for it, but more than anything else, she has desire, dedication, determination, and focus! Her Power of Performance, both on and off stage, is mighty! Our company was privileged to be Reba's agency for many years, booking her into many prestigious venues and onto a number of important television shows.

The Halsey Company held regular meetings with Reba's manager and her record company, MCA. We had just finished presenting The Oak Ridge Boys and The Judds at Radio City Music Hall, and we knew the advantages of an important New York date in terms of press, buyers, potential corporate sponsors, television producers, theatrical producers, advertising agencies, etc. Reba was beginning to happen then, and she was going to happen big. I suggested to all concerned that it was time to present her in an important date in New York. She was a star and needed to be presented in a star's venue.

I opted for Carnegie Hall or Radio City. Logistics were worked out, and finally we were informed that Reba was going to do her Big Apple debut at the Lone Star Cafe, a hip bar on 54th. It was an "in" place, but its limited capacity didn't allow Reba to be shown off the way she should be—in her great, full show, stuffed with production values.

I strongly disagreed with this decision. Reba was soon to become one of the most important artists in the music business; it was important to present her right in her premier New York engagement. Management and MCA, however, were concerned about the high costs of Carnegie and Radio City.

She needed to be presented at Carnegie Hall—and it had to be an event! I finally got my way. Judi Pofsky, senior vice president of our company, did an outstanding job of getting the right motion picture producers, advertising agency heads, television producers, and packagers—everybody important to "show biz"—to attend this event, introducing most of them to Reba for the first time.

These kinds of decisions and the responsibilities that go with them are usually the jobs of managers. But our company, while serving as booking agents for Reba, was also concerned about building her career on a positive, solid footing. The timing of a career-shaping appearance is important. So is not playing the wrong venue. Reba's Carnegie Hall appearance was an important step in the building of her career, coming at a time when she needed to take a giant step forward.

No matter how hard every member of a Star Team—manager, agent, record company, press and PR people, production & staging—works on something like this, it's still up to the artist to deliver his or her most polished and professional Power of Performance. Reba did just that, giving a spectacular show only a consummate performer could deliver. If anybody in this business ever understood the necessity of Power of Performance, Reba McEntire did!

Our efforts didn't stop once that successful show ended. In fact, they were just beginning . Our job was to follow up on all of the press that was generated and call all the buyers and others who might possibly be able to contribute to Reba's blossoming career. Our "performance" continued throughout the year, with the Carnegie Hall date an important springboard from which to launch other events.

Since that time, Reba has had whom I consider one of the best and most diligent managers in the business, her husband, Narvel Blackstock. Although husbands don't always make excellent managers, Narvel is an exception. He has guided his wife's career with the utmost polish and professionalism.

Again, I stress the importance of teamwork. Working as a booking agency team, The Jim Halsey Company complemented the other essential members of many different Star Teams, all consisting of managers, record companies, producers, music attorneys, press and PR people, promoters, and music publishers. Each of us had our specialized job to do. Mostly we had good chemistry with the other team members, and our collective ideas enhanced the Power of Performance for all concerned, including the artist.

STAN MORESS

One of my favorite managers in the business is Stan Moress. When we first met in the 1960s, Stan was a fledgling PR person employed by the great Jay Bernstein. He left Bernstein for a position with Mike Curb, then the youngest record company president in the business, at MGM. Our careers intersected again in the '80s, when Halsey Company client Tammy Wynette, along with her husband, George Richey, hired Stan to revamp Tammy's image. By this time, Stan had become a big-time manager, handling stars such as Gloria Estefan, Eddie Rabbit, and others. He became Tammy's manager.

As we booked Tammy on specific engagements, Stan stayed in daily touch with me, my agents, and our buyers. Tammy was an important client, and Stan was an effective manager, thorough and inventive, with lots of ideas.

Our company had regular meetings with Stan to plan career strategies and make plans for Tammy's future as an artist. These were held in Tulsa at The Jim Halsey Company conference room, and they usually lasted all day. At the meetings, we presented our company's ideas, discussed certain key dates, and worked with reports from Tammy's PR company, Gangwisch & Associates. All of the Halsey Company team members made a contribution. My chief of television and executive vice president, Dick Howard, would arrive from Los Angeles and focus on TV and commercials. Another senior vice president, John Hitt, our fair and special events chief, would discuss fairs, theaters, and special events, establishing a projected number of dates and the income from them. We'd listen to Stan's ideas and direction and get input from George Richey, Tammy's husband. At the day's end, we would all be coordinated on one central idea. Our goals were established, and everybody knew his or her part.

These types of "summit" meetings were very important. We held them with all our artists and managers, usually once a month. From them, we collectively established goals and set our patterns for the future, putting careers into a "road map," a picture we could all visualize. The meetings gave us a collective direction and put a new charge into all of our selling team; our daily phone calls following the meetings would always be designed to keep the artist's career on the right path.

These get-togethers with other Star Team members were power boosters, something every salesperson needs from time to time. Power boosters sharpen the Power of Performance for everyone on the team, lending collective energy to a specifically designed program.

I loved working with Stan Moress because his vision was the world. There was nothing that couldn't be accomplished with his artist. Stan himself is a little theatrical, a class act who can hold his own with the best of the biggest. Stan has style and flair. At this time in his life, Stan also smoked the biggest cigars I've ever seen, Churchill Havanas, and they put out a lot of smoke.

We also had style. And we, too, were "smoking." When Stan and other associates would come, we'd always pick them up in our Jim Halsey Company stretch limo, fully equipped with phones and VCR. We'd whisk them to our office escorted by four uniformed motorcycle officers, full sirens blowing, stopping all side road traffic along the way.

These weren't Tulsa Police Department officers, though. We used motorcycle escorts specifically licensed to escort funerals. But they wore much the same type of uniform, with helmets, tall riding boots, and black and white cycles with sirens and flashing red lights, and they would stop the traffic and let the limo carrying our important guests pass. Illegal? Yes, but it reflected our "show biz" welcome to our guests.

In addition to our all-day meeting, we'd have a luncheon in the converted boardroom we'd made into a dining room. Our outstanding Tulsa chef, the British-born and theatrical Gerard Campbell, would prepare an elaborate menu in our kitchen. All participants would be presented a printed menu, but the names would be changed to reflect each occasion. During one visit from Stan Moress, for instance, the menu featured Roy Clark Oxtail Soup, Salad with The Oak Ridge Boys' special "Elvira" dressing, Chicken ala Tammy, Potatoes Moress, and, for dessert, Gatemouth Brownies and ice cream.

As I've said, Stan smoked cigars. And even though I'd told him my entire office was a non-smoking area, it was hard for him to refrain. On this day, we all knew it was coming. We were certain he would light up after the meal, when we all relaxed for a little informal conversation.

Anticipating Stan, before the meal I had brought out a box of my very best Cuban Churchills, used just for special occasions, and gave each member of the dinner party (except Stan) one to hide in his or her coat. All had instructions not to light up until Stan did. It was going to be a real sacrifice for all my non-smokers, but we were all eager to see what would happen.

Sure enough, just as expected, Stan asked if we'd mind if he had a cigar. In unison, we said "no" and each person pulled out a Churchill, lit it, and started puffing away. Within two or three minutes, the air was so blue that we couldn't see one another across the room. It was a total smoke-polluted environment. Half of us were coughing, the other half wheezing. It was funny, and good-natured Stan laughed right along with the rest of us.

Stan did a great job for Tammy, and I enjoyed working with him. Tammy's husband, George Richey, eventually took over as her manager, and I must say that he was a great manager, too. As you can see, I've worked with some of the best.

HERB GRONAUER

Herb Gronauer was a really fine agent with our company. He'd worked with most of the very big agencies, booking lots of big acts, and before he joined us I'd known him for many years.

Herb was a great telephone salesman, one of the best I have ever known. When part of an artist's itinerary would fall out, he could always find an obscure date to plug in. He was a master of planning tours. Before leaving the office each night, his outgoing mail would be organized to prepare his buyers for his phone calls about artists he was selling.

Sometimes the idea of repetitious impressions influences not only the buyers and the public, but the artist as well. Reading newspaper and magazines articles about how great you are, having people line up after shows to tell you how much they love your music, being complimented by TV and radio hosts when you appear on their programs—all of this is repetitious impressions in action! If you're an artist, it's easy to start believing all this about yourself. This is when you should remember one of the first rules of the music business: don't believe all your own press.

One afternoon, after a particularly hard day, Herb was exhausted from the various problems, phone calls, cancellations, etc. That was the time that a big performer, whom we were representing at the time, called upon Herb in his office. This person, while still a recognizable name, was not currently in demand. His popularity had diminished, and he was very hard to sell, particularly for the kind of money he thought he was worth.

"Listen, Herb," said the aging star. "When these buyers call in for me, I don't think you're asking enough money."

Herb was having a bad day and he didn't need this type of aggravation from an artist—especially one he practically had to beg promoters to buy. "I hate to tell you this," Herb returned. "But I've been with the company for two years, and there hasn't been a 'call in' for you since I've been here. Every sale I've made on you has been a 'call out.'"

Sometimes, you just have to explain to artists that they aren't worth the money they're demanding.

Most of the performers we represented at the Halsey Company, however, understood the business. Prices on their concerts were established within the boundaries so all could make money. Again: everybody has to be a team player.

SOL SAFFIAN

We had a lot of great agents with the company, which was only right. After all, we had a list of important artists who had to stay booked. Another of my favorites, Sol Saffian, had years of big agency experience. He had the ability all good agents possess to pick up a hard-to-get date to fill an itinerary, or to find some obscure venue that would work after an important date canceled, leaving our artist dangling in the middle of nowhere with an open date and the expenses still running.

Sol always had a saying for everything. I wish I had written them all down. In discussing the Billboard record charts and some artist who was not in current demand, Sol would comment, "Yeah, their new record came out. It's in Billboard—No. 67 with an anchor." Of course, the fastest-rising records on Billboard's charts are designated by a "bullet," and all agents and managers are concerned about their artists' new record getting a bullet or keeping a bullet, because that means it's still on its way upward. When Sol humorously said a record had an "anchor," you knew he thought it was a loser.

SALES AND MARKETING

The booking agency is a sales and marketing company. It is no more complicated than that. Remember: the booking agent is the person or company who books dates and events, arranges television shows, and generally creates the cash flow. This will help you differentiate between the agent and the manager.

A lot of times, the booking agent is personified in the movies or television as a fast-talking, cigar-smoking, wheeler-dealer, slapping everyone on the back and calling people "baby" and "sweetheart." Admittedly, some booking agents fit this stereotype. But it's a fading breed. The agent's role today is much more sophisticated than before. The marketplace is more complex, and the tools, the computers and the information with which we work, are also more complex.

Making the sale and booking the date is just part of an agent's job. After getting to know their acts, agents must then research the marketplace; decide on the right territory to play; find the right venues, ticket pricing and percentages; and pick the right promoters. Cash flow created by tours and bookings is what keeps the act going in the beginning. The goal is to make the artist into a sound business property.

An agent has to know music, accounting, geography, sales techniques, and public relations, and be travel agent, negotiator, diplomat, and psychiatrist. As an agent, you must know how to use the tools of your trade just as skillfully as a carpenter, mason, or brain surgeon uses theirs. Agents also must recognize and call upon their helpers, their teammates about whom we continually talk in this book.

What are the tools needed to be a good agent?

The first one is the agent, their knowledge and personality. Before you can sell an artist, you must sell yourself. Having a pleasant personality is a good step. Being able to talk with knowledge about the artist and the business is a must. An agent must do a lot of research on their artist and the artist's style before ever making the first call. Like any good salesperson, an agent must learn both buyers and his product—the artists—thoroughly. Keeping and maintaining satisfied customers is very important. In this business, who you know is very important, but who knows you is equally important. A good agent must be versatile and able to sell any type of attraction to any type of buyer.

The next tool an agent needs is a collection of buyers—the promoters, the clubs, the auditoriums, casinos, theaters, arenas, fairs, and various venues. To be in business as an agent, you must know the places to sell your attractions. You acquire these buyers through research and experience. The internet is a good place to research too.

Another important tool is information. You can't have too much. In this day of computers, the Internet, and web pages, it is easy to assimilate, categorize, and store all types of information. There are a few information sourcebooks that list buyers of attractions on a nationwide basis. Billboard magazine publishes several different books with information necessary to help you start selling your attraction. Pollstar and Billboard magazines offer equally fine collections of special reference books. Research will reveal the type of acts your prospective buyer uses, helping insure that you don't try to sell a rock 'n' roll act to a classical music promoter.

At The Jim Halsey Company, our list of top buyers included 30,000 in America and 15,000 in Europe, the Pacific Rim, and South America. This collection of buyers was an invaluable tool. The more names you have in your database of buyers, the more prospects you have for making a sale. Note that I said "prospects." You still have to contact these prospects and make your sales pitch.

If you are going to be a good booking agent, learn the fundamentals of selling. You can pick up books on creative and imaginative selling in almost every bookstore in America. The same formulas and principles apply to selling performers as to any other product. When I give seminars on the music business, I suggest to all of my attendees that they read all of the sales and self-motivational books they possibly can, because they'll help you establish your own formula, your own plan on how to sell, how to make a pitch, how to promote, and how to advance the career of the artist you represent. Remember, success comes from acquiring satisfied customers.

Our company started every day with a sales meeting. At that time, we would discuss all of the open—that is, unbooked—dates still pending on the various artists we represented. We'd also exchange ideas about where we might be able to fill each date. Every agent within the company had his or her own territory, and our agents knew every aspect of their respective territories—every promoter, every venue, every event that was going on. But sometimes, in dealing with the thousands of dates our artists collectively played in a year, one might overlook something that would be obvious to someone else. Because of being temporarily overburdened with problems or pressures, an agent might forget about a certain venue. It was during this morning meeting that an exchange and networking among all of the agents was valuable, because one agent could make a suggestion that might help another.

Then as now, being a good agent boiled down to being a good salesperson. You had your product, your prospects, and then you made your contacts in a logical order. We had a well-oiled machine. At the sales meetings, we'd also make announcements about a new record product, a television appearance, or something similar. These announcements created what we called "sales burgers," which the agents could use when they went back to their offices. So in a short period of time each morning, 15 to 20 minutes, we accomplished three things:

1. We started the day with collective energy.
2. We all got together for an exchange of ideas.
3. We were all stimulated to go out and make that first call of the day.

The first sale each day is important, because it sets the tone for the rest of the day. To help with our calls, we made various mailings, timing them to arrive just before the agent started calling. When the call came from one of our agents, the buyer would already have that sheet of paper on his desk announcing the arrival in his area of this hot artist, and why it would be advantageous to buy a date. We called this strategy "teeing up your buyer."

We had a good sales force at The Jim Halsey Company, so good that I'm sure I could've walked into the sales meeting any morning and said, "Ladies and gentlemen, we no longer are representing people in the entertainment business. We're selling life insurance. Here are the five policies that we're now selling. These are the specifications on each policy, and why they would be advantageous to certain types of buyers. Now, instead of our regular list of 30,000 concert promoters and nightclub operators, here are names of prospective buyers for this insurance." I guarantee you that the people I had in our company could have left that sales meeting, gone to their desks and made the first phone call, selling life insurance instead of artists.

We were selling art. We were selling people who had great creative ability. But, remember my rule: no matter what you're selling, selling is the same.

LAYERED MARKETING

Understanding and implementing the philosophy of layered marketing offers you the unique opportunity to achieve spectacular results with what is, basically, a simple idea.

Layered marketing is the practice of stacking compatible partners, events, or products into the same focused campaign. When you do that, the effectiveness of the project increases exponentially, going far beyond the impact you'd have by working each marketing plan on an individual basis. It's like stacking pancakes, if you will, with each pancake representing a partner, event, or product, each of them complementing the others.

Because layered marketing has been an important philosophy of mine since the very beginnings of the Jim Halsey Company, you'll find many examples of it in these pages. Some especially good examples can be found in the section on my longtime, and continuing, relationship with the Oak Ridge Boys.

★

It is the booking agent's job to book tours. When you're involved in putting together tours, packaging different artists together and working many different venues, it's necessary to keep in mind the building process for a new artist as well as the maintenance of an established artist's career. Maintaining one career is just as important as building another.

Here are three things to remember, whether you're booking a new or a veteran artist:

1.   Carefully select the venues.

2. Have a reason to go on tour.
3. Make each date an event.
4. Make the event happen.

When you make the event happen, the artist happens, and it's just as easy to create excitement around an entire project as it is to book a date. When Reba played Carnegie Hall, for instance, we put out advertising letting people know that our artist was playing that prestigious venue. Make your show a special event. Make it more than just a date to play. It'll become much more important in the eyes of the public. Call on your Power of Performance to make it happen!

Let's say you're in a situation where the Star Team members are hitting on all cylinders. The manager's made a record deal, the record producer has cut the product with the artist, and everybody's talking about getting the artist on the road. Once the product is released—on a schedule determined by another team member, the record company—the artist must plan on touring to support his or her product. Touring helps in-store sales, stimulating interest in both the artist and the product on a national level. It helps to get radio to play the record. It creates press interest in the artist. Here's where your website becomes important and your ability to drive fans, buyers, interested parties to your website. It's through your website you are stimulating interest in your tours, music and merchandise. Your email database is important. Your ability to cross promote by linking with other web entities expands your personal network. It is big-time sales and marketing.

All of these touring benefits don't happen without a well-developed, overall plan—which is where the booking agent comes in. It is an agent's sole function to sell the artist, booking dates into venues and areas requested by the manager, who himself is working with the record company. Each artist will have different interests and requirements for touring. Whatever the demands, it's up to the booking agent to fulfill them.

The specific number of dates that are to be booked within a specified time period is called the artist's inventory. This inventory of dates must be sold—that is, an agent must book the artist into a venue for each of those dates. Booking agents usually design a sales and marketing plan for filling each artist's requested itinerary. When these tours are in the process of being booked, the agent talks almost daily with the artist's manager. The more people involved and working collectively, the better the chance for success. So the strategy of the tour is usually worked out between the artist manager, the record company, and the agent.

As I've said, sales and marketing principles are pretty much the same, whether you're selling automobiles or acts, popsicles or performers. In all cases, you have inventory to sell, prospective customers to sell to, and a method or plan for reaching those customers, explaining the benefits of the product and why they should buy it, and then making the sale.

But there's one big difference. If a salesperson selling "real" material, like cars, clothing, or electronic gear, still has inventory after an extended sales period, they then make the remaining product available at a reduced price. If some still remains, they can make further reductions and, maybe, still cover the cost of the product.

Not so with a booking agent. Once an artist's inventory period has gone by, it's gone forever. You cannot make a sale for a date on last week's calendar. This is why it's imperative that you, as agent, fill the artist's desired itinerary, and why coordination between you and the artist's manager is essential. If an inventory of dates has not been filled, then the tour will be unsuccessful, and the artist and manager will probably be looking for a new booking agent.

When a tour is planned, even before the first telephone call to a prospective buyer is made, the booking agent gets with the manager and the record label and gets the itinerary down on paper. Ideally, together they figure out the ideal tour stops and then determine the exact number of dates for the act to play, taking into consideration the performer's energy level and the amount of territory that can be covered with sensible "jumps"—that is, travel time—between each date. The tour won't always follow this plan exactly, but getting it down on paper helps pull all of the elements into place.

The manager is primarily responsible for putting together this overall plan, setting up the inventory of dates for the act on this particular tour. Then to the booking agency and they get out their maps and meet with the manager, record label, and artist. They determine the best area to tour and the best time to do it, with an eye on both selling more discs and making the artist an even bigger name. Once this is agreed on, it's then the booking agent's responsibility to deliver the tour.

Keep in mind that, as the booking agent for a tour, you might not get everything exactly as you want it. A town may not be available—it may not have the right venue, or there may be other reasons. But the town next to it might work. Hopefully, you'll get most of the dates you want to play.

Certain key cities are very important to play, and the chance to play them—even if it means rearranging a tour—should be taken. These key places include New York City, Chicago, Atlanta, Los Angeles, Seattle, and other cities that have at least one big radio station and an important record market. If your act cannot play them when he or she wants to, then you should consider adjusting the tour so these major disc-buying and press centers can still be included.

As a booking agent, you need to know geography, and you must know how to read a map. When you first start planning your tour, draw a line around the states that you want to play. Circle the cities where you have prospective buyers. A lot of times, a record company will know certain promoters, and it can help you in towns you're unfamiliar with. All of this may sound elementary, but it works. Our company did it this way every day, mapping out tours for 35 to 40 artists on an annual basis.

A booking agent's Power of Performance is easily judged by the power of the tour he or she has put together—the important cities, promoters, and radio stations involved, PLUS the cash generated! The more knowledge you have about the business and the way it works, the better equipped you are to do a good job for your artist. Learn the functions of all of the other members of your team. Again, it's important to build that teamwork among those team players. It takes a collective effort to push your artist to the top; you need the help of everyone.

In booking a tour for an artist, you, as an agent, have to make a lot of telephone calls to a lot of prospective customers, and you'd better have a good sales pitch once you make the connection. The better the salesperson, the higher the percentage of sales on each round of calling. Recognize, though, that no matter how good you are, if you only make a few calls your chances of making a sale are slimmer. Plan your sales strategy, map out your territory, and make your calls.

The booking agent has the responsibility to secure employment for the artist, but also has an obligation to the buyer—the talent buyer or promoter. You do not oversell your customers on your product. Instead, you help them make money. As a booking agent, your customers are local, regional, and national promoters as well as talent buyers for clubs, casinos, and other venues. It's in everyone's best interest to keep them in business. So deal with your promoters honestly. Give them value, and help them promote your dates. Remember: satisfied customers insure repeat business.

It's like the old story about the chicken and the egg. You have to have the artist to make the tour. But there's no tour if you don't have promoters to buy the dates. So rather than wondering which element comes first, maybe we ought to consider them equally necessary to keep things going.

Keep in mind that the buyer must have a reason to buy. Maybe the artist has a record that's getting good airplay. Maybe the artist has been on television. Or maybe he or she has created a big following some other way.

Let's talk for a moment about an established artist, one who draws a reasonable amount of people and gets a good fee. What's the procedure for booking an act like this?

First, as booking agent, you get input from the record company as to where the artist needs to play to help sell records or, conversely, where the record is hot. It is a good idea to tour in both of these areas in order to maintain or boost sales.

Second, you must carefully consider the tour plans. Will it be a 15 or 20-day tour? Should the traveling be 150 or 300 miles a day? What looks like only an inch or so on the map translates into lots of extra miles for your act to grind out in a bus or van.

Third, where do you want to go with your artist? Determine what venues are in the territory, which artists have been playing the territory, whether or not they were successful, and what the competition is.

If you're starting out to book a 20-day tour, you don't just write down 20 venues in 20 cities. List 40 or 50, and then realistically pick the most logical routing and the best venues. Every venue is different, and each one has its own particular characteristics. Different artists like different venues. You want to pick the ones where your artist will be the best received, from hardwood-floor honky-tonk to performing-arts center. Take into consideration the record company's ideas on choice of venue. Certain venues have the ability to sell records, and others do not. For instance, it may surprise you that casinos are not regarded as important venues for a record-promotion tour. They're good for cash flow and press, though.

Fourth, the next step is email, direct-mail and advertising to announce the tour. Then, you start making those telephone calls. Realize that if you want to book a 20-day tour, 50 names of prospective promoters are probably not enough. You may need 120 different names. There's a lot of competition out there on the road, and you won't make every sale, but you have to make every call. Give your prospective buyers the best sales pitch possible, offering good value.

Fifth, once a sale is made, complete filling in the other dates, one after another, until the tour is booked. Realize that there's sometimes a key or pivotal date around which the tour will be booked, and it's important to sell that date first. This engagement, for instance, could be in a city the record company feels is so important that it could break your artist into the next level.

Booking the tour is just part of it, of course. Your show's production values are just as important. Some agents think that once they've made the sale and issued the contract, the job's done. The truth is that if you want to stay in business, you have to make sure that the best possible technical production is utilized in your artist's appearances. Part of this can be done by including special requirements in the contract rider, such as technical instructions for sound and lights.

Most touring shows carry their own sound and lights and other production equipment. Some even carry their own elaborate sets. They are not going to take the chance of having their show presented improperly because of lack of technical equipment. Most acts hire specific crews or production companies that will work for an entire tour. All of this must be coordinated with the promoters on the tour to insure that each venue can properly handle the production. If you get into an area with an artist and the show doesn't have the proper production, it not only reflects badly on the artist but also the booking agent and the manager for not doing their jobs properly.

There are very few artists, with the exception of standup comedians, who can go out with one microphone and make a proper presentation. So the added value of the production that goes with the presentation is very important for a show. It enhances the audience's interest and excitement. As an agent or manager, it's your responsibility to make sure all the technical requirements are fulfilled on each tour stop. These requirements should be part of the artist's contract with the buyer. But even when they are, unfortunately they aren't always fulfilled. The agent or manager always needs to check and double-check along the way; many times, the artist's road manager has this responsibility as part of his daily duties.

I've often referred to the necessity of having a checklist. This is a good example of what I mean. Just like an airline pilot needs a checklist, the manager-agent needs something on paper that he can use to check everything and not overlook any minor details. The production values are part of the artist's Power of Performance, reflected on stage. The manager or booking agent's Power of Performance lies in the ability to make sure these production values get into every show.

Our tours with The Oak Ridge Boys, Tammy Wynette, Clint Black, and others took so many buses and trucks that they looked like circuses going on the road. Major tours take a lot of people and mean a lot of jobs. Many people get their first start in the business with one of these jobs.

Here are some examples of the services and talents necessary to put a big touring artist on the road:

- The Band/Musicians
- Vocalists
- Background Singers
- Dancers
- Chief programmer
- Lighting tech
- Riggers
- Video Design
- Video director
- Video tech
- Camera operators
- Bus company
- Bus drivers
- Trucking company
- Truck drivers
- Record representative
- Sound tech
- Tour press
- Lighting Designer
- Lighting Company
- Lighting Director
- Lighting Crew/
- Choreographer
- Travel agency
- Booking Agent
- Manager
- Tour manager
- Tour accountants
- Production manager
- Security
- Sound company
- House board mixer
- Stage monitor mixer
- Audio crew chief
- Stage techs
- Merchandise/Crew

- Local stage hands
- Wardrobe handler
- Have I forgotten anybody?

- Wardrobe design
- Star's valet
- Oh, of course: The *star!*

TERRITORIES

Now, let's talk about territories, which we touched on a little earlier. The Jim Halsey Company utilized its great number of agents by operating in a territorial style. Territories were divided up within the agency, and each agent took a certain territory. A territory could be a number of states or foreign countries. It could even be a certain specialized area, such as television and movies, or fairs and rodeos.

I learned early in my career that a salesperson with a concentrated area of focus makes more sales. They're more effective because, if they've done their research, they know their particular buyers and their buyers' needs much more intimately than any other agent. They become specialists.

Many agencies have been accused of throwing darts at a map to determine an itinerary. But if the individual agents know their respective territories and their buyers in those territories, they can coordinate a tour that looks anything but random, and makes sense to all parties concerned. An agency's Power of Performance is greatly increased by specialization.

Part of the reason that The Jim Halsey Company developed into a major agency was that I found and hired key people who were skilled in specialized areas. For instance, we wanted to help establish the idea that big-name country artists would do big-time box-office business at fairs and rodeos. I felt that becoming a specialist in the fair and rodeo business would give our company a certain reputation, enabling us not only to do a lot of business with the fairs and rodeos but also to attract other name artists to our company.

From the very beginning, one person—John Hitt—developed the fairs and rodeos for our company. John was instrumental in developing our company into a major agency, one who grew from representing a couple of artists to many. For a couple of years, we even represented an entire agency, Richard Rosenberg and Peter Grosslight's the Regency Artists Group, for fairs and rodeos. Regency had some big movie and TV stars on its roster, but it didn't have a fair and rodeo department, and we did.

Tulsa, Oklahoma, was our headquarters. Hank Thompson, Roy Clark, and I, along with Wayne Creasy, Stan Synar, and Mack Sanders, were partners in a number of ventures in Tulsa, including two radio stations and a 2,500-acre cattle ranch south of town in Mounds, Oklahoma.

When John, already a successful music-business figure, came to Tulsa to meet with me, I laid out my plans for the future. What I wanted to build, I told him, was the very best booking agency in the business, one that had skilled agents who secured the very best dates for the artists, and did the very best for the promoter as well. I wanted to do it with integrity and with the philosophy of an artist manager. As I've explained throughout this book, my focus and belief was that the artist was the key to everything. If we focused our agency on the artist and the job we could do for the artist, then everything else would fall into place.

John liked the idea enough to join the company. This was in 1972, and one of the first things we did was lay out a five-year plan, getting down on paper where we wanted to be in 1977. For John, his five-year assignment included the task of helping establish our agency as country music specialists, booking quality dates for our artists and building a name for ourselves. A major part of that was developing the fair and special event area for The Jim Halsey Company.

Not only for the first five years, but for 18 of them, John Hitt did exactly what we talked about in that early meeting. Our company built a reputation in the fair business second to none, and John Hitt, for The Halsey Company, became the most respected agent for fairs in America.

With the nucleus of the company established, we attracted other agents, and these other agents attracted other artists. We started building our global territory. We developed effective selling methods for our artists, for our company, and for the buyer these methods tied directly to timing, opportunity, patience, and persistence.

EFFECTIVE USE OF TIME

I want to stress that a booking agent or manager's effective use of time, when there are so many things to do and so many details to take care of, is an essential part of the Power of Performance.

Because it's not always possible to do everything that you want or plan to do, you must prioritize the elements involved in your work, giving the ones with the highest priority the most attention and "power." If you don't plan your time, you really can't organize properly what you want to accomplish. And how can you organize? We go back to the important method I told you about earlier: write it all down.

As a booking agent, you must take care of lots of things every day. The first thing you have to do, of course, is sell the dates. Your job not only includes selling, but also taking care of problems on existing dates and servicing the artists.

The dates you've already booked are as important as the ones you're still trying to book, and they can generate problems that must be dealt with. Maybe the promoter hasn't gotten his or her deposit to you. Maybe the tickets aren't selling, or the publicity has gotten lost somewhere. Or perhaps the artist has looked at the time and miles between two dates and told you, "That's too far of a jump for me; I want to change to another date."

To handle all these situations, you must remain organized. You must have your checklist, and you must look at it daily. You have to take care of all your dates and artists—as well as your promoters—to be effective. You must be able to prioritize and divide your time so that you can take care of a number of different facets of the agent's job.

Here are five of the most important:

1.**Selling tours and dates**—Don't throw darts at the map, literally or figuratively. Working with the manager, the record company, and the artist, collectively decide the most effective times and places to tour.

2.**Booking crucial dates**—What constitutes a "crucial date"? It's a date in the middle of a major artist's tour that falls out. It's crucial because it's directly related to the tour's cash flow. The act is already on the road and he or she has to stay on tour to keep the money coming in. The record company feels that all the tour dates are important because they're connected with the window of opportunity the artist's new disc has in the market, and the company's territorial managers are already in place with promotions. When a date in the middle of this situation falls out for one reason or another, it becomes a crucial date, and it must be filled. It's an open date, and you must book it, perhaps in a different venue in the same city or area.

Crucial dates are different from career dates. A career date is booked into a venue or market that the record company feels is important because of prestigious promotional opportunities. A New York

City date, for instance, can be a career date. Once you get New York City on your itinerary, then you must decide the most important venue for this career date—Radio City Music Hall, Carnegie Hall, the Beacon Theater? Another of the city's venues? Career dates are the ones that are important to the record company and to the overall planning of an artist's career, and they need to be developed as events.

3.**Researching for leads**—As is true with any sales organization, your list of buyers is important. These are the buyers you work with on a daily basis, buyers you cultivate with good deals, special dates, and fair and reasonable prices. They make up what is called your customer base. For you to be successful, they must become satisfied customers.

You should also research and seek buyers with whom you have not worked before. Sometimes you'll read about new promoters or venues in the trades, or a radio station or record company will give you some leads in this area. Our policy at The Jim Halsey Company was to continually build our file of buyers, promoters, clubs, and concert venues, so we could keep more and more of them informed of our artists' availability. We sent out our artists' itineraries, announcing the possibility of their being in a certain area at a certain time. Always, we kept researching, kept developing our buyers' list, picking up information about club openings, new promoters, fairs changing their entertainment policies. It was all part of the research.

This type of information-gathering never ends. This research you do with your conversations, your associations, and your membership in trade organizations (such as the Country Music Association, the Academy of Country Music, the International Association of Fair Buyers and other entertainment buyer associations, the International Federation of Festival Organizations [FIDOF], etc.) can all help you locate and identify prospective buyers.

It's very important that you and everyone working for you, right down to the receptionist, read the trades on a regular basis. The Halsey Company got many leads from newspapers and trades which our secretaries, mailroom people, and receptionists read and brought in, with the salient information circled—information that was new to the rest of us. New leads pop up all the time.

Leo Zabelin, one of my mentors, was director of our public relations for many years. On a regular basis, he would read the newspapers in libraries and retrieve all of the daily papers from the major cities, maybe as many as 40 or 50, bringing them back to our office conference room to go through them. For the next few hours, he'd be busy highlighting new venues, new clubs, new events, and new celebrations.

No other agency had Leo Zabelin, and I don't think any other agency had this service, either. It was invaluable to us. In today's world of electronic information assimilation, this can be achieved through web searches and signing up for industry newsletters. It requires constant diligence to remain up to date. Now information is much more readily accessible and available through the internet. Information on fairs, venues, casinos, other buyers of musical entertainment are available at the booking agent's fingertips on the computer.

4.**Dealing with problems on existing dates**—when you're prioritizing, remember this: take care of problems first. If you don't, they'll not only remain, they'll possibly grow into bigger problems and interfere with your flow of energy. Booking more than 3,000 appearances a year for our stars, we had problems to deal with every day. The tickets weren't selling. The tickets hadn't gone on sale. The promotion hadn't arrived. The advertising hadn't started. There was a conflict with the radio-station presenters. The deposit on the date wasn't in. The venue was closed for remodeling.

You deal with literally thousands of problems over a year's time. But as I told you earlier, I preferred then, and still prefer, to call them situations. Every now and then a real problem will arise—remember the MGM Hotel fire from Chapter 4?—and then you can make that distinction. But problems and situations are just part of the business—things that have to be taken care of regularly, just like answering the telephones or taking out the mail.

5.**Being the "responsible agent"**—Within our agency, we had what was known as "the responsible agent." Not only did each agent have a territory for which he or she was responsible, each agent had three or four artists on our roster that he or she was responsible for. All of our agents booked all the artists on our roster, but the responsible agents had the vital responsibility for their individual acts on a daily basis. Reba McEntire, The Judds, Roy Clark, Tammy Wynette, or any other of our clients knew they could call me or any agent in the Halsey Company. But they also knew that they each had one agent in the company who was their responsible agent, an agent whose job it was to know everything that was going on in their particular career, up to the minute and in-depth.

When we had our sales meetings, it was the responsible agent's duty to go over the artist's itinerary, crucial dates, problem dates, and any other situation specific to his or her particular artist. As we went around the table each morning, we discussed all of the situations for all of our artists. Each performer's responsible agent would tell what was going on, the dates that we needed to fill an itinerary, the status of contracts and deposit checks due on this particular day, special plans for the future, and any crucial dates that needed to be put on the books that day. If someone reported a crucial date, every agent we had would go out and make 10 calls regarding that particular date; with this concentration of effort, we succeeded in getting many crucial dates booked for our artists. In fact, it was highly unusual for The Jim Halsey Company to have an open date on any of our artists. Today, the effective use of emails is an essential tool for notifying buyers of open or available dates.

The responsible agents were the ones who took information from the office to their acts, which was much more efficient than having every agent in the company calling artists or managers with bits and pieces of information or dates to be cleared.

The term "clearing a date" means getting the artist's okay on an already-booked date. This wasn't always easy. We would give the performer all the details—venue, promoter, number of shows, billing, any support acts—and hope for a quick reply after our recommendation.

The responsible-agent setup made for a consistency in our operations with much less chance for error. The other agents within our company would book dates for an artist, and then take the dates they'd booked to that artist's responsible agent. We'd wait until the end of our daily business, after everybody had gathered all of the dates booked that day, and then make one telephone call to each artist or artist manager, going over everything at one time. (The only exception to this procedure occurred if a date or event came along that needed immediate attention, such as an appearance on The Tonight Show or something equally important.)

Looking at the overall situation this way, responsible agents could ascertain which dates made sense, which ones didn't make sense, whether there was enough money offered by the buyer, whether they could get a little more. Instead of making a call every 30 minutes or every hour, the responsible agents made one call to each of their artists at the end of the day and went over the day's business, which was much more sensible and organized, a more effective use of time and energy.

As the head of the agency, I was ultimately responsible for everything. But spreading my duties and responsibilities among the different agents helped me tremendously.

When you begin working as an agent, remember that you must be able to divide your time effectively among the preceding five areas, which is tough enough. But also keep in mind that the constant flow of business provides an equally constant flow of interruptions, which can keep you from spending your time the way you've planned. Something's always coming up, and it's too easy to find yourself farther behind at the end of the day than you were at the beginning.

You know how I feel about the importance of writing things down, be they dreams or responsibilities. As an agent, you should put down all the vital information you've gathered during a day. Then, write down every telephone call that you intend to make, every letter or email you intend to write. When your morning starts—whether it's with an agency sales meeting or working on your own—you should have an agenda, a list of perhaps 25 or 30 telephone calls you've scheduled to make. Add to that list as the day goes on; in addition to making phone calls, you'll receive them. Some of our agents would make as many as 200 to 250 calls per day, sticking to the plan they'd written down.

GET ORGANIZED

The solutions to problems—or, rather, situations—are usually a lot more simple than you're willing to admit. It is mostly a matter of controlling your business day, rather than having it control you, of forcing activities into the time available, rather than trying to expand the time to accommodate the activities. Once you really believe that controlling your time is not only more productive but more pleasant, the rest of it is fairly easy.

Here are five work day habits guaranteed to enhance your Power of Performance:

1. Clear your desk of all papers except those relating to the immediate situation at hand.
2. Do things in the order of their importance to your planned schedule.

3. When you face a problem, solve it then and there—if you have the facts necessary to make the decision.

4. Learn to organize. Again, organize for the next day at the end of the previous day. This gives you peace of mind at night, along with a feeling that you're on top of things. It also infuses you with real excitement about coming into work the next morning. Arrange your next day on paper, defining what you want to accomplish. Write it down! Do this, and you'll always feel that you have a head start.

5. Return all phone calls.
   Enough said!

A large part of sticking to your schedule is knowing that it's very rare something is so important, or a crisis is so urgent, that it has to be attended to immediately. Treat interruptions as you would any other time commitment. Make sure you program a space in each day for dealing with them.

CALL TO ACTION

Our agency customers were buyers for television shows, network producers, prospective corporate sponsors, fairs, rodeos, casinos, promoters, night club operators, theaters, ballrooms, colleges and universities, special events, festivals, city celebrations—anybody that used talent. And all of them had one thing in common: they knew their basic needs, which was to present talent and make a profit.

It was our job to help them buy the right attraction.

Then, as now, there were literally thousands of artists in the marketplace. Nashville alone had over 300 touring bands, singers, and recording stars. We had competition! We had lots of competition! And we had a responsibility to create a demand for the artists we represented, and to sell them—for a fair and equitable price.

We constantly needed to stimulate our prospective customers to buy our talent! The job of our booking agency was to convince the buyer that Halsey Company artists would do a better job, draw more people, get more outside support, be easier to work with, satisfy their ticket buyers, and make them money. It was our agency's Power of Performance that determined whether or not we made a sale.

Earlier in this chapter, I used the term "call to action". It refers to having a buyer call your agency to inquire about one of your acts, and you sell it by showing how your act can fill a prospective customer's needs. One of the most effective ways of creating a demand for your act, of activating the "call," is direct mail or email. Remember how it worked in our Clint Black campaign? It worked for us in many other situations, too. We sent reams of advertising stimuli to the buyers on our preferred list. It was planned. It was organized. It worked.

As an agent, you want prospective buyers to call you. Sure, an agent can call up a buyer and make a sale. But what if you have to call 10 buyers before a sale is made, or 20 buyers? Wouldn't it be easier to create some excitement so the buyer calls you? Then, all you have to do is negotiate the date and the price. When an agent originates the call, the buyer knows we need the date. No matter how much the buyer might be interested in the act, the fact remains that you're the one who's calling, and he knows that you want to make a sale.

If you instead stimulate that buyer to call you, it's just the opposite. You then know that the buyer wants to buy. Psychologically, you're better prepared to make a sales pitch, to ask for more money and make a better deal for your artist than if you had initiated the call.

Again, I believe in direct mail. But more importantly, emails are faster, to the point, and the call to action comes quicker. I believe in emailing the buyer pertinent information that stimulates them to pick up the telephone and say, "Yes, I want to buy that attraction. I'm going to call and find out if it's available and how much it costs."

This call to action principle is used every day on the infomercial pitches you see on television. They stimulate you to get out of your seat, go to the telephone, and make that toll-free call. In the same way, by stimulating your buyer with an attractive piece that tells about a new record release, a high chart position, a good review, an exciting sales figure, he's stimulated to pick up the telephone and call you.

Also called direct-response marketing, this approach saves you a lot of outgoing telephone calls, which can not only be expensive, but time-consuming as well. At the Halsey Company, we would use mailers that would include an artist's picture and give his or her history— all positive, positive, positive. "This artist is for you!" "This artist can make you money!" "You should buy this artist!" "*Call us now!*" Well, it wasn't quite that simple, but that was the gist of our message, and it was very effective for us. In today's market, even better: emails. But while we got plenty of incoming inquiries as a result of these calls to action, we still had to make lots of outgoing calls. It's a part of the business, and some agents are better at it than others.

At The Jim Halsey Company, Herb Gronauer constantly impressed me with his telephone skills. Averaging between 200 and 300 outgoing calls a day, Herb was a master at sizing up a buyer's needs and making a deal. He always planned his next day before he left at night, and he always did his own mailings, which amounted to between 100 and 200 pieces each day. His buyers were constantly teed up. Either they'd call Herb about the artist in his mailing, or they'd know about Herb's artist when he called them. Either way, they'd be prepared to talk about a deal. He was one of the best agents I ever worked with.

Ron Baird, another Halsey Company agent, was also methodical and studied with his sales approach. His method of asking for the sale—whether by phone, mail, or in person—was always very intellectual, to the point, and factual. Ron went to Creative Artists Agency after our sale to William Morris; I consider him one the best agents who ever worked for our company. Ron took the Boy Scout motto to heart: He was always prepared.

Bob Kinkead, a young man who came to our company when he was barely 21, was very aggressive and became one of the best cold-call agents I've ever seen. When our company merged with The William Morris Agency in 1990, Bob went to William Morris for a short time and then became manager of the Nashville office of the Agency for Performing Arts (APA), where he continued to make somewhere between 300 and 350 telephone calls a day, not only in the office, but in his car, on his boat, and in his home. Bob is now in the artist-management business. At our agency, Bob Kinkead made his calls only after he'd stimulated his buyers with effective direct-mail pieces on his artists. He's one of the most dedicated agents I've ever known, and both he and Herb knew the strategy of direct mail followed by a phone call.

Here's some important advice for manager and artist as well as agent: plan your mail and emails. Target where it's going and the territories it's going into. Recognize early the dates that need to be supported, and start your campaign early, too. Again, I stress that if your mailers and advertising pieces illustrate how the buyers' needs can be filled, you've got a sale. These impact enhancers should be so direct and to the point that they stimulate the buyers' call to action phone call. How can they pass up the opportunity to present this great artist you've shown them?

Read and reread your advertising copy. Is it to the point? Is it attractively presented? Is it powerfully presented? Will it generate a buyer's call to action?

My friend Joe Sugarman, the creator of BluBlocker Sunglasses, has been recognized as the king of direct-response marketing. A long time ago, he told me, "In advertising, the first sentence is the most important. The second most important is the second sentence, and so on." So, make your first sentence important!

Sometimes, you can afford to send your direct mail first class. But when you're mailing 25,000 to 30,000 pieces several times a month, you want to be able to send it bulk mail. It takes more time for bulk mail to get where it's going; sometimes it can take as much as three weeks to get to its destination, while first-class gets there in three or four days. If you're bulk-mailing, plan on when you want the item to arrive, and then work backwards, mailing the piece within the necessary time period so it'll arrive when you want it to arrive. Now, more effectively and tremendously less expensive, emails. Email is immediate and can be sent by the thousands if you have assembled an effective database.

Part of being an agent is planning ahead. Plan around certain holiday periods when you know there'll be more buying activity than at other times of the year. Start mailing early for New Year's Eve, Halloween, or Fourth of July dates. Fairs usually start buying in the fall for the next season—certainly by the time the big fair-buyers' convention is held in Las Vegas, so plan your mail to arrive accordingly. Make your mailings as creative as possible. As I keep preaching, stimulate your buyer to make the call to action.

Use email as well as direct mail to sell your ideas. Load information on your website, videos and music on YouTube, MySpace and other creative ways to present your information. Maybe you have an idea for creative packaging, putting two or three artists together on the same tour. We did it with Roy Clark and Mel Tillis. We did it with Tammy Wynette and George Jones, and several others. It gave the buyer the opportunity to buy a special event. For The Oak Ridge Boys, we put together a gigantic Christmas tour tied in with corporate sponsorship and guest artists. We had support from Larry Jones' Feed the Children charity, Amana Refrigeration, and Totino's Pizza, along with a number of other elements that made the package very attractive to the concert promoter, since it already had a lot of support going for it before the tickets even went on sale. By programming Christmas songs, special staging and effects (including snow on stage), and other elements, The Oak Ridge Boys show became a Christmas event in each city. Because of its initial success, it became an annual "happening." Beginning in 2004, Feed The Children taped the show for a Christmas television special. It and subsequent tapings have been running annually on a multitude of cable networks. Our annual Christmas tour is a much anticpated event in a lot of cities.

Other things agencies can do is stimulate hotels to do a series of shows. They can also provide the impetus for community concerts, fund-raisers, conventions, and sales meetings; colleges are another good area for agency work. These kinds of dates are booked a long time in advance, so you have to start your promotion many, many months ahead of the show in order to generate buyer interest very early. Maybe it will take more than one mailer to do it. Maybe it'll take two or three But I've seen it happen many times: an artist relatively unknown at the start of a direct-mail campaign becomes, after a series of mailings, big in the eyes of the buyers. Again, that's how repetitious impressions work. The buyers have impression after impression put in front of them, and it pays off in increased bookings for your artist.

A lot of times, you can support your emails and mailings with tie-ins to other things, such as television show appearances or ads in trade publications like Billboard, Pollstar and Music Row. Every time a Halsey Company artist appeared on The Tonight Show or another popular program, we would send out bulk mailings, usually supported by full page ads in Hollywood Reporter and Daily Variety. If we didn't have time to send our mailings bulk, we'd send them first class.

Email is another effective way to notify buyers that something important is going on with the artist. When one of our artists appeared on The Tonight Show, The Arsenio Hall Show or Late Night with David Letterman, we'd send as many as 500 faxes the morning before the scheduled appearance, saying something like, "Tonight, Clint Black is going to be on The Tonight Show. Be sure to watch. He'll be performing his latest single, 'Killin' Time,' which is No. 1 on the charts." Recently, the Oak Ridge Boys appeared on the Tonight Show with Jay Leno, we sent 5,000 emails to our VIP list and important buyers. We do the same email notification on a regular basis when the Oaks' Feed The Children specials are airing.

These email impact enhancers are very effective sales tools. They stimulate the buyer to make that call to action.

As a booking agent, you should know everything possible about each of your artists. Remember when we talked about doing research, just like you would if you were selling automobiles or refrigerators? The more knowledge you have about your acts' careers, their records. their backgrounds, the venues they've played, the gross receipts from their shows, the reviews, the crowd receptions, the better equipped you are not only to sell them but get more money for their dates as well. Get the facts in your hand. If an artist made a successful tour of the Northeast, find out the venues he or she played and how many tickets were sold. Were any sold out? If so, use that! If he or she received good press in the area, use that, too.

An agent usually deals with more than one artist, and the bigger the agency, the more acts you deal with. In the Halsey Company, I usually liked to keep the ratio of artists to agent at about three to one. When we were representing 35 to 40 artists, I employed between 12 and 14 agents. This didn't overload the agents, but because it was part of my philosophy to go in-depth with each artist, I felt it was the highest ratio of performer to agent that I wanted.

As soon as we signed a new act, every agent had to see it as soon as possible. Then they could honestly say to a buyer, "I have seen this artist. I know what they can do on stage. They can deliver to your audience, and they'll deliver for you at the box office." I don't care how good a salesperson you are. If you haven't seen a performer, you just won't have the natural enthusiasm you get once you've actually watched the act work.

Remember what I said earlier: Enthusiasm will sell more product than anything else.

INFORMATION IS VITAL

We discussed a lot of things at our morning sales meetings; it was the time for everyone to share information. Early on, before the computer revolution, all of the vital information on our artists was in books. Now, the same info is found on a computer database. Either way, your artist profile should include a picture and vital statistics, the size of the performer's band and its instrumentation, the record label, the albums he or she has had on the charts, the singles that have had chart action, awards received, important venues played, television specials, and production and staging requirements.

In this business—whether you're agent or manager—one of your most important resources is information. When someone calls you about one of your artists, you should be able to punch up your computer—or look in your book—and know instantly about the caller and his or her background. Then, when the callers asks something, you should be able to hit another couple of buttons and pull up the profile of the artist in question.

Remember these three things:

1. Know your artist inside and out.
2. Know your product.
3. Know your buyer.

If you know your artist, your product, you can sell with enthusiasm to your buyer. So write down your information on artist and buyer, put it in your computer or book, keep it at your side. It doesn't hurt to also keep a history of your act's dates, both successes and failures. Make notes of any unusual facts that might help or hinder a sale.

Also remember that booking is selling, and in selling it's not so much what you talk about as how you talk about it. Once you've got the buyer's attention, offering good service is essential. That means expedited delivery of contracts and press material, timely confirmation of dates, prompt responses to any question or request, pertinent information on staging and complete contract-rider requirements, and information on any radio or television appearances that the buyer can use to his advantage. And by all means, be honest with your buyer.

At The Jim Halsey Company, we took great pride in our company's innovative sales approaches. Our mailings were an important way of stimulating buyers—a lot of times, they were pieces of art. We gave our buyers a lot of information; as an agent, you should too. It's another way to exercise your Power of Performance.

SELL-A-THON

And now, a few words about the famous Jim Halsey Company Sell-A-Thon.

The Halsey Company had a reputation for quality direct mail, featuring good-looking pieces of advertising art. So, at one point, we thought: why not do something that was not quite so tasteful, something that would also create a lot of attention? After all, it's fun to sometimes shake people up.

We always had a lot of dates booked in the fall, which is generally a big time for shows and concerts. On the other hand, January and February of each year are fairly slow because people have spent all of their money during the holiday season, and lots of buyers and promoters think you can't sell hard-ticket shows—that is, shows that require a paid-for ticket—during this time. There's far more sales resistance to dates in the first couple of months of the year than at any other time, and buyers argue much more about paying regular prices for January and February dates.

Let's say you have an artist who wants to work 150 dates a year, which is about average for a recording act. These dates are the artist's inventory. Until you book those 150 appearances, spread out over the year with a certain targeted number of appearances per month, there's still inventory left to sell. As I've told you before, once an inventory goes by without selling, it's over. It's not like you've still got it on the shelf, and you can reduce the price and sell it next week. An artist's inventory is tied to time; if the act wants to work a certain amount in the month of March, and March passes with no dates, that artist's March inventory is wasted. You only have so many dates to sell, based on the wishes of the artist.

Although the first of the year is always slow, the artist still needs a cash flow. Many of them give bonuses to their road musicians for the holidays; some take the entire month of December off to be with their families. So, in January and February, there are bills to be paid and salaries to be met—and so dates have to be booked.

To help our artists work more in those months, we came up with a very innovative promotion, taking our cue from automobile dealers. I have a lot of respect for automobile dealers. They know how to sell! They always have a lot of inventory. In order to move it off the lot, they have to come up with hard-hitting deals and competitive prices.

So, with the car-dealer style of advertising in mind, we designed a mailing piece that got more attention than any other mailer I've ever done in my life. At the top, in cartoon-style lettering, was emblazoned the words "The Jim Halsey Company Fall Sale-A-Thon."

"Every Open Date Must Go!" shouted the flyer. "We Must Reduce

Our Inventory!" "Artists Still With Some Dates Available!" "These Dates Must be Booked Now!" "All Offers Considered!" Then we listed each of our artists and the open dates he or she still had.

We sent out a total of 30,000 copies! Using a special toll-free number for the offer, we stayed open for 24 hours a day for all three announced days of the Sale-A-Thon. While we didn't get a lot of action during the middle of the night, the promotion netted us thousands of calls. Some were laughing when they called, some complimented us on the clever promotion, some thought it too "hard-sell." But most had answered the call to action and they'd bought! Sure, it was a gimmick, but the fact that we were available 24 hours a day during the event showed we were really interested in delivering something for the buyer—and for our artists as well.

Within a week after these mailers hit, we had been deluged with telephone calls and had written several millions of dollars worth of business. We ended up having a lot of fun with the promotion, and the artists and buyers had some fun with it, too.

GETTING RADIO SUPPORT

It is statistically proven that the more calls you make, the better your chances of making more sales. To make calls, you need leads.

At The Jim Halsey Company, we had our own resource base, which included all of the promoters, all of the venues, and all of the buyers we knew. New venues and new buyers crop up all of the time, and these are particularly important in developing new artists. That's because your established acts, the big names you work with, usually have a relationship with the more established promoters and buyers. Sometimes, to get a new artist started, you have to find the out-of-the-way clubs and other venues so you can make an itinerary for them that's meaningful to the record company, which wants an act to play the cities in markets where his or her records are going to be promoted.

Part of our business at the agency every day was scrambling for new leads. We've already talked about the trade papers and Leo Zabelin, who brought in the newspapers every day. Our agents would also call contacts at newspapers and auditorium managers. Sometimes a city's Chamber of Commerce was a good source of information. Now, through Google and others, utilizing the web, much more information is available to us.

Even with those resources, though, we would sometimes get desperate for leads. At those times, we would often call the local radio station.

Radio has been a great source of help to us in our company, and I am grateful to their unselfish giving of information to our agents over the years. A good relationship with radio helped us in many ways, and it can help you as well.

As an agent, you need radio's support. You need radio stations to play your artists' records, because if they don't, it's impossible to have a hit. When you go into a community and book your date with the local promoter, it's important to work with the local radio station as well. Make sure the station gets plenty of material on your artist, and don't rely on the promoter to get it there.

The radio station is a source of information for you. It's also a resource in helping your artist date work. At The Jim Halsey Company, we kept information on radio stations across the country, When we booked an act into a city, we knew what stations could be used as resources. Although our roster carried such diverse acts as James Brown, Roy Orbison, Leon Russell, Rick Nelson, and the Woody Herman Band, the bulk of our clients were country music artists played on country radio stations. The procedure for utilizing radio, however, is the same, whether you're dealing with a jazz act, a rock act, or a country act.

Once you find the radio station or stations whose format fits your act, get the names of the station managers, program directors, and music directors. Not only can they help you with information about their cities, but they can also become talent buyers. Sometimes, big stations sponsor listener-appreciation nights, free concerts for their listeners. Even though a station usually only does that once or twice a year, it's a good way to build your artist in that area by getting him or her in front of a lot of people.

In other situations, a good promoter will get a radio station to be the co-presenter of a show or concert, which means they can use the station and its name as an exclusive promotion vehicle and, many times, use the station's hot air personalities as emcees.

It's also important to know if a station is locally owned or if it's part of a group. Over the years, The Jim Halsey Company developed a lot of friends involved with a group of stations. One was Great Empire Broadcasting Company, headed by Mike Oatman of Wichita, Kansas. Great Empire's holdings included such powerhouse country stations as Wichita's KFDI, Tulsa's KVOO, Omaha's WOW, Shreveport's KWKH and the Branson-affiliated KTTS, out of Springfield, Missouri, along with a number of others in other cities

For many years, Great Empire held listener-appreciation nights. They would buy a package of talent and run it through their different cities, giving the event a concentrated promotion in each one. For 30 to 60 days before each concert, it was nearly all you heard about on the Great Empire station in that market. These concerts were effective for both Great Empire Broadcasting and the artists doing the shows. The collective Power of Performance paid off for everybody.

Although radio can become an important member of your team, I don't list it as one of the first essential team members. Why not? Because it has a very specific role to play in an artist's development. Radio only becomes involved with your artist when—and if—it plays your artist's record. This is a specific, often temporary relationship, but it's an important one. Although there have been a few exceptions over the years, a new recording artist will not become a star without radio.

All of the other elements must be in place before radio joins the team. Once it does join, however, it's an essential member with its own Power of Performance to contribute to the making of a successful act.

★

Radio, of course, isn't your only important broadcast medium. Another one that was especially important to the Halsey Company and our performers was television. Now we include cable television and the ability to broadcast from your own website.

At the beginning of my career, I sold an Oklahoma City-based TV show starring Hank Thompson and his Brazos Valley Boys to a regional network. Its Power of Performance was amazing, and it didn't take me long to recognize the power of pictures added to audio. Our regional television program enhanced our ticket sales in those areas. Network television, with its ability to instantly reach 30 to 40 million people, became one of our keys in developing our performers' careers.

We had many ways of tapping into TV for our promotional use. Of course, we always notified our buyers when one of our acts had an appearance coming up on a big show. We also worked to get our country stars on non-country shows, crossing them over into another market. We were very successful doing this with Roy Clark in the '60s and '70s, and with the late Minnie Pearl, the wonderful country music comedienne and personality.

Despite her down-home humor and costuming, Minnie (whose real name was Sarah Cannon) was one of the most educated and classy ladies I have ever met. There also was a very hip facet of Minnie's persona that made her equally at home on The Tonight Show or The Bell Telephone Hour as on The Grand Ole Opry.

In the '60s, the standard set for a country music artist's spot on a TV show usually involved bales of hay in front of a barn. Roy Clark helped change that notion. Early on, Roy was appearing on a major network special. When he went out to perform "Malaguena" on his 12-string guitar, he was confronted by corn stalks, bales of hay, and a phony barn. Later, this would be accepted set dressing for a comedy show like Roy's Hee-Haw, but it was completely out of context for this performance.

So, I complained to the producer.

"How would you like Roy presented?" he asked.

"Just like any other good artist," I replied. That was it. The set was changed.

Once I saw how fast an artist could gain substantial stardom via television, I knew I wanted to concentrate on it. At the time, John Hitt was already in place for our specialized areas of fairs, rodeos, and conventions. We now needed a television expert, someone who would concentrate on series, specials, commercials, and movies.

Dick Howard, a young man with major agency experience, had worked with our company securing TV guest spots for our artists, and he was known and liked by all. Joining our company in the new position of vice president in charge of television, motion pictures, and commercials, he got the new responsibility of building our television department, securing as many worthwhile television appearances as possible for the artists we represented. He opened and directed our Los Angeles office.

A man of great integrity, Dick had built a fine reputation among television producers and talent buyers as an ethical person. He always wanted to sell the right person for the right show. He also had great vision and imagination and tremendous sensitivity when dealing with an artist's art. Dick had a grasp on the future; I always appreciated his ideas on building our artists as well as our company. He fully understood the Star Team philosophy and the concept of creating events with your acts. Both Dick Howard and John Hitt were essential in creating the Halsey Company's success over the next 20 years.

Television was not always a profitable area, because many times an artist would be booked on shows that didn't pay a lot of money. A performer might have to give up a lucrative concert to fly to the West Coast and do The Tonight Show—for $356! A guest shot on a major special might get an act seen by 40 million people, but the paycheck for a top-of-the-show guest-artist was only $7,500 or $10,000.

But television exposure had, and has, many other benefits besides the immediate financial ones.

I remember when Roy Clark was making a lot of appearances on The Tonight Show. When I was in Nashville, I'd run into other managers and agents, and they'd tell me, "Halsey, you're crazy. You're absolutely crazy to send Roy Clark all the way to California to do a show that pays $356. You ought to have more pride in your artists than that!"

But the reason I did it is that 40 million people were watching, and the next day our phone would just ring off the wall with buyers and promoters wanting to buy Roy. At that point, some people didn't even know his name. They'd ask for "that guy who looks like Jonathan Winters and plays a guitar."

And It wasn't long before Roy became one of the top five most-recognized people on television, just a few notches under Bob Hope.

Keeping with our company's philosophy, we specialized and focused on a target. We did not have three or four people calling up television producers and directors, giving them a pitch on our different artists, and then three or four others calling next week to do the same thing. It was important to have one person in our company establish a reputation, and then focus on selling our artists on television.

I remain very proud of the professionalism that our company built and practiced over the years, not only in representing our artists, but in our associations with buyers, producers, directors, managers, and fair managers, among others. We were No. 1, and much of the credit goes to two fine gentlemen, John Hitt and Dick Howard.

DON'T TAKE "NO"

As a booking agent and manager, over the years I learned not to take "no" for an answer. I always say it's not how many no's you get in your negotiations, but, through persistence and consistency, how many yes's you end up with.

You may remember that in my early days with Hank Thompson,

I functioned as both his manager and his booking agent. I had studied sales and marketing in school. I was a consistent salesperson. I knew how to make a presentation, how to negotiate, and how to go for the close. I encountered a lot of problems, of course, but early on, I learned to maintain a positive attitude and not to accept "no."

Here's a wonderful illustration of this attitude.

In those early days, I was taking Hank Thompson and his Brazos Valley Boys across the country, looking for new venues and new events that we could promote. One of the things I wanted to do was find venues that were not specifically country music, but hosted all kinds of different musical acts—venues that were out of the norm for country artists. In those places, I felt, we could create an event, exhibit our Power of Performance to different kinds of audiences, and build our artist to ever-greater heights.

Hank Thompson and his Brazos Valley Boys had already become a crossover attraction. Although he was a country act, with hits on Billboard's country charts, Hank and his band performed not only country and western swing numbers, but big-band standards as well. Among the songs in their repertoire were the likes of "Tuxedo Junction," "String of Pearls," and "Take the 'A' Train." It was a great band, good enough to win the No. 1 Western Swing Band from Cash Box magazine for 13 consecutive years. The Brazos Valley Boys also won similar awards from Billboard, Down Beat, and Record World, even as Hank was winning his own awards as a singer and songwriter.

THE BOB FREED STORY

Because of my experience as a promoter, playing the big bands of such top figures as Stan Kenton, Woody Herman, Harry James, Count Basie, and Guy Lombardo, I saw the potential of taking Hank's great western swing band into territories and ballrooms that had only seen big pop bands.

Salt Lake City had such a place. It was a very popular ballroom called the Lagoon, which played only the top big-name bands in the nation. Weekly big-band broadcasts originated from the Lagoon as well. I was determined to get Hank Thompson booked there, helping to expand his horizons, open up new markets, and develop new territories. It would be a good credit for Hank.

The Lagoon was operated by a man named Bob Freed. I put him on our mailing list with the idea of systematically persuading him to buy Hank and the Brazos Valley Boys for his hall. I was convinced they'd do well in his ballroom, and I hoped to convince him as well, by putting into play my method of repetitious impressions.

My first few telephone calls to Mr. Freed met with thorough rejection. He didn't just say "no. " He said, "No, not now, and not in the future." He wasn't interested in Hank Thompson—or any other country music performer, for that matter.

I've talked before about overcoming rejection. You'll encounter it in any kind of sales business; you cannot take it personally. Instead, you have to somehow discover a way of getting that "no" turned around into a "yes." You have to discover why you were turned down, revise your strategy, and try a different approach, a different sales angle.

The point is not just to convince your prospective buyer to buy what you have for sale. You have to make the sale right for a buyer's situation, so he can profit by it. You have to convince him that it is right for him and his customers. Many times that's a big job, and it's where you lose a lot of sales people. They get discouraged. They lose their focus on their goals.

My focus, however, was solidly on my goals. I was following my plan, but Bob Freed at the Lagoon in Salt Lake City was hindering my progress toward achieving those goals by refusing to buy. My Power of Performance was not effective with Mr. Freed. So, I came up with an exercise that worked for me then, and continues to work for me today. It will work for you, too.

I put myself in Mr. Freed's shoes. I examined what it would take to convince him to buy. In making a sale or in representing a client, you don't need to use hype or an exaggerated sales pitch. Just be normal, and logically give every reason that you can think of as to why this sale, this deal, should take place.

That's what I did. Over a period of three months I sent a series of letters to Mr. Freed about Hank and the band, each one telling of a recent success or containing a positive review of a new record. I sent along Billboard charts to show him that Hank had a record climbing the charts every week. I mailed him stories from metropolitan newspapers about Hank's appearances, and I notified him about upcoming television appearances that Hank was going to make.

After beginning this campaign, I heard nothing from Mr. Freed. No letters. No telephone calls. So I called him—and got another emphatic "no." I decided that before I made another call to him, he'd have so much information at hand that he couldn't say no again. I was determined to change his "no" to a "yes."

Three months after I implemented this repetitious impressions plan, I arrived at work to find a letter on my desk postmarked Salt Lake City, with the return address of the Lagoon. The message inside was simple and to the point. Bob Freed had answered the call to action. He'd decided to try Hank Thompson at the Lagoon, and for the date and the price I'd suggested. He wrote that he'd become so sick and tired of my insistent barrage of phone calls, letters, mailing pieces, and advertising on Hank Thompson that he considered booking Hank as his only way of getting rid of me. My repetitious impressions had worked! He further stated, however, that if the engagement was not successful, he never wanted to hear from me again, and that I was to take his name, address, and telephone number out of my Rolodex forever.

So, there was a lot riding on the date. But I knew that date—or, rather, that event-—would be a huge success, and it was. It surpassed my expectations, and it certainly surpassed the expectations of Bob Freed. He played Hank Thompson at the Lagoon many, many more times after that, and we became great friends. My persistence and perseverance had paid off. My Power of Performance was evident.

GEORGE AND TAMMY TOGETHER AGAIN

As an agent, you should always be trying to find new and inventive ways of marketing your roster of artists. It's just as though you have a retail store with lots of good merchandise: a lot of what you sell goes to the same satisfied customers, so sprucing up the displays, arranging several items together, or doing something new and different can create excitement. In the Halsey Company, we sometimes packaged two of our biggest stars together to make a super show aimed at Las Vegas casinos. For tours, we'd creatively package several of our artists and send them out on one bill in an effort to draw larger crowds, generate more excitement in the press, and make every tour stop an event.

I love events. And they don't get much bigger than the one the Halsey Company got involved with in the early 1980s when, after much work, negotiating, and deal-swapping, we announced that we were presenting, for a very limited number of engagements, a reteamed George Jones and Tammy Wynette. It was the first time they'd toured together since their highly publicized divorce, and they'd be singing their big duet hits, live, once again. What a natural! What an event! The press and television news went crazy, and radio was ecstatic. The George and Tammy tour was going to be one of the biggest musical events of the year, and the Halsey Company was presenting it.

The promoters and the press gave us a lot of credit for working the magic necessary to reunite these two country music giants, and I wish we could take the credit. We were the agents, the ones selling this colossal tour, but Tammy's husband, George Richey, was the mastermind. A multi-talented individual, Richie is a songwriter, musician, and a great producer; but I think his talents as an artist manager surpass everything else. He has an astute ability to guide an artist's career, and he had done so superbly with Tammy for years. He knew the potential Power of Performance of a Tammy and George tour, but nobody thought it possible to bring these two legends back together again professionally. George Richey made a deal and he made it work. Our part was easy. The hard part was in creating the event.

The pre-tour press was terrific. Promoters lined up to be among the chosen few who'd present these historic dates. Many of them, however, were skeptical of Jones. He'd been going through some rough times in the past several years, earning the well-deserved nickname of "No-Show Jones" for his failure to make all of his bookings.

To everybody's relief, however, he showed up for all the George and Tammy dates and did a terrific job. In fact, both Tammy and George were terrific, receiving glowing reviews wherever they played. With the help and inspiration of George Richey, we'd had the honor of presenting one of the most historically important touring events in country music.

We should have stopped there.

After the tour, George Richey's brother Paul became Jones' manager. He asked that we stay on as a part of the George Jones Star Team. I've always been a fan of Jones' talents, and we were excited about representing this superstar. So we signed an exclusive, three-year booking-agent agreement with Mr. Jones and announced to the world we were selling dates on this legend.

It was a booking bonanza! Dates were going on the books faster than we could issue the contracts. But as soon as we had Jones' itinerary filled for several months in advance, things started going askew for George again. He started missing dates again. Sometimes he even showed up at the venue but refused to get off his bus and go on, leaving thousands of irate customers scrambling for ticket refunds.

Naturally, after each blown date, the promoter would file a lawsuit against George Jones to try to recover the losses involved in advertising, building rental, and all of the other expenses involved with promotion of the date.

Our contracts clearly stated that The Jim Halsey Company functioned only in an agency capacity, and were not responsible for any of our artists' actions. Nevertheless, every date that George missed brought us a lawsuit. We had to hire local legal counsel in every city where he missed a date. Although the actions against us would always be dismissed, since we were not liable, it still cost our company a couple of thousand dollars each time to get our liability legally cleared. Because of this, when we were only three months into our three-year contract with the legendary George Jones, our legal fees totaled more than $30,000.

Representing George Jones hit us in the pocketbook in other ways as well. Because of his erratic behavior, all of my agents were now feeling the heat from their good buyers. Everyone who'd lost money on a Jones date now wanted a favor, a good break on the other acts he or she was buying from us.

Finally, I called a meeting with Paul Richey, Jones' manager. I explained to him that I had the greatest respect for George Jones' talent, but I could no longer afford to be involved with booking him. I returned their three-year contract with thirty-three months remaining. Richey understood. The lawsuits we were getting hit with were embarrassing for him, too.

I'd had the honor of representing the historic reuniting of Tammy and George. I'd represented George Jones, the legend, and for a short period of time his name and picture had graced our artist roster. In all, it had been a very rewarding experience for me.

About a year later, I was backstage at Opryland for a television event. A number of our artists were making guest appearances, and so was George Jones. I hadn't seen him since we parted company. Although this was still during a time when he was having some personal difficulties, he was very cordial and we had a nice visit. At one point, though, the talk turned to business and he started to chastise me. "Halsey," he said, "when your agents are booking my dates, tell them not to make the jumps so far."

I had to tell him we hadn't represented him for over a year.

I'm happy to report that since our time with George, his wife, Nancy, has helped him turn his life around, and he's doing very well, thank you. Nancy Jones has worked successfully not only to restore his personal life, but his professional life as well. Fans and promoters alike have been forgiving and have supported George's rehabilitation. By the way, I'm still a big George Jones fan and respect him immensely.

The lesson I learned from my experience with Mr. Jones just reinforced my belief that an agent needs to do a good job for all concerned. It's not a good deal unless all parties benefit. And if you're an agent with more than one artist, your dealings with the buyers and promoters will reflect on your entire roster and all their shows, not just a single engagement.

DETAILS: NEVER ASSUME

Because it involves selling and marketing, the agency business is a business of details. Details can make the difference between mediocrity and greatness, failure and success. And details can get you in trouble. Again, remember to keep and consult your checklist of details!

As an agent, you have to depend on information from other people to complete your own schedule of events. I've adopted a very important rule about this, and I suggest you adopt it also.

It is: never assume!

Never assume anything. Get out that checklist. Check it and double-check it. Make it a habit. It's a very important protection against mistakes and missteps.

Here's a checklist of general business procedures to provide you with an example for your own:

Never assume …

- someone remembers your name
- someone has the correct dates
- someone has returned the contract
- someone has your correct phone number and address
- someone has sent the deposit
- someone has sent the advertising
- someone has placed the advertising
- someone has sent the promotional material for the show
- someone has received the promotional material for the show

- your act is booked for only one show
- your act is booked for two shows
- the bus driver knows the way
- it's only an hour's drive
- everyone remembers the contract details
- the buyer's check is good (this is a big one)
- the check is in the mail
- the date is firm
- your act is getting proper billing
- your act is getting billed at all!
- your act's name is spelled correctly in the billing
- food and beverages are furnished
- hotel rooms are complimentary
- "it's been paid for"
- "it's been picked up"
- it'll be furnished when you arrive
- the sound is good
- the piano is tuned
- the lighting's adequate
- stagehands will be there
- everybody speaks English
- the car is full of gas
- a spare tire's in the trunk
- the luggage will arrive with your flight
- the airline's ticket price is the same as before
- the airplane is on time
- these are "first class" tickets
- the opening act is good
- the closing act is good
- the act does no "blue" material.
- the record-release date is firm
- plenty of rental cars are available
- the food is good
- the kitchen is clean
- the hotel is good
- that anybody knows what he or she is talking about!
  Beware of...
- home cooking
- free breakfast

- all you can eat
  It's trouble when you hear …
- "probably …"
- "it'll be a piece of cake …"
- "any moment now …"
- "you can't miss it …"
- "certain winner …"

Beware when you're told

- "no problem …"

And worst of all

- "I assume so …"

I'm sure you can think of lots of other examples. Just remember, have a checklist, and check and double-check it. It'll make your life easier with less chance for error.

BRIDGING THE LANGUAGE BARRIER

It is up to the agency to continually research and develop new markets. Since The Jim Halsey Company represented many artists with global appeal, it was our responsibility to do everything within our power to open overseas markets. Our agency was the first to go international with country music, which is now a global enterprise. Remember: you should always try to be the best and to strive for perfection, but …

Being first is always important! And it only happens once!

The recognition an artist receives from being first on a television show, at a festival or other event, in a certain venue, at a live recording, or in a country that has never had that kind of act opens a lot of doors. In this business, there's always a carrot dangling. Go for it.

Hank Thompson was the first to open my eyes to the potential of global record sales and international touring, both of which were virtually untapped by country music acts at the time. Together, Hank and I opened a lot of the international doors for the first time.

I made some mistakes, however. But I learned from them.

Roy Clark's 1976 concert tour in the Soviet Union was a great education. The first Soviet tour ever made by a major country music artist, it not only activated whole new opportunities for marketing country music, it also brought forth a lot of hazards and potential hazards that had to be corrected on the spot. Even though we were furnished good escorts and interpreters by Gosconcert, the official USSR concert bureau, the language barrier was almost impenetrable at times. I had failed, in all of my negotiation, to include the provision of a bilingual crew. Our interpreters spoke excellent English, but they were unfamiliar with much of the technical language we needed to use to communicate with our all-Soviet production crew, who spoke only Russian. After that experience, I vowed that next time, wherever we went overseas, I would insist on a bilingual crew.

MONTREAUX JAZZ FESTIVAL

You can achieve a lot of success in this business by doing something completely unexpected—and by being the first to do it.

Roy's Soviet tour was important because it was a first. Country music in the USSR was something unexpected, and we were the first to do it. We accomplished it and it was a press and cultural bonanza.

Nobody had ever tried to do country music at an international jazz festival, either—especially the most prestigious one in the world. Country music at the Montreaux Jazz Festival in Switzerland? Why not? It would really be a first, and certainly worthy of worldwide press.

You can measure Power of Performance in many ways, but it all boils down to accomplishment. Ideas and dreams are great, but they have to be followed and implemented.

This dream was totally off the wall—a superstar-driven country music package, playing the stage of the Montreaux Jazz Festival.

Claude Nobs has for years been Montreaux's imaginative and capable creator/impresario. His consideration for his artists and his audience is tops. His striving for quality artistic entertainment is constant and ongoing.

I met Claude Nobs at the annual music convention, MIDEM, in Cannes, France. This meeting, held each January, brings together all of the top recording and publishing executives to exchange ideas and sell product. Many managers, artists, and impresarios attend. Each night during the five-day conference, the record companies present a gigantic gala, studded with their biggest stars.

In 1979, our company, in conjunction with Jim Foglesong and ABC Records, presented a country music gala at MIDEM—another first. Roy Clark, The Oak Ridge Boys, and Don Williams gave one of the best gala performances ever staged at the convention, and I had Claude Nobs in the audience. The performers followed that with still another first—a gala for Princess Stephanie of Monaco at the Sporting Club in Monte Carlo.

After seeing our acts perform, Claude caught the vision The Jim Halsey Company had for Montreaux. We made a deal to present, for the first time ever, a country-music show at the Montreaux Jazz Festival, which was coming up in six months. Once again, I needed support from the record company. And once again, Jim Foglesong got on board.

Sensing Claude Nob's attention to detail and commitment to excellence, I made a trip to Switzerland to finalize our show for the coming summer. We put together a huge concert studded with quality performers: country superstars Roy Clark, The Oak Ridge Boys, and Barbara Mandrell as headliners, packaged with legendary acoustic performers Doc and Merle Watson and enhanced with special appearances by blues and R&B stars B.B. King, Gatemouth Brown, Taj Mahal, Lonnie Brooks, Little Milton, and James Brown, Buck Trent, and Jana Jae.

Wow! What a show!

It was very important for me to give Mr. Nobs and the Montreaux Festival audience a top-quality concert, so during my advance trip to Montreaux, I investigated everything: stage facilities, sound and lights, hotel accommodations, transportation from Geneva to Montreaux, food facilities, stagehands. My own Power of Performance was on the line here. I wanted to be respected for my thoroughness and professionalism and, as the saying goes, I left no stone unturned.

When I returned to the United States, I found out that my L.A. associate, Dick Howard, was going to be able to sell this concert for television, which meant it was going to be an event, for sure. But it also meant even more logistical details to check out and firm up. I made a checklist of everything that needed to be accomplished.

Jim Foglesong was excited. Three major acts on his ABC Records label were the show's stars. Together, we anticipated the grand breakthrough we were about to accomplish. Our press and public relations company, Gangwisch & Associates, and the ABC Records press department worked hand in hand to make this a big press event, as well. Again, all of the Star Team elements were coming together to deliver a consolidated performance.

I felt so clever. My attention to detail extended to the smallest components of the event: specially designed bags, stickers, and luggage tags, and special shirts and tour jackets, posters, stage passes and other paraphernalia tied in with the event. We put together a tour book that included every piece of information anyone could possibly want, from the beginning flight numbers to our exact arrival time back home. It was a terrific compendium of information, and we gave it to every person on the tour.

Because I had done other international shows—particularly those on the Soviet tour—I'd picked up some useful experience. This time I was pretty smart. I wasn't going to experience the same difficulties as I had in Moscow and Leningrad, where Russian was the only language spoken by the stage and technical crew. This time, I insisted to the Montreaux producer, that the crew—from stage manager to floor manager—had to be bilingual.

That was just one of the details we took care of. We had transportation waiting when we arrived at the airport. When we got to the hotels, we were already registered and our rooms were already assigned. Bouquets of fresh flowers awaited our stars. Meals were arranged. Luggage and instruments were handled precisely and accurately. Nothing was misplaced or lost. Everything was fine, until we reached the stage for rehearsal. Then I learned one of the greatest lessons of my life.

Fred Woods, my dependable tour and production manager, strode excitedly toward me as I arrived at the auditorium for the first rehearsal and camera run-through. I waited for him, anticipating our fantastic spectacle, feeling pretty proud of the way things were going.

"We've got a problem," Fred said.

"What's wrong?" I asked.

"Nobody speaks English," he replied. "Not the stage manager, not the hall manager, not the TV director, none of the stage hands—nobody."

"Fred, get your contract out," I said. "Read what it says."

He looked at me. "Oh, they've followed the contract to the letter. We certainly have a bilingual crew. But the languages they speak are French and German!"

Well, it hit me. I had failed to make English one of the required languages. They'd followed the instructions in the contract, certainly, but I'd been too smug to realize that not everyone speaks English. We overcame the problem by an ingenious method of sign language. It was hard, but it worked.

I was embarrassed, but I'd learned a good lesson. Always have a checklist, and always double-check everything! You cannot check the details too many times in your negotiations. You must double-check even the things that seem obvious. Go over the details of the plan with your associates, and check each other! It's all part of being a good impresario, and a part of your expected Power of Performance. Attention to detail puts you on the road to excellence, and certainly keeps you from making some very, very humiliating mistakes.

The biggest hit of the Montreaux Festival was Roy Clark, as always the master showman. Interestingly enough, the Montreaux audiences seemed disappointed with the more poppish, modern sounds of the Barbara Mandrell show and The Oak Ridge Boys. They wanted pure, down-home, American country music. That meant, of course, that Doc and Merle Watson's set was a big success. Roy, of course, tailored his show to fit the audience, and his joint performances with Doc and Merle were well-received.

While our country-pop acts didn't go over as well as we planned in the first ever country show at Montreaux, country music has since expanded considerably throughout Europe, and all kinds of country music are now well received overseas.

MERVYN CONN

A London-based impresario named Mervyn Conn was instrumental in helping establish country music in Europe. Mervyn's festivals, held throughout the U.K. and Europe, were for many years "the place" to get an artist started overseas. At this time, I wanted to build an international demand for artists like Don Williams, Tammy Wynette, Roy Clark, The Oak Ridge Boys, Donna Fargo, Freddy Fender, and Hank Thompson, and I wanted to expand it beyond the traditional European ideas of what country music was.

I liked Mervyn and got along well with him. I also saw the importance of what he was developing—even though, at his early festivals, his audiences were the real hardcore country-music devotees, not the crossover audiences coveted by the record companies. A great promoter, Mervyn had established a successful annual event in London, the Wembley Country Music Festival (later shortened to simply the Wembley Festival), and he drew large audiences not only in the U.K., but also in the Scandinavian countries, Germany, Holland, and eventually some of the Eastern European nations. I felt it was important for us to tap into this base audience, and then add our own special touch.

Mervyn was difficult in negotiating deals, always haggling over some of the most minute details, right down to the last plane ticket or hotel room. But with Mervyn, whatever was negotiated and agreed upon was always fulfilled. He had his Power of Performance fine-tuned.

In 1980, The Jim Halsey Company had more artists on tours with Mervyn Conn than any other booking agency in the world. Seeing an opportunity to achieve some great worldwide press, Mervyn and I decided to announce our 1981 booking agreement by holding a large international press conference at the prestigious Mayfair Club in London. Our agreement, officially drawn on parchment and done in calligraphy, stated that in 1981 The Jim Halsey Company would supply and Mervyn Conn would accept a combination of artists to appear in the U.K. and Europe, with a total guaranteed amount in excess of $2 million. At the time, this was the largest contract for country music outside of the United States ever written.

Many contracts are simply sent through the mail, signed by all parties, and put into force. But this was something much more than just the signing of a personal appearance contract. When we announced this new association, our press conference was jam-packed, and the news reverberated around the world. A large contingency of worldwide press witnessed the actual signing. It was a monumental association, and the impact it had on country music reflected the Power of Performance of The Jim Halsey Company, Mervyn Conn, and Gangwisch and Associates, our PR company.

Our story broke in the global press, giving us all an international Power of Performance before any of the artists involved had even set foot on a foreign stage in fulfillment of the contract. This is the way it's supposed to work. We had called attention to this record-breaking contract through the press. There was Power in this collective Performance.

A chapter is upcoming on press and public relations, but I want to note here that we would usually invite the press to an elaborate cocktail party, exclusive of Mervyn's press receptions, when our own artists were working overseas. Gangwisch had established an association with a U.K. press outfit called Byworth-Wooten, comprised of two energetic and accomplished young PR pros, Tony Byworth and Richard Wooten. Between Gangwisch and Byworth-Wooten, we were able to garner enormous amounts of press for our artists. One gathering, in fact, was so well attended by British and other European media that we had continual stories for the next three months on Roy, Tammy, George Lindsey, Hank Thompson, Freddy Fender, Donna Fargo, Don Williams, and The Oak Ridge Boys. We usually held these parties in the Roof Garden of the Royal Garden Hotel in London, inviting press and entertainment VIP's. (And our company picked up the tab for these costly events, not the artists.) We'd arrange individual interviews with the stars we represented, achieving a press coup and giving our performers some extra punch.

The Wembley Festivals were the stepping stones to Europe and individual tours and concert appearances overseas. They also afforded us opportunities to establish relationships with television producers. As a result, our Dick Howard—working his Power of Performance on an international level—was able to sell a number of TV specials, and even a series of six 30-minute shows starring Don Williams, and three starring Roy Clark.

Mervyn Conn was successful in many ways, not only for our company and our artists, but for all of country music. He deserves more credit than he gets for helping to establish the success of American country music in Britain and the rest of Europe today.

We also worked with another important impresario, Jeffrey Kruger. Jeffrey flung his promotional net wide; he was the one to establish both Glen Campbell and Don Williams as huge international stars. Over the years, Jeffrey and Mervyn Conn have taken turns in promoting a lot of our acts. Jeffrey, for instance, was the first to introduce Dwight Yoakam to the European market through his Peterborough (UK) International Festival.

As I've said, we wanted to get our stars in front of European audiences that weren't exclusively country fans. At this point, I'd already presented our stars in a lot of the world's most prestigious venues, from Las Vegas casinos to the Montreaux Jazz Festival, Carnegie Hall to Moscow's Rossiya Theater. I was looking now for an important, prestigious venue in the U.K. for The Oak Ridge Boys. Of course, the most prestigious would be the Royal Albert Hall in London, a venue reserved almost exclusively for the biggest stars in the world. What better place to exhibit the Power of Performance of our stars?

Impresario Jeffrey Kruger took the lead in this case. He was presenting Johnny Mathis in concert at the Royal Albert; we convinced him to put The Oak Ridge Boys in to do the show's first half.

As we've discussed, an important part of any event is the press it receives. After all, while only 6,000 people would actually attend the concert, we needed to let the whole world know about it, thereby boosting the power of the act. We accomplished this through teamwork, with our important team member Kathy Gangwisch and her press and PR company going into action, coordinating with the promotion team from The Oak Ridge Boys' record company. We made the event larger than life with press parties and conferences, interviews in both the US and in London, and a combined Power of Performance contributed to by every involved team member. The Oak Ridge Boys did their part, too, and the show was a huge success!

I might add that both Mervyn and Jeffrey would often have special events or tours, or would top one another by offering us better money and amenities. Those things determined which one we signed with each time around. I have a lot of respect for and I'm enormously grateful to them both for helping us establish our artists internationally. We continued to view Europe as a great opportunity, not just for personal appearances, but also for television, records and music publishing. And we continued to introduce our artists to European audiences through those two fine impresarios, as well as others.

The UK and Europe became such a big market for us that we eventually opened an office in London, becoming the first country music agency ever to do so. Records, TV, personal appearances, specialized tours, and music publishing all needed immediate attention in this region, and a young, energetic record-company executive, Charles McCutcheon, became our man in London, doing a great job for us.

When we were starting to develop Dwight Yoakam, we looked for an impresario who was working with younger, more contemporary alternative acts. We chose to work with an aggressive and capable young man named Paul Fenn, who ran a company named ASGARD. For Dwight, we took a totally different approach than we had with our other, more established artists. We played him in more alternative venues and went for coverage in the alternative rather than mainstream press. Paul Fenn did his job thoroughly, and Dwight became a successful international act.

Why was it so important to me to reach out around the world? You may remember that even when I was a beginning impresario with my very first artist, Hank Thompson, I believed that the world was linked by artists and their art. I saw no barriers or restrictions, no boundary lines that an artist couldn't cross. Even language couldn't deter music, the universal language.

Over the years, I'd often recall reading about Sol Hurok, whose story had reached out to me, a high school boy in Independence, Kansas, inspiring me to become an impresario. For Sol Hurok, the world truly was his stage. I was developing it to be Jim Halsey's, too!

THE THREE "S" PRINCIPLE

In summing this chapter up, I'll tell you that becoming a successful booking agent boils down to a simple formula. It's called the Three "S" Principle, and it's as important as it is simple.

THE THREE "S" PRINCIPLE

1. Sign 'em
2. Sell 'em
3. Service 'em

I have seen a lot of booking agency offices with a simple framed sign that states, "Remember the three S's." When I see that, I see a dedication to where that company is going. We can sometimes get so complex with our explaining of theories, methods, formulas, and philosophies that we overlook the fact that it's really a simple, straight-ahead business that yields many rewards to its successful practitioners.

When I give lectures and seminars, I often conclude with a story that brings our lofty discussions back to earth. It's about a friend of mine who was walking down 57th Street in New York one busy noontime. He saw, approaching from a distance, a veteran of one of the big booking agencies named Irv Dinkin. Now Irv Dinkin is the personification of what a booking agent is all about; he works at selling tours and one-nighters for his acts just about every day of his life. You know he has problems. You know he has open dates on his mind.

As my friend passed Irv, he said, "Hi, Irv. How're you doing?"

Without hesitation, Irv answered sharply, "Looking for a Tuesday night," and passed on by.

I think that says it all.

★

I'll finish this chapter with some wisdom from an agent I consider one of the very best, Bill Elson. The former executive vice-president of International Creative Management (ICM), Bill is now a partner with Ascendant Management Consultants.

Not long ago, I did a lengthy video interview with Bill. We discussed agents and agentry from all sorts of philosophical, intellectual, and methodological standpoints. But finally, he said, it boiled down to this: "If somebody wants to be an agent, they just need a telephone and someone who's out of work who plays the guitar."

That may sound simplistic and even arrogant, but it's really what being a booking agent is all about. It's about seeing economic opportunity and personal fulfillment in finding somebody a job. And that's something you can do anywhere in America.

FEES AND CONTRACTS

How are agents paid? In most cases they're paid a booking agents fee of 10%. This is pretty universal. Sometimes if a band is just getting started the percentage can be more. If you're an artist or band raking in the megabucks, the artist or their manager may negotiate a lower fee. The booking agent is an integral part of the team system. The booking agent's term of contract with the artist/band is usually three years. Sometimes less, or sometimes based on a performance clause that requires the agent to produce certain results per the agreement. The contract between the artist/band and the agent is almost always exclusive. There could be exclusions if the agent does not work in certain areas. i.e. Television, commercials, endorsements, etc.

As the title states, they are bookers, sellers of dates. We've explained how solicitations of prospective buyers are made and when the *call to action* is answered. The agent will complete their own form, "offer to contract" with all of the buyer's pertinent information. Name of venue or club, hours of performance, date of performance, price and terms negotiated, payment method. This "offer to contract" information is presented to the artist or band for their approval. Comments are made back and forth between the agent and the artist/band. Any comments or compromises go back to the buyer that has made the offer. When the offer is accepted, the booking agent issues the "contract for a performance" to the buyer. Sometimes, the booking agent will hold on to the offer before accepting so other dates can be attached that would help make the itinerary more sensible. In almost every case, the booking agent will ask for a 50% deposit from the buyer when the buyer returns their contract signed. Here again the contract may be held for the artist/band signature until more dates can be scheduled in a compatible itinerary.

There is another attachment, "rider to the contract." This doesn't include the "terms," but includes the "conditions" the artist/band will expect when the date is played. This generally includes all technical requirements, staging, dressing room facilities, catering for artist/band and crew, stagehands required, even down to types of meals and menu to be served. The rider is also the place to request specialized musical equipment, if needed.

'Twelve year old 'General' Jim Halsey, extreme right,
reviewing his Junior Marines, Washington school grounds,
Independence, KS, 1942.' *Photo by Norvel Couch*

'Radio City Music Hall, 1986–Follow your dreams and
visions, I did with this one.' *Photo by Kathy Gangwisch*

'The Oaks show off their Blublocker bus wrap sponsored by infomercial guru, Blublocker Corp. Chairman, Joseph Sugarman.'

'Oak Ridge Boys' Magnum Blublocker Sunglasses specially designed as part of their corporate sponsorship.' *Oak Ridge photo by Joe Sugarman*

'L to R: Claude Nobs, creator/director Montreaux Jazz Festival and Jim Halsey, Montreaux, Switzerland.' *Photo by Kathy Gangwisch*

'L to R: Mervyn Conn, Jim Halsey, At the time signing the largest contract for country music stars' personal appearances in Europe' *Photo by Kathy Gangwisch*

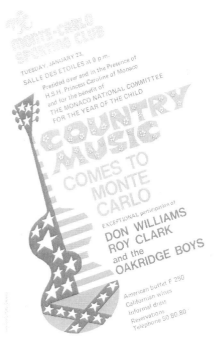
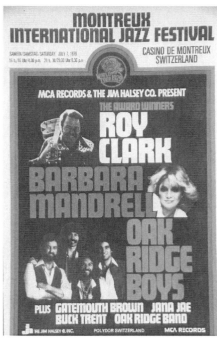

'Poster for Country Music Comes to Monte Carlo, another first ever event.'
'Montreux Jazz Festival, 1979'

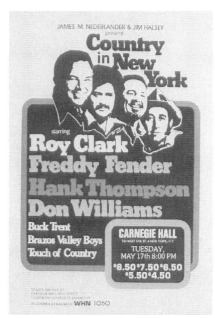

'Country in New York–Co-produced with James M.
Nederlander.' *Photo courtesy of Jim Halsey Co. archives*

'Jim receives Oklahoma Governor Frank Keating's award for 'Excellence in Art and Education,' recognizing Halsey as Director of Music and Entertainment Business program, Oklahoma City University. L to R: Betty Price, Director, Oklahoma Arts Council, Jim and Governor Keating.' *Photo by Travis Caperton*

'Jim Halsey and Little Richard backstage at Oak Ridge Boys' television series 'Live From Las Vegas." *Photo by Gina Halsey*

'L to R: Frederico Mayor, General Director of UNESCO, Leon Davico, Chief of Information for UNESCO, and Jim Halsey, President of FIDOF at UNESCO headquarters, Paris, France.' *Photo courtesy of Jim Halsey Co. archives*

'Recording of 'Making Music' with Gatemouth Brown, Roy Clark and producer Steve Ripley.' *Photo by Gina Halsey*

'Jim with daughters Gina and Crissy. Occasion–Halsey receiving Doctor of Fine Arts Honoris Causa Baker University, Kansas.' *Photo by Minisa Halsey*

'19 year old promoter and big band leader Jimmy Dorsey at a Jim Halsey promoted event.' *Photo by Huff*

'The Tulsa partners, Tulsa, OK, 1972. L to R: Hank Thompson, Wayne Creasy, Roy Clark, Jim Halsey' *Photo courtesy of Jim Halsey Co. archives*

'Hank Thompson and his Brazos Valley Boys and their new Flex touring bus, state of the art circa 1952. Far left is Jim Halsey' *Photo courstesy of Jim Halsey Co. archives*

'Tulsa International Festival produced by the Jim Halsey Co. L to R: Madam Jean Shu (Korea), Professor Armando Moreno, Secretary General FIDOF-UNESCO, Jim Halsey, President FIDOF-UNESCO and Kenny Rodgers.' *Photo courtesy of Jim Halsey archives*

'Jim and Minisa Halsey' *Photo by Kathy Gangwisch*

'Working with artists involved in restoring Ford's Theatre. President
George H. W. Bush greets Impresario Jim Halsey and his wife Minisa
Crumbo-Halsey, 1990' *Photo courtesy of Whitehouse Archives*

'Oak Ridge Boys giving a nod to their manager, Impresario Jim
Halsey' *Photo by Libba Gillum/ courtesy Country Weekly*

'One of my favorite clients, Rick Nelson' *Photo by Kathy Gangwisch*

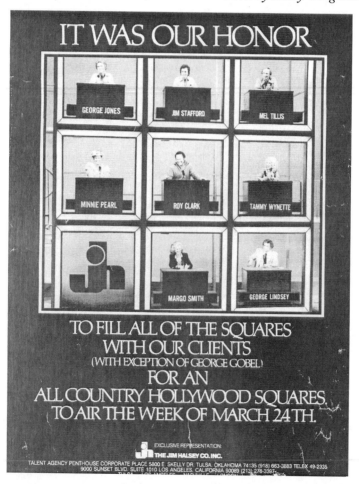

'Roy Clark Friendship Tour cast, Moscow, USSR, Thanksgiving Day, 1988. L to R: Fred Woods, Bridget Dolan, Roy Clark, Jim Halsey, Minisa Halsey, Cris Carter, Judy Pofsky, Gina Halsey.' *Photo by Gina Halsey*

'Frontier Las Vegas, a Halsey package' *Photo courtesy of Jim Halsey Co. archives*

'Jim Halsey with students of the Halsey Institute at Oklahoma City University.' *Photo courtesy of Jim Halsey archives*

'Jim with Bulgarian singing star, Bisser Kirov, at Halsey home, Independence, Kansas.' *Photo by Minisa Halsey*

'Jim and daughter Gina Halsey.' *Photo by Kathy Gangwisch*

'Jim and Minisa in Moscow.' *Photo by Gina Halsey*

'Big band leader Ray Anthony promoted by young
Impresario Jim Halsey, circa 1950' *Photo by Huff*

'Impresario Sherman Halsey and Impresario Jim
Halsey.' *Photo by Kathy Gangwisch*

'Jim and client Waylon Jennings' *Photo courtesy of Jim Halsey archives*

'Neewollah Celebration, Independence Kansas. L to R: Jim, country music star and Halsey client Don Williams, celebration chairman 'Generalissimo' Jerry Webb' *Photo by Kathy Gangwisch*

'Vying for entertainment industry record, The Jim Halsey Company is proud to announce the renewal of the near 40 year management/booking relationship between Jim Halsey and Texas cowboy Hank Thompson. Thompson was Halsey's first client in 1952 when the two posed for a photo (left) with Miss Minnie Pearl. On a recent get together at Halsey's corporate headquarters in Nashville, the three reenacated the scene for the camera.' *Photo courtesy of Jim Halsey Co. archives*

'Jim Halsey, Halsey Associate Troy Bailey with President George W. Bush.' *Photo courtesy Jim Halsey Archives*

'Entertainer Roy Clark and manager Jim Halsey (far left) picked up a few health tips during Roy's concert tour of the Soviet Union when they met up with these Soviet Cossacks at their hotel in Moscow. In town for a convention, these Soviet gentlemen, all 100 years +, agreed to pass on their youthful secrets–"vodka once a day, a fur hat ten months out of the year and a closed mouth.' *Photo by Gina Halsey*

'L to R: Jim, Louis Armstrong and Hank Thompson circa 1953' *Photo courtesy of Jim Halsey Co. archives*

'Jim with superstar clients Woody Herman and Roy Orbison.' *Photo by Kathy Gangwisch*

'Leo Zabelin, Jim Halsey friend and mentor.'
Photo courtesy Jim Halsey Co. Archives

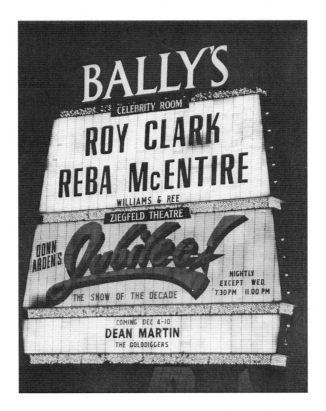

'Bally's Grand Las Vegas, a Halsey package.' *Photo courtesy of Jim Halsey Co. archives*

'Ceasar's Las Vegas, a Halsey package.' *Photo courtesy of Jim Halsey Co. archives*

'Hilton Las Vegas, a Halsey package.' *Photo courtesy of Jim Halsey Co. archives*

'Sahara Las Vegas, a Halsey package.' *Photo courtesy of Jim Halsey Co. archives*

'Frontier Las Vegas, a Halsey package.' *Photo courtesy of Jim Halsey Co. archives*

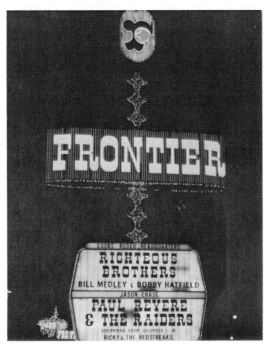

'Frontier Las Vegas, a Halsey package.' *Photo courtesy of Jim Halsey Co. archives*

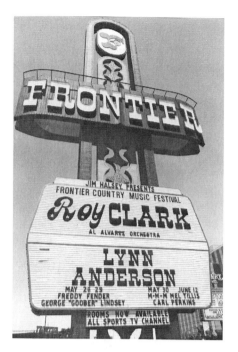

'Frontier Las Vegas, a Halsey package.' *Photo courtesy of Jim Halsey Co. archives*

'L to R: Mervyn Conn, UK Impresario; Victor Sakovich, Cultural Attache' Soviet Embassy, Washington DC; Walter Kane, Entertainment Director, Howard Hughes Hotels, Las Vegas; Impresario Jim Halsey.' *Photo by Kathy Gangwisch*

'Oral Roberts, Las Vegas' entertainment czar Walter Kane and Jim Halsey during Roy Clark's Celebrity Golf Tournament, Tulsa, OK, 1981' *Photo by Kathy Gangwisch*

THE OAK RIDGE BOYS *and* THE JUDDS

MARCH 21 & 22

RADIO CITY MUSIC HALL
A ROCKEFELLER GROUP COMPANY

THE OAK RIDGE BOYS AND THE JUDDS ARE REPRESENTED EXCLUSIVELY BY THE JIM HALSEY CO.

'Oak Ridge Boys and The Judds, Radio City Music Hall, a Halsey package. Commissioned poster art by Al Hirschfeld' *Photo courtesy of Jim Halsey Co. archives*

'2009. The Oak Ridge Boys still reinventing themselves at the giant South by Southwest Conference.' *Poster design by Kathy Harris*

'The Oak Ridge Boys with godfather' *Photo by Celeste Winstead*

'Oak Ridge Boys MCA multi-million dollar contract signing celebration.
L to R: Wm. Lee Golden; Jim Halsey; Irving Azoff, President
MCA; Duane Allen; Jim Foglesong, President MCA Nashville; Joe
Bonsall; Richard Sterban.' *Photo courtesy Jim Halsey Archives*

'President Jimmy Carter, First Lady Rosalyn Carter and Jim Halsey
at White House reception, 1979.' *Photo by Kathy Gangwisch*

'Halsey talks to client Reba McEntire backstage at Universal Amphitheatre performance. L to R: Narvel Blackstock, Reba's husband and manager, Halsey Co. executive Terry Cline and Jim Halsey.' *Photo courtesy of Jim Halsey Co. archives*

'Roy Clark greets a sold out Soviet audience, 1976, Sports Arena, Riga, Latvia' *Photo by Kathy Gangwisch*

'May 1977, Jim Halsey receives the Jim Reeves Memorial Award from the Academy of Country Music, ABC Network telecast. Presented by Roy Clark.' *Photo by Kathy Gangwisch*

'Roy Clark inducts his friend Jim Halsey into the Oklahoma Music Hall of Fame, 2000' *Photo by John Southern*

'L to R: Roy Clark, Walter Kane and Jim Halsey at the Halsey Ranch Party' *Photo by Kathy Gangwisch*

'Sherman Halsey and Dwight Yoakum' *Photo by V. Lee Hunter*

'Video Producer/Director Sherman Halsey on the set as they're shooting the award-winning "Live Like You Were Dying" video.' *Photo by Melinda Dahl*

'L to R: Sherman Halsey, Roy Orbison and Jim Halsey prior to Orbison's Bulgarian Tour, 1982.' *Photo by Kathy Gangwisch*

'White House Entertaiment, L to R: Sound Generation from John Brown University in Siloam Springs, AR, President Gerald Ford, Jim Halsey, Roy Clark, singer Diana Trask, banjoist Buck Trent.' *Photo by Kathy Gangwisch*

'Hank Thompson band beginning a 13 year run at the largest fair in the nation.' *Photo courtesy of Jim Halsey Co. archives*

'Rossiya Theatre, Moscow, Roy Clark / Oak Ridge Boys Soviet Union Tour 1976. L to R: Madam Alla Butrova, International Director of Soviet Cultural Exchange, Mrs. Barbara Clark, Vladimir Popov, Deputy Minister of Culture for the USSR, Roy Clark, Jim Halsey.' *Photo by Kathy Gangwisch*

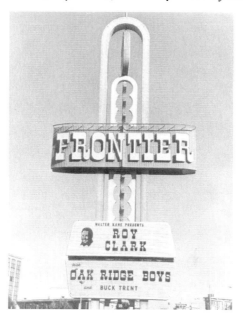

'Frontier Las Vegas, a Halsey package.' *Photo courtesy of Jim Halsey archives*

'1872: Halsey owned stagecoach line Oswego, Kansas.
L to R: Driver unknown, H.E. Halsey Sr. (Jim's grandfather),
Stephen A. Halsey (Jim's great-grandfather).'

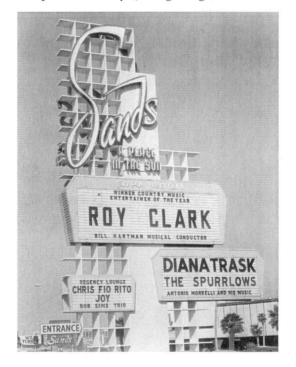

'The Vegas Sands, a Halsey package.' *Photo courtesy of Jim Halsey Co. archives*

'1957. L to R: Jim and client Wanda Jackson sign long term contract with Bill Greene, owner Las Vegas Golden Nugget' *Photo courtesy of Jim Halsey Co. archive*

'Halsey Company Ranch Party.'

'Ranch house, event headquarters.'

'L to R: Roy Clark, Jim and Bob Hope at Roy Clark Celebrity Golf Tournament, Tulsa, OK.' *Photo by Kathy Gangwisch*

'Senator Ted Kennedy (L) and Jim.' *Photo courtesy of BMI*

'Jim with Russian Rock superstar Alla Pugachova at IMOF
Conference and Festival in Nashville, TN, 1989.'

'L to R: Minisa Halsey, Jim and Eric Clapton. Grosvenor House
late night jam session with Clapton, Pete Townsend, Hank
Thompson, Don Williams.' *Photo courtesy of David Montgomery*

chapter 18

PRESS AND PUBLIC RELATIONS

The Five "W's"

I f you've ever studied journalism, you've heard about the five W's: Who? What ? Where? When? and Why? These are the five questions a newspaper reporter must answer in every story.

The five W's are also very important to another member of the Star Team, the press and public relations (PR) person. In the last chapter, we talked a little about this important team member. Now, it's time to examine the role in detail.

Please keep in mind that at the beginning of an artist's career, press and PR is sometimes handled by the artist manager or the artist's record company. Performers, in fact, may have to handle their own press until they're financially able to hire a specialist. So everyone involved in an artist's career needs to learn how it's done.

First, a simple definition: a press person, also known as a publicist and still occasionally called a press agent, is the member of the team whose job is to get your artist's or company's name in newspapers and magazines and on radio and TV, to spread "the good word" about your clients. Publicists are also helpful in designing media campaigns for events and causes.

These team members are important during all phases of an artist's career. In the beginning, the stories they release to the media will help build the performer's name recognition—getting, in a sense, free advertising for an act, free advertising that sells the public on your performer. In the beginning, people need to know about an artist, and the publicist must release interesting stories to the media.

Recognizing the value of using a publicist is important, but understanding how to use one is essential. You must include your publicist in the overall planning of an artist's career. As we've said before, involving all the team members in the master plan gets everybody's energy working in the same direction and opens the channels of communication, which leads to the reception of more helpful ideas. When you're directing the publicity for an artist, you must determine your overall goal and desired results.

Generally, publicists generate news stories to the media so the public will become more aware of the artist. An upcoming tour, a new record release, a television appearance, a major contract with a corporate sponsor, or an outstanding sold-out performance are all worthy of stories, and should be publicized.

After the publicist writes the story, he or she releases it to a media list. In addition to the traditional electronic and print media, the Internet has become another media outlet—and perhaps even email and computer networking are included. A good publicist will have personal contacts in all media, which helps him or her get stories placed. And when you're developing a campaign to build an artist, a publicist's stories can be used effectively in conjunction with paid advertising and personal appearances.

Hank Thompson was responsible for many "firsts" within the country music business. He was, for instance, the first country music artist to record a "live and in person" album. In fact, Hank did three live albums, all big successes: the award-winning Hank Thompson at The Golden Nugget (produced by Ken Nelson for Capitol Records), Live at The Texas State Fair and Live at The Cheyenne Frontier Days. These weren't just records by an important act—acting in accordance with my philosophy, we turned each one into an event.

Hank was a unique talent, and so was Roy Clark. At this time in my career, I represented them both. Hank was established, but Roy wasn't. I knew that what we did early in Roy's career would be essential in helping determine how far and how long his career would go. I also knew the career of the famed Grand Ole Opry comedienne Minnie Pearl, whom I was also handling, could be expanded to a larger audience.

I felt that if we could reach beyond the country music audience, Hank, Roy, and Minnie all had a good chance of breaking into the mainstream. I visited with several people who did press and PR for country stars, but they couldn't grasp what I envisioned for Hank, Roy, and Minnie. Finally, I told my artists I wanted to hire a "Hollywood press agent," someone who could get their names in publications besides the country music magazines. Of course, it was important not to lose our country music press, but I wanted to get stories in mainstream publications all over the country. A story picked up by a major newspaper syndicate—the New York Times, Los Angeles Times, or Chicago Tribune—would be ideal. At that time, you simply didn't see syndicates like those running stories on country artists.

I wanted to hire the best, and we did. We hired Jay Bernstein in Beverly Hills. He was expensive, but he was worth it. It was the first experience Hank, Roy, Minnie, or I had with a press and PR person, outside of what we did in-house or what was furnished by the record company, and our association with Jay Bernstein opened my eyes to the importance of using a top mainstream professional. Through Jay's office, I also met a couple of other impressive young men.

Stan Rosenfield did a lot of the groundwork on Hank, Roy, and Minnie's behalf, working the trade publications Hollywood Reporter and Daily Variety and making daily visits to various television shows. Stan also worked closely with our television agent, Dick Howard.

Hey, we were beginning to build a team!

Stan was an important part of our building process, getting Minnie, Roy, and Hank lots of press. Now Stan Rosenfield heads his own Beverly Hills-based PR agency, and it's a very big one.

Stan Moress (remember the cigar-smoking incident?) was also with the Bernstein office at the time. He was just beginning his career. Later, he'd move to record companies and then to his own business, working as a personal manager for many big stars in both the pop and country fields. I consider him one of the best managers in the business. He is bright, imaginative, dedicated to his artists, and best of all, he's a person of integrity.

Jay Bernstein became a super-important manager and producer, a true Hollywood star-maker. Sadly, he is gone. He was an ingenious innovator for his profession.

See how this business works? You start by building relationships. As you grow in the business, most of the people you come in contact with also grow. If you're in the music and entertainment business, you're in the relationship business as well. As a beginning manager, agent, or promoter, you often have to be your own publicist. That happened to me. As a young promoter in southeast Kansas, I knew that when I was bringing a show or dance to town, advertising was important. But I also knew it was important to have newspaper stories—ideally with pictures—giving the who, what, when, where and why as a complement to the advertising. It was the same thing with radio.

I knew I had to establish personal relationships with people in the media, so I would always personally take my news releases to the editors and always with a generous supply of tickets for good seats to the event. This was not "payola." The shows I would bring to town were always worthy of a good story, and the tickets served as a common courtesy, a means of saying thanks. It was equally important to get good press reviews from the show, which would help build audiences for my next event.

A competitor in a neighboring town once asked how I got so much press on the shows I was promoting. In his hometown, he said, the papers never mentioned his shows. I asked if he took good complimentary tickets to the newspaper. He said he hadn't thought of it, but he'd try it the next time.

A couple of months later, we visited again. He was really unhappy with me. He'd given out comp tickets to the newspaper, and it hadn't worked. Not one story in the local paper. Not even one mention.

I told him I couldn't believe it.

It was true, he insisted. "I gave good complimentary seats to every newspaper delivery boy, " he said heatedly. "I gave tickets to all 35 of them, and still no story."

I had to explain to him that the tickets should go to the people responsible for getting his stories in the paper: the editor, the managing editor, anyone who writes columns, specializes in music, or has a lot of influence over what stories run. Believe it or not, he was so disgusted that he never tried to place a story again, choosing to rely only on paid advertising. And that brings us back around to a point I made earlier. In promoting a show or building an artist, paid advertising is important, but you enhance the power of advertising with editorial copy, copy not paid for. It authenticates the event or product.

It's the same thing with radio. Stations and air personalities can enhance the power of your paid advertising with on-air plugs or comments about your forthcoming show or artist. Perhaps they'll even do an interview with the artist. Everything doesn't have to be paid advertising. And getting publicity, which is essentially free advertising, is part of the publicist's job.

Throughout this book, I've emphasized how important it is to have a goal, have a purpose, and then establish a plan. Publicists needs to know the master plan for an artist's career. They need to know when stories are to be released, and where they should go, and why this publicity is important.

They always need to keep the five W's in mind: Who? What? When? Where? and Why?

By knowing the master plan, and the direction of a performer's career, and by utilizing the five W's, publicists can creatively unleash their own Power of Performance.

They can increase the dimension of an event. They can even create one.

I'm not saying that a publicist should exaggerate or blow things out of proportion, although that sometimes does happen. A good press and PR person, however, can craft a story that emphasizes an event's importance and makes it appear to be bigger than life.

Positive images of artists or a company can be built by using a good press agency and getting the story in front of the targeted audience. Accumulating a lot of stories, advertisements, and television appearances in a short period of time, combined with effective direct mail, telemarketing, and use of electronic media, will create the repetitious impressions that are so important in launching an artist's career, or taking it to the next level.

★

In the first part of this book, we talked about putting together a press kit. Whether you are a publicist, a manager or an artist doing your own publicity, one of the first things you must make available to the media is a good press kit. Think of it as a business card you can leave with your media contacts—a short, concise package of information. When they open it, they should have all the vital information on your artist, material that answers the questions raised by the five W's: Who? What? When? Where? and Why?

In addition to media, the press kit is used to service concert buyers, prospective corporate sponsors, and others you want to tell about your artist or company.

The most effective press kit for an artist contains:

1. At least one good 8 x 10" picture.
2. A brief biography of no more than two pages.
3. A discography (listing the artist's recorded work).
4. Reprints of reviews and articles and/or quotes from important figures.
5. A current tour itinerary (if applicable).
6. A business card or the printed name and address of the publicist
7. A current CD or video.
8. EPK

All these materials (except the EPK) should be packaged attractively in some sort of folder. The established attractions have custom-designed press kit folders; those just getting started can go to a discount or office-supply store and find inexpensive, attractive folders in a variety of styles and prices.

An EPK (electronic press kit) contains essentially the same elements of a traditional press kit, a photo, bio, press clippings, audio demo, contact information and booking requirements. This material now is prepared for the digital domain and can be placed on the artist website, emailed and/or posted on sites specializing in artist promotion. It is common to include video of artist performance to enhance market appeal. Much like a traditional press kit, the look and presentation of this material in the digital domain will impact the ability to market and sell the artist product and inventory.

PRESS RELEASE

Like the press kit, a good press release addresses the questions Who? What? When? Where? and Why? It should do that in a simple and effective way.

Remember my telling about Joseph Sugarman, creator of Blu-Blocker sunglasses? As you'll recall, when Joe creates advertising, his theory is to always put your most important statement in your first sentence, the second most important in your second sentence, and so on. That method applies to press releases as well. If you can grab the readers' attention in the first sentence, they'll stay with you for the rest of the text. Positive first sentences such as "Roy Clark will appear at Carnegie Hall" or "The Oak Ridge Boys have scheduled a concert at Royal Albert Hall to kick off their spring tour" sets your readers up for the rest of the pertinent information.

Before sending out your press release, always check and double-check for accuracy, spelling, and grammar. Double-space the printed message so editors and others will be able to read it easily and can make additions or deletions in the copy before they print their own version. Always include the name or names of people who can supply more information, if needed. Put all of that right below the letterhead, before the main body of the release: Contact (Name, address, telephone number)

Below that should be the release date, either

For Immediate Release

or

Release On (date)

or

Release After (date)

A good press and PR person will have a specialized list of contacts. Usually, these are broken down into several areas:

1. The trades (papers and magazines dealing with the music and entertainment business, including Billboard, Music Row, Hollywood Reporter, Variety (in both weekly and daily editions), Gavin Report, Radio & Records, Pollstar

2. Local newspapers

3. Newspaper syndicates (i.e. Los Angeles Times, New York Times, Chicago Tribune, Knight-Ridder. Reuters)

4. Magazines (Rolling Stone, Entertainment Weekly, People, US, OK, Spin)

5. Wire services (Associated Press, Reuters International)

6. Broadcast media (TV, cable and radio)

7. Cable news conferences (interactive), uplinks

8. Direct mail still effective, but is becoming more and more expensive.

9. Electronic distribution (faxes, e-mail, Internet, etc.)

Although a beginning publicist may not have, or even need, contacts in all of these areas, it's important to use the contacts you do have and to build more as you go along.

THE IMPORTANCE OF A GOOD WEBSITE

The Jim Halsey Company, Inc. had a press department. Even though we had Gangwisch & Assoc., an outside press and PR company, under contract, we needed our own department as well. After all, we represented 40 artists, and daily handled requests from the press and other media. And whenever a Halsey Company contract was signed for a date, we immediately sent out a full press kit on the artist.

Press kits are constantly updated, and it's as important to delete old material as it is to add new material. When you're sending a press kit to a promoter, always include more than one picture; this kit will be one of his basic tools for promotion, advertising, and publicity, and he'll need extra photos for his newspaper and other ads.

Working with their artists, publicists can come up with other ways to help a promoter. Some artists will be willing to make custom advertisements on audio and video for each engagement. Most will do interviews with local newspapers, radio, and television. It's the publicist's job to set up these interviews, which are usually done by telephone in advance of the date.

Another way to get coverage from newspapers, television, and radio is to hold a press conference. This is an invitation for the press to meet at a designated time and place for an important announcement—a special tour, an upcoming big event, the signing of an artist to a new record contract or to a new agency—and it's always more effective to have the artist present for the conference. It gives the press a chance to ask the artist questions, and there's always something magical about the in-person handshakes and greetings.

The publicist organizes these press conferences, notifying his or her media contacts and following up with phone calls to make sure the invitations got where they were supposed to go.

Press conferences should be short and to the point. You should announce the reason for the conference, refer to the handouts given the attendees, and have the act on hand to answer questions.

For many years, we did a very successful series of Christmas dates with The Oak Ridge Boys. Then we decided to go the extra step and make the next Christmas tour an event. We held a press conference in Nashville to proclaim just that, and when the press showed up and asked what made this particular tour any different, we were prepared with our list:

1. We'd added new Christmas music as well as traditional favorites to the regular show.
2. We'd added special production numbers with sleighs, animals, and snow.
3. Special guest star Marie Osmond had been added to the concert.
4. Santa and his elves would appear in person.
5. We'd tied the entire tour in with Larry Jones' Feed the Children charity. (We not only gathered tons of food each night for the effort, but distributed it to the needy in the cities we played the next day, which was a media event in itself.)

Because of these things, each of The Oak Ridge Boys dates turned into a fantastic holiday event. Pre-concert news conferences in each city we played insured us of additional press.

None of The Halsey Company events in this book would have been as successful without the effective use of the press. Press is a power booster. Unless you are trying to create some sort of mystery about an act by not doing press, you must make your artists accessible to the media.

There are electronic, interactive news conferences organized via satellite. These can be especially effective when announcing a major concert tour by a big artist. An increasingly popular way of bringing news to a multitude of people is via the Internet. While not nearly as personal as a press conference, it still gives people opportunities to ask questions of a performer and find out news about a tour or other event.

A website on the Internet can be very effective, too, if you remember to update it daily, and to make it personal.

Press and PR people are specialists, most of whom work on a contract basis. Some are hired for specific jobs or tours. Others remain as part of the essential team on a year-round basis.

It takes an imaginative and creative person to do this job. Good publicists are experts who've accessed their Power of Performance. If they have—and you don't want them if they haven't—you will see absolute magic happen.

★

For more than 25 years, the same press and PR person represented The Jim Halsey Company, Inc. It was Gangwisch & Assoc. in Kansas City and Nashville, headed by Kathy Gangwisch. A person who understands the value of team energy, she worked with many of our artists—including The Oak Ridge Boys, Roy Clark, Mel Tillis, Tammy Wynette, and Don Williams—and was involved with almost every event project our company has conceived. (Since her retirement in 1995, The Brokaw Company, Los Angeles has been exclusively involved). We have recently double teamed with Nashville based Webster PR headed by energetic Kirt Webster. His associate, Jeremy Westby, was a Halsey student at OCU.

While the terms "publicist" and "public relations" seem synonymous, they are really two different things. Public relations involves work, projects, or events that enhance an artist or company's image in a positive way. Most of the artists represented by our company were involved with public relations endeavors that would elevate their status as human beings: collecting food for Feed The Children, playing in golf tournaments for charities, and lending their name to worthwhile fundraising events.

Several years ago, our company launched a major campaign on The Oak Ridge Boys that included extensive press, radio, promotion, and advance on all dates. It was just like a circus promotion. As The Oak Ridge Boys' public relations firm, Gangwisch & Assoc. was getting enormous amounts of major national and regional press on the group. At the same time, we were heavily involved in doing the same types of promotions with Roy Clark, Reba McEntire, Mel Tillis, The Judds, and some of our other superstar attractions. It was a busy summer.

We were heading into the fair and rodeo season, with these artists playing the biggest fairs and rodeos in the nation. It was going to be a very big-grossing time for us. Naturally, all avenues were covered, and press releases went to all the big national magazines, including Time, Life, Esquire, and People. We were trying to saturate them with the fact that country music was happening, and that our names were the biggest names in country music, the ones making the biggest grosses, playing the biggest venues, drawing the biggest crowds.

Pouring all of your energies into a campaign like this is a little like blowing up a balloon. You hope you do the things that can make your project fly while avoiding the things that will make it blow up in your face. If you believe in yourself and the value of your project, and you've accessed your Power of Performance, you know it's going to fly. You know the "big call" will come.

One hot summer evening, the "big call" came. I was working in the yard some distance from the house. It was just beginning to get dark when my wife, Minisa, called excitedly to me from our second-floor balcony.

"Jim," she shouted, "Time magazine is calling from New York!"

Time magazine from New York! We both knew what that meant.

I dropped everything and hurried up the hill. As I jogged toward the house, my mind raced through all of the possible reasons for the "big call."

"Is it about The Oak Ridge Boys?" I wondered frantically. "Roy? Reba? The Judds? Maybe it's about me. Time magazine—hooray!"

I teased myself with the possibility of stories on more than one of my acts, knowing that at least one Halsey Company client would be the lucky recipient of some Time magazine ink. I hardly dared to dream of a cover piece—but I did. Time seemed to stand still as I hurried along, all these possibilities flashing in front of me. Time magazine ... from New York. All the years of hard work and dedication, all of the artists' sacrifices of time and energy, was about to pay off. Time magazine would not call at nine in the evening for a casual quote. No, nine p.m. meant something big. When I finally reached the top of the hill, I was out of breath—not just from the physical exertion, but from the excitement and anticipation. I could feel my heartbeat in my mouth, throat, and fingertips. I felt almost giddy. Leaping up the front porch steps two at a time, I ran into the house. My wife, who seemed just as excited as I was, handed me the phone.

"Hello?" I gasped.

"Mr. Jim Halsey?" asked a pleasant voice that seemed to hold promise of wonderful news.

"Yes, this is Jim Halsey."

"Good evening, Mr. Halsey. I'm Nancy from Time magazine in New York City, and I have good news for you."

Time magazine in New York has good news for me!

"I'm calling to offer you our very special subscription bonus," she continued. "Thirty-six weeks of Time magazine at half the price. No money now; we'll bill you after you receive your first issue."

Suddenly, the cover story with Roy Clark, The Oak Ridge Boys,

Reba, The Judds or Mel, exploded and fluttered away in my mind like so much confetti.

"And what's even better," Nancy from Time magazine in New York said, "if you give me your order right now over the phone, we'll give you a free pocket calculator."

I took a deep breath and gathered the strength to decline the offer, then I returned the phone to its cradle.

I sat down.

I laughed. Hard. And my wife joined me. It was a good joke on us both.

I share this story with you because I'm a dreamer. I always have been and always will be. Our dreams take us places where other people are unable to go. Being able to accept a disappointment or rejection with a good laugh is part of making your dreams into realities. For a dreamer, nothing is impossible, even a Time magazine cover.

★

Advertising and promotion is not the same as press and public relations, but it all ties together. Effective use of the media, in both paid and unpaid forms, builds your artist, band, or project. In fact, in the music and entertainment business, effective use of the media is essential to success. Press is an impact enhancer for any campaign. Whether it's career building, tour planning, record promotion, or the maintenance of a career, how effective you are is determined by how well you've employed the media in your overall plan.

At The Jim Halsey Company, our plans included using every media opportunity, along with an in-depth advertising campaign. Together, they created the repetitious impressions you've heard so much about in this book.

Please understand the term "impressions." When one person sees or hears an advertisement or a media mention, that's one impression. If the same person sees or hears it again, that's two impressions. If a thousand people see one ad, that's a thousand impressions. When you hear advertising agencies talking about a certain campaign getting, say, 10 million impressions, that means through ads and other mentions in the media, their product was seen or heard 10 million times.

To get the maximum number of repetitious impressions, we'd design campaigns for our artists using every method we had available, including guest appearances on television, radio interviews, newspaper and magazine stories, record releases, and direct mail. A typical campaign would bunch together as many as six to eight television guest shots, with our artist appearing on everything from network series to local shows within a three- or four-week period. Usually, these appearances would be coordinated with a record release or some other important event. During this time of concentrated television exposure, our press and PR people would schedule as many interviews as possible with national publications, important daily newspapers, radio shows, cable news shows, magazines, etc.

Additionally, this activity would be designed to tie in with a specific record company promotion aimed at rack jobbers (record distributors who have racks in a variety of stores), distributors, and giant retailers such as Wal-Mart, Target or Best Buy. During this time, our method of repetitious impressions would also include a systematic direct-mail campaign regarding that particular artist.

To maximize the effect, direct-mail advertisements using three different artistic treatments should be mailed to the same list, so that the buyers and promoters receive these three different pieces spread over a six-week period—the same period that encompasses your artist's concentrated TV appearances, the accompanying flurry of press, and the record-company promotion. The first piece of mail should arrive at the beginning of the campaign, and the third, or last, piece about two weeks after the campaign has peaked. If you time everything right, for that four to six weeks it will seem like there is nobody more important in the world than your artist.

I developed this method of repetitious impressions early in my career and have used it effectively with every one of my artists at one time or another. The same can be done with email.

In the early days of building Roy Clark's career, for instance, I used it quite effectively. For some artists, you actually have to be careful about having too many repetitious impressions, especially too many television appearances in a short time, because of overexposure. If your performer is one-dimensional, too many appearances too close together could have a negative effect instead of a positive one. This, of course, wasn't true with Roy. He could do so many different things that the audience never got tired of seeing him.

I remember one campaign we did in which Roy started with an appearance on The Tonight Show with Johnny Carson, followed it up with a guest shot on Mitzi Gaynor's special, and made additional appearances with Merv Griffin, Dinah Shore, Mike Douglas, Joey

Bishop, and the Hollywood Squares. During this time period he also did interviews with a writer for the Associated Press, with Jack Hurst for Hurst's syndicated column in the Chicago Tribune, and with such major daily newspapers as the Detroit Free Press, Kansas City Star, and Las Vegas Sun. He had a new album out and a current show at the Frontier Hotel in Las Vegas. While Roy always had a lot going on, this was an especially good time for us to maximize his efforts with a repetitious Impressions campaign.

The Jim Halsey Company used repetitious impressions on a year-round basis, making more direct mailings than any other agency in the business. I took great pride in developing our list of talent buyers and promoters not only nationally, but internationally as well. I firmly believed that if my target list of buyers could be kept informed on a regular basis of the artists we represented and what they were doing, they would be more stimulated to buy.

It worked. They called, we called, and they bought!

Our direct mail would go out at least twice a month to every name on the list. Special campaigns or new record releases might bump it up to once a week. It was sometimes directed, sometimes generic, but always on a regular basis.

This was a lot of mail. We always hit at least 60,000 pieces a month, and sometimes sent out 120,000. The cost was considerable, but we had help, with the artist, the record company, or the music publisher often helping financially. Now email provides the same type of campaign and virtually no cost of postage. We also complemented our mailings with full-page ads in Billboard, Amusement Business, Cash Box, Radio & Records, and other trade publications.

One time I took out a two-page spread in Billboard to announce that our combined artist roster had achieved, through the press and television in the past 12 months, total impressions of 280 billion, a phenomenal amount of impressions that illustrated the importance of our agency as well as the artists we represented. The advertisement also noted that somewhere in the world, every minute of every day, one of our artists was being played on the radio.

This two-page announcement was targeted toward advertising agencies, prospective corporate sponsors, and television and cable TV programmers. We specifically targeted other promotions as well, including ones for annual events such as the Fair Buyers Convention in Las Vegas, held at the end of November.

While these were advertising campaigns, you can understand how they became much more effective when coordinated with a press and PR campaign. Advertising is paid media exposure; publicity and public relations is unpaid media exposure. Together, they work hand-in-hand. Now, effective methods will also include email notices and innovative website designs.

PHOTO SESSIONS

Even these days, when a press kit is just as likely to be an EPK (electronic press kit) with photos on a disc or even a website, good photographs are still a very necessary ingredient of press, PR, and promotion.

Having good photographs–or good "art," as it's known in the newspaper business–is very important to both beginners and established acts. An act's music is a signature, a brand, its identification. But equally important is that act's look, or image. As you–whether artist or artist's representative–submit your demo CD to various labels, the people at those labels will want to know what the performer or group looks like. As the act becomes established, the photos become important tools in booking dates and getting press.

Often, the kind of photos available to newspaper and magazine editors will go a long way in determining how big the publication plays the story. One or two good pieces of "art" may get you on a magazine or newspaper entertainment-section cover, with a big photo drawing attention to the story. On the other hand, a substandard picture may relegate the story to the back pages, where the picture of the act may not be much larger than a postage stamp, or not even used. Sometimes, a good photo will also be used as what's called "wild art," spicing up an event listing or upcoming-show column in a newspaper or magazine, getting the artist even more attention. For these and other reasons, good pictures are very important. Here are 10 tips that will help you get the best photo session for yourself or your act:

1. **Get a good photographer.** You're going to make the best demo you can, using the best studio and technicians you can afford, aren't you? Then do the same with your photos. Most cities of any size have some excellent photographers experienced in shooting entertainment-related photos. Make sure to have examples on hand of the kind of pictures you want.

2. **Pick an interesting location.** You may want to shoot in a studio, but

publicity shots these days are often taken on location—maybe on the street, in front of interesting buildings, or at a farm or ranch, airport or bridge or railroad tracks. Use your imagination to come up with a nice visual image. Look at other CD cover art as well as posters and other promotional material—not to copy them, but to inspire a style that works for you. A good photographer will also have some creative ideas.

Over the years, we've had some intriguing photos done with the Oak Ridge Boys. One of my favorites was an album cover, suggested by Kathy Harris of the Oaks' marketing department, which depicted the four guys, all in tuxedos, being briskly led on a walk by a cheetah! Another shot we used for an LP cover, lots of ads, and even a Sunset Strip billboard, had the Oaks all riding in an MG convertible. These two images are still talked about today.

3. **Consider performance shots.** These are always interesting, whether they're taken during a show by the act, in the recording studio, or at a television or video performance.

4. **Get photos with other performers or celebrities.** If your act is working or associated with other performers, perhaps on a package show or at a charity event, be sure to get photos of your client with them—especially if they're well-known. Then—with permission, of course—make those photos a part of your press kit.

5. **Plan your photo session.** If you're just starting out as an artist or artist representative, you may have to plan the session by yourself. Later, that task may be taken over by a record company representative, booking agent, or other member of your team. Regardless of who plans it, the plan must include how the session will be shot, by whom, where, and how it will be used.

6. **Plan your wardrobe.** An artist should know what he or she is going to wear to the shoot. It should be clean, of course. Remember that dark colors usually don't photograph as well as bright ones, and details like special stitching sometimes don't translate to a picture.

7. **Bring a change.** So all of the photos won't look alike, bring a change or two of wardrobe.

8. **Show up on time.** If you're an artist representative, make doubly sure your act gets to the session at the appointed time and place.

9. **Have a good attitude.** A professional shoot may take several hours. An artist should make sure to smile both on and off camera, to be relaxed and natural. After all, this will be the act's visual image, sometimes for several years.

10. **Be prepared.** There's that Scout motto again. A photo session should *never* be preceded by a late evening of dissipation. It will definitely show on camera. Artists should get a good night's rest before the shoot so there won't be bags, sags, lines, or a washed-out look. This is also good advice for those shooting a music video or a television show.

Finally, if the top-drawer photographers you want are out of your price range, look around and ask around. There may be a good amateur in your circle of friends and acquaintances. If you do use a nonprofessional, however, make sure they shoot lots and lots of photos, giving you plenty to choose from. The more shots you have available, the more the chances increase of your finding one or two great ones. It's simply the law of averages.

And here's a trade secret: Even the very best photographers shoot an abundance of photos at every session.

chapter 19

THE MUSIC PUBLISHER

t this point, we've attached almost all of the spokes to our Star Team wheel. Beginning with the artist—the hub of the wheel— we've added the artist manager, the record company, the record producer, the booking agent, and the publicist, all necessary components of any Star Team.

Now it's time to add another essential member: the music publisher. Although many people would be hard-pressed to explain exactly what this team member does, a music publisher is often one of the main ingredients in developing a star.

A music publisher represents the songs created by a songwriter, collects the revenues for their use, and splits it with the songwriter. What usually happens is that the publisher collects 100 percent of the revenue generated by a song, and then gives 50 percent to the songwriter.

The music publisher copyrights the material, registers it with a performing-rights organization (BMI, ASCAP, or the smaller SESAC), stays up to date with the current compensation policies, and negotiates licensing fees for the songs. Publishers are a crucial part of the business, although I must add that they—along with the rest of us—wouldn't be necessary if there were no songwriters.

In many ways, the relationship of a music publisher to a song is like the relationship between a booking agent and a performer. The publisher, in other words, represents a song. It is the publisher's responsibility to get a song recorded. It is the publisher's responsibility to get a song in commercials, on television, in a film, or on stage. When the music publisher obtains a song from a songwriter, the publisher gains full control of that song, taking the responsibility for promotion and deciding where the song's potential can best be utilized. Publishers have the ability to make money off a song in many, many ways!

Music publishers have great resources at their command. They also stay on top of national and international regulations regarding the use of songs. These regulations can change rapidly, and a publisher helps the songwriter by always being aware of the parameters that define the way a song can be used.

Publishers can also be very instrumental in helping a new singer/songwriter get a record deal. Some have their own publicity department, which can supplement the record company's promotion on a new release. That's just one way a music publisher's Power of Performance can and should be coordinated with that of the rest of the Star Team.

Music publishers are found in cities where there is a lot of musical activity, places like Los Angeles, New York, Nashville, Austin, Atlanta, Chicago, and Seattle. You can find their addresses in the yellow pages of the telephone book. Most local phone companies have books for other cities; you can also check your local library or Chamber of Commerce.

The Internet is also an excellent source of information on music publishing, copyrighting, and songwriting. Much of the information an up-and-coming songwriter needs is out there for the finding.

Good music publishers are busy. Many are reluctant to accept unsolicited new material. If you know anybody in the business who can give you a referral, that would be a great help. Sometimes, attorneys who specialize in the music business (we'll talk about these in the next chapter) will, for a fee, represent you and your songs to a music publisher or record company.

Write letters! Try to see publishers. Do anything you can to see anybody, even if it's the secretary, the security person, or another office worker. Many times, people like these can introduce you to a publisher or recording executive. Once again, it's up to you to actualize your Power of Performance.

★

Now let's discuss how you will make money with your songs.

As we've said, the music publisher functions for your song or songs in much the same way that a booking agent works for a performer. Publishers represent your music and pay you a portion of what your song earns. Their efforts on your behalf are important.

We mentioned BMI, ASCAP, and SESAC earlier. These are not music publishers, but organizations that license copyrighted music to users and collect fees for the writer and publisher. These users include radio and television stations, nightclubs, casinos, arenas, amusement parks, hotels, and any other commercial establishment in the US where music is played publicly. The form of payment to the publisher and songwriter is called a royalty.

The term has an interesting origin. Music publishing started in 15th century Italy. Because all musical compositions were printed at the time, the term "music publishing" came into use. The kings, princes, and other members of royalty bestowed exclusive rights to musicians and composers to print sheet music. Those musicians and composers, in return, paid their benefactors from the proceeds of their work, and since they were paying royalty, that's how the term came to be.

Today, songwriters and publishers have a number of potential sources for royalty income. Here are eight of the most common:

1. **Mechanical Royalties.** These are paid to the publisher / copyright owner by the record company on the amount of record sales. Sales are determined through SoundScan. Mechanical royalties are paid either by song or by song length. If the song is less than 5 minutes then the mechanical royalty rate is 9.1 ($0.091) cents, and if the song is greater than 5 minute then the royalty rate is 1.45 ($0.0145) cents per minute. The mechanical royalty rate for each copy of the record, CD, or tape made and distributed are as follows:

Mechanical Royalty Rate by Year
Per Minute
(if song is greater than 5 minutes)
2007   9.1cents1.75 cents

Mechanical Royalty Rate by Song (2007 - rates)
Song LengthRoyalty Rate
Less than 5 minutes   9.1 cents

Less than 6 minutes	10.20 cents
Less than 7 minutes	11.95 cents
Less than 8 minutes	13.70 cents
Less than 9 minutes	15.45 cents
Less than 10 minutes	17.30 cents

Mechanical Royalty Rate by Album (2007–rates)

Number of Songs
per Album Royalty Rate
(All songs under 5 min.)

1	9.1cents
2	18.2 cents
3	27.3cents
4	36.4 cents
5	45.5 cents
6	54.6 cents
7	63.7 cents
8	72.8cents
9	81.9 cents
10	91.0cents

Example: If there are ten songs on a CD or cassette, each running five minutes or under, the total payment by the record company to the music publisher (or publishers) would be 91.0 cents per CD & cassette sold. If this album goes platinum and sells one million copes, then mechanical royalties would equal $910,000. The music publisher, in turn, then pays the songwriter a portion of the revenues. This portion is usually a 50/50 split, depending on the arrangement between the songwriter and music publisher.

There are exceptions to this schedule of payments. If the artist recording the songs is also the songwriter, co-writer or publisher, the record company looks at this situation as "controlled" material, and if more than an average number of "controlled" (i.e. written by the recording artist) are included on the album, the record company will ask for a reduced mechanical royalty. Usually of over half the songs on a CD are "controlled," they will pay only 75% of the statutory rate, or will also limit the number of songs on the CD, or both. These reduced rates are negotiated between the record company and the artist/songwriter.

2. **Performance royalties.** These are divided into two categories: broadcast performance and non-broadcast performance. These royalties are collected and paid by the performing rights organizations mentioned earlier: BMI, ASCAP, and SESAC. Radio and TV broadcasters have a system in which the songs they play are periodically logged. From this, they compute a song's average airplay. Every broadcaster pays a blanket licensing fee to all three performing rights organizations for the right to broadcast copyrighted material. Each organization then pays its songwriters and publishers a portion of the fees collected as broadcast performance royalties, based on the average airplay reported by the stations.

In a 2005 decision, the United States Copyright Royalty Judges determined internet radio rates should be thus: 2007 - $.0011 per performance; 2008 - $.0014 per performance; 2009 - $.0018 per performance; 2010 - $.0019 per performance; 1 performance equals 1 play of one song multiplied by the number of listeners tuned in for any part of it. SoundExchange was then tasked with the responsibility of distributing royalties to copyright owners. SoundExchange is a non-profit performing rights organization that represents thousands of record labels and artists who have specifically authorized SoundExchange to collect royalties on their behalf and was, at that time, an unincorporated division of the Recording Industry Association of America.

Though it is a non-member organization, SoundExchange is authorized by over 12,000 performers, 3,000 record labels and 800 record companies to collect royalties on their behalf. SoundExchange distributes royalties to nearly 15,000 copyright owner and performer accounts and, as of September 20, 2005, has processed over 650 million sound recording performances.

For complete documentation of the U.S. Copyright Royalty Judges proceedings on this subject, visit http://www.loc.gov/crb/proceedings/2005–1/final-rates-terms2005–1.pdf and for further reading on this issue visit http://www.techdirt.com/articles/20070304/223155.shtml.

Keep in mind that a songwriter can only belong to one performing rights group, either BMI, ASCAP, or SESAC. The organization a songwriter belongs to is responsible for paying his or her broadcast-performance royalties.

A non-broadcast performance occurs whenever copyrighted material is played in public for profit. This covers both recorded music and live performances, and it can happen almost anywhere: theaters, arenas, auditoriums, fairs and rodeos, concert halls, restaurants, theme parks, casinos, night clubs—even elevators and funeral homes. BMI and ASCAP have been very successful in compelling every one of these venues to comply with the federal law and secure a license to play copyrighted material. They, of course, must pay for the privilege, which assures songwriters and music publishers more revenue.

3. **Jukebox royalties.** Another important source of revenue licensed by BMI, ASCAP, and SESAC, royalties from jukebox play are paid out to publishers and member songwriters.

4. **Sheet music royalties.** When there were more pianos than stereos in American homes, sheet music sales were an important part of a publisher and songwriter's income. Sheet music has become less and less important over the years, but some is still being created on a mass-market basis, mostly in the form of songbooks and folios by popular artists. Usually an average of 12.5% of retail is paid to the publisher.

5. **Grand rights royalties.** This isn't one of the better-known sources of songwriter income, but it generates a lot of revenue for certain writers. The term grand rights refers to Broadway shows and musicals. Once a writer has music in a hit show, these royalties can last a long time. Shows can travel for years following a Broadway run, with "bus and truck companies" crisscrossing America on tours and repertoire and college theaters picking up a show. They all have to pay the publisher grand rights before the curtain can go up.

Look at the continuing popularity of such shows as Guys and Dolls, Showboat, Oklahoma!, Music Man, Annie Get Your Gun, and, of course, all of the Andrew Lloyd Webber shows. They will be around for years, making money for those who created their songs.

6. **Synchronization royalties.** When your music is used in movies or on a television show, you get a synchronization fee. Generally paid to the publisher (who splits it with the writer), it's not a set fee. Instead, the fee amount is negotiated with whoever wants to use it.

7. **Special permissions royalties.** Now this is an interesting one. These are licenses worked out with merchandisers that want to use a song in a disc or tape for a special marketing program.

Companies often put together special albums to be sold through service stations, convenience stores, or large supermarket chains. You've seen these around, especially at Christmas and other holidays. Like synchronization royalties, the fee for this kind of song use is usually negotiated, and the songwriter and publisher—along with the artist, of course—get the money.

8. **Foreign rights royalties.** A lot of songwriters today have universal appeal: their songs have the potential to become popular all around the world. So foreign rights can be very important. As a songwriter, you must try to get a publisher with experience in making deals outside the US so that you can have your songs promoted internationally, with international royalties the result. Revenue can be exceptionally good in the European market, as well as in South America and the Pacific Rim countries.

9. **Mechanical DVD Royalties.** Putting a song on a DVD which is then made available for sale requires a negotiation between the record company and the publisher. There is no statutory rate of royalty for DVD sales.

A beginning songwriter may not have access to a publisher with worldwide offices, but a savvy publisher can make sub-publishing deals with other publishers to license your material abroad.

We should also note that the performing rights organizations, BMI, ASCAP, and SESAC, have reciprocating agreements with other performing rights societies around the world, which helps when it comes to international performance royalties.

★

Let's step away from the publisher for a moment and answer the question most asked by beginning songwriters: how do you protect your original material?

Under the Revised Copyright Act of 1976, you have an automatic copyright on your song the moment you have completed your material, either on paper or on tape. For further protection, you may register your copyright with the Library of Congress. To do that, write the Copyright Office, Library of Congress, Washington, D.C., 20559 and request Form PA, returning it with the required payment.

Realistically, it's usually not necessary to register your copyright until your song has been recorded; however, it's always a good idea to put the copyright symbol, that little "C" with the circle around it (©), along with your name, address, and date, on each of your lyric sheets or on any label of cassettes that contain your songs. Under the most recent copyright laws, a copyright is good for the life of the writer plus 70 years.

★

There are pitfalls that await you in this business. At every turn, unscrupulous operators are, ready to take advantage of the unwary. When you're assembling your Star Team, be very careful about the people you add. Make sure you are getting value received for any money you pay out, and be very careful when paying anyone anything.

Let's take the music publisher as an example. A legitimate music publisher will publish your song and try to generate income from it, royalties that will be split with you. Never pay a publisher to publish your song. The publisher should be earning money for you, not from you.

This is generally true in the recording business, as well.

If you have a song or a performance that is worth being recorded, a record company will, in most cases, advance the money for the recording session, hoping to get a return on its investment in the form of marketable music. If you are asked to pay for the recording or for the manufacturing of so many cassettes or CDs, watch out—that's a red flag!

Examine what you're getting in the deal. Is it up to you to pay the recording costs? To get your product manufactured and distributed to the record stores? To promote your records on radio? If you are paying for everything, you have gotten into the record business, and your chances of succeeding are slim indeed.

Here's one of the most common ripoffs. A songwriter or singer sees an ad in a newspaper or magazine soliciting "new songs and new artists." The address on the ad gives the name of a record company in some major recording center—New York, Los Angeles, Nashville. So the artist sends in some material.

Unfortunately, no matter how good or how bad the material is, a glowing report soon arrives from the "record company." It says, this could be the next big hit. All you need is to record it professionally and get it on radio stations. And, of course, that's where they come in.

They'll tell you what they're going to do, and they'll do exactly what they say they will. They'll record your song, and they'll get it to radio stations. But it's going to cost you. And your cost to record with them will almost always be much more than if you simply went to a recording studio of your own choice and hired a bandleader and musicians yourself.

They'll send your song to a certain number of radio stations, just to remain legal. But the program directors and music directors at radio stations don't usually listen to new material from a record company that's not in the mainstream. They're also familiar with these kinds of labels and know what they represent. And what's more, they don't usually listen to anything on cassette, which is the way many of these companies distribute your material.

So before paying anyone anything, find out who you're dealing with. Get some recommendations from other people who have worked with them. Check with the Better Business Bureau, the Chamber of Commerce, music publishers, or trade organizations. It may save you thousands of dollars.

★

Remember that part of my method for success is being persistent and consistent? Well, I've found over the years that songwriters, to their credit, are a very persistent lot. If songwriters are really serious about their craft and believe in their songs, hardly anything will discourage them. And the most persistent ones have an uncanny ability to penetrate even the most secure backstage areas of giant superstars. I know. It has happened on some of my own shows.

The backstage has been tightly secured, with no friends, no family, no business associates allowed. There's not enough room and the show's on a tight schedule. And there I'll be, standing in the wings, watching my superstar Oak Ridge Boys wow an audience. Then suddenly, a tug on my sleeve, the feel of a CD pressed into my hand, and the familiar words:

"Excuse me, Mr. Halsey. I've written this song especially for The Oak Ridge Boys. Would you see that they get it after the show?"

This is one of the lessons of this book, and of the Halsey method: If you are persistent, if you want it badly enough, you will make your own breaks. You will open the doors that seem to be closed.

This kind of tenacity is what gets songwriters into closed recording studios and sessions and onto the sets of TV shows. For a persistent songwriter, every meeting with a music-business person is an opportunity to get his or her songs heard. I have been pitched songs by bankers, doctors, and college professors. Waiters and waitresses have brought me material in restaurants. I've been slipped tapes at funerals, weddings, concerts, movie theaters, on airplanes, and even late at night by an undiscovered songwriter who had discovered my home address.

These are the ones who will remain enthused about their songs after suffering untold rejection. These are the ones who, after having been turned down dozens of times, will still submit their songs with the firm belief that they are hits waiting to happen. These are the ones with a good, strong pair of shoes who can take them down endless pavements in search of success, who can get their feet inside of doors. These are the ones who won't quit until they have a legitimate publisher and are seeing royalties from their work.

These are the ones who will make it.

★

These same guidelines, by the way, apply equally as well to performing artists as they do to songwriters. I remember presenting one of my seminars in Tulsa back in 1993 on October 18th, where I talked to the crowd about the same things I've just told you here: make the calls, get your foot in the door, and don't be afraid you are bothering someone by pitching your song or your talent—it's the persistence that will pay off.

About a quarter to seven the next morning, the phone in my hotel room rang. "Good morning, Mr. Halsey," said the masculine voice on the other end. "I attended your seminar last night, and I have three talented sons who write and play music. They want to become stars."

I said, "Fine. Send me a tape and I'll listen and give you my opinion."

"Mr. Halsey," he returned. "I paid 50 dollars to hear you last night. I'm following the advice you gave. I'm getting my foot in the door, so to speak. I have my three sons downstairs in the lobby. Would you please come down and hear them?"

Well, what could I do but say yes. He was, after all, following the method I'd given him the night before.

Twenty minutes later, in the lobby of the Tulsa Marriott Hotel, I was watching and listening to one of the greatest young groups I'd seen in a long time. The three boys were brothers, and each boy had star written all over him. Their father, Walker Hanson had told me over the phone that his sons were talented; Zach, Isaac, and Taylor proved him right. It was a winning act.

Walker asked me if I'd be interested in helping his boys, and I gave him the name of my Los Angeles attorney, Bill Coben, along with lots of encouragement. I knew they'd make it. Coben became their lawyer, and an important part of their Star Team, helping Walker assemble the other team members. The Hansons, as they were known when I saw them that morning, became Hanson—a household name in millions of homes all over the world, a huge teen-idol band, and a multi-platinum-selling recording act.

I feel fortunate to have been there at the beginning with advice and encouragement for them, and I'm proud that they thank me in their official biography for helping them along the way. They persevered, they got a foot in the door, and they made it.

chapter 20

THE MUSIC AND ENTERTAINMENT ATTORNEY

Our Star Team is coming together now, with only two more elements to add. Have you found your place on the team yet, or are you still looking?

Next chapter, we'll talk about the promoter, the final spoke in our Star Team wheel. Now, however, it's time to talk about the music and entertainment attorney. As we begin dealing with contracts, record deals, videos, royalties, guarantees, and percentages, the team needs somebody to look over each of these deals, to check the contracts, and maybe even to help negotiate a contract, or at least fine-tune some of its language. Remember how important my attorney, Bill Coben, was to the success of Hanson, helping Walker and the boys build their own Star Team.

It's important to make sure that this music and entertainment attorney is a specialist. I don't care if your uncle is the most famous attorney in Cleveland—if he doesn't know the music and entertainment business, he is basically useless to your Star Team. Get somebody with experience. Good music attorneys are not going to cost that much more than any other good attorney without the necessary specialized knowledge. Because they know the nuances of the music business, and know about the kinds of deals made in it, a music and entertainment business attorney will be worth what he or she costs. Many good music attorneys deal with record companies on a daily basis. They have close relationships with decision-makers within the companies, so they might even help an artist get a record deal.

At the very least, a music attorney is essential in dealing with contracts. An emerging artist will usually have to forge contracts with a manager, a booking agency, a record company, and a music publisher—all members of the Star Team. Contracts may also come up for music videos, commercials, product endorsements, and corporate sponsorships, among many other things.

Dealing with these contracts calls for the in-depth knowledge of a music and entertainment attorney. There are, in fact, whole law firms that concentrate their expertise in these areas. Most entertainment lawyers work on an hourly fee basis. Some may become more involved and require a monthly retainer. Others may take a personal interest in the artist's career and work for a percentage of the artist's earnings. And sometimes, if an attorney believes in the potential of a new artist, he or she will help the artist assemble a Star Team—as Bill Coben did for Hanson. Accessing the specialized music attorney's Power of Performance can play a major role in the success of an artist.

Since 1967, I have been blessed with good attorneys. Dan Sklar and Bill Coben, based in Los Angeles, negotiated many entertainment-business contracts for The Jim Halsey Company. Warren Jackman and Eric Grimshaw, of Tulsa, represented us in corporate and other areas of business. Ralph Gordon has represented some of my Nashville business, and Joel Katz and his firm have worked with me, and son Sherman in other specialized areas. It's been a good combination. Jeff Biedermann on board in certain areas and Gary Spicer is The Oak Ridge Boys corporate attorney.

As a manager, I've negotiated a lot of record contracts, but I've always been smart enough to include my attorneys, Bill Coben and Dan Sklar, in the process. Record contracts can be several hundred pages in length, and they're always tilted in favor of the record company. To get the best deal possible, the manager and the artist must be knowledgeable and very alert, and the music attorney must be on board to help protect the artist's rights.

★

Many performers, upon getting their first recording contract, are so eager to seal the deal that they forget about their rights. They'll sign anything just to start recording.

Obviously, this is a bad idea. At the very least, an artist must be able to recognize the basic language of a recording contract and to understand things enough to ask questions. So it's in every Star Team member's best interest to know the meanings of the following words:

Services: The record company engages the artist for exclusive or non-exclusive personal services as vocalist and/or instrumentalist according to the agreement.

Term: This is the length of time for which the record company is signing the artist, expressed in a number of years and/or number of albums. But this can be deceptive. There's a big difference between a firm term and a term with options. That is, an artist may think he or she has a seven-year, seven-album deal, but it may only be firm for the first year and first album, with an option for the remaining six. The option can also be expressed only by year or album, instead of both. A lot of people think they've signed a long-term deal, only to be cut loose when their first one or two discs don't perform up to expectations and the company decides not to pick up their option.

Remember this: whether or not to pick up an option is always the record company's choice.

Recording Commitment: This spells out number and length of songs, who owns the masters, how the record company may package and release the product, time frame of recording and delivery schedule.

Recording Procedures: Budget, producer, recording studio, technology involved.

Guarantees and Advances: These terms represent the amount of money the record company pays the artist. In most cases, this amount is usually recoupable (see below) against sales. In other words, if an artist gets a $40,000 guarantee or advance for a recording session, that artist won't get any more money until he or she has earned more than that $40,000 back from royalties (see below).

Recoupable: If an artist sees the term "recoupable against royalties" on a contract, it means that the record company will recover everything it advanced or spent on the artist's behalf before the artist receives any more money. Areas where the record company might spend money include tour support, independent promotion (to supplement in-house promotion), videos (sometimes split 50–50 with the artist), transportation, wardrobe, supplemental musicians, and almost anything else it wants to charge an artist for. The company will withhold all funds from the artist until its expenditures have been recovered.

Royalty: This is an amount, either a percentage of sales or an exact dollar amount, paid to the artist based upon the number of records sold. And the artist may not receive money for a long time if all of his or her disc sales are cross-collateralized (see below).

Cross-Collateralized: What this means is that all of an artist's recorded product must be paid for before the artist receives any money. One disc's costs are charged against, or crossed with, the costs of all of the others. If the artist has one good-selling album and one poor seller, the sales of the two are added together, and nothing is paid to the artist until the total sales of both albums are enough to cover costs.

Name and Likeness: Uses and restrictions on how the record company may use the artist's likeness, logo, and name.

Reserves: Before a record company will pay an artist for album sales, it will put an amount of the money owed the artist into reserve for a specified period of time—sometimes as much as 12 months or even longer. So the artist won't be paid all the monies actually owed him or her until the record company is absolutely certain this money won't have any encumbrances against it.

Free Goods: Free goods are supposedly product used for radio-station promotions, press and PR, or as a sales incentive to move the artist's product with retailers. Since the artist's contract calls for payment on product sold, there's no payment for product given away—free goods. If, to sell 100,000 CDs, the record company gives away 10,000 copies, does this mean the sale of 110,000 copies has been discounted or that full payment of royalties will be paid only on the 100,000 and no payment on the 10,000 free copies? In a worst-case scenario, the record company sells 100,000 copies of one artist's disc, but gives away 10,000 free copies of another artist's CD. The "free goods" provision on any contract should always be carefully examined by a qualified music attorney!

Packaging Charge: This is the amount deducted for the cost of packaging each CD or cassette into a case with cover photo, liner notes, etc. This cost is deducted before royalty payments are made to an artist. We should note that this charge is usually inflated in favor of the record company.

Artist Product Purchases: Establish the price artist may purchase product from the record company (merchandise sales at appearances is an important source of revenue; artist needs to be protected here).

Cutouts and Deletes: Cutouts and deletes are old albums that have outlived their sales potential, the discs and tapes you see in "bargain bins" of just about any music store. Usually, the record company stipulates in a contract that no royalties will be paid on these albums.

But shouldn't there be some form of payment to the artist on these, especially if they're discounted to someone overseas, or to stateside dealers who buy junk? And if an artist sells merchandise on the road, as most do, he or she should always have the contractual option to buy their own cutouts and deletes at the same deeply discounted price the record company offers to anyone else.

Controlled Compositions: These are songs controlled by the artist, either as a writer, co-writer, or publisher. In some cases, if more than 70 percent of the songs on an album are controlled by the artist, the record company will pay the music publisher a reduced rate. Consequently, the songwriter receives less.

Also, some record companies now pay publishing royalties for only ten songs on a CD. If an artist wants more than ten, the publishing royalties will be divided among however many songs are on the CD. This has nothing to do with the royalty the artist receives as a singer or performer, just any songwriting royalties he or she may have as composer.

Best-of Albums: Most recorded product is cross-collateralized, but a "Best-of" album can be treated as a separate venture. If the artist is hot enough and has had a lot of hits, the record company may treat the "Best-of" CD as separate, not "crossing" it with any other of the artist's albums, so the artist could receive payment for just that disc. This is something, however, that has to be negotiated at the time of an artist's initial contract with the recording company.

Joint Recordings: These may prove artistically interesting and quite commercial—just ask Willie Nelson—but they should always be done at the artist's discretion. An artist should look for a "favored nations" clause in a contract. This assures the artist payment and billing equal to that of whomever he collaborates with on a joint recording.

Record Clubs: Since record clubs sell albums for less than retail price, royalties will be less. An artist needs to be careful about promotion and free goods here as well. Most ads for record clubs let you pick so many CDs for free, or for a penny, when you join the club. The record club doesn't pay royalties on those records—they're considered free goods to the record clubs. Thousands of your CDs can be given away to promote someone else's catalog.

In most circumstances, I'm opposed to that. I recently negotiated a contract for a one-album deal, and the label included the stipulation they would be able to give so many thousand copies of the disc to a record club for use as giveaways in attracting new members. We did not accept this.

If you have a big catalog—if your act has, say, 15 or 20 albums in the catalog—you've got a chance to make that back, because people will order something else recorded by that act. But if you've got only one album in the record club, and people can get it free, there's no way they're going to order a second one and pay for it.

Record clubs can sell a lot of product for an artist, and in a lot of ways they're good. But you have to be careful of what you're giving them when you negotiate a contract.

Direct-Response Sales: Any contract should include a provision for payment for CDs offered for sale in TV ads, whether it's an artist's entire CD or individual tracks included on a compilation disc with other artists. A lot of product can be moved by direct-response marketing programs on television—many of us remember the successful TV promotions for albums by the likes of Andy Griffith, Tennessee Ernie Ford, and Slim Whitman, or have seen spots for the endless repackagings of classic rock 'n' roll hits. If an artist has other discs in stores, television-sales albums will usually stimulate their sales.

Video: The contract should stipulate the number of music videos to be made and the cost. It should also tell who's going to pay for them. Often the record company will advance the money for a video and then recoup it from the artist's royalties. Sometimes the company will recoup half the cost and pay the other half itself. Maybe it'll even pay the whole cost of the video. It depends on how hot the artist is. The record company will always own the copyright to the video. An artist should check a contract carefully to see who has creative control—who can pick the production company, producer, director? Does the artist have a choice? And what about the royalty structure for sales of music videos?

Favored Nations: We've mentioned this in the "joint recordings" section. It means that an artist's payment, treatment, and billing will be equal with the highest ranking contract in a collaborative artistic venture.

Tour Support: In a first-record deal, it's usually not known how much, if any, tour support will be needed. Once an artist is established, however, tour support is absolutely part of any record deal. This support, which comes from the record company, can involve promotion, advertising, additional musicians, travel arrangements, tour press, lights, sound, production, costumes, instruments, and anything else necessary to make the artist's presentation acceptable and that he or she can't afford to pay up-front. The tour-support portion of a recording contract can be flexible, but it is necessary. The dollar amount can be fixed or it can be advanced per tour; but either way it will probably be recouped from the artist's royalties. In other words, it's a loan the record company makes to the performer that has to be repaid—but only by royalties from the sales of the artist's records.

Accounting, Right to Audit: Artists are entitled to an accounting of their album sales at regular intervals. They are also entitled to audit their record company's books. Both of these rights need to be spelled out in the contract.

Merchandising Rights: Most record companies now want the right to sell the artist's merchandise, and they'll try to get that privilege in their contracts. Many record companies have their own merchandising arms; the artist still gets paid for merchandise sold, but only a percentage. If possible, a performer should keep his or her own merchandising. This is called the right of choice, and it means that the artist must approve anything with his or her image on it, including such things as T-shirts, photos, and tour books. Sometimes, the artist can make a more advantageous merchandising deal, getting an advance directly from the merchandising companies and recouping it through sale of merchandise instead of records. A merchandising company might give a star, say, $250,000 for merchandising rights, which all has to be recouped by the company through sale of the merchandise.

In some cases, that money comes from the merchandising company in the form of a personal loan, and the artist has to be very sure that what he or she signed to get the advance is not going to have to be repaid. If it is, and the artist doesn't sell enough merchandise, he or she can be on the hook for thousands of dollars. That's a very important point, and it's another reason why performers need good managers and lawyers.

Promotion Budget: This is the money the record company is willing to spend itself to promote a record via such things as ads, special promotions, graphic arts, in-store displays, special sales bonuses, and television, newspaper, and radio campaigns and contests. Establishing a budget for this is the responsibility of the record company, but many times the amount is not spelled out in the contract. A disc might need more promotional input than the record company believes is necessary. Or worse, the company could drop the ball and do nothing. For both these reasons, a specific promotion budget must be in the contract.

Independent Promotions: Sure, the record company people are always convinced they have everything covered, so promotion outside of the company won't be needed for a disc. This, though, is debatable. In many instances, once a record starts to happen the artist needs all of the help he or she can get, and fast! Performers should ask for a contractual provision guaranteeing a certain amount of money for "independent promotion," jointly administered by the artist's manager and the record company.

Ownership of Masters: Unless an artist is a superstar, and is leasing his or her master recordings to the record company, or the record is being done through a production deal, the record company always owns the masters. Of course, if the company wants an artist badly enough, deals can be made in which ownership of the masters reverts back to the artist or production company after a certain length of time or when the company's investment has been recouped.

Sometimes a record company may be interested in releasing an artist's master recording, but not interested enough to pay for the session or advance the money. The company may then opt to license the songs on the master recordings and pay the artist a royalty.

So a lot of times a producer will have enough faith in an artist to go in and make a whole album without knowing where he or she is going to sell it. The producer, or the artist and producer together, invest the money, do the session, then go out and shop the masters to see if some company wants to release it. But a company may say, "We're not going to give you money up front for this, but we'll pay you a royalty." That's licensing a master, and it's usually done for a specified period of time, after which the producer and artist get the masters back and the company no longer has any interest in the masters. They're leased for a period of time for a percentage of royalty. It's a good way to get an album out there, too, if you know what you're doing and you believe in yourself.

Foreign Payments and Rights: Many times royalty payments will be different in each foreign territory that sells an album. If artists aren't with a multinational company, their record companies will have to negotiate with other companies for pressing and foreign distribution. Because we're living in a global marketplace, with almost any product today carrying the potential for worldwide sales, it's important to have a music attorney on the job here.

Assignment of Contract: This is almost always the right of the record company, but there are certain restrictions that may well apply, and artists must understand them. They must know whether the company has the right to assign their entire contract (if the company sells out to another record company, does the artist have to go to the new company?) or just certain masters or tracks. In the case of a buyout or merger, artists should have the opportunity to decide where they go themselves.

Keep in mind that a record-company contract can be assigned to almost anything—not just another record company, but a bank or some other entity. Record masters and publishing contracts are almost like chattel these days, traded like stocks and bonds. An artist may not have much to say about whether or not his or her catalog can be sold to someone else, but the company shouldn't be able to piecemeal it out without the artist's approval.

Breakage: Are they kidding? In this age of CDs, cassettes, and DVDs, are there still massive broken shipments? Many record companies think so. Some will pay only 90 percent, even 85 percent, of royalties on sales, deducting 10 or 15 percent for breakage.

This practice goes back to a time when records were fragile and easily broken. It hasn't really had any validity since the advent of the vinyl LP, and certainly not since the introduction of cassettes and CDs. If the artist is big enough, he or she can usually negotiate for payment on 100 percent of the sales.

Finally, an essential piece of advice: Never sign any agreement or contract until your specialized music and entertainment attorney has examined and approved it. Usually, there'll be a lot of changes.

In this chapter, I've identified some of the basic contractual terms; it may be just enough information to be dangerous! Again, any Star Team needs a specialized attorney. Don't be without one. I never have been!

Following is a list of definitions used in most contracts with an explanation. These are for you understanding so you may intelligently converse with your specialized music business attorney.

DEFINITIONS

"Advance" shall mean prepayment of royalties. Company may recoup Advances from royalties (other than mechanical royalties) to be paid to Artist or on Artist's behalf pursuant to this Agreement or under any other agreement between Artist and Company or its affiliates relating to recordings embodying Artist's performances, unless otherwise expressly set forth herein. Advances hereunder include the prepayment of any applicable union scale wages.

"Album" or "LP" shall mean an audio-only long-playing Record which is not an EP, Single, or Long-Play Single, and where the context requires, Master Recordings sufficient to constitute a long-playing audio-only Record.

"Artwork" means, without limitation, photographs, graphic designs and related materials created or used in connection with this Agreement, including all packaging, marketing, promotion and publicity materials for of each LP released in the United States during the Term hereof.

"Audiovisual Record" shall mean a Record embodying an Audiovisual Recording. Without limiting the generality of the foregoing, any CD-ROM, DVD or other interactive audiovisual Record which is not intended primarily for audio playback shall be deemed to be an Audiovisual Record hereunder. For purposes of the preceding sentence, so-called "enhanced CDs" and CD-Plus Records are intended primarily for audio playback. The term "Audiovisual Recording" shall mean every form of Master Recording embodying visual ima"es.

"Budget record" shall mean a Record which is released under any label designation, and bears a SRLP in the applicable country of the Territory which is currently less than or equal to fifty-five percent (55%) of the SRLP of a majority of Company's or Company's licensees,' as applicable, then-current newly-released Albums.

"Compact Disc" shall mean a disc record (presently 120mm diameter) reproducing sound alone the signals on which are read and transmitted by laser.

"Club Operation" shall mean any sales to consumers through record clubs or similar sales plans or devices.

"Composition" shall mean a single musical composition, irrespective of length, including all spoken words and bridging passages and including a medley.

"Configuration" means each particular format in which Phonograph Records are now or may in the future be manufactured or distributed, including, without limitation, 7-inch disc singles, 12-inch disc singles, analog cassette tape albums, digital audio tape albums, digital compact cassette albums, each format of direct transmission, disc albums and CD albums;

"Controlled Composition" shall mean a composition, or that part thereof, written, owned or controlled by Artist or any person or entity in which Artist has a direct or indirect interest.

"Cybersales" shall mean the act of selling and distributing a physical copy of a Record to an end user consumer via on-line Internet services.

"Delivery" or "Delivered" when used with respect to Master Recordings, means the actual receipt by Company of fully mixed, edited and equalized Master Recordings, commercially and technically satisfactory to Company in Company's reasonable business judgment and ready for Company's manufacture of Phonograph Records, and all necessary licenses and applicable approvals and consents, and all materials required to be furnished by Artist to Company for use in the packaging and marketing of the Records.

"Digital Records" shall mean all Records embodying, employing or otherwise utilizing any non-analog technology and shall include, without limitation, compact discs and New Media Records (including Electronic Transmission Records).

"Electronic Transmission Record" shall mean a Record sold via the distribution, transmission or communication of such Record over a communication medium (including, but not limited to, wired and/or wireless systems, broadband, narrowband or other, Internet, satellite, optical fiber, wire, or cable), whether now known or hereafter devised, from one location to a remote location, in such a manner that the Record when received at the remote location is sufficiently permanent or stable to permit it to be perceived, reproduced, or otherwise communicated to the recipient at such remote location, without regard to whether the sound recording or audiovisual work embodied in the Record is simultaneously performed in an audible fashion during such distribution, transmission or communication or whether, when performed, such sound recording or audiovisual work embodied in the Record is performed in its entirety, and, for the avoidance of doubt, shall be deemed to include transmission or communication of Records in connection with mobile devices or services, or by cybercast, webcast or any other type of so-called audio or audiovisual "streaming."

"EP" shall mean a long-playing disc-type record or the tape equivalent thereof embodying between five (5) and six (6) Masters.

"Full-Price Albums" shall mean Records sold by Company as top of the line recorded product.

"Joint Recordings" means Masters embodying the Artist's performance and any performance by another artist with respect to whom Company is obligated to pay royalties.

"Master Recordings" or **"Masters"** means any recording of sound, whether or not coupled with a visual image, by any method and on any substance or material, whether now or hereafter known, which is intended for use in the recording, production and/or manufacture of Phonograph Records.

"**Mechanical Royalties**" means royalties payable to any Person for the right to reproduce and distribute copyrighted musical compositions on Phonograph Records.

"**Mid-line or mid-price record**" shall mean a Record which is released under any label designation, and bears a SRLP in the applicable country of the Territory which is currently less than or equal to seventy-three point nine percent (73.9%) and greater than or equal to fifty-five percent (55%) of the SRLP of the majority of Company's or Company's licensees, as applicable, then-current newly-released Albums.

"**Multiple Album**" means a Record containing two (2) or more Albums packaged as a single unit or equivalent.

"**Net Royalty**" or "**Net Flat Fee**" shall mean the gross royalty or gross flat fee, as the case may be, received by Company in the U.S. from a Person solely attributed to the exploitation by that Person of rights in the applicable Masters (excluding any catalog, handling and/or administrative fees), less all costs paid or incurred by Company in connection with the licensing and/or exploitation of those rights and the collection of those monies. For the avoidance of doubt, in calculating any Net Royalty or Net Flat Fee hereunder, Company shall not deduct the cost of any royalties or other sums payable to producers of those Masters (and/or any other similar third party royalty participants), it being agreed and understood that all such royalties and other sums shall be borne solely by Artist.

"**Net Sales**" shall mean ninety percent (90%) of the aggregate number of Records sold to wholesale and retail customers for which Company has been paid or finally credited, less returns, rebates and credits, and reserves against anticipated returns, rebates and credits.

"**New Media Records**" shall mean all Records in the following configurations: mini-discs, digital compact cassettes, digital audio tapes, laser discs, solid state memory devices, digital versatile discs (i.e., "DVDs"), compact discs capable of bearing visual images (including, without limitation, Enhanced CD, CD-Plus and CD-ROM), Records sold via "point of sale" manufacturing, Electronic Transmission Records and any other configurations other than conventional vinyl records, cassette tapes and audio-only compact discs, whether such Records are interactive (i.e. where the user is able to access, select or manipulate the materials therein) or non-interactive, and whether now known or hereafter devised.

"Net Receipts" shall, where customary and appropriate, also mean "net royalty," and such terms shall mean actual receipts as computed after deduction of all "out of pocket" costs paid or incurred by Company in connection with the exploitation of the applicable rights, including, manufacturing costs, copyright royalties, union and other applicable third party payments, taxes and collection costs, if any.

"Performance" means singing, speaking, conducting or playing an instrument, alone or with others.

"Performance Track" shall mean a Recording containing one (1) or more Master Recordings of the music track of a Master Recordings without vocals used as a musical background wither during public performances or to aid in rehearsal for a soloist or choir which are distributed by Company under any trademark or trademarks.

"Person" means any individual, corporation, partnership, association or other organized group of persons or legal successors or representatives of the foregoing.

"Records" and "Phonograph Records" means all forms of reproduction now or hereafter known (including reproductions of sound alone and audio-visual reproductions) which are manufactured or distributed primarily for home use, institutional (e.g., library or school) use, jukebox use or use in means of transportation including, without limitation, any computer-assisted media (e.g., a CD-ROM, CD-I and similar disc systems, interactive cable, telephony and so-called "streaming" and/or "downloading" or any similar or successor form of transmission on the Internet or on any system which is similar to or is a successor to the Internet).

"Royalty Base Price" means the suggested retail list price less all excise, sales and similar taxes included therein and less the applicable Container Charge.

"Side"–shall mean a Master Recording embodying Artist's performances of not less than three (3) minutes of continuous sound. If any Album (or other group of Master Recordings) Delivered to Company in fulfillment of a Recording Commitment expressed as a number of Sides includes Master Recordings of more than one (1) arrangement or version of any Composition, all of those Recordings will be deemed to constitute one (1) Side.

"Single Record" or "Single" shall mean an audio-only seven-inch (7") disc Record or its tape or other equivalent, embodying no more than two (2) Compositions. The term "Long-Play Single" shall mean an audio-only Record embodying no fewer than three (3), and no more than four (4), different Musical Compositions.

"SRLP" or "Suggested Retail List Price" or "Retail Price" shall mean (1) with respect to Records, sold in the United States, the suggested retail list price established by Company for the particular price series of the Record concerned in the configuration concerned from time to time during the accounting period in which the sale occurs; and (2) with respect to Records sold outside of the United States, Company's licensees' suggested or applicable retail price on which Company is paid with respect to the country of sale. If Company is not paid on the basis of a suggested or applicable retail price in any particular country, including, without limitation, the United States, for any particular sale, the SRLP will mean the retail-based price as may be established by Company, Company's licensees or affiliates from time to time in conformity with the general practice of the record industry. In such event, without limitation of the foregoing, Company may, but will not be obligated to, use the retail equivalent price, less handling fees, adopted by the local mechanical copyright collection agency for the collection of mechanical royalties, or the applicable wholesale price or published price to dealer multiplied by an uplift factor. Company may elect to utilize a different method of computing royalties on Net Sales of Records from the SRLP. If Company elects to discontinue designating SRLPs for Records in any country or elects to compute royalties on a wholesale price basis for any reason, then, for the purposes of computing royalties hereunder, the SRLP of a particular Record will be deemed to be a dollar amount computed by multiplying Company's then-current wholesale price (before consideration of any discounts resulting from the distribution of free goods) of that particular Record in the country concerned by a fraction, the numerator of which is the SRLP of a Comparable Record (as defined below) immediately prior to Company's discontinuance of designating SRLPs (or, if applicable, immediately prior to the election to compute royalties on a wholesale price basis) and the denominator of which is Company's wholesale price (before consideration of any discounts resulting from the distribution of free goods) in the country concerned of a Comparable Record immediately prior to Company's discontinuance of designating SRLPs (or, if applicable, immediately prior to the election to compute royalties on a wholesale price "asis). A (Compara"le Record) means a Record of the same configuration, with the same packaging, and in the same price category as the Record in question.

"Territory" shall mean the Universe.

"Video" shall mean a film, videotape or other device used for the reproduction of a combination of Artist's audio performance of one (1) selection and a visual rendition of Artist's performance (and/or other visual accompaniment), including a dramatization of the applicable selection.

"Videogram" means an audio-visual record intended primarily for home consumer or institutional (e.g., library or school) use, jukebox use or use in means of transportation, including, without limitation, videocassettes, videodiscs, DVDs or other media or devices that allow the consumer to control the viewing of or to interact with the Videogram, including without limitation, transmission directly into the home that enables the consumer to view the Videogram at any time.

chapter 21

THE PROMOTER

There's a reason I've listed the promoter as the final Star Team member. It's because he or she is usually the last component to be plugged into an artist's master plan, the last spoke in the wheel. All of the other Star Team members, from manager to attorney, should be in place first. Collectively, with their combined Power of Performance, they give the promoter something to promote.

What does a promoter do? He or she puts the artist on stage, in front of an audience. He or she presents the artist. Usually relying on ticket sales for payment, the promoter is the risk-taker, a team member whose performance relies on time, money, ingenuity, energy, and friendships. Without the promoter, there would simply be no show.

Many music-business professionals have started out as promoters. I'm one of them. When I was 19 and still a college student, I began bringing every imaginable type of show, band, artist, and production to my hometown of Independence, Kansas. The city had a great auditorium, and I took it upon myself to fill it.

When I started, I knew enough about the retail business to see an analogy that helped me make the transition to the entertainment business. I saw the auditorium as my store, the attraction as my merchandise. I would notify my customers—the potential ticket buyers—and try creatively to convince them they would like my show; that it was a good value, and that they should make the decision to come—to answer the call to action and purchase a ticket. It sounds simple, and it was. All I had to do was my homework on the attractions I was bringing in and figure out the potential audience for them.

You've read earlier how important I think it is to create an event with your shows. I learned instinctively how to do that. The first show I promoted featured regional western swing star Leon McAuliffe and his Cimarron Boys band. My finances dictated that I had to be inventive about my advertising and promotion. So I examined every possible way to inform the public: radio, newspapers, posters, handbills, mailing lists, special contests. I left absolutely no avenue unexplored.

I will never forget the night of the dance, my first night in show business. I wasn't sure how it would go. In those days you didn't do a lot of advance ticket sales; the people who heard about an event would just show up at the box-office right before it was supposed to start. On this night, there was a long line waiting to get in by the time the box office opened. In fact, the dance had been going for 30 minutes before the last person in line could buy a ticket. That place was jam-packed with people; my first promotion was a success. Somehow, I'd done enough things right. And I realized right then that I was in the music business for good!

Early on, I established some important criteria for my business. Good ethics was one, the continual pursuit of the satisfied customer was another. I gave the people what they wanted: a good show at a good value. Truly, the Power of Performance was there.

Then, when I was 20 years old—with a number of successful promotions under my belt, but still learning—I had the Power of Performance dramatically demonstrated to me. It also was something I'll never forget. Neither will I ever forget the man involved, legendary big-band leader Woody Herman, who would later become my client and mentor.

I had been very successful in my first year and a half as a promoter. But since I was still in college while I was operating the business, I was using every penny I made, and everything I promoted had to be cost-effective. I was always looking for great deals, ones that offered small risk but high potential profits.

I got my opportunity when Woody Herman and his great 19-piece jazz band came through. They were playing the major cities in Kansas and Oklahoma: Wichita, Topeka, Kansas City, Tulsa, and Oklahoma

City. What was most important was that they had an open date during this time—and they'd be close to Independence.

Usually when there's an open date, the agent will offer promoters in the area a special price, below the normal asking price, just to fill in the date and help meet some of the road expenses.

That's what happened to me, and that's how I got Woody Herman. I'll always remember the date: February 21. It was shortly after the New Year holiday, I was short of money, but the deal was so good that I couldn't resist. Under regular circumstances I wouldn't have been able to afford him, but with this special "routing" price, Woody's guarantee was low and I could see myself making some pretty good money.

I did one of my most thorough jobs promoting this date, turning it into an event, working my Power of Performance as a budding impresario. I made sure that everybody in southeast Kansas and northeast Oklahoma knew that the great Woody Herman and his band were coming to Memorial Hall in Independence, Kansas. Local merchants offered special "Woody Herman" sales prices. The mayor proclaimed February 21 "Woody Herman Day" in Independence.

Most managers call the promoter the day before an engagement, requesting that the promoter have the guaranteed amount , in cash, ready for the act. When Woody's manager called, I assured him there wouldn't be any problem. I was sure myself. In fact, I was sure that after Woody got his guaranteed amount, he would also pocket lots more money on his percentage of the take. (Most big acts get a percentage of the gross from box-office receipts, after the guaranteed amount is reached.) We were getting calls from all over the territory inquiring about tickets.

The day of the concert, Woody was coming in from Topeka, 125 miles to the north. Since I'd taken the date on short notice—one of the reasons I got a good price—I hadn't sold a lot of tickets in advance. But I had literally hundreds of people asking me to hold their tickets at the box office. It was going to be a big success.

Then the unexpected hit, and it was a promoter's worst nightmare.

Just a few hours before the show was to begin, a huge blizzard and ice storm hit northern Kansas and roared southward, right toward Independence.

My heart sank.

By the time I opened the box office at 7 p.m., it was snowing so hard I couldn't see across the street. The storm was becoming one of the worst blizzards Kansas had seen in 20 years, and my event was turning into a disaster.

No cars moved on the streets. A few loyal Woody Herman fans braved the weather and walked to the auditorium. But I could see what was going to happen. There would be hundreds of reservations for tickets that would not be picked up. The elements had displayed their own Power of Performance!

I was sick to the soul. All my hard work, all my great promotion, all my time—wasted. Minutes before showtime, fewer than 100 hardy Herman fans had trekked through the blinding storm to get to the concert. At least they were warm inside the auditorium.

I checked the time. At 8 p.m., when the show was scheduled to start, I planned to take the stage and explain that Woody and his great band weren't going to make it. I knew everyone would understand. There wasn't anything moving in southeast Kansas that night. I knew some people had braved the elements that night hoping that Woody had arrived earlier in the day, but that's not the way things work with traveling musicians. They work late, sleep late, and travel late, usually arriving just in time to set up and play.

I was going to take a big loss on the night, as well as learn a good lesson: a promoter should never promote a show or enter into an obligation unless he has the funds to pay it off. Although I wouldn't have to pay Woody Herman his guaranteed fee, I was still financially obligated to the hall and the stage hands, and to my advertising and promotional expenses. I had enough to pay these costs, but barely. At least, I thought, I wouldn't be buried by the blizzard.

At 8 p.m., I started for the stage, ready to tell the sparse audience that Woody couldn't make it because of the storm, and all tickets would be refunded. Then, suddenly, I saw two large headlights barely visible through the falling snow. It was the sole vehicle moving on the streets. It could only be the bus!

Sure enough, it was Woody Herman and his Thundering Herd fighting the elements, and, like the U.S. Post Office, making their appointed rounds despite the weather, arriving at Memorial Hall in Independence at exactly 8 p.m.

My heart sank again!

Now the concert would go on as advertised—but with only a bare handful of brave souls there to see it. Much more important, I was now again obligated to pay Woody Herman his guaranteed fee. How could I do it? Where was I going to get the money? I'd counted on the box-office receipts to pay off, but with this record-breaking winter storm, I'd collected only few hundred dollars in ticket sales.

Woody Herman was one of my musical idols. How could I tell him I couldn't pay him?

The only option I had was to try and get a loan for the amount at the local bank the next day. But I knew that wouldn't happen. My banker, Mr. Ernest Sewell, was conservative, and he didn't much approve of the risks involved in promoting shows.

I finally realized this could be my last date as a promoter; I guessed I might as well enjoy it. So when the lights went up and Woody's great band struck its first note, I was sitting in the audience. And did I enjoy it! In spite of everything, that night was one of my finest musical memories.

Woody's powerful concert that night did just what it was supposed to do; his Power of Performance transformed me, put me in a different space. And when it was over, I pulled my spirits together, got my positive attitude in shape, and swallowed hard, mustering up the courage to tell Mr. Herman I only had a few dollars on hand to pay him. I'd have to try to raise the money the next day.

Had it been only yesterday that his manager had talked to me, insisting that the guarantee be paid in cash? Everything had seemed so rosy then, and I'd been so confident about raising plenty of money on the date. Now, just a day later, my whole world had turned around.

I stood in the box office, waiting uneasily for Mr. Herman. I had to tell him the truth.

Then he entered the room. It was the first time we'd met. In a gruff voice, he asked for the promoter.

"I'm that person," I blurted out, desperately working up my courage.

He looked surprised to find that he was working the date for a 20-year-old kid. And before I could say anything else, Woody asked in that matter-of-fact style that was his trademark, "How much did you take in tonight, kid?"

"About $350, Mr. Herman," I answered.

Without hesitation, he said, "Listen, kid, why don't you give me that, and we'll call it square."

I almost fell on the floor.

Was this man a mind reader? Did he really understand that because of him, a miracle had just happened? Woody Herman had not only just exhibited masterfully his Power of Performance on the stage of Memorial Hall; he'd also encored with that power to me, a grateful audience of one, in the box office.

Because of Woody Herman, I was still a promoter—and a wiser one. The lesson I learned that night is an important one: never extend your resources beyond what you can pay. And remember, while it's good to look at all the possible scenarios, never forget weather as a possible trickster on the day of your event.

Instead of ending my career as a promoter, this potentially disastrous meeting foreshadowed a relationship between Woody Herman and me that would last for decades. Later on, I promoted many more of his dates; I even became his agent in the 1980s, almost exactly 30 years after we first locked eyes in that Independence, Kansas, box office, with the blizzard raging outside. I found Woody to be a man of great integrity, with the ability to pick promising young musicians from around the country—recognizing their potential Power of Performance—and shape them into real players. I enjoyed being his agent and was proud to have represented this great musical organization.

I learned a lot from Woody Herman, beginning with that encounter in Memorial Hall. Decades later, when our business relationship had blossomed into a personal one as well, I finally told him that the young promoter for that long-ago date had been me. I explained that, because of his grace in accepting a far lesser amount than his guarantee, my career had probably been saved.

Woody remembered the date well, and he confessed that he was surprised that the impresario had been only 20 years old. He'd sensed that it would be bad news for me if he demanded his full amount. So on the spur of the moment, he saved everyone embarrassment, and more, by asking for only the box office receipts. He told me he was glad to get that much "gas money" from the job.

We both had some good laughs about our first meeting, but it set the tone for a major part of my philosophy when I later formed my booking agency: it's in everyone's best interest to keep a promoter in business.

Perhaps even more important, I learned from Woody Herman on that icy night that the Power of Performance is just as important off stage as on.

Since then, I have worked to develop my own Power of Performance as a manager, agent, impresario, businessman, and human being. And as I built my own company, which would employ many people and represent many fine artists, I always tried to pass on the theory of the Power of Performance, and how accessing it will put you on the road to success.

★

My next few years as a promoter provided a good education for me. I promoted everything—concerts by jazz groups, big bands, and symphony orchestras; classical events; wrestling matches; circuses; ice shows; and performances by rhythm & blues and country acts. I learned by doing—by making mistakes and failing as well as by getting things right and creating events with my shows. By starting as a promoter, one of the essential Star Team members, I was able to learn all of the facets of the business, and what made them all work.

Very early in my career, I learned that it takes a lot of cooperation from all concerned. Almost instinctively I began finding out who the important team members were and observing how they all worked together. I was learning how to be successful, developing my Star Team method, exercising my Power of Performance.

As a promoter, you learn about cutting the right deals with the venues, and about the right venues for an artist. You must know about whatever or whomever you're promoting. Who's the audience for what you have? How do you reach that audience? If you have a choice of venues, what is the best venue for this particular act?

Here's a simple formula every promoter should remember. First, figure expenses carefully, taking into account the cost of the venue, the artist, any co-headliners, advertising, promotion, the stage crew, staff salaries, box-office commissions to the agencies that sell your tickets, ticket sellers, lights and sound, possible traveling expenses, and taxes, and fulfilling all of the requirements of the artist's contract.

Add all of these up. This amount represents your expenses.

Next, find out the number of people your venue will hold. You can now establish the ticket price. My own advice is to base the ticket price on how much it will take you to make a reasonable profit (the amount after your expenses) if you sell enough tickets to fill three-fourths of the venue's capacity, or three-fourths of what you anticipate your artist will draw. Of course, if you sell more, so much the better.

This is a reasonably safe formula. But, as you know, if you sell far fewer tickets than you need to make a profit, you not only lose money, but a lot of time and energy as well. For this reason, being a promoter carries a certain amount of risk.

In dealing over the years with a lot of music-business professionals, including agents, managers, and record company and music publishing executives, I've found that many of them started as I did, as a promoter on a local or regional basis.

I think Sol Hurok, the legendary impresario who was my first inspiration, would approve.

chapter 22

CREATING EVENTS

A large part of this book is about creating events, and every good promoter must know how to produce one. To create an event, you take something special, add a number of complementary elements, and transform this something special into something extraordinarily special, expanding it far beyond what it would be if the extra elements were absent—and many times exceeding even your own expectations. How do you create a true event? My experience has taught me that you can do it best if you do it in these eight stages:

1. Inspiration
2. Goal and Purpose
3. Planning
4. Expanding the Elements
5. Implementation
6. The Event
7. Review
8. Follow-up

Let's illustrate the method with an event that meets the criteria of something extraordinarily special. In the early 1970s, when we were establishing The Jim Halsey Company in Tulsa, we convinced our client, partner, and friend Roy Clark, to join us in Oklahoma. He and his wife, Barbara, moved from Annapolis, Maryland, and established a home in Tulsa. Meanwhile, our group of partners—including Hank Thompson, Wayne Creasy, Mack Sanders, and Stanley Synar—had many investments in the community. We owned and operated two radio stations and a large apartment complex, built several office buildings, and purchased a large ranch south of Tulsa. Because of our high profile—and highly leveraged financing—we had been able to acquire many businesses and properties; because of our high visibility, we were the subject of much press, both local and national.

Most of the investments we made fit within our philosophy of synergy, in which one plus one can sometimes equal not two, but 20. We were all contributing to an overall plan, and among the things we were trying to do was build Tulsa into a music center.

Tulsa had our support, and we had Tulsa's support. Now, with our collective energies and high visibility, was the time for a community public-relations event. Not simply something that would get us press, but something that would benefit the whole community. And so, we began thinking in stages:

1. **Inspiration:** While I'm not especially sports-minded, I had a vision of establishing a major sporting event in the name of Roy Clark. The sport was golf; the idea was a celebrity golf tournament. Many of our friends within the music and entertainment industry had heard so much about our projects in Tulsa, they were eager to see for themselves. This would give them a great excuse to visit.

2. **Goal and Purpose:** Establishing a golf tournament in Roy's name would be an opportunity to invite any industry-related associates to Tulsa, to have a good time playing golf, to give our community high national visibility, to raise some money for a local charity—and to do some business as well.

3. **Planning:** Since the organization and planning tasks fell mainly on The Jim Halsey Company, this signaled the beginning of the hardwork phase. Roy, a good golfer, liked and supported the idea. My main man in Tulsa, John Hitt, was also a good golfer; he became an important member of our planning team. Warren Jackman, our attorney, got on board early. When we needed a good local charity, he got Children's Medical Center (CMC) of Tulsa involved. That worthy hospital was not only a beneficiary, it supplied us with our golf course as well.

We planned to end the weekend of celebrities and golf with an all-star celebrity concert. Famed Tulsa evangelist Oral Roberts contributed by furnishing his beautiful, state of-the-art, 10,000 seat Mabee Center on the campus of Oral Roberts University for the concert event. Dr. Roberts and his son Richard have always supported us, and we them. They're good golfers, too!

We were beginning to roll, and we were still six months away from the event. That sounds like plenty of time, but there's no such thing as too much time. The more time you have to plan and work, the more elements you can add.

4. **Expanding the Elements:** We were set with the Roy Clark Celebrity Golf Tournament, our dates were scheduled, our goal and purpose in place. Now, it was time to expand the elements.

With a special event like this, it's always good to get as many prominent citizens involved as possible. We established a big committee, staffing it with community leaders, members of the board of Children's Medical Center, media executives, bankers, lawyers, automobile dealers, and others. There was a lot of work to be done, and a lot of volunteer help was needed. One of the best moves we made was getting the Women's Auxiliary of the CMC involved. They had some great ideas and made important contributions.

For nearly six months the office staff of The Jim Halsey Company was involved daily with the planning and work. Everyone contributed to the team effort that turned this into an extraordinarily special event. As we went along, we invited a lot of major talent buyers to our weekend extravaganza, people we dealt with all year long: television producers; fair and rodeo buyers; casino operators from Las Vegas, Reno, and Tahoe; club operators; and concert promoters.

We brought these folks into Tulsa as our guests for two reasons. Number one, it was a way of saying "thanks" for the business they had given us over the preceding year. Number two, we were going to have most of the artists we represented involved with the tournament. Subliminally, having the buyers on hand worked as our own private sales opportunity for our artists' upcoming dates.

Since we had so many of our artist roster involved—Roy Clark, Hank Thompson, The Oak Ridge Boys, Mel Tillis, Freddy Fender, and others—we enlisted the support of their record companies. Since most of our artists were with ABC Records (later to become MCA), that label became our most active record-company team member. ABC

Records' president Jim Foglesong, whom I talked about earlier, always supported our events when they made sense to him and his company. (I must add that he was also a good golfer.) He came on board for the tournament, and ABC Records invited many top radio personalities and performers from across the nation to spend the weekend in Tulsa. Some would play golf, some would just play, but all would have a good time, rubbing shoulders with TV and movie stars, country and pop music greats, and Tulsa's industry and community leaders in a relaxed and informal atmosphere.

Now for the press. As we continued expanding the elements, the time came to plug in Kathy Gangwisch, our press and PR person extraordinaire! With Kathy providing input, we invited a number of national and international press representatives, getting leading newspapers and magazines to cover the golf tournament. In addition, many of the visiting radio personalities planned remote broadcasts to their home stations from the golf course, our headquarters hotel, or backstage at the Mabee Center during the all-star celebrity concert we had dubbed "Star Night." Ralph Emery, America's No. 1 country-music radio personality, would be doing live interviews with the stars over Nashville's clear-channel WSM as well as for the stations that carried his syndicated shows.

5. The Implementation: All of the ideas were in place. We prepared a written manifesto covering all of the elements. Included in it was a chronological schedule of events; where they were to take place; schedules for various artists and celebrity rehearsal times and appearances; airport pickups and hotel times; scheduled parties and receptions; interview appointments; tee-off times—every minute detail. We hoped fervently we hadn't left anything out.

The week of the event, the Halsey Company offices were like the nerve center of a military operation, with every single member of our staff armed with a full list of instructions. Our office was the focal point for all of the weekend's business, and it took our entire staff. We were, of course, only one of several elements, each with its own responsibilities. Also on the team were the local committees, the local board of directors, Jim Foglesong's group at ABC Records, and Roy and Barbara Clark, who were acting as hosts.

6. The Event: If the first five stages are completed well, an event should run smoothly, even though unexpected situations will always arise. This event unfolded and played itself out like a great circus, with everything happening and everyone functioning at full capacity. For a great three-day weekend everybody was working, playing, having a good time, and doing some good for the Children's Medical Center! It was a success!

I'm sure some people think something like this just happens. They have no idea of the hours, days, weeks, and even months that go into planning a three-day event, and the teamwork it takes to pull it off. We couldn't have done it, nor would it have been the huge success it was, without the effort of hundreds of Tulsans working and contributing their time and money … or the six-month-long efforts of many of The Halsey Company employees … or the stars with their talents and time … or the contributions of many sponsors. We had a particularly special relationship with Amana Refrigeration, who supported with money and hundreds of prizes.

In return, many Halsey Company artists—including Roy, The Oak Ridge Boys, and Mel Tillis—lent their support to Amana's annual charity tournament. Roy played golf, signed autographs and, with Barbara, hosted a dinner and reception for the contributors and celebrities; he remained busy the next year returning favors to many of the celebrities who came to play in his tournament. Bob Hope, for instance, has probably given us more "free" dates than any other celebrity. Roy, in turn, would give a "free" date to any request Bob would make for his own celebrity tournaments and events. That's how it works.

7. The Review: Here's the test. Did the event meet the criteria of your goal and purpose? To find out, review all of the elements involved. Have a meeting of the principal planners and workers as soon after the event as possible—at least within the following week. That way, everything will still be fresh in their minds. Note mistakes both large and small, and get suggestions for improvement. If you plan for your event to be an annual one—as the Roy Clark Celebrity Golf Tournament and Star Night turned out to be—it's not too soon to start planning for the next one.

Annual events are good for a couple of reasons. First, so much energy goes into the initial start-up of any event that subsequent annual events get the benefit of residual planning. Second, any event can be improved and enhanced every year that it's staged.

Regardless of what kind of event you have, always answer these questions:

1. Was it a success with the audience?
2. Was it a success within the business?
3. Was there good media coverage?
4. Did the event meet your own critical criteria and standards?
5. Did it bring great recognition to the artist or artists involved?
6. Did it bring great recognition to sponsors or charity involved?
7. Did it have a lasting cultural effect?
8. Did it represent all concerned with integrity?
9. Was it financially successful?
10. Were the customers satisfied?

In the case of The Roy Clark Celebrity Golf Tournament the answer to all 10 questions was "yes."

8. The Follow-up: A lot of the important work is done after a successful event's over. Among the things you must do is make sure there are follow-up stories for the press, that the money pledged is collected for your charity, that thank you's go out to all concerned.

In most music industry-related events, many of the important business contacts are not made until the actual event occurs. Acquaintances made at performances and the accompanying receptions can be the starting place for follow-up meetings with prospective buyers, corporate sponsors, or potential television projects.

By the time the Roy Clark Celebrity Golf Tournament came along, I had further developed my theory of the Power of Performance, and I was learning how the combined energy of each element, each member of a team, is essential for success. The golf tournament illustrated perfectly both of these ideas, as well as showing the benefits a promoter reaps when he or she is able to create a true, real event.

WE DO MAGIC

The Jim Halsey Company created another huge event in Tulsa. In fact, you could call it our Event of All Events. It incorporated everything we've talked about in this book: the call to action, the power boosters, the impact enhancers, the repetitious impressions, plus a sophisticated level of other sales and marketing techniques, all fueling an event of gargantuan proportions!

Let's start by reiterating that an important part of all sales and marketing is maintaining satisfied customers and building repeat business, and that an agent or agency constantly has inventory of an artist's dates to fill. As you've already read, The Jim Halsey Company was constantly keeping our buyers informed through direct mail, trade ads and good and ongoing press and public relations campaigns. It was also very important for us to develop events for our artists and our company—just as it's important for a promoter to transform his shows into events wherever possible.

With that idea in mind, we developed a combination event and promotion of such magnitude that it almost defies description. Dubbed the Halsey Ranch Party, it was not only a gigantic thank-you celebration for our best customers—the promoters and other talent buyers—but also the biggest three days of the year for selling our artists.

We invited talent buyers, television producers, record company executives, and radio personalities to spend a weekend in Tulsa as our guests. While they were there, we showcased new talent for them, and each of our major stars also gave a tasteful performance at some time during the big weekend.

The Halsey Ranch Parties were held south of Tulsa at our 2,500-acre ranch, which my partners—Roy Clark, Hank Thompson, Wayne Creasy, and the late Stanley Synar—and I jointly owned. Although we were raising cattle there, none of us lived in the ranchhouse, which looked like something out of the Bonanza television series. Instead, we used it for entertaining. When you sat on top of the hill overlooking the swimming pool, patio, and thousands of acres of beautiful, rolling Oklahoma pasture land sprinkled with contentedly grazing cattle, the atmosphere was super-conducive for relaxation, informal socializing—and big-time sales.

The 2,500-acre spread included a natural amphitheater, which provided a memorable place to present our artists. We had chairs available, but most people ended up sitting on the ground, enjoying the fantastic barbecued ribs, brisket, links, turkey, and chicken expertly prepared by our partner Stan Synar—whose profession was real estate, but whose specialty was outdoor cooking. Proud of my Cherokee heritage, we had Indian tepees scattered around the property with Native American art also on display. We always featured Indian dances as part of the weekend's entertainment.

This was no set created by a Hollywood designer. It was our place, a real place, a place to bring and entertain our guests.

We held our Halsey Ranch Parties in early autumn. The timing was designed not only to take advantage of the beauty of the season in Oklahoma and celebrate the harvest, but to entertain all of the important state fair buyers before their annual late November meeting in Las Vegas. A lot of fair buyers decided on their headliners for the following year during Halsey Ranch Party festivities, and my ably equipped chargé d'affaires of the fair department, John Hitt, along with his staff, was always on hand to arrange the bookings.

In this unique setting, our buyers enjoyed live shows from the likes of Roy Clark, Hank Thompson, The Oak Ridge Boys, Mel Tillis, Tammy Wynette, Minnie Pearl, Freddy Fender, Donna Fargo, Don Williams, and Jimmy Dean. By the time our guests were heading back to their respective homes in Los Angeles, New York, Las Vegas, Reno, Nashville—and London, Tokyo, Moscow, Sofia, Budapest and Prague—our artists would have much of their coming year's itineraries already booked.

There was nothing high-pressure about our sales methods, but who wouldn't be in a mood to buy after a weekend at the Halsey Ranch Party? The Jim Halsey Company hosted a good party, and everyone on our staff knew who was coming and how important these guests were to our artists and to us. No one lived in the ranchhouse, but it was fully furnished, with the bedrooms outfitted as offices. Those were used for private sales meetings, where my expert agents would get down to the business of discussing itinerary and money for the artists who had caught the eyes and ears of our Halsey Ranch Party guests.

Dick Howard was in charge of inviting our guests from the television industry. During the event, his staff was equally busy booking television deals, guest spots, guest-host jobs, and commercials. What a bunch of deals were made during the gigantic Halsey Ranch Party weekend! The tally of future bookings always ran into the millions of dollars.

And you never knew what other benefits might come out of that colossal weekend.

In one of our early Halsey Ranch Parties, for instance, we presented a show by The Oak Ridge Boys. Many of the buyers for the big state fairs were seeing The Oak Ridge Boys for the very first time, and it's an understatement to say that The Oak Ridge Boys wowed 'em. Before the weekend concluded, John Hitt had written The Oak Ridge Boys deals for more than 30 major fairs!

That was the magic of the Halsey Ranch Parties. Deals were

struck left and right. Nothing was left to chance. We were all prepared with our sales plans before any of the guests arrived—what we wanted to sell, who we wanted to sell, where and for how much was all in our heads. We all had our artists' routing books in our hip pockets. When a buyer expressed the slightest interest, we were ready. If interest wasn't forthcoming within a sufficient time period, we tactfully made suggestions. We didn't want to force anything, but we wanted to be effective. We had our inventories of dates for the following year, and the Halsey Ranch Party was the big sales event that filled our artists' itineraries.

It was a sales event without parallel in the industry, a private showcasing of Halsey Company artists before the most important buyers in the world. And it upset many of our competitors, because we had the first opportunity to book our acts with fair buyers for the coming year.

We covered many, many different bases with this one gigantic weekend. We invited members of the press in from everywhere, and got stories for the next three months in return. A limousine company from St. Louis, Jed's, asked to be included, so our guests were greeted by 25 new white Cadillac limousines to transport them from Tulsa hotels to the ranch.

Ralph Emery's broadcasts from the Halsey Ranch Parties reached all across the country. Dick Howard sold a taping of Ranch Party highlights every year as a syndicated TV special. To further gild the lily, Hank Thompson, Roy Clark, Mack Sanders, and I were owners of two radio stations in Tulsa, one AM and the other FM. We invited our very best sponsors to this invitation-only affair, and many advertisers helped with party supplies. Pepsi furnished the soft drinks, Pringles the chips, Hunts the ketchup, local auto dealers the cars; the list goes on and on. Nowhere in America could a Tulsa radio advertiser see such shows and rub elbows with stars of such magnitude. Our radio stations booked a lot of heavy advertising dollars for the coming months. The Halsey Ranch Party worked for everyone.

There was magic at the Halsey Ranch Party. Not only sales and marketing magic, but the real thing as well. One of our frequent guests was the Amazing Kreskin, the renowned mentalist. He wasn't represented by our company, but he was a good friend and welcome at our gatherings. He did a lot of one-on-one entertaining and was a delightful addition to the event.

I'll never forget when one of our guests inappropriately asked Kreskin if he was going to do any tricks.

"I don't do tricks," Kreskin replied. "I do magic."

This he does, and so did we at the Halsey Ranch Parties.

The overwhelming success of these events illustrates how planning carefully, setting a goal, and having a distinct purpose will result in success far beyond anyone's imagination. Each Halsey Ranch Party took a year of planning and included the thoughts and ideas of everyone within our company. It took coordination with our in-house PR Director, Leo Zabelin, and our Company's PR firm, Kathy Gangwisch and Associates, which was able to bring in a large contingency of quality press representatives from around the world for this event every year.

It took thought, planning, and coordination, much as you would see in a military campaign. Our goal was the same: to win. We always won, but in our case the winning made our world a better place to live.

EVENTS

As you learn about the building of events, creating interest, stimulating attention and elevating the importance of the project, examine the potential elements that can be layered to enhance the overall. Throughout our lives we have grown up with events, city celebrations, state and county fairs. It's always a meaningful life event to attend Disneyland, Disneyworld and local and national events such as homecomings, annual community celebrations, Fourth of July, Veterans Day. These are all events that have been organized and promoted as something we want to attend. There's always excitement in the air.

When movies are released, big campaigns are planned. It's a big event planned with promotion to stimulate your interest and ticket sale. Car dealers, grocery and furniture stores all design special events to get your attention and your purchase with flags and banners waving, special prices.

Hollywood Squares "Layered". We did a similar type of magnanimous grouping of our artists wherein we, the company, through the efforts of our super-agent Dick Howard, filled all of the squares in the popular Hollywood Squares television quiz show. This feat certainly was worthy of lots of press attention. No other agency had done this before (or since, that I'm aware of). This all-country Hollywood Squares included our clients Roy Clark, Minnie Pearl, Mel Tillis, Tammy Wynette, Jim Stafford, George Lindsey, Margot Smith and George Jones (permanent square, host George Gobel was not our client).

Celebrity Golf Tournament. This star-studded tournament was held in Tulsa for a number of years, hosted by Roy Clark. The entire community got behind us. It added another element to our weekend Halsey Ranch Parties, layered with press, TV and networking with our own celebrity clients and important buyers.

Country Goes to England. We were able to utilize Mervyn Conn's important Wembley Festivals in the Spring of the year. It garnered important press, TV and European buyers. Our company always had a contingency of our stars present which enabled us to network and promote the UK and European continent for records, publishing, TV and personal appearance tours. Besides Mervyns important conferences and press events, the Halsey Company always hosted a VIP reception, usually on the roof garden on the Royal Garden Hotel in London. The festival and events became the featured subject of a network television special "Country Goes to England," produced and directed by Sherman Halsey.

Oak Ridge Boys Live in Las Vegas. Another television event consisting of fifteen one-hour specials produced by Sherman Halsey that ran on cable network TNN intermittently for the two years. It was taped at the Hilton Hotel on the former "Elvis" stage featuring the Oak Ridge Boys and important guests. It received high ratings, but also was an event for press. The stimulation of Oak Ridge Boys buyers had the effect of a top five record. It's still producing lasting effects.

Bulgaria Spectaculars. The prestigious Golden Orpheus Festival held annually at Sunny Beach, Bulgaria created huge notice for the appearances by Roy Orbison, and later by Roy Clark.

The televised event was the number one show in what was then known as the Soviet Satellite countries. It brought even more attention to Orbison and Clark in the Western world because of their unusual scheduling in an Eastern European country.

The MIDEM Event. The largest professional music conference, MIDEM, is attended annually in Cannes, France by the very top professionals from nearly every country in the world. Never had Country music been represented, and certainly not presented in live concert until the Halsey Company put together a spectacular combination of artists to attend MIDEM '79. Our presentation of Roy Clark, Don Williams, The Oak Ridge Boys along with banjoist sensation Buck Trent was the first. The old opera house was the scene and was filled with music dignitaries plus over two hundred international press. We heard and read about this for years following the concert. We were able to connect this event with Princess Caroline's 19th birthday party at the Sporting Club in Monte Carlo. What a coup! Other events fell into place because of these prestigious appearances. It was here, at a meeting with impresario Claude Nobs, we were able to secure our invitation to the *Montreaux Jazz Festival plus the Brussels (Belgium) Millennium Celebration.*

Recognize how important these events are? A first for our artists and a first for Country music. Others might treat these engagements as just another date on the itinerary. Wrong! These are "for the first time only" and being first is *always* important. Sometimes, it's not just one date or one event, it's a project that lasts for a period of time. For The Oak Ridge Boys, being the national celebrity spokesperson for The National Anthem Project lasted for two and a half years, sponsored by MENC (Music Educators National Conference). This opened doors to many other events and eventually led to The Oak Ridge Boys being featured on the National Anthem Project Float in the Rose Parade, New Years Day 2007. This float was provided by NAMM (National Association of Music Merchants). There were nearly 2 millions viewers on the parade route, but television carried the parade around the world to 1.5 *billion* viewers. *Now that's an event!*

The Billboard Special. Even print can be presented as an event. Billboard Magazine, bible of the industry, honored the Jim Halsey Company with a special edition. Many times these are looked at as vanity affairs. I didn't want ours to be that. We agreed to participate, but I had two requests. Number one, the advertisement would be slanted toward the achievements of the artists that were asked to participate, not the Halsey Company. It was a selling piece for them and in turn the Halsey Company would use it as such. My other request was the special edition would coincide with the Billboard issue released and promoted at the important MIDEM conference. Up until that time this was the largest special edition that Billboard had produced, *54*

Pages of Jim Halsey Company Edition! This was very prestigious for us and our artists and we totally maximized its potential.

This event philosophy is meant to guide your thinking toward taking normal everyday events, adding to them and turning them into extraordinary events. In the development of your business and that of your artists, consider every possibly way to enhance what's already on the table. Pay special attention to unique and unusual circumstances that will build a creative and special presentation into an *event*.

Calling attention to being first in situations and events is always worthy. Such as, my stellar client Hank Thompson was the first country artist to record in high-fidelity. Hank Thompson was the first county artist to record in stereo. He was the first Country music artist to record a live and in-person album, "Live at the Golden Nugget." Likewise, his "Live at the Frontier Days Rodeo," was the first to be recorded live at a rodeo, and his "Live at the Texas State Fair" the first to be recorded at a state fair. These three album firsts are in the history books. There are lots of other live country music albums, but none have that "first" distinction. These all became big events at that time and remain so today.

Country in New York. An event our company produced with New York impresario James Nederlander was another big event that became another first, Hank Thompson, Don Williams, Freddy Fender and Roy Clark, all in concert at Carnegie Hall. It was also recorded live and released on an album. But for the first time, broadcast simultaneously live over network of 50,000 watt radio stations. A media event, for sure!

Neewollah. Neewollah is a spectacular Fall event that takes place around Halloween. This event was co-created with my good friends Jerry Webb, Bob Wholtman and Don Dancer in my hometown, Independence, KS. This extravaganza includes stage shows, bands, gigantic parades, queens, home talent events, and of course, celebrities. This has continued over 50 years and is recognized as Kansas' largest annual celebration. It's been the subject of two nationally televised specials (Sherman Halsey produced), one for HBO and more recently for Larry Jones and Feed The Children.

There are hundreds of regular concert appearances that include National Anthem singing at ball games, ribbon cuttings, historic events, Feed The Children food distributions, fishing tournaments, queen's coronations, charitable situations. Almost anything can be structured or turned into an event that creates attention and makes the project more worthy. I've just illustrated a few here. There have literally been thousands in my life. And there are thousands in your life, too, if you recognize that the most important event everyday in your life is the sun coming up over the horizon. Now *that's* an event!

chapter 23

VISION TO REALITY: RADIO CITY MUSIC HALL

can point to many projects and events—and even artists—that have been developed as a result of dreams and visions. As I've noted throughout this book, it's important to recognize dreams for what they are: inspirations that come to us to tell us how something could be. With good and careful planning, we can turn them into reality.

Years ago, I had a vision of developing an important event in New York City, something that would attract the attention of advertising agencies, commercial producers, convention producers, prospective corporate sponsors, television and radio executives, record company executives, members of the press and media, and concert, casino and fair buyers. It was a vision of a showcase that would elevate the image of my artists and pay off for years to come.

My vision? To put The Oak Ridge Boys and The Judds into Radio City Music Hall.

Our company had already done a number of shows at Carnegie Hall, another internationally recognized venue. Even The Oak Ridge Boys had played there. But my vision this time called for Radio City Music Hall.

At this point, our company was just beginning to break The Judds. Wynonna and Naomi had two successful records under their belt, they'd won some awards, and we felt a prestigious engagement with The Oak Ridge Boys at Radio City Music Hall would give them a big boost. We figured it could even be the push they needed to catapult them into bona fide stardom.

As you know from previous chapters, part of the secret of developing artists into stars is getting them seen and heard by people who can do something for them. A lot of times, you can do this by packaging shows, putting a developing act on the front half of a big superstar's concert. This was what we did with The Oak Ridge Boys and The Judds, figuring that the combination of the two would not only be dynamite for the New York market, but also something that could explode The Judds' career. In addition, it would be an impact enhancer for The Oak Ridge Boys, who were launching both a new album and a new tour.

Before any work began on this project—before, in fact, anyone else knew anything about it—I started my meditation and prayer, formulating exactly what it was I wanted to accomplish. As I had seen Radio City Music Hall many times before, I knew exactly what the stage and the exterior, marquee and all, looked like. During my meditation, I envisioned The Oak Ridge Boys on Radio City's giant stage, with all of the lights, sound, and production imaginable. I also imagined The Judds on that stage, standing and performing in warm, perfect, lighting. I visualized a sold-out hall with thunderous applause and standing ovations. I then envisioned that wonderful neon marquee of Radio City Music Hall with the names of my artists, The Oak Ridge Boys and The Judds, emblazoned in white-reverse across the front.

I was determined to make this date happen, and I was determined to make it an event.

It became one.

We actually did the date—the event—almost a year later. It took that much time to work it out properly. First of all, we needed the support of The Oak Ridge Boys' record company, MCA, and The Judds,' which was RCA. We convinced both companies of the merits, and long-term benefits of doing a gigantic promotion. They understood exactly how important this date could be and pledged full support.

Our next step was to coordinate the dates of the two groups along with the venues with the proposed record release schedules for both artists. We planned to book them together for not only Radio City Music Hall, but other selected dates.

The Radio City date would be most effective if it coincided with the release of their new albums. We scheduled planning meetings between The Oak Ridge Boys and The Judds and Kathy Gangwisch and Assoc., our PR firm.

We all knew that this was our opportunity to showcase our two acts in one of the most prestigious venues in the world, in one of the most important entertainment cities in the world, something that wasn't expected of country music performers at the time. So the promotion from all aspects had to be enormous and elaborate.

First I contacted Margo Fieden, the agent for the great caricaturist, Al Hirschfeld. I wanted a centerpiece, if you will, a symbol to speak for the event. A Hirschfeld caricature of The Oak Ridge Boys would be exactly that, something that could be used constantly to create repetitious impressions in posters, program books, newspaper ads, billboards, invitations, and, eventually, in a live album recorded by The Oak Ridge Boys on the Radio City Music Hall stage.

In fact, we had plans for Hirschfeld's masterful caricature to continue to work after the event was history. We arranged with Felden to do a limited number of serigraphs of the piece; our idea was that Hirschfeld would sign and number and The Oak Ridge Boys would autograph each copy. This limited edition would then be sold, with proceeds going to our favorite charity, the Oklahoma City-based Feed the Children.

Remember how, in Chapter 12, I told you never to assume anything? You'd have thought that a project like this, with proceeds going to a good charity and everyone involved benefiting in various ways, would be easy to accomplish. Unfortunately, it wasn't. In fact, it never happened. The difficulties that grew out of The Oak Ridge Boys' personality differences were reaching critical mass at the time, and shortly after the engagement, William Lee Golden left the group. The limited-edition serigraphs were never sold, the charity funds never raised, and the great Hirschfeld caricature was used only for the Radio City event. Thank goodness William Lee Golden returned to The Oak Ridge Boys in 1996.

Still, the promotion became enormous and was a great success. Press, radio, the record and publishing companies, management, and our PR firm all had a synergistic effect on one another and on the event itself.

Ron Delsner, one of New York City's finest promoters, handled the concert (along with Radio City Music Hall), and he took care of all of the public promotion. Equally as important to us, however, was promoting the event within the industry. We started working on press many months before the date in order to obtain space in the weekly and monthly publications. Both The Oak Ridge Boys and The Judds made themselves available for press, radio, and television interviews.

On a broader basis, we ran ads using the Hirschfeld caricature in many national and international magazines and newspapers, plus all of the trades. We knew that most of their readers were not going to flock to New York City from around the world for our concert, but we wanted to make a "prestigious announcement," letting everyone know this was an important event with two important acts.

At the same time, radio was being worked on a nationwide basis. MCA Records held contests over many country radio stations, flying the winners into New York City for the show. Also flown in were important talent buyers from around the world, whom we specially invited.

One of the major pre-concert events was a party and reception held in the Time-Life Penthouse directly across from Radio City. Five hundred of the biggest music, broadcasting, advertising, and press and media executives from around the world attended, along with heads and chief executives from some of America's top corporations. It was a big success. The artists' "performance" at this reception was as important as what they would later do on the Radio City stage, and I'll bet The Oak Ridge Boys and The Judds shook hands with every single one of the 500 invited guests.

Time finally came for the concert, and it was just as I'd envisioned it nearly a year earlier. Radio City Music Hall, with the names of our acts emblazoned across its marquee, was completely sold out, and both The Judds and The Oak Ridge Boys received thunderous applause and standing ovations. In every sense of the word, it was an event.

Sometimes, after everybody has worked so hard for so long on a project like this, there's a letdown feeling after it's over, a sense of disappointment in knowing that the euphoric space occupied by the event is no more. That wasn't the case for me. Sure, I was tired, but I was filled with a wonderful feeling of satisfaction and success.

Still, there was one more thing I wanted to do.

The Oak Ridge Boys and The Judds were packed and gone. The audience members, carrying their own memories of this marvelous show, had all dispersed when Minisa, Kathy Gangwisch, and I walked out the front door of Radio City Music Hall into the neon night of

New York City. We looked back at the marquee, still ablaze with "The Oak Ridge Boys and The Judds." It was a symbol of a dream and vision I'd had almost a year earlier, and I wanted Kathy to take a picture of it.

She did, and that picture still hangs prominently in my office, an illustration of the power of a dream that comes true, an example of how to go from dream to vision to reality.

Again, the Radio City Music Hall show is a graphic illustration of what an event should be. We created it by following the right steps and revising our plans over and over again, perfecting them, tuning them, until we finally put them into operation. We had our goals established. We focused upon them. We were successful.

You can do the same thing. As I've told you before, part of the secret of success is to constantly strive to go beyond what you might think of as your limits. Extend your energies and abilities to achieve new goals and broaden new horizons. Project your goals. Put them in writing and look at them frequently. Then, formulate your plans for achieving them.

Most of all, have the courage to follow your dreams, because that is where it all starts—for you, for me, for everyone who wants to succeed in this business.

chapter 24

THE LAS VEGAS EVENT

"Jim Halsey's most recent accomplishment deserves a place in the Guinness Book of World Records.*"* —*Joe Delaney,* Las Vegas Sun

Imagine a glittering showroom, abuzz with quiet conversation and the clinking of glasses. Then suddenly the lights dim, the spangled curtain shimmers, and the announcer's voice booms from the speakers: "Ladies and gentlemen, Bally's Grand Hotel is proud to present … The Oak Ridge Boys!"

If your act is good, it will only be better in Vegas.

Casino areas are always well covered by the local press and major news services. The reviewers for papers in places like Las Vegas and Atlantic City have important voices; usually seasoned entertainment writers and journalists whose reviews and comments are respected throughout the country and the world. Most of them bring years of seeing what works and what doesn't work to their reviews and stories, and they are usually very consistent with their standards. A good review from one of them can be used as an endorsement for your artist's talents. A bad review gives you something to work on. Even negative reviews can contain a good comment or two, and those can be used in your news releases and other publicity material for your acts.

Las Vegas, Atlantic City, and other casino areas are better than normal places for creating promotions and making your shows into events. As an artist, manager, or booking agent, you shouldn't just accept a booking in one of these places and rely on normal avenues of promotion. Las Vegas, for instance, is a great place for a presentation, but you also have more competition. There are all kinds of promotional avenues to examine, including airlines, bus benches, taxi tops, billboards, newspapers, and special television and radio campaigns. A big Vegas or Atlantic City engagement is a great opportunity to market an artist internationally, and you should let the world know that your act is appearing in one of these showrooms. If you're a booking agent, invite everyone on your buyer's list, even if you know some or most can't attend. While these areas usually aren't of major importance when it comes to record sales, bookings in major casinos and hotels are impressive and should be publicized.

WIN ROY, MEL OR TAMMY

For artists, managers, and booking agents, Las Vegas takes on a special importance each November. The last week of that month is the date of the annual convention of the International Association of Fairs and Expositions, when all the fair and rodeo buyers from across the United States and Canada gather to exchange ideas and select attractions for the coming year.

The Las Vegas convention is much like any other trade show, with various booths where agencies and other fair vendors display their wares. Our Jim Halsey Company booth held pictures of and pamphlets about all our artists. A lot of times, we gave away merchandise, including tour jackets and T-shirts, to various fair buyers. We prided ourselves on having a unique marketing program on display at the convention—always something different, something spectacular.

The Jim Halsey Company was an entertainment agency, of course, but first and foremost, it was a sales organization. We had to devise ways of attracting attention so we could sell our artists for the coming season. For that week in November, our Power of Performance had to be the best. We expected it from ourselves. Our artists expected it from us. And the attending fair buyers always expected it, too!

One of our more successful ways of standing out from the crowd was our use of a jumbo slot machine, which Bally's—where the convention was held—was always kind enough to loan us. One of these slots stands as high as a human being, and that in itself was an attention-getter. But it was the way we used it that made it such a great promotional tool.

What we did was allow every fair manager and talent buyer to have a pull on the machine. If any of them proved lucky enough to line up the three bars and hit the jackpot, he or she would win a performance from any one of our stars—absolutely free! Imagine having a chance at a free show from Roy Clark, Mel Tillis, The Oak Ridge Boys, Minnie Pearl, Tammy Wynette, Reba McEntire, The Judds, Ronnie Milsap, or Merle Haggard, among many others. If you were a talent buyer, wouldn't you be interested?

The slot-machine promotion, needless to say, captured the imagination of the attendees, with a constant line of the top fair buyers in the United States and Canada in front of our booth, waiting for a turn at the slot. Those who didn't win a free show—which, of course, was almost all of them—were able to win records, videos, jackets, T-shirts, and other paraphernalia belonging to the different artists.

THE VEGAS BLITZ

The Halsey Company booth was always the most popular one at the convention, and the slot machine was a wonderful promotional tool, year after year. But as good as that was, we came up with an even greater promotion. We were able to book most of the big casino showrooms with Halsey Company artists during the run of the convention, which created a real event. What better way to sell your stars than to have them playing Vegas, at one of the main venues, with all those buyers in town? Each year, we concentrated heavily on getting as many of our artists as we could into these showrooms while the convention was going on. Once, in the six major hotels that were presenting headline attractions at the time, our acts headlined in five of them. It made Vegas look like a Jim Halsey Company town. Those arriving in Las Vegas for the International Association of Fairs and Expositions convention were hit from all sides with the names of our artists, the marquees of major hotels advertising them in letters as big as those on billboards. At Bally's Grand, it was Roy Clark and Reba McEntire plus the great comedy of Williams and Ree. The Hilton offered The Judds and The Nitty Gritty Dirt Band; Caesar's Palace, The Oak Ridge Boys and the Forrester Sisters; the Frontier Hotel, Lee Greenwood and Bill Medley; and the Sahara Hotel, Mel Tillis and the Statesiders.

What an array of entertainers, and all Halsey Company artists!

If we'd put the names of our stars on every billboard in town, we couldn't have launched a more impressive campaign. These major marquees advertised our headliners 24 hours a day, and when the fair buyers hit town for the week, all they could see were the major acts we'd be selling them for their coming fair season. It took almost a year to put that multiple-act event together. It was a major coup for us, one that no other agency had done before—or has done since.

Besides being impressive to all the fair buyers, this multiple-venue event attracted a lot of flak from our competitors, especially after Joe Delaney, the important entertainment-business columnist for the Las Vegas Sun , wrote, "Jim Halsey's most recent Las Vegas accomplishment deserves a place in the Guinness Book of World Records."

It was all part of promotion, of creating events. It was a perfect example of the Power of Performance.

PLANNING, PLANNING AND MORE PLANNING

Our company developed an outstanding rapport with fair buyers and fair managers around the country, and fairs became a major source of revenue for our artists. John Hitt, who you'll remember headed The Halsey Company's fair department, built us into the No. 1 fair booking agency in the world. Some of that ranking came because of the big stars we handled, but much of it was because of the great service that John and the rest of the Halsey Company associates gave to the fair buyers. A born salesperson, John knew the eternal value of a satisfied customer.

John and his sales crew always did a tremendous business at the fair buyers' convention in Vegas. With Halsey Company acts headlining in the main showrooms, we had the opportunity to entertain the fair buying committees and make sales at the same time. John and his staff always prepared several months in advance, arranging personal interviews with the fair buyers during the convention. It took a lot of preparation to make all those connections, but when John and his crew hit Vegas, they were set up for one meeting after another—and one sale after another.

Once again, one of the keys to success is planning, planning, and more planning. Not only were the names of our artists shouting out from marquees, but also from ads, pamphlets, promotional pieces, and billboards. If you were a talent buyer, you couldn't miss them. And as icing on the cake, before any fair buyer arrived in Las Vegas, he or she received a personal invitation from us to one of the showrooms where our artists were appearing, or to play our giant slot machine for a chance to win his or her fair attraction for the next year.

We had confidence in our product. We had confidence in our promotion. And we had confidence in our presentation. We were always successful at gatherings like the International Association of Fairs and Expositions convention because we maximized every promotional element available to get our artists in front of the buyer as well as the public. In this case, the bookings in these top Vegas venues provided prestige, international recognition, and cash flow, and helped us develop new artists, which we used to open the shows for our headliners.

It's always advantageous to sellers to present their wares to prospective buyers in the most favorable light. Automobile dealers do it. Furniture and appliance dealers do it. They present their cars or sofas or stoves in beautiful settings, with lighting designed to enhance whatever special features of a product might be especially noteworthy.

Any manager or agent can apply this same principle. Selling your act to a prospective buyer can be aided by lighting, staging, and special presentation. Las Vegas was the perfect place to bring buyers, television producers, record-company executives, columnists, and magazine writers to see our shows. Any of the big showrooms offered a well-dressed stage with special effects, an impressive strip marquee with our star's name, comfortable seats, and of course, the best sound and lights. A deal could almost always be closed in one of the comfortable booths at one of these shows as the buyer watched Mel, Roy, Tammy, The Oak Ridge Boys, Reba, Lee Greenwood, The Judds, Freddy Fender, Merle, or any other of our star artists play to a receptive full house. There was something about the glamour of Las Vegas, with the lights going, the neon flashing, and our artists' names in big letters on the marquees, that enhanced the Power of Performance and set the mood for deal-making.

In the '70s and '80s, country stars were not always easy to sell to network television shows, because some L.A. executives were still unconvinced of their drawing power. Taking advantage of the easy access from Southern California to Las Vegas, we often flew in TV producers and talent coordinators who we knew were in the process of putting together network shows. When these people saw our country acts in a Las Vegas atmosphere, we were able to close many a television deal.

The Jim Halsey Company was a pioneer in getting country acts on mainstream television programs. Thanks to my associate and executive vice president, Dick Howard, selling country music artists to non-country TV shows was a constant goal of The Halsey Company. Running our L.A. office, Dick not only made a name for himself as the expert country music agent in Southern California, but also established our company as the No. 1 agency for getting country artists on network television—and kept us there.

chapter 25

NICE IS NICE

Fulfillment with Purpose

A good project or promotion should have a worthy conclusion—a fulfillment of the goal and purpose I've spoken about before in this book. If things work out right, many will have benefited, including all of the artists and companies involved.

Any good manager or impresario is always looking for the right date or promotion to present itself, so it can be turned into an event. Remember: Most events start out as simply concerts or personal appearances, and the difference between something ordinary and something spectacular is based on the degrees of imagination and inventive planning involved. As you know, I was always looking for some type of happening that could be turned into an event for one of my artists. Sometimes, one just fell into my lap.

That was the case with one of our best Halsey Company promotions. It began with a casual meeting in the lobby of the Carlton Hotel in Cannes, France, during the MIDEM Music and Entertainment Convention. Jacque Mediciene, mayor of Nice (pronounced "niece"), France, Oak Ridge Boys principal William Lee Golden, and I were discussing the MIDEM convention, and Jacque Mediciene suggested that The Oak Ridge Boys would be perfect to open the new convention center in Nice, a state-of-the art creation called the Acropolis.

Projected to be the most modern facility in the south of France, it was to house a concert stage, exhibit halls, a shopping center, recording studios, and broadcast facilities.

We arranged a meeting the next day with Mediciene, who would make the final decision about The Oak Ridge Boys. After meeting and negotiating with him, we got an official invitation.

Everything about the deal was good. The Oak Ridge Boys were to play one show for a fee of $50,000. In addition, we would get deluxe hotel accommodations and meals; 35 round-trip, first-class airline tickets on Air France; sound and lights for the show, and all internal transportation. The problem was fitting the date into The Oak Ridge Boys' itinerary. It was isolated, and there was not enough time to book any other meaningful dates on either side of it.

Still, I hated to pass up this opportunity to further expand our European visibility and potential record sales. If we couldn't turn this booking into something meaningful and practical, it would be just another personal appearance.

We contacted an old friend, Larry Jones, whose Oklahoma City-based Feed the Children charity does such outstanding worldwide work. "Any suggestions?" we asked him.

He had a good one. At the time, Kenya, Africa—where Larry's charity was helping feed the people of the Rift Valley—was in the midst of a long, severe drought. If water could be obtained in the area, the people could begin planting crops and start growing some of their own food.

Larry asked us a question. If he could deliver matching funds, would The Oak Ridge Boys donate their $50,000 performance fee to Feed the Children for the express purpose of drilling a water well in the Rift Valley?

Duane Allen, Joe Bonsall, Richard Sterban, and William Lee Golden, the four members of The Oak Ridge Boys, readily agreed. Everyone liked the idea of putting the performance fee into drilling a well for a drought-stricken area. One of the most satisfying things about it was that the event would, in a significant way, live for a long time after the actual concert concluded. The well would stand as its symbol .

As the opening of the Acropolis grew near, it was becoming an event in itself. Press members from all over Europe were invited to witness the opening. Television was going to cover it, and many TV news departments were sending crews for live "bites" of the event .

The Halsey Company did its own brand of promotion, inaugurating a 90-day campaign built around the slogan "Nice is Nice!" All of our promotional material was geared to this phrase. Our news releases, special press kits, radio packages, T-shirts, and anything else dealing with the concert went out imprinted with the slogan, The Oak Ridge Boys' logo, and the image of crossed American and French flags.

Kathy Gangwisch, our PR person, was on a roll, getting lots of TV, radio, and newspaper interviews. The television magazine shows were all covering the event. Halsey Company senior vice president Judi Pofsky, working out of Los Angeles, sold the live gala broadcast internationally and to ABC radio in America. The coverage was worldwide and enormous! It was a media event, just as we'd wanted.

Prior to the performance, the city of Nice held a press conference and reception. As Larry Jones made prayers for the opening of the Acropolis and the success of the concert, he gave a startling announcement: instead of one water well in the Riff Valley—our goal—Feed the Children had been able to raise enough money to drill four wells! Further, he said that each well would be named after one of The Oak Ridge Boys!

There were many other welcoming remarks, but nobody could top that.

Joseph Rael, a Picuris and Mountain Ute medicine man who had accompanied our entourage to France, performed a beautiful blessing of the new Acropolis building and the concert. Larry Jones videotaped the entire proceedings and the concert for inclusion on his own television show, carried in 110 markets. Portions of the event were broadcast over Eurovision and on almost every TV network and channel throughout the world.

This is a magnificent example of what can happen when you practice Power of Performance. Everyone concerned combined their talents and, working together, turned an ordinary concert date into an event of monumental proportions. To this day, the four wells are producing precious water for the residents of the Riff Valley.

See how important projects are born? Sometimes they can come from something as casual as a conversation in a hotel lobby. You should always listen closely to the details of any proposal or idea. There may be some hidden benefits beneath the surface.

Learn to use and expand your imagination. Recognizing the potential of an idea is at the heart of perfecting your Power of Performance. And remember also that when an opportunity is presented to help people, we are always helped in the process. It is possible to have fun, take care of business, and do good all at the same time. Our experiences in Nice once again showed The Jim Halsey principle that a deal is good only when it's good for all concerned.

Nice was nice!

chapter 26

ORBISON MAGIC IN BULGARIA

Around the time of the first Roy Clark Soviet tour, I became interested in FIDOF, the International Federation of Festival Organizations, and its charismatic founder and leader, Professor Amando Moreno. Founded in 1967 in Cannes, France, simultaneously with MIDEM (the Music Business Industry Conference), FIDOF's umbrella expanded to include more than 360 major music festivals in 80 countries.

FIDOF introduced me to festivals and organizations that were not familiar with country music (but soon would be). As the organization broadened my scope, I became more active in pursuing my goals on an international basis. In fact, I served as FIDOF's president from 1984 through 1990 and currently hold the title of president of honor, in recognition of my service to FIDOF.

Many of my artists, aware of Roy Clark's then-recent great success in the USSR, were interested in the world festival arena. One of them was the legendary rock 'n' roller Roy Orbison. Already a big international record seller, he had at the time toured extensively in Asia, Great Britain, and Western Europe, witnessing the effect of his own Power of Performance on international audiences. He had not, however, appeared in any Communist countries.

We were able to secure Mr. Orbison an invitation to perform in Bulgaria.

From his Nashville home, Orbison would travel halfway around the world to give a show. That wasn't so different for him, a seasoned traveler and international performer. What was different was that this would be his first-ever concert behind the Iron Curtain. He was to be the headliner at the final gala performance at the Golden Orpheus Festival in Sunny Beach, Bulgaria—the prestigious talent showcase of the Communist world. Outstanding young talent from Bulgaria, the Soviet Union, China, Hungary, Romania, Poland, East Germany, Czechoslovakia, Albania, Cuba, North Vietnam, and Yugoslavia made up the festival's roster, along with a handful of performers from outside the Soviet bloc—England, Holland, France, and West Germany.

But now, for the first time, it would be an American artist who had the honor of closing the festival's final night, the Gala Performance. Roy Orbison wasn't a communist, of course. But he knew music was the international language, and he also knew that through music and art, an atmosphere of peace and harmony could be created and perpetuated.

Although The Jim Halsey Company was known as the largest country-music agency in the world, with many superstars on our roster, we also represented other major artists from other musical genres, including rockers Leon Russell and Rick Nelson, R&B icon James Brown, and big-band legend Woody Herman, who had helped me through that snowed-in Independence, Kansas, date at the beginning of my career. All of us were bound by one common thread: we believed peace and harmony could be achieved through music and art, and that the Power of Performance could change lives.

At the time, The Jim Halsey Company had become involved with many international projects. We had been, for instance, producing an international festival in Tulsa and Oklahoma City (at Oklahoma City University), as well as at Independence (with the Neewollah Festival) and Baldwin (at Baker University), Kansas. Through these events, we became aware of fine Bulgarian singers like Bisser Kirov and Nelly Rangalova, each of whom took our grand prize in successive years.

Now, for the first time, America was coming to Bulgaria—in the person of Roy Orbison, creator of such immortal songs as "Crying," "Pretty Woman," and "In Dreams."

It was a long and grueling trip for him. As we got closer to Sunny Beach, the airplane and airline changes grew more and more frequent, and the planes seemed to get smaller each time. Finally, arriving in

Sofia, Bulgaria, 24 hours after the start of the trip, we got into a Balkan Airlines twin-prop job of near-antique vintage, which was to take us to Bourgas. From Bourgas, it was on to Sunny Beach by official government limousine.

Finally, we made it to the festival site. Exhausted from hours of flying, no sleep, irregular food, and the constant changing of planes, Roy Orbison emerged from the limo and looked around a moment. Then, in an uncharacteristically gruff manner, he asked me, "Halsey, where are we?"

"Sunny Beach, Bulgaria, Roy," I answered. "You are the first American to ever perform here."

"Bulgaria?" Orbison said incredulously. "You told me we were going to Bavaria."

I never found out if he was kidding.

THE FIRST AMERICAN

As I've said before, it's always important to be the first at something, and our company liked to be first with programs, events, and projects. Our artists liked to be first, too. Roy Orbison was the first artist to represent America as a performer in the prestigious Golden Orpheus Festival, and he did a superb job.

Before sound check on the afternoon of Orbison's performance, he and I, along with officials from both the American Embassy and the Bulgarian Ministry of Culture, were walking down the Avenue of Flags in front of the concert hall in Sunny Beach. Flags from all of the nations represented at the festival flapped in the sea breeze. There was the Bulgarian flag, of course, as well as those from the Soviet Union, East Germany, Hungary, Romania, Poland, Czechoslovakia, Albania, Yugoslavia, North Vietnam, Cuba, and China. And for the first time ever, we saw Old Glory flying proudly over Sunny Beach, right next to the Soviet flag.

The Deputy Minister of Culture, who was hosting our sight-seeing walk, turned to Roy.

"Look, Mr. Orbison," he said. "Because you are here, your American flag is flying today in Bulgaria."

I don't need to tell you that this was goosebump time for all of us Americans, walking on the Avenue of Flags that day, far away from home.

Roy's performance that night may be one of the best he ever gave.

In Europe, audience members will often bring flowers to the stage when they particularly respect and appreciate an artist's performance, and I have never in my career seen as many flowers as I saw that evening. The entire stage—and it was gigantic—was totally buried in flowers, all brought to the stage by members of the enthusiastic crowd. And Roy's ovations were tremendous. After each song, the audience would break into rhythmic clapping that lasted for many minutes. His show was delayed so many times by the delighted crowd that I didn't think he'd be able to finish.

Perhaps the most touching thing about his concert, however, was that everyone in the audience knew all of his songs, singing along with most of them and making for a very emotional evening.

The concert attracted press from all over the world, and the entire show went out over Eurovision, which broadcast to an audience of 200 million viewers in Western Europe. In addition, Soviet TV beamed it to more than 500 million Eastern Europeans, giving Orbison's performance a potential audience of more than 700 million people!

Again, it's easy to understand the importance of the Power of Performance by a great artist on a prestigious stage, but the performance we have to give in our everyday lives is equally important, because that performance can change lives as well.

After the gala concert, my wife, Minisa, and I hosted a dinner at the leading hotel in Sunny Beach. We had champagne and caviar, shopska salad, and virtually everything else we could get on the menu. After all, we were celebrating Roy Orbison's overwhelming success—a success for America!

Our party included several guests from the American Embassy as well as Eastern European superstars Bisser Kirov of Bulgaria, Alla Pugachova of the USSR, and Iosif Kobson, known as the "People's Artist of the USSR." We were also honored by the presence of the Bulgarian Minister of Culture, who had become an instant Roy Orbison fan. We witnessed magic that night, with American, Bulgarian, and Soviet performers and artists all sitting at one table, talking music and art, transcending their political boundaries, respecting and enjoying one another.

As a result of the banquet and Roy Orbison's fantastic success at the festival, some very positive things happened. The cultural attaché with the American Embassy had been in Bulgaria for three years without ever being able to get an appointment with the Minister of Culture. Now, here they were together at the same table with the rest of us, making champagne toasts to Roy Orbison's success, to each other's countries, to peace, to art and music, to expanded friendship, to those who were not with us, to everything that came into anyone's mind.

The final toast? As is the custom, we all made it to our mothers—an appropriate finish to this magical, emotional, joyous evening.

The next week, the cultural attaché had an appointment with the Ministry of Culture. Interestingly enough, they discovered that they lived in the same apartment complex. Meanwhile, we had made a deal for Bisser Kirov to tour in the United States, and we'd started the wheels in motion for another American superstar, Roy Clark, to perform at Sunny Beach.

All of this and more happened because of Roy Orbison's Power of Performance, and all that went with it. .

Let me stress again that I really believe art and music can make the world a better place to live, a place of peace and harmony. The artists and musicians of the world can contribute greatly to this process, but those of us who don't take a stage to make our living can make contributions of equal value. It doesn't have to be a monumental event happening halfway around the world, like the concert at Sunny Beach. It can happen in your home, your neighborhood, your local concert hall, your church or temple.

Music is a feel-good profession that can change lives. Those of us on the presenting and business side have just as much obligation—and can get just as much gratification—as the artists themselves. We must find out how to be the best we can possibly be, learning by experience to be bigger and better than our last performance.

chapter 27

THE SECOND SOVIET TOUR

"The Friendship Tour"

n November of 1988, Roy Clark returned to the Soviet Union. There were a lot of reasons it took so long to get him back there. For one thing, the Soviet Union was in a constant state of financial flux, and hard currency—that is, currency exchangeable on the international money market—was becoming more and more scarce there, because of less and less trade with other countries. Of course, the Russians wanted Roy back—but they wanted someone else to pay for it. Also, funding for the State Department's cultural-exchange program, never lavish by any standards, had dried up completely as far as the Soviet Union was concerned. (This was, you'll remember, an era of harsh diplomatic relations between our two countries.)

We were going to have to be resourceful in funding our event this time, but we couldn't even begin looking for funds until we had the official invitation from the Soviets, and at least some idea of what they could offer.

For more than a decade, between 1976 and 1987, I made numerous trips to Moscow, trying to get both the invitation and a deal that would work for everyone. It proved to be a unique and unprecedented deal-making experience for me. Setting up a major tour usually follows a pattern: you find a promoter, establish the venues and dates for your act, coordinate any record releases, set up a TV show, and start to work. With the Soviets, though, I had tried to delicately mesh all the government organizations, the times, and the events.

All tours came under the direction of the Ministry of Culture. But it was necessary to coordinate things not only with the Ministry of Culture's concert bureau, Gosconcert, but also with the government-owned Gostel Radio (for TV and radio broadcasts). Then, all of these agencies had to work with Intourist, the USSR's official hotel and travel agency. Since the officials at every one of these agencies constantly disagreed with one another, putting the tour together was a lot harder than just finding venues, getting the dates approved, and arranging the logistics of the tour.

It took a great deal of negotiation to even get the invitation. Several times, I flew to the USSR to make formal negotiations only to get home and find that the heated political differences between the US and the USSR had caused the cancellation of the State Department's cultural-exchange program. These cancellations were always temporary, but they were maddening, and when the ban was lifted I'd have to start over again at square one.

I don't think most people would have kept going with it, but, knowing how important this would be to Roy's career—among other things—I called upon one of my big helpers: patience.

Finally, in late 1986, after four days of steady meetings with top Soviet officials, we got the invitation for Roy to do a two-week series of concerts, with one week in Moscow venues, and one week in Leningrad. The kicker was that the Soviets had no hard currency—nothing available that would convert to US dollars; they had only rubles to pay for the tour, and rubles weren't worth anything outside the USSR. They would finance all internal travel, hotels, allowances for meals, and certain other logistical items—but in rubles, not dollars.

All along we had been negotiating for dollars, but Soviet circumstances had changed drastically, and dollars were no longer available for artist exchange. What few they did have were needed for wheat and other goods essential to the Soviet people—not entertainment. Remember, that on our 1976 tour, the State Department, through its cultural exchange program, had paid the band members and bought the airline tickets. By this time, however, that funding had dried up. If we wanted to tour now, we'd have to finance it totally, without a penny from either government.

After the years of negotiations to set this tour and the thousands of dollars our company had invested in trips for me to the USSR, this event had become too important for me to drop. I had to figure some resourceful way to make the trip happen and to make it pay off. How could I do it?

Finally, I made another trip to Moscow. If I couldn't get it done, I'd already decided to put the Soviet tour on the back burner. But I had to make it work.

Meeting with Mr. Ostakovitch, director of Gostel Radio (the television branch of the Ministry of Culture), I explained the circumstances and insisted that we be given the television rights to our shows. Normally, the Soviets kept the rights, did their own taping, and sold the product. I wanted to work a compromise that would allow them to save face and still give us the deal. We finally agreed that they could televise the event for the Soviet Union and its satellite countries, and let us have broadcast rights to the rest of the world. They would furnish us certain live-concert footage, and we would have total access to anywhere we wanted to film, within reason. It was a great meeting with Mr. Ostakovitch, a true gentleman and a good negotiator. I think we both ended up with what we wanted.

Now I had everything we needed from the Soviets to make the tour—except money. Which, of course, meant my work was really just starting. It would be another two years before Roy Clark set foot on a Moscow stage, because it took that long to coordinate all of our efforts. We had to do some real planning, because we had to pay for the tour ourselves: transportation, salaries, hotels, meals, and all. As he had with the previous tour, Roy agreed to go without a fee. But everything else, including the salaries of his musicians and crew, had to be paid.

The total amount needed was somewhere around $200,000, which would pay for our airline tickets, our excess baggage, and the salaries for our musicians and crew. All the USSR could pay for were our hotel bills.

Now the real planning began, and we did it according to the Halsey method of using eight distinct steps, in the same way we created the Halsey Ranch Party events I wrote about in Chapter 16.

1. **Inspiration:** This was already in place. Inspired by the tremendous success of our first Soviet tour, we would call this one the "Friendship Tour."

2. **Goal and Purpose:** The goal was to create a self-financed tour. The purpose was to create peace and harmony through the musical performance of Roy Clark, with a secondary purpose of providing a vehicle for an enormous amount of press and PR for Roy.

3. **Planning:** In this stage, my main associates—John Hitt, Judy Pofsky and Sherman Halsey—met with me to lay out what we hoped to accomplish. The major question: how were we going to get it paid for?

We had four ideas to put on the drawing board.

1. Get several corporate sponsors.
2. Sell the show for US broadcast.
3. Enlist the aid of Roy Clark fans and other American citizens.
4. Stage a fundraising banquet in Nashville

BLUBLOCKERS TO THE RESCUE

The very first corporate sponsor we signed came from a "cold call," which in the sales business means calling up a prospective buyer who doesn't know you and trying to make a sale. I decided to write a letter—to make, if you will, a cold call—to a person I considered the foremost marketing expert in America: Joe Sugarman. I didn't know him personally and he didn't know me. I had been impressed, however, when I'd read the text of a speech Mr. Sugarman had given—the one in which he'd said that the most important sentence in any piece of advertising was the first one, followed in descending importance by the second, the third, etc. And I'd been a fan of Joe Sugarman every since I'd first read and ordered from his JS&A advertisements in the airline magazines. I was, in addition, truly mesmerized by his inventive and creative new form of marketing, the television infomercial—a half-hour ad that looked like a regular program—which a marketing genius Richard Sutter had invented for Joseph Sugarman to sell BluBlocker sunglasses. And sell them he did. BluBlocker became and still is the top-selling sunglasses brand in the world, and Sugarman's infomercial started a revolution in telemarketing.

In my letter to Mr. Sugarman, asking him to become one of our corporate sponsors, I tried to use the principle I'd read about in his speech. Here, then, are the first two sentences of my letter to him:

"Dear Mr. Sugarman:

Obviously, you are the most inventive salesman in America today. I think you will have a great appreciation for the patriotic marketing program I am proposing in this letter…."

I think you'll agree that I was quick to learn his technique—and it worked! We heard back almost immediately. Yes, he would come on board, providing funding in the dollar amount we had asked for. In addition, he would give us 5,000 pairs of BluBlocker sunglasses, specially imprinted with the words "Roy Clark Friendship Tour." These sunglasses normally cost $69 a pair, but these would not be for sale. They'd only be used to promote Roy's tour.

Wow! In addition to helping finance the tour, Joseph Sugarman had provided us with nearly $350,000 worth of BluBlocker sunglasses.

His gift of sunglasses gave us another idea. Now we wanted to involve all of America in this tour, using the vehicle of country radio.

We formed the Friendship Radio Network, designing a large Friendship Book with pages three feet high and two feet wide, which Roy would take with him to the USSR. Loose pages for the book were sent to radio stations, who in turn asked their listeners to sign one of the pages. For a gift of two dollars, those signing would receive a postcard sent by Roy from Moscow during the Friendship Tour! Four thousand pairs of the special BluBlockers would be sent as gifts to the stations on the Friendship Radio Network (which would leave us 1,000 to take to the USSR as gifts). The stations were free to use the glasses in promotions, but BluBlocker had to be mentioned.

THE FRIENDSHIP BOOK

Nearly 500 radio stations across America became part of the network, each collecting signatures for the pages of the Friendship Book. When it was time to take the book on tour, it contained more than 25,000 signatures—and the signees had given us a total of $50,000, a full one-quarter of the money we needed to raise.

We displayed the Friendship Book with its 25,000 signatures, at each concert, making sure the Soviets understood that the tour was made possible by a combination of contributors, including the 25,000 Americans who'd signed the book. This show of goodwill and support, seen in page after page of signatures, was a big hit with the Russian people.

It was a hit with us, too. We were very grateful—frankly, we hadn't expected such a huge response. And now we were obliged to send 25,000 Roy Clark postcards from Moscow!

We found a good photo of Roy, taken in front of Moscow's St. Basil's Cathedral during his previous Russian trip. It made a great visual for the postcards. We put that photo on 25,000 postcards, addressing each one before we left. When we got to Moscow, we figured all we'd have to do is put on stamps and drop them off at the nearest post office.

That was what we figured. Unfortunately, it was easier said than done. When we arrived in Moscow, our trusted Gosconcert tour manager, Inna Sanovich, informed us it would be impossible to get that many stamps. They just were not available.

But we had to have them! She had to get them! We explained the situation, and she understood.

To this day we are not sure how Inna, as resourceful as she was, came up with 25,000 Russian stamps. But she did, and for the next two weeks—at every rehearsal, every show, every news conference, every place where more than two people with two hands and a wet tongue gathered—we drafted anyone we could find to help us lick and stick 25,000 stamps on the 25,000 postcards. On the last day of the tour, we finally finished—only to have Moscow's Central Post Office refuse to handle the cards. But once again, the invaluable Inna Sonovich prevailed, and most of the cards arrived in the US about six weeks after we did.

It was a great promotion. People still talk about receiving Roy Clark postcards from the Soviet Union, and they have become keepsakes in thousands of homes. Thanks go to Joseph Sugarman for inspiring this great promotion and, with his BluBlocker sunglasses, helping make it possible.

4. **Expanding the Elements:** Even with the great assistance of Joe Sugarman and the Friendship Book signees, we still needed more cash—or more help. We got the latter from American Airlines, which had helped us fly in celebrities to our golf tournaments. A sizable portion of our budget was set to go toward the almost 50 international round-trip airline tickets we needed. To help with that budget item, American agreed to give us round-trip tickets from Nashville to Frankfurt, Germany, where we would have to buy tickets to get from Frankfurt to Moscow. In return, American Airlines would be a part of the television show arising from the event.

Another of our long-time corporate friends, Amana Refrigeration, came aboard. Amana had helped us in numerous other projects, including the Roy Clark Celebrity Golf Tournament, where the company was a major sponsor. Liberty overalls and jeans, a first-time sponsor, gave us major help as well some cash and blue jeans.

Meanwhile, Judi Pofsky, the senior vice-president in our Los Angeles office, was busy pitching this tour for television. A big TV sale was important for several reasons. First, the only money Roy would take would come from the television show. Second, we needed it for documentation of the tour. Third, its use as a vehicle for generating press would further enhance Roy's image as an international peace diplomat.

Jim Owens Productions of Nashville became the buyer and producer. The Nashville Network (TNN) agreed to multiple runs. The musical documentary would be a co-production between the Owens and Halsey companies.

Things were coming together pretty fast now, but our tour dates were also fast approaching—and we were still $50,000 short of our projected budget. So we created another event to help kick off the main event. We envisioned it as a black-tie banquet, at $150 a plate, to be held in Nashville, and asked Bob Hope to emcee. He agreed, provided we furnished him a private jet. Industrialist Armand Hammer, who had earlier turned down our requests for help with the tour, furnished his Oxy Petroleum Jet as transportation for Hope and his entourage.

Preparation for the Friendship Tour banquet was a masterful project in itself, taking everyone in our company to make it happen. When it did, everyone in Nashville's music and entertainment business turned out.

Our own entertainment was superb that night, as well as being unusual for a Nashville banquet. Among the acts performing were the Ellis Island Band, a klezmer group from Los Angeles that performed Eastern European music. Roy's friend, the classic entertainer Phil Harris, also took the stage, and there wasn't a dry eye in the place when he finished his version of Tom T. Hall's, "Old Dogs, Children and Watermelon Wine."

Many entertainment and sports personalities who'd supported Roy's Celebrity Golf Tournaments in Tulsa were surprise arrivals, including actor David Huddleston (of Santa Claus fame), who was not only a friend, but a recruiter of many of the celebrities for the tournament. In addition, every star and up-and-comer in Nashville attended. Opryland gave its full support. Frances Preston, president of BMI, had several tables. Tennessee congressman Bob Clement, along with Senator Jim Sassor and Senator—and future Vice President— Albert Gore.

The reception progressed, with a wonderful job of emceeing from Bob Hope, who, after talking about the funds that were being raised for the Roy's tour, asked, 'Wouldn't deporting him be cheaper?" And then, midway through, came the biggest surprise of the night. I'd reached back into my bag of tricks to come up with it, and I knew it was a sure-fire show-stopper.

For years, at our Halsey Ranch Parties, golf tournaments, and a few of our international festivals, we'd hired a marching band to come through at a certain time, and it always grabbed attention and brought everything to an absolute halt. The marching-band stunt hadn't, to my knowledge, ever been done in Nashville, and things did screech to a stop when the Tennessee State University Marching Band came parading through the party. They were sensational and a great surprise to the guests.

It was a fun time. Roy and Barbara Clark were perfect hosts and, with the banquet and party, we raised the final amount we needed to cover tour expenses—not to mention getting tons of international press coverage from the event.

5. **Implementation:** Now our expenses were covered, the logistics taken care of, and we were ready to go. We had our special touring cases, suitcases, hanging garment bags, patches, stickers, posters, bag tags, tour books, and matching all-weather slickers—everything emblazoned with the Roy Clark Friendship Tour logo. As we were making final preparations to leave, Christie Cookies of Nashville—whose owner, Jim Christie, was a big supporter of the tour—delivered numerous tins of outstanding cookies for us to to take along as presents for the Soviets.

6. **The Event:** Finally the day arrived for our departure from Nashville International Airport aboard American Airlines. A big crowd came to see us off, and those who showed up had a final chance to sign the Friendship Book, in case they'd missed the opportunity before.

Then we were airborne, and with a different sense of anticipation than before.

This was truly an event, and not just because it had taken six years to plan it. One of the biggest reasons was the participation of the Voice of America radio network. Listening to VOA broadcasts had been officially forbidden in the USSR since 1976, but, in conjunction with Roy's tour, Soviet officials had lifted the ban. Judy Massa's popular VOA country music program was going to be broadcast live from Russia featuring music from Roy's concerts. His playing and singing would circle the globe in this historic, first-time broadcast. Just as Roy Clark had blazed cultural and diplomatic trails 12 years before in his earlier Soviet trip, he'd be setting some new "firsts" on this trip also.

7. **The Review:** It's important to understand the preceding six steps in creating an event. Even if your event is of a much more modest nature than a trailblazing international tour, the steps still apply. And it still goes that any event can be extremely important to the career of an artist, as the Roy Clark Friendship Tour was to Roy's career.

It's essential for Star Team members to review any promotion, campaign, or event after it concludes. After all, something like this is part of the history, and our futures are based on our history. After the Roy Clark Friendship Tour was finished, every single person involved with it met and examined what had happened in minute detail. We all studied, talked, and contributed notes (which are still in my files, just in case I ever want to mount this type of tour again), deeming the tour a success in virtually every phase.

8. **The Follow-up:** This step prolongs the benefits of the event and opens the door to other elements in an artist's career. Because of the Roy Clark Friendship Tour, Roy was now fully recognized as a world-class entertainer and diplomat. This recognition opened the doors to countless press and TV interviews and kept Roy in the public spotlight in more ways than just as a performer. Because of his great humanitarian works, his involvement with the Children's Medical Center, his charity golf tournaments, and the world-wide recognition he'd earned from his global tours, UNICEF, the United Nations International Children's Fund, named him a special ambassador for the organization, and even sponsored his next Tulsa golf tournament. I also served for years on UNICEF's board of directors.

See how all of this works? What started out to be just a tour of one-night concerts in the USSR ended up as a life-changing and career-enhancing experience. It was an important tour from the beginning, but its importance grew exponentially through exhaustive planning and development.

I've only covered its high points here. There could be a whole book written about the two Soviet tours, and I may just write it someday.

★

Many rewards come from a successful project. They can be emotional, material, financial, and spiritual. Sometimes, you get them all.

Many of Roy's rewards from his Friendship Tour came as recognitions of a job well done. Before the fund-raising banquet, I wrote a letter to every US Representative and Senator telling them about the upcoming trip, noting that Roy had given both his time and his celebrity endorsement to the US State Department's cultural-exchange program.

Nearly every member of the US Congress sent a note of support to Roy; he received almost 500 different messages from political figures. I had them all bound in a book and gave the book to Roy so he'd be able, in future years, to reflect on how much his efforts were appreciated.

★

As you know, much of my philosophy has to do with following your dreams and visions. Again, it's important to note that some will work, and some won't. But the important thing is to follow them all, and to learn to work with them.

The event I've just written about, one of my best, started with just that: a dream. And as the rest of the Star Team and I worked with it, it grew into an event of such magnitude and lasting impact that it's still talked about.

It was a major event, but it began with a dream. And when you start with the raw and exciting material of your own dreams and visions, and follow through with my eight-point plan, you'll be able to create your own events, as important and unique to you and your Star Team as the Roy Clark Friendship Tour was to us.

So get started!

chapter 28

CORPORATE SPONSORSHIP

What is corporate sponsorship? Essentially, it's a cash and/or in-kind payment to a property (in the case of sports, arts, entertainment, or various causes), artist, or celebrity in return for access to the exploitable commercial potential associated with that property, artist, or celebrity.

That's the definition. Now, let's take a closer look.

Corporate sponsorship is a fast-growing marketing medium especially suited for organizations, events, artists, and celebrities that are focused on sports, the arts, entertainment, or causes. It gives companies a way to cut through all the media clutter, replacing commercial messages with meaningful alliances.

That's an important distinction. Corporate sponsorship is *not* advertising. Instead, it's the opportunity for a company to be associated with a selected organization, event, artist, or celebrity. Sponsorships come with a title like "Presenter" or "Also Presented By," "Sponsor" or "Co-Sponsor." These titles, along with the sponsor's name, can show up in a wide variety of places, including signs, posters, billboards, buses and other rolling stock, television and radio spots, websites and website links, even on travel bags, uniforms, airplanes, and equipment. There are a lot of benefits to this association, and those are what you must be able to explain in order to successfully solicit sponsors.

Here are some things that a potential sponsor will consider:

1. **Tangible Benefits.** These include impressions in both measured and non-measured media. i.e. records in the charts, press and television coverage (impressions), and touring schedules. Program books, advertisements, signage, tickets, and hospitality, as well as on-site signage and sampling. The sponsor may provide samples of product, coupons, soap, shampoo, chewing gum and inventive contests. Sampling can also include specific time and place promotions that can be analyzed and involved to expand on a more broadened scope.

2. **Intangible Benefits.** These have to do with the level of audience loyalty, category exclusivity, and the recognizibility of event/talent marks and logos. Good press, fond memories and positive reputation can go a long way in creating interest in the corporate sponsor's product.

3. **Geographical Reach and Impact.** The reach reflects the size and value of a market or markets in which the event/talent marks and logos are usable and relevant at the point of sale.

4. **Established Track Record.** Does the act or event have a good track record?

5. **Newsworthiness.** Is the event or act newsworthy? Will it generate positive media attention, which can benefit a sponsor?

6. **Cost-to-Benefit Ratio.** The sponsorship needs to reflect the amount of promotion and the expected audience. "Friendly reception" assets are expanded to more impressions through press and PR, television, radio, and personal appearances. My attraction, the Oak Ridge Boys are exceptionally friendly to media interviews. It helps that there are four of them, so usually one of the Oak Ridge Boys would always be available. It's easy to schedule media for them and they want to do it.

7. **Prestige of Property.** For instance, the Oak Ridge Boys are a very prestigious property. They have long running popularity with a good reputation. Many big hits. Twenty seven top 5 records, sold over 30 million records, every year work national tours, associated with charities (mainly Feed The Children for twenty years), national celebrity spokespersons for The National Anthem Project. All of this has accumulated "impressions" of enormous magnitude. The Feed The Children television shows represent hundreds of millions of television "impres-

sions" each year. The Oak Ridge Boys are a "prestige" property. The Oak Ridge Boys are an important *brand* themselves. Get the idea?

8. **Awareness and Recognition Factors**

9. **Category Exclusivity.** With this, the sponsor has an exclusive association with the event or talent on a worldwide basis.

10. **Level of Audience Interest and Loyalty.** In one study, 60 percent of audience members said that the sponsorship of an act would impact their purchasing decisions.

11. **Ability to Activate.** This means that the sponsor can tie the purchase of its product to discounts on tickets for the sponsored event.

12. **Limited Degree of Sponsor Clutter.** Each sponsor should have a proprietary program and designated area at the event. The attention span is limited. So make the focus on the corporate sponsor and the artist identification. It is important to note, simpler is better.

13. **Networking Opportunities.** The potential exists for sponsor and co-sponsors to cross-promote events, workshops, classroom instruction and videos.

14. **Numbers.** The number of markets for the event or act is important, as are the size and value of those markets.

15. **Image.** To be attractive to a major sponsor, an act or event must project a good image.

Corporations may be interested in sponsorship for a variety of reasons. Here are a few:

1. Heightened Visibility.
2. Potential to Shape Consumer Attitudes
3. Communicating Commitments to a Particular Lifestyle
4. Business-to-Business Marketing
5. Having a Different Sponsorship Than Competitors Have
6. Entertaining Clients
7. Showcasing Product Attitudes: Family?, Youth?, Masculine?, Feminine?, Homey?, Patriotic?, Mass Appeal?, and so forth.
8. Demographics–Most products appeal to specific demograph-

ics (age, financial, gender, geographic factors). Campaigns are designed are designed to target these specific areas.

9. Entertaining the Public! This is why corporate sponsors get involved with artists, bands, personalities, etc.

When I talk about corporate sponsorship, I speak from years of experience. You'll notice I said *experience*, not *expertise*. Getting corporate sponsorship is a tricky business, with uncertain guidelines and inexact ways of measuring its effectiveness. It can work well for both the talent/event and the sponsor, but getting to the point of commitment can be challenging.

Some corporate sponsorship deals are straight-ahead. The sponsor knows what benefits it's looking for and the amount of money it wants to spend. Those are the easy ones.

In my 50 years of dealing with corporate sponsorships, I've observed that most deals have been consummated by emotion rather than reason, by chance meetings between a celebrity and prospective sponsor on an airline flight, in casual conversation over coffee at Starbucks, or in lounges and bars at conventions or conferences, like the ones presented by the International Events Group (IEG), which bring, clients, agencies, and prospective sponsors together. Corporate sponsorships have even sprung from the son or daughter of a CEO, telling Dad that his company should really sponsor the tour of a certain artist. I've personally seen every one of these examples happen.

Although I've made a lot of corporate-sponsor deals in my time, I still can't tell you precisely how it's done. Remembering the guidelines I've listed in this chapter can help.

HANK AND CORPORATE

If you're this far into the book, you know that two of my chief interests in life are sales and marketing—how to connect the consumer with the seller and how both parties can benefit from that connection. With that and the idea of corporate sponsorship in mind, let's go back to the beginning of my career and my first management client, Hank Thompson.

In another example of good timing, I connected with Hank in December of 1951, after successfully promoting several of his tours in the previous two years. When I became his manager, I was still learning the business, but a quick study of the clubs and ballrooms he was playing showed me that beer consumption at the shows was just about as important as ticket sales. The success of many of our dates was not only judged by how many people we got in the door, but how much beer they drank.

Hank's Capitol Records releases were breaking big, and just as I was joining him, the company released what would become one of country music's all-time biggest records, Hank's "Wild Side of Life." As it soared toward the top of the national country charts, it increased his demand, his price, and his crowds. This was 1952, and while television was still a novelty, it was fast becoming a necessity in homes across the country.

I realized early in my career that visual promotion via television was going to be the way to reach millions of people instantaneously–not just the fans of a particular act, but general audiences from all walks of life. I knew if I was to succeed with Hank Thompson in a big, spectacular way, I had to expose him to the masses, and that meant television.

Enlisting the help of my newly made acquaintances at Capitol Records, as well as other industry associates, I was able to secure appearances for Hank on a couple of big network variety shows–*The Kate Smith Evening Hour* and *The Perry Como Show*–where he performed "Wild Side of Life" for millions upon millions of viewers. (He was able to use his own band, too, which was not normal procedure for singers' television appearances at the time.) The record jumped to No. 1 on both the *Billboard* and *Cash Box* charts. It remained at No. 1 for well over three months, staying on the *Billboard* chart for some 30 weeks. Sales climbed to a million. "Wild Side of Life" was a huge hit that proved to me the power of television. And since those early days, I've used that tool effectively with every artist I've represented.

As I thought about how to expand the popularity of Hank Thompson, I was inspired by the movie cowboys who had made very successful moves to TV–Gene Autry, Roy Rogers and Hopalong Cassidy. I saw that they were appearing before their audiences in commercials, endorsing products like breakfast cereal and pet food. There had to be money there. Why not take my own "cowboy," Hank Thompson, connect him with a product, and see what happened?

You'll remember how beer consumption at Hank's live shows was sometimes as important to the promoters as ticket sales. A lot of our dates were in ballrooms throughout the South and Southwest, and those places moved a lot of brew. So it seemed obvious to me that a beer company would be the perfect product for Hank to endorse.

One of the biggest beer brands in that area at the time was Falstaff. It was sold at every ballroom and nightclub we played. I thought, "Wouldn't it be great if we could get Falstaff to sponsor Hank Thompson?"

The lesson I learned early in life—*write it down*—then came into play. I filled several legal pads with ideas and notes for a presentation to Falstaff. Refining my material with the help of Hank's creative genius, I finally felt I had something to present to the head of the company. So, I called Falstaff's president in St. Louis, seeking an appointment to make my pitch. I was quickly turned over to the director of sales and marketing, which made me feel I was getting the brush-off. Although disappointed, I continued the pursuit—and was thrilled and a bit surprised when I got my appointment.

As I traveled to St. Louis, with great excitement and anticipation, I reviewed my presentation material. I'd made up press kits that included pictures of Hank, biographical material, newspaper and trade-magazine reviews, photocopies of the *Billboard* and *Cash Box* charts that showed "Wild Side of Life" at No. 1 and letters of praise from people in charge of fairs and rodeos where we'd recently appeared. Accompanying these kits were copies of Hank's latest 10-inch LP, which was also a hit recording.

I arrived at my destination a few minutes early, giving me just enough time to take one last review of the proposal and how I'd make it. Then, preparing myself mentally, emotionally, and spiritually, I took several deep breaths and walked into the office.

The director of sales and marketing was there. So was the director of advertising, the director of public relations, and a couple of other people, all gathered around a highly polished conference table—and all focused on me. I took another deep breath and waited a moment or two, allowing silence to descend on the room. And then I spoke.

As they leafed through my presentation packets, I told them about Hank, and how important his endorsement of Falstaff would be. I talked about how we could get clubs where we were appearing to feature Falstaff beer the night of our appearance, and how the posters advertising our shows would carry the Falstaff logo. Even the stage clothes of Hank's band (created by the famous designer and tailor Nudie) would feature the Falstaff logo embroidered on their shirts.

My plan also called for the company to buy radio spots advertising our performances. We would hold contests, where legal, in conjunction with Falstaff. And the final *piece de resistance*–a network radio show, featuring Hank and sponsored, of course, by Falstaff Beer.

I embellished all of this with the idea that Hank and his Brazos Valley Boys, sponsored by Falstaff, would appear at the Texas State Fair on the stage at the head of the midway for the fair's entire 21-day run. What a promotion! And talk about impressions–the Texas State Fair crowd numbered more than 100,000 every day!

The state-fair idea was enthusiastically received by the executives that day. In fact, my whole presentation went over well. No decision, however, was to be made immediately. It took several more trips and on-site visits to the various sales and marketing decision-makers before they made the deal. But they made it! I didn't get everything I'd asked for, nor did I get all the money I'd requested. But it was enough.

That began a relationship between Hank Thompson and Falstaff Beer that lasted for a long time. We played the Texas State Fair for 18 consecutive years. The radio show ran for three years, three times a week, over 650 stations. And, as a bonus, Hank got a new bus, which we needed. In return for buying the bus, Falstaff got to put a logo on it.

The day I walked into the Falstaff offices for the first time, my inexperience and hope changed into knowledge and reality. After that, I not only understood the positive aspects of making an intelligent presentation; I also realized just how important a corporate sponsor can be to an artist's career–and to the bottom line.

I was lucky. I felt I'd made a decent presentation, and that Falstaff was interested in what I had to say. They realized–probably before I ever got there–what a big name like Hank could do for their product.

That was the beginning. Where did we go from there?

BLUBLOCKER SUNGLASSES

We'll talk about other big-name artists, events, tours, and spectaculars later. Right now, let's fast-forward half a century. Instead of anxiously composing myself outside a door to an office in St. Louis, I'm sitting in the corporate headquarters of BluBlocker sunglasses in Las Vegas, making a presentation to chairman Joe Sugarman and president Mary Stanke.

I start things off with the Oak Ridge Boys' "Got A Minute?"

video. It's got music, voiceovers, performance footage and other visuals that cover touring, record sales, impressions, and what we can offer a corporation. The video runs exactly one minute.

When it's over, Mr. Sugarman turns to Mrs. Stanke. "This may be what we're looking for," he says. Then, I listen to this master marketer tell me how the Oak Ridge Boys and BluBlocker sunglasses could fit together.

First of all, our coast-to-coast touring—in two big Oak Ridge Boys buses—was appealing to him. We could endorse BluBlockers from the stage and sell them at our merchandise table, thus becoming Blu-Blocker ambassadors. The buses could become traveling billboards for BluBlocker, parking at high-visibility locations like fairs, ballparks, theme parks and auditoriums, where they get approximately 10 *million* passerby impressions every year.

We struck a deal, and the public launch of our association was a newsworthy achievement, with Joe Sugarman, the Oak Ridge Boys, and the Belmont University Music Business School hosting a breakfast for Nashville business leaders and students in Belmont's marketing classes. Sugarman, an accomplished motivational speaker, and the Oaks talked about how important the Red, White and BluBlocker tour was going to be, and our talented PR person, Sandy Brokaw, made sure the story got out to the national press.

There are side benefits to these sorts of partnerships. For many of our major promotions, often including fair dates, we would run contests in conjunction with the local radio stations. Prizes would be things like tickets, meals, CDs, and T-shirts. BluBlockers made a great addition to the prize mix. After all, everybody likes sunglasses, and the presenting radio stations were happy to have brand-name items for prizes and giveaways.

In some areas, BluBlocker purchased billboard advertising. But the Oaks' buses were really rolling billboards themselves—the faces of the guys on both sides, looking as though they belonged on Mount Rushmore, and big red, white and blue artwork featuring the Oaks' logo and the words, "Red, White and BluBlocker Tour." These buses were so spectacular that they could literally stop traffic. When they were parked, people would line up to get their pictures made in front of one of the buses. Once, the Oaks were on the *Fox and Friends* TV show, and the bus sat squarely behind the Fox TV hosts for the entire broadcast.

Although it wasn't spelled out in the contract, another big benefit from the buses was their being used in the opening of two of our Feed the Children TV specials. Because these specials are seen all across America, the accumulated impressions ran into the millions.

Lots of fun things happened during the partnership. Mr. Sugarman arranged an Oak Ridge Boys day at Wrigley Field, in conjunction with a Chicago Cubs home game. It was the biggest crowd of the season, and the Oaks performed three different times. They did an opening number, then "The Star-Spangled Banner," and, during the seventh inning stretch, the traditional "Take Me Out to the Ball Game." It was the first time a single act had performed in all three spots at a ballgame there.

The BluBlocker-Oak Ridge Boys corporate sponsorship program lasted two mutually productive years. Mr. Sugarman still supports our special events, charitable work, and other high-profile appearances.

In between the Hank Thompson-Falstaff Beer partnership–one of the first-ever instances of corporate sponsorship–and the BluBlocker arrangement with the Oaks a half-century later, we helped link many other corporate sponsors with appropriate acts.

HUNT'S KETCHUP

Remember the Hunt's Ketchup campaign with Roy Clark? These colorful television and print ads ran for a solid decade, keeping Roy constantly in front of an audience. Added to his hosting of the popular *Hee Haw* TV show, it helped make him one of the most recognized personalities in the world. That particular sponsorship came from a solicitation to advertising agencies. We actually wanted our relationship to expand into a corporate-sponsor arrangement, but that didn't happen. While I'm grateful for the success of this advertising campaign–and another one, in which our client Minnie Pearl had her picture prominently featured on a Kellogg's Corn Flakes box—the Ketchum Agency, which handled Hunt's Ketchup, had its ideas of what it wanted, and it was not going to get involved in corporate-sponsorship deals.

Sponsorship deals of this nature are usually handled by special-event and celebrity-marketing divisions of corporations, not ad agencies. When you're dealing with a company with a big brand name, you'll often find many divisions, each with its own audience and budget. In one sense, this may work to your advantage. If the people in the advertising end of the business aren't interested, maybe the marketing people will be.

KODAK

When we first started working with the Judds, we wanted to make a deal with Kodak. These were the days before the Internet and all its easily accessible information, so we simply called the company to find out the names of the Kodak head of marketing and the advertising agency that handled its account. It was about 7 p.m. when I placed the call to Eastman Kodak in Rochester, Minnesota, hoping the operator who answered would give me the names of the proper contacts.

The phone rang and rang. Finally, a gentleman's voice answered with a simple "hello."

"Is this Eastman Kodak?" I asked.

"Yes," returned the voice.

I identified myself, and asked him for help in locating the right person to contact regarding the Judds. Then, he identified himself—as the president of Kodak! The offices were closed and, for some reason, my call had rung through to his private number. He was very pleasant—not irritated, as you might expect—and even better, he happened to be a fan of the Judds. He gave me the name of the company's marketing person. When I called the next day, that person had already been told of my prospective call. Many things developed from that connection. Talk about luck, timing, and fate. It all happened there!

You may remember that Barbara Mandrell, a huge act from the '70s into the '90s, was for several years the national television spokeswoman for Sunsweet Pitted Prunes. How did this connection happen? The way I've heard it is that the company president was interested in getting a country-music star for Sunsweet's commercials. He got up one morning, turned on his radio, and the first voice he heard was Barbara Mandrell's. That, as the story goes, is how she was "scientifically" selected to star in the company's TV spots.

You'd think the selection process would be studied and exact, with lots of research and focus groups. But there really isn't a set formula.

Sometimes, you hunt and hunt and hunt for the right corporate partnership, and it seems like you never make any progress. It's always the wrong time, the wrong budget, the wrong demographic, the wrong money, and the wrong images. But you can't give up. Keep calling. Keep soliciting. Keep making presentations.

WHATABURGER

For years, we had a deal with the Whataburger hamburger chain for Mel Tillis' services. The association produced some great TV spots, and even though it seemed each year that we might lose the account, we were able to come up with some new, creative suggestion that enabled the relationship to continue. We were, however, never able to move into corporate sponsorship with the company. We tried hard to make that happen. We made lots of presentations. But the executives at Whataburger were only interested in the visual of Mel on TV, representing their product, and so they budgeted only for commercials.

Although it hasn't always happened when we wanted it to, we've been generally very successful in securing corporate sponsorship over the years. One of the biggest corporate-sponsor presentations was the Roy Clark Friendship Tour to the Soviet Union in 1988.Elsewhere in this book, there's a whole chapter devoted to Roy's Soviet tours, so here I just want to tell you that BluBlocker Sunglasses, Christie Cookies, Liberty Blue Jeans, American Airlines, and Amana all came to the table to help make Roy's tour possible. It was an ambitious and expensive project that took a lot of help.

It took a long time to put together our solicitations to prospective tour sponsors, but it was worth it. People are still talking about Roy's groundbreaking visit to our Cold War foe.

With one exception, we made elaborate presentations to the tour's potential sponsors. The exception was BluBlocker, the company that later became such an integral part of the Oak Ridge Boys' tours. At the time, I was enamored of the provocative 30-minute infomercial for BluBlocker sunglasses, and I wrote company chairman Joe Sugarman an impassioned letter about Roy and all the good this tour would do for what was then a strained relationship between the USA and the USSR. The day he received my letter, Sugarman called me to tell me he was on board—with money as well as 5,000 pairs of BluBlocker sunglasses. That was the beginning of both our friendship and our business relationship.

CLARK CANDY BARS

The same was true for Clark candy bars—a natural tie-in with Roy Clark. We always had mountains of Clark Bars backstage during Roy's Vegas engagements, and we handed them out at press conferences and when he played venues like fairs and rodeos. We even took Clark Bars to the Soviet Union.

TOTINO'S

Then there was Totino's Pizza, whose executives used the Oak Ridge Boys' image and name value to help launch their new product on television and radio and in print. When the new line of frozen pizzas started appearing in grocery stores, they were endorsed by the Oaks. For a number of dates, Totino's was a corporate sponsor, generating plenty of promotion in all media. Totino's bought full-page ads in newspapers to make the public aware of the new product, always including pictures of the Oak Ridge Boys and notes on where they were performing. We sent pizzas to radio stations. We gave away pizzas on the air. We talked about how good they were from the stage. We even did cross-promotions with our record company–and the folk at Totino's paid the Oaks very well.

You always try to find a product or sponsor that fits with your artist. When we signed Clint Black, whose signature hat happened to be a Stetson, we knew that company would be the obvious choice for a corporate sponsorship. We went after the company, Clint got a deal, and Stetson not only paid him some money, but made a special hat for him.

ROY CLARK: WYLER'S AND PRINGLES

Roy Clark's endorsements have included Wyler's Lemonade and Pringles Country Style potato chips, both of which fit his image. We got the Wyler's ads through a solicitation to an ad agency, and it turned into a lucrative print campaign. The same was true with Pringles.

Since all musicians use instruments in their work, endorsements with companies that make those instruments is a natural. Many times, they'll supply an artist or group with instruments or equipment in exchange for an endorsement. While no money is typically exchanged, they'll usually sweeten the deal by paying for advertisements in trade papers and other magazines. These ads feature the act, linking it with the company's musical product.

On the other hand, some endorsements just don't fit. For many years, tobacco and alcohol companies have been big spenders when it comes to corporate sponsorships. They've sponsored performers, sporting events, and even paid for naming rights to arenas and coliseums.

Years ago, through my friendship with promoter Harvey Goldsmith, I was put in touch with a cigarette company that wanted to sponsor an Oak Ridge Boys tour. Their offer was huge—seven figures, plus the money necessary for elaborate staging and sound.

The Oaks turned it down. From the beginning, they have been solid in their refusal to accept either tobacco or alcohol sponsors.

FEED THE CHILDREN

They have, however, forged a two-decade relationship with Feed the Children, the charitable organization headed by Larry and Frances Jones.

As a charity, the Feed the Children relationship with the Oaks isn't technically that of a corporate sponsor. However, in many ways the benefits are the same. Over the years, the Oak Ridge Boys have been featured on a series of Feed the Children television specials. In adding the Oaks, Feed the Children expanded its focus. The specials were still primarily concerned with the tragedy of the world's hungry and starving people, and how they can be helped by donations to Feed the Children. But the Oak Ridge Boys added uplifting musical presentations to the programs, performances that not only fit with Feed the Children's message, but also helped expand the audiences and keep viewers tuned in longer. Donations increased. The Oaks helped feed more children.

These quality television specials continue to run on a variety of cable networks and broadcast stations, each one airing numerous times. Usually, within a given year, three specials will run: a patriotic-themed presentation, a Christmas special, and a variety show. The total viewership for these specials is nothing short of awesome! More than 100 million viewers will tune in to one or more of the shows over the course of a year.

The Oak Ridge Boys believe in what Feed the Children does. In addition to performing inspirational material on the specials, they've helped pass out food boxes in many locations. A by-product of their commitment to this cause is positive press and PR, building their prestige and reputation and, at the same time, helping raise awareness of, and contributions to, Feed the Children. The Oaks' exposure on these specials increase ticket sales as well as sales of their CDs and books, Because of their TVQ (a term that rates a celebrity's visibility and recognizibility because of frequent television appearances) they also have more touring dates, and for better money. Even though Feed the Children is a charity, these are the same sorts of benefits you can expect from a corporate sponsor.

THE RECORD COMPANY

A record company can also function as a corporate sponsor. If you have a record deal, the company helps market and promote your CD. This is called *tour support*. It's another form of sponsorship, and it can include buying radio spots, cash advances for expenses, posters, pictures, stand-ups, bin buys, and end caps (an advertising piece used at the *end* of a store aisle. You've seen them, special buy on batteries, cereal, shampoo *and* CDs, DVDs.). The space is sold by the store to the product manufacturer. You've seen them in Wal-Mart, Target, Best Buy and so forth. It is an added incentive to help stimulate sales on down the aisle space. Tour support can also include road expenses, hotel rooms and meals, staging, light and sound support, paying for an opening act, and transportation (buses, limos, etc.). Many times, the record company support will be limited to certain cities or geographical areas; often, an artist needs the help of the record company to expand internationally. All of this promotes the product—the CD—but it also enhances the image of the artist.

When it comes to tour support from a record company, however, *be careful!* Some or all of the payment for this support, while benefiting the artists, is also recoupable advance money. That means it comes out of the artist's royalties–before the artist receives any payment. This isn't subterfuge or deceit on the part of the company. It's just another aspect of sponsorship that you should be aware of.

The sponsorship deals I've made over the years have all come from hundreds upon hundreds of solicitations, winnowing down to a few positive responses. From there, we've followed through and found the most interested prospective buyers. And the subsequent sponsorships have always helped the artist's bottom line.

There are a couple of simple but important questions to ask yourself before you pursue a corporate sponsorship. First, what do you have to offer a potential sponsor or a commercial or endorsement prospect? Second, how can you most effectively accomplish the desired objective? Companies that associate themselves with celebrities via endorsements, commercials, or sponsorship hope to enhance the value of their product, and a celebrity act–like my clients, the Oak Ridge Boys–

brings greater public awareness of that product. The Oaks have an important and immediately recognizable brand name, bringing integrity and believability to anything they endorse.

How easy will the endorsement or sponsorship be to implement? The answer to that question is always important to a sponsor. Your artist's personal-appearance itinerary, interview schedule, and the ability to create events and interest in both the artist and endorsed product are all a part of what the endorsement fee covers. Collaborating with co-sponsors or business partners also enhances the value of the acts and their business relationships. Such things as cross-promotions on websites and cooperative use of email announcements will make the final results more satisfactory for all.

Now that you know what corporate sponsorships and endorsements are, how do you get them—especially if you're just getting started? Well, if you have a CD that's getting local or regional play, and you're working dates and getting a little publicity in the local media—if you're occasionally recognized at the grocery store or the gas station—then you have a value in your local market.

First, find out who spends money advertising in your area. These entities could include retail and convenience stores, car dealerships, grocery stores, jewelers, and many more. Look at the ads in the newspapers and on television and radio. Check out billboards. Then, try to get involved with one of these prospective sponsors. You can do that by offering endorsements, doing local commercials, or putting up signs and other acknowledgements of the sponsor at your personal appearances. If you have a bus or van, you can wrap it with the sponsor's logo and contact information—just like the Oak Ridge Boys did with BluBlocker. Your act can give a show, perhaps in conjunction with a live broadcast, at the business site itself. (Weekends are an especially good time for this.) If you have a fan club, get the members to turn out. Bring your CDs to sell, and see if you can leave some of them at the business itself, to be sold on a continuing basis. As you do all of this, you build your relationship with sponsors, so that you become increasingly important to them.

Who do you call to make these kinds of deals? In a local market, it's usually the general manager, marketing and advertising director, or the big boss him- or herself—the one whose name is on the marquee.

If your act already has some solid name recognition beyond the regional level, a good following, and a nationally released CD, you're in a position to ask for a substantial endorsement. Most corporations have specific departments or managers to handle this. The titles vary from business to business, but some of the ones to look for are director of event marketing, advertising director, promotions manager, business development, corporate branding, brand management, conventions, sponsorship management, and public affairs. You can go online and look up the corporation or product you're interested in. Most of those websites will show you the appropriate contact person.

There's also a professional organization that provides a lot of valuable information in this area. It's the International Events Marketing Group, or IEG, founded and ably operated by Lesa and John Ukman. IEG publishes many source books and informative bulletins. It also sponsors workshops and conferences dealing with sponsors, properties, agencies, and suppliers. IEG is a *must belong*. You can visit the website at www.sponsorship.com. Their land address is IEG, Inc., 840 N. LaSalle, Suite 600, Chicago, IL 60610–3777.Phone (800) 834–4850, or email at ieg@sponsorship.com

part three
SECRETS OF THE JIM HALSEY COMPANY

chapter 29

THE HALSEY METHOD

n the rest of this book, we'll look at some of the methods and secrets I used to make The Jim Halsey Company, Inc., the biggest country music agency in the world. To paraphrase what my friend the Amazing Kreskin told a guest at one of our Halsey Ranch Parties, these are not tricks. We didn't do tricks. However, many times we did magic. And with the knowledge in this book and your own Power of Performance, you may be able to do some magic yourself.

★

Previously I briefly mentioned four things: goals, research, timetables, and following your dreams. Because these have all been important components of my career and my life, I now want to take a little more time on each one of them.

First, goals. You know that I advocate writing down your goals and putting the list into a place where you can encounter it every day. I caution you to make sure that the goals you set are your own. Many people get off the path by trying to achieve goals someone else has set for them. You must build your future on where you want to go and on what you want to do.

Make your goals realistic and reachable, and put a timetable on them. Start out marking time in increments of 6, 12, 18, or 24 months and then expand to three-year and five-year goals. Your plan begins when you get it down on paper—this is part of the Halsey method.

Our large staff at The Jim Halsey Company always represented at least 40 important artists. This roster included the high-caliber, big-name performers I've mentioned throughout this book. Each had his or her individual desires and goals, and it was up to us to implement a plan that would help these stars achieve what they wanted. In every case, we would consult with the artists—and sometimes with the performer's other Star Team members, especially managers and record-company executives—to determine where they wanted to go with their careers. We'd write down all of the desires, potential opportunities, realistic—and sometimes seemingly unrealistic—goals, and, most important, their dreams. By writing down each artist's "want list," we had something tangible to focus upon. We then had the opportunity to build a plan, using the idea of "events" and the talents of other team members for achieving those goals.

Here's a secret: My method requires that 90 percent of the goals you write down have to be realistic. You also need to have a certain number of goals that are attainable in a short period of time. Early in life, I learned that establishing a lot of unrealistic or unattainable goals will discourage even the best salespersons, so you need to make sure that most goals are always within reach. That makes it easier to eventually attain the unattainable.

At The Halsey Company, our lists always contained goals that could be achieved, many of them relatively quickly. There was a lot of the possible, and a little bit of the impossible. When our salespeople and agents achieved the possible, all that was left was the impossible. As a result, we were always achieving the impossible.

The specific goals and timetables were important; they made the list a guidebook, a road map giving everyone the right direction to follow. At the Halsey Company, we always shared these written directions with each artist involved.

Again, put your goals in writing. The reason I stress this so many times in this book is that writing down goals is one of the most important parts of my method.

Now, to research. Once you get your goals down, pursue a diligent pattern of research. Investigate every means that might possibly help propel you to the conclusion of your plans. If a lot of avenues of research aren't immediately available to you, do as much study as you can and then start to work. As you work toward your goals, you'll hit some roadblocks. Solutions to these problems will often present themselves as you continue to work; research can help you get past some of the pitfalls as well.

Always pay attention to what's happening with your plans. Many times, a new direction will present itself in the middle of the project. Sometimes a complete change of plans or a new direction will be necessary.

As I said, you should establish timetables at the beginning. Remember that it's not necessary to follow these down to the second. They do, however, give you important guidelines for achieving your goals.

MAINTAIN GOOD HEALTH

Part of my method, an important one that never seems to be addressed in most "How To" books is *maintaining good health!* Of the hundreds on the market telling about setting goals, staying focused, dedication, diligence and resolve, including my own *"Ten Keys to the Power of Performance,"* they mainly boil down to "Success and Where to Find It."

Equally important, in my opinion is that quality of life comes from one thing, discovering "Life and How to Live It"…mentally, physically and spiritually.

To function at your maximum proficiency, maintaining good health is a must.

Eat right, sleep right, get the right kind of exercise. Think right, keep the right mental attitude, keep your thoughts and attitude elevated. Most of all, get right with the Creator.

WHAT IS FAILURE

One foreign critic once described my book as the typical America way— all about success. True, but success only comes with failure, maybe lots of them before true success. That's why I encourage all of you to fail. What did I just say? I don't mean to fail and just lie and wallow there in self-pity and destruction.

To fail means your project, your music, your product has not met the expectations of success. Maybe you have been embarrassed, gone broke, lost your job, sold 25,000 CDs and had 50,000 of them returned (yes, that's happened), got bad reviews for your music, stage performance, or job performance. Maybe you've been deserted or back turned on you by your (you thought) friends. Maybe your car has been repossessed, maybe you've lost your home.

Yes, you have failed, and from these or many other failures you're going to learn. This learning is going to be the most important of your life. Depressing, I'm sure, but to overcome your setback with the knowledge you have gained is going to be priceless. It is from failures that most successful ventures have been formed.

I'm a reader of biographies, and I have not read one–not one biography of any important, successful people that had not, I repeat, had not experienced failure; failure many times for some of the biggest and most successful, important people you can imagine.

Yes, I too, have failed many times. But from each failure has formed the seeds of inspiration for a successful project or venture that was better that what I had envisioned for the failed project.

Did I suffer disappointment? Yes. Was I discouraged? I would say, set back a little, because I viewed my failed project as a learning project. And from it, I could design something better, and hopefully, and usually, successful. Sometimes there will be a whole series of failures before success.

If you can understand that failure is a part of a learning process, you'll understand how to turn it into a positive for you.

Caution, if you accept failure and failures as a personal rejection, or of your ability or lack of it, and you resign yourself to that condemnation, you need some help.

Start by reading some biographies of very successful people, go to some lectures, and watch interesting biographies on television. You'll find most of the super successful people have gone through many failures before achieving success.

Success is there for all of us, but we have to want it, we have to work for it. It's not like a "free delivery pizza" that is ordered up and expected to be delivered to your home.

Finally, I again stress the importance of following your dreams. Following dreams is a very effective way to access your personal Power of Performance. My own dreams have been a source of expansion for my life, for The Jim Halsey Company, and for the artists we represented. Dream your dream of dreams. Nothing is too great to conceive. I sincerely believe that anything is possible when you follow your dreams.

I have always been a dreamer, relying upon my visions to identify where I wanted to go with my life and my career. These include visions about developing projects and events as well as going to unexpected places. Dreams have fueled my life and provided much of what this book is about.

chapter 30

BUILDING IDENTITY

The Halsey Rose

As we continued our direct-mail campaigns, our coordinated promotions with record companies, regular TV and cable appearances, and identification with corporate sponsors, we found that our repetitious impressions were creating an identity for The Jim Halsey Company as well as for our artists. I wanted us to be known as a major company that represented major stars, but I also wanted the company to be remembered on its own.

In order to do this, I used a couple of methods, both with the idea of creating a kind of instant identity. I learned one way to do this from my good friend, Walter Kane, entertainment czar for the Howard Hughes-owned hotels in Las Vegas. Walter had a gimmick of affixing a little embroidered rose on the lapel of every person he encountered. I believe he first used this as a means of identifying people who were cleared to go backstage at his shows; however, it quickly grew past that into one of his trademarks, one of the things he was remembered for.

When we made the first Soviet Union tour in 1976 with Roy Clark—an important landmark not only for country music but for diplomatic relations as well—Mr. Kane gave me hundreds of these roses to take along.

"A rose is a symbol of friendship," he told me. "Pass these out in the

USSR. " And I did. As I met various officials and government dignitaries and exchanged greetings, I'd make a point of sticking one of Mr. Kane's little roses on the front of their clothing. That personal communication, that physical touch, was an instant success. Truly, our hosts saw the roses for what they were: small, sincere symbols of friendship. Opening night in Moscow's Rossiya Theater was packed full of government dignitaries, medal-bedecked officials, television crews, and all of the top representatives from Gosconcert, the official concert agency that was handling our visit. By that time, we were a week into our trip, and many of the officials sported the friendship rose—sometimes right next to their rows of military medals.

At the official reception before the concert, Madam Butrova, the Minister of Culture, was our host. We exchanged greetings and I ceremoniously pinned her with what had now become "The Official Rose of Friendship." As I did, I felt the importance of what the rose was becoming—a way that two people could communicate personally, physically, and spiritually, without having to speak each other's language. I think the first full significance of the rose came home to me at that moment.

That night at intermission, a Ministry of Culture attaché came backstage, seeking me out.

"Excuse me, Mr. Halsey," he said in excellent English. "Madam Butrova would like to know if it would be possible for you to give her 12 more roses?"

While part of the magic was the personal contact of putting the rose on somebody, I was flattered by her request and certainly honored it.

I continued using the rose in my extensive travels around the world, becoming known as not only an impresario, but as the man who carried the Friendship Rose. Always, the rose instantly broke through social or political barriers, magically bringing everyone involved into an immediate area of peace and harmony.

I became quite well known for my roses. People who hadn't yet gotten a rose from me would come up and ask for one. At conventions and trade shows, buyers would come to our booth seeking both me and a rose. People in elevators would spot the rose on my lapel and ask if I was Jim Halsey. Of course, I would always extend the rose of friendship.

One day, my wife Minisa and I were having lunch at New York's

Plaza Hotel, in its crowded Oyster Bar. I couldn't help noticing that a gentleman sitting a few tables away kept staring at us. Finally, he got up and came over.

"I noticed the rose on your lapel," he said. "Do you know Jim Halsey?"

I told him I was Jim Halsey.

It turned out to be Gil Cates, brother of Joe Cates. The Cates brothers were big producers of TV specials, and they were fond of Roy Clark, The Oak Ridge Boys, Minnie Pearl, Mel Tillis, Tammy Wynette, and many of our other stars. I had worked mainly for Joe, who knew about my roses. However, I'd never met Gil, even though Roy had sung the title song for a Gil Cates-produced movie, "I Never Sang For My Father", for which stars Gene Hackman and Melvyn Douglas and writer Robert Anderson received Academy Award nominations.

Gil Cates knew about the rose, too, and I was happy to extend one to him at the Plaza Hotel Oyster Bar.

Another Halsey secret is to establish something you'll be remembered for. It can be an unforgettable advertisement, a hit song, a great performance—in my case, it was the Friendship Rose.

All of those roses out there illustrate my method of repetitious impressions. The rose was an impact enhancer, with its own Power of Performance.

All of that was important to me, because when it all boils down to the essentials, I'm a salesperson. I have good product for sale and I want to make a deal. I'm also the man with the rose. Remember me?

Yes, they did—and it worked! I still use the rose today! Thank you, Walter Kane!

THE HOT ONE (TABASCO)

When you're in the music and entertainment business, it's important to become known and remembered within the industry. It's just part of selling yourself, your artists, your company. The Friendship Rose was a very personal gift—and people always like receiving gifts. The little lapel roses became worldwide symbols of our company, and significant examples of the Power of Performance.

After I had been giving out the roses for quite a while, I began looking for something extra to give out on our trips abroad. I wasn't trying to detract from the power of the roses, but wanted something in addition that would be fun and remembered by people, something that would cause talk and attention. The roses had become my personal gift, my identification. Now people expected them from me.

I wanted some new pass-out promotion that we could tie in with one of our artists, or with some of our events. The idea I ended up using didn't come immediately, but it came naturally.

I've previously mentioned, one of my favorite condiments in the world is McIlhenney's Tabasco, the famous brand of hot pepper sauce. Whenever I traveled out of the country, I would always purchase miniature bottles for my own personal consumption, since it was hard to find overseas. I always ended up sharing it, too. Members of my traveling entourages constantly requested the Tabasco; diners at neighboring tables in some of the finest restaurants in France, England, Hungary, Russia and Bulgaria, upon seeing me produce a bottle, came over and asked for samples. The piquant sauce was so popular overseas that, as I was preparing to leave on a European tour with Roy Clark, I requested a thousand miniature Tabasco bottles from McIlhenney to give away. President and CEO, Paul McIlhenney graciously granted our request. We placed small stickers on the backs of the bottles that read, "Roy Clark, The Hot One," and took off on tour with something that would get us more notice than a full-page ad in an international magazine.

The miniature bottles of Tabasco sauce didn't just make for a good promotion. It was a great promotional idea. All of our artists liked it, and we used the miniature bottles many times for specific promotions: The Oak Ridge Boys, The Hot Ones; Tammy Wynette, The Hot One; The Hot Show, Hilton Hotel and The Judds. We used these little bottles everywhere. McIlhenny furnished them, and in return got its own publicity as well as implied endorsements from the artists whose names were used on the bottles.

We ended up using Tabasco in lots of different ways. As a radio promotion for one of The Oak Ridge Boys' singles, we once sent 2,500 miniature bottles to stations through the mail. On several other occasions, I purchased giant, commercial-sized bottles of Tabasco from restaurant-supply houses and put them in specially constructed wooden boxes lined with velvet, where they looked like bottles of fine, rare wine. When one of our acts performed in a foreign country, we would give these as gifts to high-ranking officials. I'll bet some of those large bottles still have a few drops left. As long as they do, and for a time afterwards, we will still be remembered as "The Hot One."

The practice of the Power of Performance works in wondrous

ways. All you have to do is use your imagination and proceed. The Tabasco promotion shows that it's more important for a promotion to be inventive and creative than it is to be expensive. Those little bottles were simple, but effective.

What were we looking for? Identification, pure and simple. The Tabasco promotion is a good example of the techniques we've discussed in earlier chapters: Repetitious Impressions, Power Boosters, and Impact Enhancers. The promotion was used to sell our artists, to sell our company, to be remembered so that we'd get the call to action.

I love Tabasco sauce. It's the Power of Performance—with a bite.

Eagle Dancer, Woody Crumbo

chapter 31

LOGO AND TRADEMARK: OUR SPIRITUAL SHIELD

Eagle Dancer, Woody Crumbo

A good company logo or trademark should not only represent your company's philosophy, it should also have personal meaning for you. It is, in a symbolic way, your shield.

An effective logo or trademark will help others remember you. It's an important part of your Power of Performance, and it should be powerful itself. I believe that I have one of the best logos in the business: Woody Crumbo's Eagle Dancer.

I should explain that my own heritage is Cherokee. In 1999, I was a recipient of the Cherokee Medal of Honor; of all the awards I've received in my life, it means the most to me. For many of my events, including overseas tours, I have included Native American dancers on the program.

I also love Native American art; I've collected it for a long time. In fact, it was through my love of this art that I met my wife, Minisa Crumbo, who is one of the finest of the Native American artists herself. Through Minisa, my interest in this art form was expanded even further.

Then, because of my association with Madam Butrova, the Soviet Minister of Culture who loved my embroidered roses, Minisa had the opportunity to do a one-person exhibition in the USSR. I brought

Minisa's art to Madame Butrova's attention, and she became very interested, inviting Minisa to Moscow to talk about a possible Soviet showing. After the ministry examined samples of Minisa's work, looking for a hidden political agenda and finding none, she received an official invitation to show her artwork in Moscow, Leningrad, and Kiev.

She exhibited her art for nine months, to great public and critical acclaim, becoming only the second American artist to be extended an invitation for a one-person show by the Soviet Union. (The other was the acclaimed artist Jamie Wyeth.) Minisa and her work were featured extensively in television and press throughout the Soviet Union. She was even on the cover of Soviet Life magazine.

Of course, since there is no longer a Soviet Union, she was also the final American artist to be accorded this great honor.

Minisa's father, Woody Crumbo, was the dean of American Indian artists; his work is exhibited in museums all around the world. I was a big fan of Woody's—not only because he was such a fine artist, but a great man as well.

One series he did that I was particularly fond of showed dancers in various costumes, performing different dances. Three paintings of Eagle Dancers, each facing a different way, were a part of this series.

Very few of Woody's originals were available. Most of his art was available as limited-edition lithographs, silkscreens, and etchings. Over a period of time, however, I was able to find and purchase two of the three original paintings of the Eagle Dancers, and one of them became the logo trademark of The Jim Halsey Company, gaining fame throughout the world. I used Woody Crumbo's Eagle Dancer in our ads and on posters, pins, and business cards. I knew we had something very special when people began asking us for several of our business cards at once.

The Eagle Dancer image gave us another way for people to recognize and remember us. Whenever I gave my business card to someone for the first time, I got reactions that reminded me of Joe Sugarman's famous TV ads for his BluBlocker sunglasses: "Wow! Look at this!" "Can't believe this!" "I've never seen a business card like that!" "This card is beautiful!" The Eagle Dancer trademark has become so well-known and so identified with me that the recognition is there forever.

Because of our extensive collection of Native American art and the number of people who identified with Woody Crumbo's Eagle Dancer, our company for years published a calendar reproducing 12 beautiful pieces from our original art collection, which further enhanced our identification with Native American artwork.

When you design a logo or trademark, make it something that's important to your company, and something that not only identifies you, but with which you identify. To me, the Eagle Dancer had a deep spiritual significance, augmented by the fact that it was created by a member of the family. It is a great piece of art, one that has not only made a deep impression for The Jim Halsey Company, but is a well-known and respected work from a major American artist. I'm very proud to have this Eagle Dancer as the logo that identifies our company.

'Minisa Crumbo Halsey one-person art exhibitions in Moscow, Leningrad and Kiev. First Native American artist invited to exhibit in Soviet Union.'

chapter 32

THE ART OF NEGOTIATION

Don't Oversell

I n the music and entertainment business, negotiating deals is an art. In this chapter, I'd like to give you some examples of the art of negotiating—both good and bad—taken from my own experience.

In the building stages of Roy Clark's career, it was my strategy to expose him to the largest audience possible. Even then, Roy possessed enormous and varied talents. In addition to his mastery of many different instruments and his distinctive vocal style, he had an engaging stage presence and an innate flair for comedy. I wanted people to experience the whole package. We had Roy on records, we did press and public relations, we packaged him with other artists, we did radio benefit appearances and other free shows with him, just to get him seen and heard. Of course, his multiple talents made him a natural for television—and he did lots of it.

In the beginning, though, when we were both novices in the business and I was serving as both his manager and agent, it wasn't always easy to get our message across to the important television producers.

In 1967, Roy's "Yesterday When I was Young" hit the top of both the pop and country charts, enabling us to place him on a lot of television shows. At the same time Roy's song was going through the roof, movie star Mitzi Gaynor was contracted to host a network television special, which would also feature other big-name stars. To me, this special would be the perfect vehicle to enhance Roy's career and help him find an audience beyond country music.

The producer was Jack Bean, Mitzi's husband. But after several meetings with him, sincerely pitching Roy and all of his comedic, musical, and acting abilities, I could see that I wasn't getting anywhere. Finally, because I wanted this show for Roy so badly and knew how we needed it, I resorted to a little hard-sell—which definitely is not my style. That's when I made the mistake that dooms many salespeople. I focused too hard on making the sale, on selling Roy, rather than concentrating on filling the need of my customer, the buyer, who in this case was Jack Bean.

I finally played my trump card and used my last sales tool. I told Jack Bean that Roy Clark's current single, a Top Ten record, had just reached sales figures of over one million copies. I felt that if all the other reasons I'd given to make the sale had failed, this one would be the one that changed his mind.

After I dropped that bomb in Mr. Bean's office, there was a long silence. Finally, he leaned back in his chair.

"Sold a million copies, huh?" he asked.

"That's right," I returned.

Folding his arms behind his head, he looked me straight in the eye. "I guess that means he's only going to appeal to a little over two percent of our audience," he said.

The room fell silent again. A little uncomfortably, I pondered his words.

"We are very interested in Roy Clark," he finally added. "But it's not because he's sold a million records. We have to appeal to 40 million people. That's our audience. We like Roy's talents and think he will appeal to this 40 million."

I was embarrassed, but I'd learned a valuable lesson. Being over-anxious to close a sale, I had almost blown the whole deal by not sizing up my buyer properly. I'd deviated from my normal style and become impatient, overlooking the very basic point of selling that I'd been teaching my own salespeople for years: fill the needs of your customer and you've got a sale. If I'd been graded on my Power of Performance in this negotiation, I don't know if I would've passed.

Fortunately, Mr. Bean saw the qualities in Roy. He'd just been slow in making a decision because so many other pieces of the production had to fit into place.

The Mitzi Gaynor special turned out to be a major showcase for Roy's ta"ents. He sang (Yesterday Wh"n I wa" Young,) "e played (Malagueña) on the 12-string guitar, and he did some comedy. He even danced a little.

This experience taught me that an important element of being a good manager, agent, promoter, or any other member of a Star Team dealing with contracts, obligations, selling, marketing, advertising, or promotion is knowing the art of negotiation. Good deal-makers understand the fundamentals of sales and marketing, as well as knowing and applying simple rules of etiquette. They know their product, understand the needs of all involved, and organize their presentations. They're concise and truthful, they listen to concerns, compromise when needed, and they ask for the sale.

There are two key words in any deal-maker's vocabulary: patience and persistence. And remember: It's not a good deal unless it's a good deal for everybody.

BEST TO BE UNDERWHELMING

I have accomplished much, thank you, God! I have been blessed with good fortune of family, friends, good business colleagues, lots of stars and superstars involved, on a worldwide basis, too!

Most will describe me as low key and quiet. Certainly I don't see myself as the typical promoter-impresario type. I'm not really a salesman either, although my whole life has been about sales and marketing.

If I represent a good artist or product, my best sales presentation is to clearly and honestly present the facts and why someone should buy. My "call to action" is soft but forceful. Just tell the advantages and benefits in a positive and enthusiastic manner. That doesn't mean theatrics of jumping on top of a table, although I have done that to make a point.

My personality has been described as quiet, soft, persuasive. I like that. My old friend and colleague, Dick Howard preferred to call it "Dull!" I didn't take offense.

Merle Travis, the guitar great and dear friend, in an interview issued one of my favorite descriptions, "Jim Halsey is the type of person that would write a bomb threat in pencil." In today's world that's probably not too well said, but I think Merle meant I could be effective even if soft spoken. I hope so.

I've never been considered "overwhelming." I think it's more effective to be "underwhelming." In selling and representing the artist and their art, your straight forward presentation of facts and need will be more effective and respected.

This business of the music business is a sensitive one. Treat it as such.

Go out into the world and underwhelm somebody today!

BE A GOOD LISTENER/ BE PREPARED

Every person in the sales business has a style. Some are forceful, some are bombastic, some are high-pressure, some merely make a presentation.

What are The Jim Halsey secrets of selling and negotiation? First of all, be a good listener. Find out your prospective customer's needs and then determine how to fill them. Get your buyers to open up. Learn their priorities, time frames, budgets, and special requirements, Then you can make an intelligent presentation.

Remember the Scout motto: Be Prepared. Do your homework. Present to your buyer an artist and a program that will be to his benefit. Never use high-pressure tactics. Never sell something your buyer does not need or that won't benefit all the parties involved.

It's simple: if you can fill the need, you can make the sale. Make your presentations, ask for the sale, and trust your Power of Performance to make it happen.

LEARN FROM THE BEST

I've written earlier about my long-term relationship with the Howard Hughes-owned hotels in Las Vegas, including the Frontier, Desert Inn, Sands, Landmark, Castaways, and the Silver Slipper. And you've also already met my friend Walter Kane, the originator of the Friendship Rose, in these pages.

In 1971, Hughes asked Kane, his friend and business associate for half a century, to become the entertainment director for all of his Vegas hotels. In taking over as "entertainment czar" for the six hotel showrooms, Walter Kane became one of the most influential and powerful entertainment buyers in the world.

Mr. Kane was a promoter, an impresario of the first magnitude. He deserves a whole book. Describing him as a "colorful show-business impresario" doesn't begin to indicate the spectrum of color and energies this unique character exuded.

Walter Kane was a master negotiator. He liked nothing better than to make a deal. Much of my learning in selling, marketing, and negotiating came from my experiences with Mr. Kane. He was an absolute master of the Power of Performance, always giving a better performance than any of the big stars he hired for the main showrooms. He was one of my teachers, one of my mentors, and certainly a valued friend.

You can usually count the individuals who created turning points in your life and career on the fingers of one hand. For me, Walter Kane is one of those people. Through all the years I was associated with him, over countless hours at dinners and show openings, we had many discussions that transcended business. Some of the best were about his personal history. His stories and life were so interesting to me that spending even a few hours with him was always the high point of a trip to Las Vegas. Many times, while we were enjoying a dinner together, it would be interrupted by a telephone call for "Sir Walter," originating from the Bahamas. That would be the big boss man, Howard Hughes, inquiring about the show counts, how the showroom audiences were receiving various stars, etc. I never met Howard Hughes, never spoke to him, but I was impressed with the detailed information he'd always request about the artists and the shows in his hotels. I was intrigued that this mysterious man, who ruled such an empire, wanted to know things like how many people Roy Clark had in the showroom that night, their reaction to him, and whether or not he got a standing ovation. He always did. Plus, it was energizing just to be across the table from a man who was talking directly to Howard Hughes.

After one of these important calls, Walter Kane and I would get back to business as usual. But the whole aura of the evening would invariably be changed, the air charged by the call from Howard Hughes. I was there, and I experienced it. Talk about a Power of Performance!

Even today, many a manager and agent is mumbling to himself about his dealings with Mr. Kane. Because of his age—he was 82 at the time of his death, in 1983—many of the agents he dealt with underestimated his fine memory. I learned early in my dealings with him that his so-called "bad memory" was a convenience he used at the negotiating table, and always to his advantage.

From the beginning, Mr. Kane and I were friends, with mutual respect for each other. He made deals the way a good musician plays his instrument: with grace and beauty, and as often as possible. His countless stories about his different deals and negotiations over the years were invaluable to me in creating some of my own style, and I'll confess now that on our countless evenings together, I'd usually lead him into talking about his deal-making secrets.

Upon first taking over the entertainment-buying responsibilities for the Hughes hotels, Mr. Kane inherited a number of contracts with performers he was obligated to honor. One of these contracts was for a two-week playdate with Roy Clark. Walter was not a country music fan, so you can imagine his surprise when he first saw Roy's show-stopping performance. But even that show and its reception by the Landmark Hotel audience didn't change his mind about country music. He just wasn't interested in buying any more country artists. He wasn't even interested in seeing me so we could talk about more time for Roy. When Roy finished his obligated two weeks, Kane wanted to change the entertainment policy at the Landmark to one that would not include Roy, or anybody else considered "country."

As strange as it sounds, Las Vegas wasn't aware of the entertainment world outside its own city limits. At this time Roy was already a big star, guest-starring on network television shows, drawing big crowds nationwide, and cutting records that invariably climbed the charts. But in Las Vegas, with Walter Kane, he was still a hard sell.

At this time, Kane was looking for a musical format that would work consistently at the Landmark. I knew if I could ever establish a working relationship with him, I could sell him not only Roy, but a lot of the other artists on our roster. He didn't want country music. I thought I could change his mind by applying one of the basic principles of selling and marketing: educate your buyer.

Remember my advice about having a good pair of shoes, strong enough that you can get them in the door without getting your foot mangled? I wore out a pair or two of those trying to get established in the Hughes hotels. I was seeing some success selling other artists to different Vegas hotels and clubs, but not in the ones owned by Howard Hughes. Walter Kane wouldn't even see me. I would always call ahead for an appointment, only to be told that he had no appointments available. Furthermore, he let it be known that he wasn't interested in any of the artists I represented.

Did that stop me? No. Every trip I made to Vegas would include a visit to his office in the Sands Hotel.

Walter Kane had six secretaries. Eleanor Grasso, Carolyn Wallace, and Barbara Kelly were the three in charge. They all sat in one large room, which contained the entryway to Kane's plush office. Every time I came in and reintroduced myself, they would restate the fact that it would be impossible to see Mr. Kane. He had an opening that night. He had a meeting with an act. He was tied up. He just wasn't interested in my artists. And all the while, I could hear him through the door to his office, talking energetically on the phone, sometimes shouting, making deals. I had to get into Mr. Kane's inner sanctum. If I could just meet him face to face, I knew I could sell him.

After I'd visited Kane's office a few times, Eleanor, Carolyn, and Barbara began recognizing me. I'd always bring them gifts—flowers, or boxes of Godiva chocolates. Once, I filled up a big five-gallon canister with hard candies and took it in; other times, I'd bring in a five-gallon can of popcorn and leave it for them. After awhile, they began to chat informally with me. I began to know them. In a way, they were glad to see me each time, because I always brought them a little something.

Still, I couldn't get in to see Walter Kane.

Finally, on one of my visits Eleanor Grasso—the head secretary—stopped me as I was leaving the office. "Wait just a minute," she said.

I stood stock still as she opened the door to Mr. Kane's office and slipped in. Listening intently, I heard her say, "Mr. Kane, can't you give Mr. Halsey just five minutes of your time? He's come here every week for the last six weeks. You've refused to see him. I think, as a courtesy, you could give him five minutes."

The door opened. Had I made it? Yes! With a smile, she beckoned me in, and in a moment I was standing in front of the entertainment czar of Howard Hughes' hotels. Finally, I had my chance. And I knew I'd better not mess it up.

At the time, there was a little ray of hope for country music acts at the Landmark. Jimmy Dean had been successful at a number of Las Vegas venues, and he currently had a Landmark contract. But although he was a country music recording artist, he was also a television star and wasn't really considered "country" by the Vegas buyers. I told Mr. Kane that Roy Clark had the same kind of crossover appeal. Mr. Kane wasn't really familiar with Roy, even though Roy had just finished playing two weeks for him. But I gave him my best sales pitch, and he listened intently.

We spent little more than five minutes together at our first meeting. But somehow, we connected right then, beginning the long relationship we would have. From the first, we each recognized that the other had a "performance" to give.

I did not, however, immediately get an additional two weeks for Roy at the Landmark. That was what I'd wanted, but Mr. Kane wasn't ready. I'd done my best. He wasn't buying.

But I wasn't discouraged. In fact, I was elated! I had made contact. I had made my presentation. I had given my Power of Performance. And I knew that one of the formulas for a successful sale was persistence. I would be back (and sooner than I thought).

At the end of our meeting, I excused myself, thanked him for the time, and headed back to my office in Tulsa. That's when a strange thing happened—the first of many that would occur throughout our relationship.

I had no sooner returned to Tulsa when I got an urgent call at my office. It was Walter Kane. He wanted me to sit down with him in his office in Vegas and talk about a Roy Clark deal at the Landmark Hotel!

I had to make a decision. Did I want to get right back on a plane and travel another four hours back to Las Vegas, without even unpacking my bags? Or could I try to do it by telephone, or set it up for a later time?

In the business of selling, you have to be able to recognize an opportunity for a sale when it's presented to you. It was a time to act, not hesitate. It was my opportunity to sell Roy Clark to Walter Kane and the Hughes hotels.

So I hauled myself and my unpacked bags right back to the airport, got on a plane, and returned to Vegas where I met with Mr. Kane. That meeting began a long relationship between Roy Clark—and the other artists I represented—and the Hughes line of hotels. It also began my educational experience with Walter Kane.

One of the most important things I learned from Mr. Kane is that learning by experience is one of the best ways to learn. In the business of entertainment, it's sometimes the only way to learn. That's why this book is autobiographical, telling you about some of my experiences in the music and entertainment fields. I learned from these things; you can too.

Out of our meeting came two more weeks for Roy at the Landmark Hotel—exactly what I'd hoped for. The crowds there loved him. He sold out his shows, and the Landmark was always getting calls and letters, wanting to know when he'd be back. Prior to his playing the Landmark, Roy had co-headlined with Petula Clark at Caesar's Palace for two weeks, but no long-term deal was forthcoming. We couldn't get the money we needed, or even any interest, from a lot of the other big Las Vegas hotels because they didn't think country music would sell on the Strip.

The Landmark was actually two blocks off the Strip, but it was still considered a major hotel and showroom, even if it didn't have quite the same stature as the rest of Hughes' hotels. However, as long as we did good business at the Landmark, and my relationship with Mr. Kane continued to grow, I felt that sooner or later our Landmark successes would open the door to the Strip for us.

Walter Kane was always thrilled with Roy's sold-out business at the Landmark, and I eventually convinced him to put Roy at the Frontier Hotel, one of the major venues on the Strip. But I couldn't convince his superiors. They all liked Roy, but they were afraid country music just wouldn't make it there. Walter Kane knew it would. Roy Clark knew it would. I knew it would. Still, no sale.

Then our big break came. You always have to watch for these times, and when they come, you have to act.

During one of Roy's opening-night engagements before a capacity crowd at the Landmark, Walter Kane and I were enjoying Roy's show in Sir Walter's private booth, complete with a red hot-line telephone.

Suddenly, it rang.

Mr. Kane answered and turned ashen in color, visibly upset with the information he was receiving. After he hung up, he turned to me.

"What will I do?" he asked. "Robert Goulet is opening tonight at the Frontier, but he's unexpectedly become ill. The showroom is packed and dinners are being served; in fact, customers are eating right now, waiting for the show to start.

"We can't cancel now, and the opening comic can't carry the show beyond thirty minutes."

Goulet probably wasn't nearly as sick as Mr. Kane was at this moment. There was no time for a replacement. Or was there?

Without asking Roy if it would be acceptable to him, I suggested we whisk Roy to the Frontier—two blocks from the Landmark—by limo immediately following his show, so he could fill in for the stricken Goulet. If our timing worked, the staggered showtimes would allow Roy just enough time to get from the Landmark to the back stage of the Frontier as the opening comic was finishing his act.

There wasn't time to ask Roy or even explain the situation. He just had to trust Mr. Kane and me. And he did. Just as Roy finished his Landmark show, we ushered him into a limo—guitar, amp, and all. As we sped the two blocks to the Frontier, we explained the situation briefly, and Roy understood. He got out of the limo, his guitar and amplifier were rushed to the Frontier stage by Jack Yenchek and his great stage crew, and Roy Clark, without rehearsal, stepped center stage to present one of the best shows of his life.

He winged it. The band winged it. And the audience loved it. When he finished his show, with (Malagueña,) he got a standing ovation.

What a show! It had worked!

That night was a turning point in our Las Vegas career. Roy Clark had proved once and for all that he could entertain anybody, anywhere. The powers that be believed it now, and suddenly we were talking multiple weeks and a long-term deal. Now it's a part of entertainment history. Strange to think that so many people were afraid to take a chance.

But Roy Clark wasn't. I wasn't. And thank God, Walter Kane wasn't.

This situation, once again, proved that patience is a virtue in this business. It also illustrated the value of cooperation between all parties—manager, artist, and buyer. In this case, as it should be in all cases, we had one common goal—the satisfied customer!

Our relationship with the Hughes hotels lasted for many more years, ending only when the chain started selling off its properties. We played to capacity audiences in all of their main hotel showrooms, including the Frontier, Desert Inn, and Sands, but we still fondly remember those early sold-out days at the Landmark, where our Walter Kane association began.

COUNTRY MUSIC USA

Later, after Roy had graduated to the Frontier Hotel, where he headlined for many years, the Landmark became a source of frustration to Mr. Kane. He'd tried several different entertainment policies for the Landmark, but none had been really successful, and there was no continuity in the programming. I'd suggested several artists I thought could be successful there, but none had been acceptable to him.

At this time, I was constantly in Las Vegas working with Roy and two of our other artists, Mel Tillis and Tammy Wynette, at the Frontier, Desert Inn, and the Sands. I had a lot of meetings with Mr. Kane, trying to figure out a solution for his Landmark situation. I couldn't come up with the right idea for him, even though I made a number of suggestions. After one completely frustrating session, I returned to my office in Tulsa, knowing I had the right answers for a successful Landmark show, but unable to sell them to Mr. Kane.

Soon after I'd arrived back home, I received a frantic call from Mr. Kane requesting my immediate return to Las Vegas. Colleagues of mine at other agencies thought it was ridiculous that I would make these long flights, do a turn-around, and return to Las Vegas. They told me if it were them, they wouldn't give Walter Kane any more time. But I'd proved over and over again that it was worthwhile for myself, my company, and my artists. Once again, I saw an opportunity to be of service to Walter Kane and Howard Hughes' six Vegas venues, so I caught the first flight out.

As I flew to Las Vegas I tried to put a picture together, using everything I knew about the situation. I knew I hadn't yet been able to come up with the entertainment idea Mr. Kane would buy for the Landmark Hotel. I knew the kind of problems he might be facing. I knew the kinds of venues our artists needed for best exposure. Finally, I knew if I could find the right solution to his problem, I could provide a real service to both our artists and the Hughes hotels.

I knew all of that. But the question was, what could I possibly pitch him that I hadn't pitched before? What could I offer Mr. Kane that would be unique to his Landmark operation? Most of all, how could I be of service to him?

That last question seems obvious enough in any situation, but its importance is often overlooked by an over-zealous salesperson. Too often, we forget that we're in the service business—service to our buyers, to our artists, and to our public. And when I viewed the Landmark problem from that perspective, I finally saw the solution. It was an idea I've put forth several times in this book: Don't concentrate on simply trying to sell an act to headline somewhere. Instead, put together an event.

Arriving in Las Vegas, I knew what I wanted to sell. Now, all that had to be done was sell it, and between the airport and Mr. Kane's office, I got my "performance" together.

When I arrived at his office in the Sands Hotel, I was very excited about presenting my plan for an event in the Landmark. But I didn't start right in with my presentation. Instead, I did something very important to any negotiation. I listened. He told me his needs and what he wanted to accomplish. He complained about the high cost of artists, of production, of advertising. As he talked and I listened, he was, in essence, preparing himself for my presentation. When he finally finished, I explained my plan for the Landmark. It was no accident that I said exactly what he wanted to hear. He had let me know what he wanted, and I'd heard him and responded with a plan.

My idea for the event was a production show called Country Music USA It would feature country music stars on a rotating basis, showcased in a Las Vegas-style production, allowing for variety as well as stability.

Mr. Kane bought it. It became our opportunity to prove that country music would work in Vegas, and it did. Country Music USA was good for the Landmark, and it gave major hotel-showroom exposure to established country music artists. It also became a developing ground for many emerging artists. Running two years straight at the Landmark (except for three months at the Silver Slipper while the Landmark underwent remodeling), it was great for all concerned.

Because of Country Music USA, many Halsey Company artists got their first Vegas exposure in a big-name showroom. These included The Oak Ridge Boys, Ferlin Husky, Hank Thompson, Freddy Fender, LeRoy VanDyke, Bob Luman, Mel Tillis, Johnny Paycheck, Tommy Overstreet, Skip Devol, Ray Price, and "Hee-Haw" TV regulars Guinella Hutton, Grandpa Jones, and Archie Campbell. It was a good illustration of how a good deal can be good for everyone involved, and it showed that putting elements together to create an event creates something far more special than just packaging some acts together for a show. It also demonstrated another point, one that I simply can't stress enough: never underestimate the value of your product.

Give the person sitting across the table a chance to tell you his or her needs. Listen to the problem, then give your solution. That, in a nutshell, is the secret to successful negotiating.

★

After the success of Country Music USA, country music became a staple of the Las Vegas entertainment market. Once our show broke the ice, we were able to sell our other big-name country stars to headline venues on the Strip. Because many of our artists were not only there in the first wave, but successful there as well, we were able to move into other hotels, including Caesar's Palace, Bally's Grand, The Hilton International, Sahara, Desert Inn, and the Sands. Continuously, The Jim Halsey Company had one or more major stars headlining at these big Strip hotels. We were the only ones booking name country artists into Vegas. We were specialists.

And always, we tried to make each date an event. Whenever we played our big stars at these major hotels, we would try to tie in a promotion or a contest. Working with radio stations in Arizona and California, we'd promote free trips into Las Vegas for listeners to win. We came up with the idea of offering "Have Dinner with the Star" contests. We'd negotiate with the hotels for free rooms and bargain with airlines for free tickets. We'd work with the record companies and various corporate sponsors. Somehow, each engagement had to be more than simply a date; it had to be an event.

A Vegas date with one of our acts became something customers and fans anticipated with excitement. They knew The Oak Ridge Boys' show at Bally's Grand or Caesar's Palace, or the Vegas shows with Roy Clark or Mel Tillis, wouldn't just be plain old shows. There'd always be something unique to go along with them, a special event or new promotion. On several occasions, for instance, we cut live albums with our acts at the hotel showrooms. Other times, we'd broadcast over a radio network. Always, we'd invite press from around the world to view our major artists' shows, which usually assured us glowing reports and reviews.

All this, as you can probably see, was simply another manifestation of my philosophy of the Power of Performance.

The casino areas of Las Vegas, Reno, Lake Tahoe, and Atlantic City are not for every artist, but they were important and right for our company. These showrooms helped us develop such acts as Roy Clark, Mel Tillis, The Oak Ridge Boys, Freddy Fender, Dwight Yoakam, Tammy Wynette, Ray Price, Reba McEntire, The Judds, and Clint

Black into major stars. They also provided good cash flow. And perhaps most important, they gave us the chance to showcase the Halsey Company star roster under the most favorable production situations, with good lights and sound, special production facilities, big flashy marquees, and lots of press. And because we were able to bring in television and motion-picture buyers, fair producers, rodeo producers, special events producers, prospective corporate sponsors, and convention buyers to see these great artists in very comfortable situations, these dates were springboards to many more sales.

part four
NOW IT'S YOUR TURN

chapter 33

WRAPPING IT UP

Finally, the Star Team wheel is complete: the talent at the center; the eight spokes, each representing a different team member, radiating out from it, forming the support that enables the wheel to roll down the road to success.

As you go along in your music-business career, you'll see that others will become members of your team from time to time. These will be extended-team members. The ones we've discussed in this section, however, are the essential nine. The order that they're brought in will not always be the same as we've listed here, and some members of a team will often perform more than one function, as I did when I was both the booking agent and manager for Hank Thompson. The important thing is that, to be successful, each member of the team must combine his or her energy with that of the other team members. This is what the team's Power of Performance is all about.

No matter which one of these Star Team members you want to be, it's important for you to know about them all. With what you've learned in this section as a guide and foundation, continue to educate yourself on the functions of each team member. That way, you'll know what to expect from everyone involved. You'll know what to look for, and you'll be able to determine if the other team members are doing their parts. If you decide to be a promoter, you'll have a leg up on this; promoters and other talent buyers usually have the most well-rounded knowledge of the team, simply because they routinely work with all members of a Star Team.

Whatever job you choose, learn it better than anyone else. If you do, there'll always be a place for you in the music business

★

While most of what we discuss in this book is about business, all of it is about life. No matter what you do for a living, you should learn to pay attention to things going on around you, to signals that indicate change, or acceptance. A lot of what we learn comes simply from experience. Education and discovery comes when you try new things and do new things—when you live.

As you know, I'm a great believer in lists. Establishing a plan with chronological timetables gives you a path to follow in any endeavor. When you've written it down, step-by-step, go back over it, do research, flesh out details. Make sure to put your list where you can see it several times a day, to refresh your memory about what it contains. And then remember that if you strive to go beyond your projected plan, you may even surprise yourself with your own abilities.

Be ready to make sacrifices, extend your energies, take chances, and put a lot at risk. Be ready even to take a new direction in the middle of a project. And then, follow your dreams. Pay attention to them, give them respect, and believe them possible.

Maintain faith in yourself and your projects.

Let nothing discourage you from following your dreams and reaching your goals.

chapter 34

THE FIRST JOB: YOUR POWER OF PERFORMANCE

Mentors: Nobody has ever done it alone. *Nobody*. If you've gotten anything out of this book, it should be the realization it's about teamwork and your ability to network.

We all need help, and we all need the special kind of help that mentors can give us. Find a mentor. We learn from them, follow them, emulate them. Sometimes they come to us in a secondhand way: from books, lectures, classes, and the Internet. If we're fortunate, others come along to help us first-hand, guiding us personally through our stages of development. I've been blessed all my life with good mentors, good teachers–and good friends–who've done just that for me.

We should always be going through some developmental stage or another. If we're not, we're not growing, and it's important for us to continue to grow throughout our life. You grow as you develop, and you develop as you learn—if there's one key to success in any business, it's learning. In the entertainment business, the only thing constant is change, and you'd better be able to keep up as it evolves. The way to do that is by being always willing, and even eager, to learn. As I write this, for instance, the music business is evolving with technology like never before, and to survive under these new and ever-changing circumstances you need to continue learning about the latest developments and how they relate to what you're doing, and what you want to achieve.

This book is primarily about the music business, but the methods and suggestions you read here apply to any business. After the first edition of *How To Make It in the Music Business* came out in 2000, I had a *dentist* tell me that it was a more valuable tool for becoming successful in his profession than any of the instruction he'd gotten in college. He had certainly learned how to become a good dentist from that instruction, but until he read the book, he was clueless about how to establish and market his practice and how to find potential patients.

Lots of great and successful people are willing mentors. They don't advertise, though, and you can count yourself lucky if you find a good one. Sometimes, the opportunity will present itself through your job. Remember that your biggest reward from any job comes from the people you meet. Any business–including the entertainment business–is about relationships, contacts, and networking. You can find mentors by joining on-the-job or after-work organizations, participating in volunteer projects, or getting involved in organizations related to your job. Never overlook a networking opportunity.

Many times, your mentor will find *you*. You can help the process by trying to meet or do some work with someone who deeply impresses you. You can even ask if they'd help you, or become your mentor. Most real professionals are always willing to help interested people.

In my years in entertainment, I've been helped by a number of mentors. They're *still* helping me, even as I pass it forward by mentoring young people myself. And I can say from experience that it's one of the most rewarding things I've ever done.

Use this book as a guide to find your place in the business. Don't pass up an opportunity in your initial job search to work as an assistant, apprentice, or in the "mail room" of a big company. This is where you meet and learn. Your first job in this business most likely will not be your dream job, but accept it and view it as your continuing education. The first and most important thing is getting your foot in the door. Then go from there.

Now that you've finished this book, you should have a good understanding of the elements that make up the music and entertainment business. And you should know by now that it all boils down to sales and marketing.

This business is about people. It is about common sense. It is about getting as much knowledge and education as you can. It is about discovering your own Power of Performance, how to access it, and how to master it.

There's a lot of vital information in this book, things I've learned over the decades I've been in the business, and I suggest that you reread the chapters you're most interested in, marking or underlining the points you feel are important. I hope you found the personal stories I told to illustrate some of these points both entertaining and educational as well.

One of the keys to making it in this business is knowing that it's never a one-person show, but a team effort. Another key is knowing that you're probably not going to step directly into the team-member role you want, despite your training and education. That doesn't matter! The important thing is to get into the business. Get your foot in the door, get past the receptionist, get on the inside. Then you will be able to start working toward the job you really want.

Some years ago, a young law-school graduate came to see me. He wanted to be an agent, and he wanted to work for The Jim Halsey Company. But even though he had a law degree, he had no agenting experience, and I was looking for a seasoned agent at the time.

"We'll keep your application on file," I told him, giving him the time-honored, polite turndown. "If something comes up, we'll call you."

Just as he was getting ready to leave my office, my assistant interrupted the meeting. It seemed we had a "situation" that needed attention. Our company always maintained a limousine and a full-time driver to pick up important guests, artists, and visiting buyers and executives. But the driver had just quit—and ABC Records president Jim Foglesong would be arriving at the airport shortly!

"What should we do?" my assistant asked.

Before I could offer any suggestions, this young law-school graduate jumped to his feet. "I can drive the limousine for you!" he announced.

He was hired "on the spot" because he was on the spot—in the right place at the right time. It may not have been the job he came to our offices looking for, but it was an opportunity for a music-industry job. Knowing instantly he'd be better off learning the business from the inside, he accepted the challenge.

For the next few months, this young man chauffeured artists, record company presidents, promoters, nightclub operators, casino managers, and fair and rodeo buyers for us, coming in contact with nearly every important person the Halsey Company was dealing with then. He listened and he learned, and after those months we hired him to start training as an agent.

His name was Terry Cline. He was capable and ambitious, and he stayed with The Jim Halsey Company for 15 years, becoming one of our major executives.

See how important it is to be able to recognize opportunities, and to act on them? They may not always seem right at the moment. They may not even seem to be anything you want. But you must examine all of them closely. If there's a possibility one will open the door to other opportunities, give it lots of consideration.

★

It's now time to put your own plan into action. Decide where you want to go, and whom you have to contact to get there. Use this book's description of essential Star Team members as a map. Then determine the real-life team members, the players you want to contact. Write their names down on a piece of paper. This sends a subliminal message to them, telling them you want to make connections.

How can you find these people? How can you get to know them? For starters, read the trades, which tell you about the major executives of record companies, booking agencies, management companies, and publishing companies.

Then make lists of these names. Study them. Find out all you can about who they are and how they operate.

Once you determine who it is you need to see to advance your career, the next challenge arises. How do you get an appointment with them? How can you make them notice you and pay attention to you?

Remember persistence? It's one of the 10 keys to the Power of Performance. And being persistent in making your contacts, or trying to make your contacts, comes into play at this time. Frankly, it's very unlikely that you'll get to see the executive you want to see on your first try. You must call on all of your history, education, and memory, and on what you've learned from the trades and the books on the business you've read—including this one—to finally get through the door and past the receptionist or secretary. That's the first person you'll meet in an office, which means that he or she is your first hurdle. It's very important to be clear and straightforward when you approach this first contact.

When you encounter the receptionist, be very courteous and state exactly what you want. Be positive and firm. Show him or her that you have self-confidence, but also show respect. Stand up straight, look him or her in the eye, and project the image of being both focused and grounded. Have your resume and a photo with you. And don't be afraid to make a cold, in-person, call.

It's very easy to be turned down over the telephone. The person you're calling may have a full schedule, there may be no positions available, etc. If you walk instead into an office, projecting positively and clearly, you stand a much better chance of seeing the person you want to see.

If you cannot see that person, try to see someone else in a position to help you. At least try to get past the receptionist so you can get inside.

Once you're inside, make your presentation as short and concise as possible. Do not take a lot of time. Don't hang around, lounging in a chair. Sit up straight. After you have said what you want to say, stand up, thank the person for seeing you and for the time, and see if another appointment is called for. Then leave. You aren't there for conversation, and it's usually a good idea to depart before the person begins signaling you that the meeting is over.

When you exit the office, always leave your name and telephone number, as well as a business card. Next, make call-backs. Keep the person informed about what you're doing. Remember the idea of repetitious impressions. Without being overbearing about it, make a repetitious image in the mind of that person. It will help you when he or she is looking for someone to fill a position.

There are a lot of ways to try to make your entrance into this business. Do not overlook the opportunity of getting into the business you want by accepting a lesser, more menial, job—as Terry Cline did with us. Once you are in the door and begin to know people, you can show them your abilities and skills. If you're actually working for a music or entertainment company, no matter what your position, you stand a thousand-percent better chance of advancing within the company than somebody from the outside does. An entry-level job that gives you the opportunity to meet people—in a mail room, as a delivery person, as someone who runs errands or chauffeurs a car, or even as a waiter or waitress in a restaurant frequented by music-industry people—can be a real asset. Who you know and what you learn are equally important in this business.

If you still can't land a job, try to find someone who knows a person in the company where you've interviewed. You don't want to be just another name in a file drawer full of resumes; making someone on the inside of the company aware of you can help you stand out from the pack.

Remember, when you call on the people you want to work for, your first impression may be your last. So make that first impression good—good enough to be a stepping stone to successful future contacts. Make them want to see you again, or at least let them investigate you and see what you are about and what opportunities you may hold for them as an employee. Your Power of Performance may never be needed as much as it is on your first interview.

★

The Power of Performance is really what this book is about. In these pages, I've told you about the way I've built my life in show business, music, and entertainment—utilizing my own Power of Performance, and that of the other members of the Star Team, to achieve my goals.

This concept can just as easily be used by those interested in any other career involving sales and marketing: electronics, real estate, insurance, furniture, banking, computers, automobiles, advertising—anything where success is derived from interaction with people and teams.

There are thousands of creative, stimulating, and financially rewarding jobs in the music and entertainment business. The better educated and better prepared you are, the more knowledge and experience you have, the more available you are to success. Learn, study, work, concentrate, have a goal with a purpose—and stay focused! Learn about your Power of Performance and access it to make your personal dreams and visions into your own realities.

Learning how to use your personal Power of Performance will help you understand success and where to find it. Most important, the Power of Performance is the key to life and how to live it! It is a gift. It is your gift. You have it now. Use it! The path from your dreams to your goals may sometimes be difficult to navigate, but the trip will never be dull.

Take it from another dreamer.

Good Luck!

—Jim Halsey

appendices

Acetate Dub: An individually cut record (as opposed to pressed records).

Administration: The supervision of all financial, copyright and contractual aspects of either an entire catalog or a particular song.

Advance: Money paid before the recording or release of a song, to be deducted against future royalties of that song.

AF of M: American Federation of Musicians; unions for musicians, arrangers, copyists, contractors and orchestras.

AFTRA: American Federation of Television and Radio Artists; union for singers, actors, announcers, narrators, and sound effects artists.

AGAC: American Guild of Authors and Composers; a songwriter's protective association.

Angel: The financial backer of a play.

A&R Director: Artists and repertoire; record company employee in charge of selecting new artists, songs and masters.

Arrangement: The adaptation of a composition for performance by other instruments and voices than originally intended.

Arranger: One who adapts a musical work to particular instruments or voices.

Artist: Individual or group under recording contract.

ASCAP: American Society of Composers, Authors and Publishers; a performing rights organization.

Assignment: The transfer of rights to a song or catalog from one copyright proprietor to another.

Biography: A concise account of an artist or group's industry related experience or background.

BMI: Broadcast Music, Inc.; a performing rights organization.

Booking Agent: One who finds employment for artists from buyers of talent.

Bootlegging: The unauthorized recording and selling of a performance of the song.

Bullet: Designation of a record listed on the charts, referring to increased record sales.

Casting: The selection of actors, musicians, or dancers for an artistic project.

Catalog: All the songs owned by a music publisher considered as one collection.

Charts: Lists published in the trade magazines of the best-selling records. These are separate charts for pop, soul, country, western, etc.; musical arrangements.

Chord: Three or more notes sounded simultaneously that imply a harmonic function.

Chorus: A section of the song that repeats itself at certain intervals.

Clearance: The right of a radio station to play a song.

Clearance Agency: See performing rights organization, ASCAP, BMI, SESAC.

Click Track: A perforated soundtrack that produces click sounds that enables one to hear a predetermined beat in synchronization with the movie.

Collaborator: One of two or more partners in the writing of songs.

CD (Compact Disc): Digital audio recording

CMA: Country Music Association; organization devoted to promoting country music.

Commercial: The potential to sell; that which has mass appeal.

Common-Law Copyright: Natural protection of a song based on common laws of the various states. To be superseded by a single national system effective January 1, 1978.

Composer: One who writes the music to a song.

Composition: A musical work; the art of writing music.

Co-Publishing: The joint publication of one copyrighted work by two publishers.

Compulsory License (Phonorecords): Statutory mandate given to a copyright owner to permit third parties to make sound recordings of the copyright owner's song after it once has been recorded.

Consumer Publication: Entertainment oriented periodicals written and published for a general public readership i.e., Rolling Stone, Spin.

Copyright (n): The exclusive rights granted to authors and composers for protection of their works; a song or musical composition.

Copyright (v): To secure protection for a song by filing the proper registration forms with the Copyright Office.

Copyright Infringement: Stealing or using somebody else's copyrighted song.

Copyright Notice: Notice comprised of three elements:

1. The symbol of copyright, the word "copyright," or the abbreviation "Copr."

2. The year the song has been registered for copyright or the year of first production of the work.

3. The copyright owner's name.

Copyright Office: Federal government department, one of whose main purposes is to file and supply information regarding copyrights.

Copyright Owner: The owner of any one of the exclusive rights comprised in copyright.

Copyright Royalty Tribunal: A committee created by Public Law 94–553 to determine adjustments starting January 1, 1978, of royalty rates with respect to compulsory licenses for educational television, cable television, jukeboxes, and sound recordings.

Cover Record: Another artist's version of a song already recorded.

Co-Writing: Joint authorship of one work by two or more writers.

Cross Collateralization: Means of recouping the money spent on one song or recording against the earnings of another song or recording.

Crossover: A song which receives airplay in more than one market.

Cut: To record; a recorded selection.

C&W: Country and Western

Date: A recording session or live engagement.

Demo: A demonstration recording of a song used to show its potential to music industry personnel.

Demo Firm: An organization specializing in the production of demo tapes.

Distributor: Company that exclusively handles the sale of a record company's product to jobbers and retail outlets for a certain territory.

D.O.R.: Dance-Oriented Rock; a categorization of popular music utilized by radio stations.

Employee For Hire: Contractual basis whereby a motion picture producer or company employs a composer or lyricist to create music or songs for a movie with copyright ownership to be retained by the producer or company.

Engineer: Individual who operates studio equipment during the recording of a song.

Exclusive Songwriting Contract: A contract which prohibits the songwriter from writing for more than one publisher.

FIDOF: The International Federation of Festival Organizations.

Folio: A collection of songs offered for sale to the public.

Gold Album: Certification by the Recording Industry of America that an album has sold half a million units.

Gold Single: Certification by the Recording Industry of America that a single has sold half a million units.

Grammy: Music industry awards presented by the National Academy of Recording Arts and Sciences (NARAS).

Groove: Rhythm or tempo that helps create the "feel" of the song.

Harmony: The combination of musical notes to form chords that serve to enhance the melody line; the art of combining notes into chords.

Harry Fox Agency: An organization which represents music publishers in connection with the mechanical reproduction of their copyrights as well as the use of their compositions for motion picture synchronization.

"Head" Arrangement: An arrangement devised spontaneously. No charts are prepared for instrumentalists and vocalists. Instead, they read off lead sheets and an arrangement is made from various experimental styling devised at the studio.

Heads Out: Manner in which a reel-to-reel tape is stored, with the loose end at the beginning of the tape, enabling the tape to be played immediately.

Hit: A record that sells many copies; a description applied to records that achieve top 40 status.

Hook: A phrase or melody line that repeats itself in a song; the catchy part to a song.

Heavy Metal: A category of popular music characterized by high-volume, maximum guitar presence.

Impresario: An entertainment entrepreneur

Ink: To sign a contract.

Jingle: A short phrase of music usually accompanied by lyrics used to convey a commercial message.

LP: A long-playing record played at 33 1/3 revolutions per minute (rpm).

Label: A record company

Leader: Conductor or person in charge of the band.

Lead Sheet: A musical notation of a song's melody along with the chord symbols, words, and other pertinent information.

Leader Tape: Reel-to-reel tape which contains songs separated by white tape for easy access.

License (n): A legal permit.

License (v): To authorize by legal permit.

Lick: A brief, improvised musical interpolation.

Logo: An artistic design found on records and album covers that identify the company issuing the product.

Lyrics: The words to a song.

Lyric Sheet: A (typed) copy of the lyrics to a song.

Lyricist: The writer of the works to a song.

Manager: One who guides an artist in the development of his/her career. Same as artist or personal manager.

Market: Selling place; medium where only one type of record is played (i.e., pop, R&B, C&W, etc.)

Master: A finished recording of the song from which records are pressed and distributed to radio stations and record stores.

Mechanical Right: Right granted by the US copyright law to copyright owner to profit from the mechanical reproduction of his song.

Mechanical Rights Organization: Collection agency for copyright owners of money earned from the mechanical reproduction of their songs.

Mechanical Royalties: Moneys earned for use of a copyright in mechanical reproductions, most notably records and tapes.

Mix: Blending together the tracks of a multitrack recording.

Modulate: To change from one key to another in a song.

MOR: "Middle of the Road"; songs that may be classified as easy listening.

Motif: The shortest significant melody of a song or theme.

Moviola: A projection machine that reduces film to a small viewing screen.

Music Publisher: The individual or company who:

1. Screen songs and gets them commercially recorded.

2. Exploits the copyrights.

3. Protects the copyrights.

4. Collects income from performance, mechanical synchronization, and printing rights both in the United States and in foreign countries.

Neutral Demo: A demo that doesn't sound like it's for one particular artist, but best represents the song whereby it can be recorded by anybody.

One-Stop: Wholesale record dealer that sells the records of several manufacturers to jukebox operators and record stores.

Overdub: The addition of instruments or voices to pre-existing tracks.

Packager: One who selects and combines talent for shows.

Payola: Secret payment to broadcasters to play certain records.

Pen: To compose or write.

Performing Right: Right granted by US copyright law which states that one may not publicly perform a copyrighted musical work without the owner's permission.

Performing Rights Organization: Society whose purpose is to collect monies earned from public performances of songs by users of music and to distribute these to the writers and publishers of these songs in a proportion that reflects as accurately as possible the amount of performances of each particular song.

Performance Royalties: Monies earned from use of one's song on radio, television and other users of music.

Phonorecord: Any device which transmits sound other than that which accompanies a motion picture or other audio-visual work.

Photo-Offset Reproduction: Reproduction of musical manuscript by printing press.

Pick: A song that has been reviewed by the trades and projected to have success.

Pirating: The unauthorized reproduction and selling of sound recordings (i.e., records and tapes).

Pitch: To audition or sell; the position of a tone in a musical scale.

Platinum Album: Certification by the Recording Industry Association of America that an album has sold a minimum of one million units.

Platinum Single: Certification by the Recording Industry Association of America that a single has sold a minimum of one million units.

Plug: Broadcast of a song; to push for a song's performance.

Plugola: Secret payment to broadcasters for free mention of products on the air.

Points: A percentage of money producers and artists earn on the retail list price of 90 percent of all records sold.

Press: The manufacture of a large quantity of records duplicated from a master for commercial sale.

Printed Edition: A song published in the form of sheet music.

Professional Manager: The person in charge of screening new material for music publishers and of obtaining commercial recordings of songs in his company's catalog.

Producer: The individual who oversees the making of a single or long playing record, radio, television or stage show from inception to completion.

Production: The technical aspects of the music industry, including sound systems and lighting requirements as well as video and recording processes.

Program Director: Radio station employee who determines which songs shall be broadcast.

Promoter: One who secures talent from an agent for the production and presentation of a performance; the primary risk taker in the event.

Prosody: The marriage of words and music.

Publication: the printing and distribution of copies of a work to a public by sale or other transfer of ownership, or by rental, lease or lending.

Public Domain: Unprotected by copyright due to an expired copyright or caused by an invalid copyright notice.

R&B: Rhythm and blues; "soul" music.

R&R: Rock and Roll.

Rack Jobber: Dealer that supplies records of many manufacturers to certain retail outlets such as drugstores, variety stores, and supermarkets.

Release: The issuing of a record by the record company.

Road Manager: Traveling supervisor hired by artist to coordinate details of concert tours on behalf of the artist.

RIAA: Recording Industry Association of America.

Royalty: Money earned from use of the record or song.

Self-Contained Artist: An Artist who writes and performs his own material. Also refers to artists who require no production or personnel assistance from promoters.

SESAC: A performing rights, mechanical rights, and synchronization licensing organization.

Session: Meeting during which time musicians and vocalists make a recording.

Sheet Music: Printed editions of a single song offered for sale to the public.

Showcase: A presentation of new songs and/or talent.

Single: A small record played at 45 rpms containing two selections, one on each side; record released because of the expectation by the record company that "A" side would achieve success.

Song Plugger: One who auditions songs for performers.

Song Shark: One who profits from dealing with songwriters by deceptive methods.

Speculation: The recording of a song with payment to be made to the recording studio, musicians and vocalists when a deal is consummated.

Split Publishing: When the publishing rights to a song are divided among two or more publishers.

Staff Writer: One who writes exclusively for a publishing firm and earns a salary in this capacity.

Standard: A song that continues to be popular for several years.

State-Of-The-Art: Contemporary or current.

Statutory Copyright: Status acquired by a composition when it is registered with the Copyright Office or is published with the proper copyright notice.

Studio: Place where a song is recorded.

Subpublisher: The company that publishes a song or catalog in a territory other than that under the domain of the original publisher.

Subpublishing: When the original publisher contracts his song or catalog to be handled by a foreign publisher for that territory.

Sweeten: The addition of new parts to existing rhythms and vocal tracks such as strings and horns.

Synchronization: The placing of music in timed-relation to film.

Synchronization Right: The right to use a musical composition in (timed-relation to) a film or video tape.

Tails Out: The manner in which a reel-to-reel tape is stored, with the loose end at the end of the tape, requiring the tape to be removed before playing.

Time Reversion Clause: Contractual agreement in which a publisher agrees to secure recording and release for songwriter's material within a certain period of time. Failure to secure recording and release triggers reversion of the song rights to the writer.

Top 40: Radio station format where records played are only those contained in lists of the best-selling records.

Top 100: Lists published in the trades of the top-selling singles for a particular market.

Track: One of the several components of special recording tape that contains recorded sounds, which is mixed with the other tracks for a finished recording of the song; the recording of all the instruments or vocals of a particular music section; music and/or voices previously recorded.

Trades: Music industry publications, i.e., Billboard, Pollstar, Variety, Hollywood.

Union Scale: Minimum wage scale earned in employment by members of AFTRA, AF of M, SAG, etc.

Verse: The selection of a song that precedes the chorus or is the A section in AABA pattern songs.

Writer's Signature: Unique style of the writer.